Developments in American Politics

Developments in American Politics

**Gillian Peele, Christopher J. Bailey,
Bruce Cain** *Editors*

MACMILLAN

First published 1992 by
THE MACMILLAN PRESS LTD
Houndmills, Basingstoke, Hampshire RG21 2XS
and London
Companies and representatives
throughout the world

ISBN 0–333–49437–7 hardcover
ISBN 0–333–49438–5 paperback

A catalogue record for this book is available
from the British Library.

Filmset by Wearside Tradespools,
Boldon, Tyne and Wear

Printed in Hong Kong

Contents

Preface   x
List of Contributors   xii
List of Tables and Figures   xiv
List of Abbreviations   xvi
Map of the United States of America   xviii

Introduction   1

Part One: The Sources of Political Change

1 Values, Institutions and Policy Agendas   14
    Gillian Peele
    Political Institutions and American Values   15
    Party Divisions and American Values   17
    A Value Shift in the 1990s?   20
    The Evolution of the Conservative Movement   22
    A Revived Liberalism?   27
    Political Movements and American Values   29
        The Feminist Movement   29
        The poverty issue   31
        Blacks   33
    Conclusions   35

2 The American Electoral System   *Bruce Cain*   **37**
    The Fracturing of the American Electorate   37
    Racial and Ethnic Division in the American
        Electorate   47
    Institutional Fracture   55
    Conclusion   61

3 American Political Parties   **63**
    Daniel Hays Lowenstein
    Weakness and Strength   64
        The party in the electorate   64

The party in government	65
Party organization	66
Progressive Party Reform	72
Party Renewal	80
Conclusion	84

Part Two: The Governmental System

4 Presidential Leadership   *Colin Campbell*   **83**

Reagan and the Decline of Policy Competence	90
Managerial Style and Administrative Organization in the White House	94
The Reagan White House	95
The cabinet councils	96
The onset of the 'Regan' administration	99
The Bush Presidency	102
Organizational stress	108
Congressional relations	109
The Gulf War	112
Conclusion	113

5 Congress and Legislative Activism   **115**
   Christopher J. Bailey

Constituency Attentiveness	117
Emphasis on constituency service	117
The parochial Congress	122
Strengthening Congressional Capacity	126
The increase in resources	127
Strengthening the political parties	129
The Role of Congress	134

6 Constitutional Legitimacy and the Supreme Court   *Richard Hodder-Williams*   **138**

Introduction	138
The Problems of Divided Partisan Control	140
Interest Groups, Policy Preferences and the Use of the Supreme Court	147
The Reagan Administration and Attempts to Influence the Judicial Branch	152
The New Debate over Jurisprudence	156
Conclusion	160

7 **Public Bureaucracy in the American Political
   System** *B. Guy Peters*   **165**
   Structure and Performance   167
      Public employees   168
      Organizations   171
         Autonomy   171
         Links to the outside   172
      The policy role of the bureaucracy   174
   The Reagan Years   177
      The personnel system   177
      Pay and perquisites   178
      The private sector as exemplar   182
      Utilizing the private sector   184
      A Civil Service for the Year 2000?   185
      Morale, recruitment and retention   185
      Hopes for the future   187

Part Three: Public Policy

8 **The Changing Federal Balance**   **190**
   Desmond S. King
   Approaches to Federalism   191
   President Reagan and the New Federalism   195
      Federal welfare programs   195
      Federal grants   196
      Reforming federal regulatory policy   197
      Reforming urban policy   199
      Federal housing policy   201
      Tax and economic policy   202
   The New Federalism and the New State Policy Role   203
      State welfare policy   205
   Conclusion   207
      The empowered states and persistent center   207
      Institutional incentives and the New
         Federalism   208

9 **Economic Policy**   *Joseph Hogan*   **210**
   The Institutional Structure of Economic
      Policy-making   211
   Postwar Economic Policy   216
   Conclusion   225

10   Social Welfare Policy   *Robert X. Browning*   **229**
The Nature of Social Programs   230
Patterns of Growth   232
   Entitling new groups   233
   The elderly   236
   In-kind growth   236
The Limits of Reform   238
The Reagan Agenda   240
   The social security issue   242
   Housing programs   243
   Increase in poverty   244
The Post-Reagan Period   245
Social Policy in Transition   248

11   American Foreign Policy   *Miles Kahler*   **250**
President and Bureaucracy: Conditions for
   Coherence   254
Congress and Foreign Policy: Consolidation or
   Retreat?   260
Passions and Interests in Foreign Policy   267
Public Opinion and Foreign Policy   271
The New Politics of American Foreign Policy   274

Part Four: Current Issues

12   The Budget Deficit   *Stanley E. Collender*   **280**
The Legacy of the Reagan Years   280
   The numbers tell the story   281
   Procedural and political changes follow the
      numbers   283
Challenges for the 1990s   287
   Spending   288
   Taxes   290
   Process   290
The Real Legacy of the Reagan Years   291
   Stalemates   291
   Slow progress on the deficit   292
   Limited ability to respond to new
      contingencies   292
   Hidden taxes   292

13 Civil Rights in the United States *Gillian Peele* **294**
   The Reagan Legacy on Civil Rights 295
   The Bush Administration and Civil Rights 301
   The 1990 and 1991 Civil Rights Acts 305

**14 Immigration Reforms: A Mexican–American
   Perspective** *Rodolfo O. de la Garza* **309**
   The 1980s: The Decade of the Hispanic 309
   Immigration and the Mexican Community 312
   1980–1986: The IRCA Debate 316
   Conclusion 320

Part Five: Conclusion

15 An Era of Divided Government **324**
   Morris P. Fiorina
   Divided Government in Historical Perspective 325
   Explanations of Divided Government 328
      Incumbency 332
      America is fundamentally a Democratic
         country 335
      Purposeful explanations 338
      Summary 345
   Consequences of Divided Government 345
      Efficiency and effectiveness 346
      Responsibility 348
      Intellectual challenge 350
   Notes to Chapter 15 353

Guide to Further Reading 355
Bibliography 360
Index 385

Preface

Developments in American Politics shares with its companion volumes the goal of combining the comprehensiveness of a textbook with the liveliness and contemporary relevance of articles by leading scholars. Thus, although the student or teacher seeking a single volume treatment of the government and politics of the United States will find *Developments in American Politics* an accessible introduction to the subject, the volume is also suitable as a supplement to other texts and for use in more advanced classes.

The authors are all specialists on their chosen subject areas and are drawn from both sides of the Atlantic. The topics chosen reflect the editors' ambition to provide the reader both with an overview of some of the important scholarly debates about the key trends in American politics and with sufficient background information to understand the nature of those changes.

Writing about the United States and using a team of British and American authors presents certain stylistic problems. The editors have decided that spelling should be Americanized throughout in order to promote consistency. On the other hand, some specifically American usages have been excised. Where appropriate the party and state of members of Congress have been included. The references to works cited in the book are collected together at the end of the text. There is also a short guide to further reading for each of the chapters.

The editors would like to thank our publisher Steven Kennedy for the help and encouragement he has given with this volume. We are extremely grateful for the secretarial help given by the College Office at Lady Margaret Hall. Pauline Shepheard, Elizabeth Martin, Frances Wilson, and

Jenny Harker assisted in a variety of ways, not least in keeping that essential tool of transatlantic collaboration – the fax machine – under control. We also thank Seamus Tucker and Samuel Woodhouse who provided research assistance at earlier stages of the project.

The editors acknowledge with gratitude the intellectual support given by their colleagues at the University of Oxford, the University of Keele and the University of California at Berkeley. Chris Bailey would also like to thank Senator Reid and his staff for their kindness during his tenure as an APSA Congressional Fellowship in Washington.

The editors are also grateful for the constructive criticisms of the anonymous readers of this proposal.

On a personal level the British editors realize how much they owe to the hospitality and the friendliness of American scholars. We would particularly mention Nelson Polsby, James Thurber, Roger Davidson, Paul Herrnson, Maggie Fish, John and Leslie Francis, Chris Deering, Vincent Buck and Austin Ranney.

Finally, we would like to thank our contributors, whose patience and prompt responses to queries have helped to get this book to the finishing line.

Gillian Peele
Chris Bailey
Bruce Cain

List of Contributors

Christopher J. Bailey is Lecturer in American Studies at the University of Keele. He was an APSA Congressional Fellow in 1989–1990. Among his publications are *The Republican Party in the US Senate, 1974–1984*, and *The U.S. Congress*.

Robert X. Browning is Professor of Political Science at Purdue University. Recent publications include *Politics and Social Welfare Policy in the United States*.

Bruce Cain is Professor of Government at the University of California, Berkeley. He is the author of *The Reapportionment Puzzle* and a co-author of *The Personal Vote*, which was awarded the Richard F. Fenno Jr. Prize of the American Political Science Association.

Colin Campbell is Professor of Government at Georgetown University. He is the author of *Governments Under Stress* and *Managing the Presidency*.

Stanley E. Collender is Director of Federal Budget Policy, Price Waterhouse, Washington DC. He is the author of *The Guide to the Federal Budget 1992*.

Morris Fiorina is Professor of Government at Harvard University. He is the author of *Congress: Keystone of the Washington Establishment*, and a co-author of *The Personal Vote*, which was awarded the Richard F. Fenno Jr. Prize of the American Political Science Association.

Rodolfo O. de la Garza is C. B. Smith Fellow in Latin American Studies and Professor of Government at the University of Texas, Austin. He is the author of many articles on the politics of Mexican Americans.

Richard Hodder-Williams is Reader in Politics at the University of Bristol. Among his publications is *The Politics of the Supreme Court*.

Joseph Hogan is Professor of Government and Politics at Birmingham Polytechnic. He is the editor of *The Reagan Years*.

Miles Kahler is Professor of Government at the University of California, San Diego.

Desmond S. King a former Lecturer in American Politics at the London School of Economics is Fellow and Tutor in Politics at St John's College, Oxford. He is the author of *The New Right* and the co-author of *The State and the City*.

Daniel Hays Lowenstein is Professor of Law at the University of California, Los Angeles.

Gillian Peele is Official Fellow in Politics at Lady Margaret Hall, Oxford. She is the author of *Revival and Reaction*, and a co-editor of *Developments in British Politics*.

B. Guy Peters is Maurice Falk Professor of American Government at the University of Pittsburgh. Among his publications are *American Public Policy*, and *Politics of Bureaucracy*.

List of Tables and Figures

Tables

2.1	Presidential vote by race and ethnicity	48
2.2	Citizen voting by race and ethnicity	53
5.1	Votes in Congress showing party unity, 92nd to 101st Congresses	130
10.1	State–federal social welfare comparisons	232
10.2	Federal social welfare expenditures by category	234
10.3	Federal social welfare expenditures by category as percentage of total	235
10.4	Spending for major federal social welfare programs	237
10.5	Changes in poverty, 1979–82	245
12.1	Steady growth in U.S. revenues and outlays, 1981–88	282
12.2	Steady growth in the U.S. deficit, 1981–88	282
12.3	Dramatic changes in U.S. budget components, 1980–88	283
12.4	Gramm–Rudman–Hollings deficit maximums	284
15.1	Control of national institutions, 1832–1992	326
15.2	Major periods of divided government	327
15.3	Divided government by type of election	328
15.4	Congressional districts carried by House and presidential candidates of different parties	331
15.5	Patterns of President–House ticket splitting	332
15.6a	Gubernatorial and legislative victories, 1978/ 1982 and 1986	337
15.6b	Patterns of state government control	337

15.7   Voter policy positions compared with
        perceptions of party positions   341
15.8   President/House ticket-splitting   344

Figures

2.1   Ticket splitters in American elections, 1952–88   40
15.1   Divided states, 1946–90   329
15.2   House–President ticket-splitting   330

List of Abbreviations

ACLU	American Civil Liberties Union
AFDC	Aid to Families with Dependent Children
APA	Administrative Procedures Act (1946)
BEA	Budget Enforcement Act (1990)
CIA	Central Intelligence Agency
CBO	Congressional Budget Office
CRA	Civil Rights Act (1964)
CRC	Civil Rights Commission
CRS	Congressional Research Service
D.	Democrat
DNC	Democratic National Committee
EPB	Economic Policy Board
EOP	Executive Office of the President
ERA	Equal Rights Amendment
ES	Executive Schedule
FBI	Federal Bureau of Investigations
FDA	Food and Drug Administration
FIA	Freedom of Information Act
FOMC	Federal Open Market Committee
GAO	General Accounting Office
GRH	Gramm–Rudman–Hollings (Balanced Budget and Emergency Deficit Control Act (1985))
GS	General Schedule
HUD	Housing and Urban Development (Department of)
IRCA	Immigration Reform and Control Act (1986)
LULAC	League of United Latin American Citizens
MALDEF	Mexican–American Legal Defense Fund

NAACP	National Association for the Advancement of Colored People
NASA	National Aeronautics and Space Administration
NCLR	National Council de la Raza
NGA	National Governors' Association
NSA	National Security Agency
OBRA	Omnibus Budget Reconciliation and Economic Recovery Tax Acts (1981)
OIRA	Office of Information and Regulatory Affairs
OMB	Office of Management and Budget
OPEC	Organization of Petroleum Exporting Countries
OPM	Office of Personnel Management
OTA	Office of Technology Assessment
PAC(s)	Political Action Committee(s)
PHS	Public Health Service
R.	Republican
RNC	Republican National Committee
SDI	Strategic Defense Initiative (Star Wars)
SES	Senior Executive Service
SIGs	Senior Interagency Groups
SSA	Social Security Administration or Social Security Act (1935)
SSI	Supplemental Security Income
UDAG	Urban Direct Action Grants
VRA	Voting Rights Act (1965)
WIN	Work Incentive Program

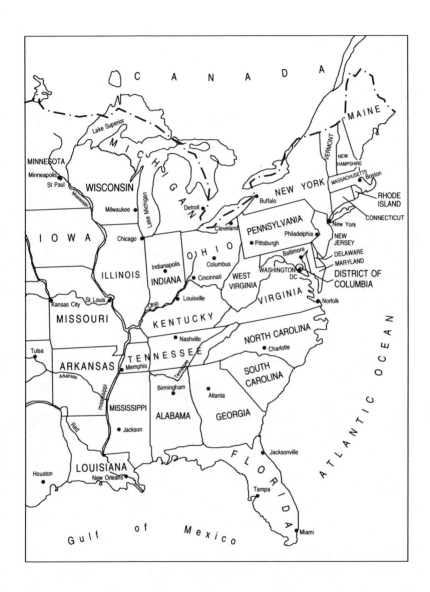

Introduction

Developments in American Politics is designed to provide an
accessible but theoretically informed exploration of the
changing character of American political life. American
politics have to be understood as the result of a complex
interplay between the institutions of government and the
demands of a highly heterogeneous society. This interplay
produces a politics which is at once relatively stable in outline
but subject to rapid transformation in detail. Against the
apparent longevity and stability of a system of government
confidently celebrating its bicentenary, must be set the
underlying reality of a dynamic political culture, the product
of rapid and profound social changes in the United States
over the last quarter of the twentieth century.

The sources of change in American society are many –
technological, demographic and cultural. Some of the
changes are exogenous to the American system; others are
the distinctive products of American society itself. In particular, immigration and the effects of ethnic diversity have left a
major mark on the political life of the United States.
Although the American political system has always been
affected by such changes to a degree which sets it apart from
other comparable democracies, their impact on American
politics has recently become more marked.

The 1990 census figures reveal how dramatically the non-
white population has grown in the last decade. Even though
the *actual* number of whites in the United States has grown by
11 million, the *percentage* of whites dropped from 83.1 per
cent to 80.3 per cent. The Latino population has increased
from 6.4 per cent to 9 per cent and the Asian from 1.5 per
cent to 2.9 per cent. The black population has grown only
slightly from 11.7 to 12.1 per cent. In some states, the

1

changes are even more dramatic: in California, the Asian population increased by 127 per cent between 1980 and 1990 and the Latinos by 69 per cent. Greater demographic diversity has several effects. It changes the mix of interest groups competing for power at the local, state and national levels. As the various racial and ethnic groups reach a threshold population size, the prospect of mobilizing for political power becomes realistic. Demographic diversity also adds to the already rich array of political cultures in the United States. Even when groups are large enough to be politically influential, they must develop the strategies, leadership and commitment to political participation needed to be effective in the rough and tumble of politics. Some groups are further along that path than others. Finally, the changing mix of the American population places wider demands on public services and programs at all levels of American government.

The focus of the first part of this book is on the sources of political change in the United States and on the ways in which such changes are integrated into the political system. Although politics in the United States have generally been seen as less dominated by ideological conflict than European political systems, ideology does play a part in American political debate so that some of the most important shifts in American politics are the result of changes in the values dominant in the United States. In particular, the rise of a self-conscious conservative movement in the late 1970s and 1980s transformed and sharpened public debate about a range of issues including the organization of the economy, the global role of the United States and a host of questions related to personal morality and culture.

The role of ideology in the United States should not, however, be exaggerated. By contrast with many other countries, the source of the values which drive political debate is less likely to be some explicitly articulated doctrine (such as conservatism or liberalism) than the changing agendas of significant groups within the system. Thus, although broad ideological movements and American political parties can shape values in the United States, periods in which value change occurs in this way are unusual. The period of the

New Deal (1933–1940) and the more recent period of the
Reagan presidency (1981–1989) thus stand out as atypical
years of political controversy when placed in the historical
perspective of the twentieth century as a whole. Much attention will be paid in this book to the so-called 'Reagan
revolution' and its legacy; but this attention should not
obscure other features of American politics – for example,
the perennial appeal of the value of equality and the potential strength of economic populism – which have a longer
pedigree in the history of the United States. Similarly,
although the conservative movement generated some important policy shifts in the 1980s, in the 1990s, other movements
and interests (such as the women's movement, and the
concerns of ethnic minorities) must be taken into account in
any assessment of America's contemporary political agenda.

An understanding of the priorities of particular interest
groups and movements has long been seen as an essential
component of any attempt to capture the reality of the
American policy process. But in the United States interest
groups do not *merely* advance the particular sectional concerns of their constituencies, although of course they perform that function with varying degrees of effectiveness.
Interest groups also shape the language of political discourse
and structure public debate, sometimes to a greater extent
than do the political parties. Moreover, the activities of
interest groups affect the way in which virtually all of the key
institutions of American constitutional life – notably Congress, but also the courts, the parties, and the bureaucracy –
operate. The debate about the effect of interest group
activity on the quality of American democracy is as old as the
Republic itself. For some observers, interest groups pose a
threat to the health of American democracy; for others their
activities constitute a vital link between society and the
structures of government. Whatever the diagnosis of the role
of interest groups in American politics, it seems unlikely that
their role will diminish. Although we have not included a
separate chapter on interest groups, the significance of
interest groups in American politics is one of the central
themes of this book and is addressed from different stand-
points in many of the chapters.

On one level, the demands of the variety of groups which constitute the mosaic of American society are translated into political power via the electoral system. But the process is by no means a simple one. Different ideas of representation prevail at different times. Is it essential to ensure the representation of distinct groups such as Hasidic Jews, blacks or Latinos? Or should Americans simply be treated as the language of the constitution implies as individuals? Such questions are not, however, academic: reforms such as the Voting Rights Act of 1965 can restructure the environment of political competition profoundly. The strength of support for the two major parties in the different regions of the country varies considerably but is everywhere sensitive to the effects of demographic change. The process of electoral reapportionment which follows each decennial census offers a regular insight into the political consequences of demographic change both for the United States as a whole and for its component parts. As the 1990 gubernatorial races in California, Texas and Florida underlined, the struggle to control those consequences can be extremely bitter.

The extent to which groups define the American political agenda (and the relative weakness of linkage mechanisms such as parties and ideologies) means that in the United States politics is fractured and public opinion is fragmented. Certainly on occasion the American public can be bullied or cajoled into apparent consensus; but broad consensus across a range of issues is hard to sustain. And it seems that in the 1990s the institutions of American government will increasingly reflect and reinforce this fractured pluralism. The decentralization of Congress, the shift of many responsibilities to the states from the federal level in the wake of fiscal constraint, and the apparent preference of the American electorate for divided partisan control of its political institutions all contribute to concern about the continued ability of American government to cope with the problems which it faces in the 1990s. In fact as Morris Fiorina's essay at the end of the book shows, the problem itself is many faceted. We need to know to what extent the outcome of divided government is the product of a conscious preference on the part of a portion of the electorate. We need to know the extent to

which it really does affect the quality of policy-making; and
we need to know whether there are any convincing remedies
for the current governmental *malaise*, if *malaise* it be.
One popular remedy for the perceived weaknesses of
contemporary American government is a return to a stronger party system. Yet the strategies of those who have argued
for a strengthening of political parties in the United States
frequently seem out of touch with the political reality of
modern America. Some minor party-building reforms may
occur. But American parties, it could be argued, are weak
because the functions which parties traditionally perform in a
democracy have either been shared with other agencies such
as pressure groups and campaign consultants or have been
eroded in an attempt to democratize the party structure. In
these circumstances, although parties may perform residual
functions, it is a mistake to see them as the answer to the
problems of contemporary American politics. Indeed the
unravelling of party coalitions and the absence of realignment constitute an environment in which the parties themselves find it difficult to operate.

The second part of this book looks at the impact of some of
these changes in the dynamics of American politics on the
key institutions of American government. The presidency is
the one institution which clearly has a national constituency
and can on occasion integrate the disparate parts of the
American constitutional system. But much depends on each
individual's conception of the presidency and the personal
strategy which he adopts both in relation to Congress and to
his administration. The Reagan presidency highlighted features of modern American government which trouble many
observers. First, it was a presidency which was of a different
partisan complexion from at least one chamber of Congress
for the whole period, although the Senate was in Republican
hands from 1981–6. At the very least this limited the capacity
of the executive to forge a coherent policy with Congress and
allowed responsibility for such crucial problems as the deficit
to be deflected.

Secondly, the problems of securing administrative co-ordination and control remained substantial despite a successful first-term working relationship between senior staff

members and an imaginative use of cabinet councils. Yet, as
the various inquiries into the Iran–Contra scandal in 1986
showed, the management of the executive branch was imper-
fect and there was a degree of anarchy within the government which could have politically disastrous consequences.

Finally, although the president could provide leadership in
a fragmented system and although Reagan did have an
unusually explicit agenda for the United States, the difficulty
of translating an agenda into policy inevitably tempted a
president to abdicate any responsibility for producing legislative agreement. Thus the president might adopt a so-called
'public strategy' which would allow him to by-pass the representative institutions of American government and appeal via
the media to public opinion when political resources really
needed to be mobilized. In routine matters presidential goals
would be achieved by less visible administrative strategies,
including the careful use of the executive power of appointment to control the bureaucracy.

The advent of the Bush Administration has produced a
slightly different version of this scenario. While more clearly
engaged in the details of administration, Bush was criticized
for his failure to articulate a clear vision of what he wanted to
achieve in his presidency. Inevitably therefore the presidency
has been in no position to transcend the immobilism which
appears to have gripped American political life. Even in
international affairs – where events such as Panama and
more recently the Iraqi invasion of Kuwait obtained a decisive presidential reaction – Bush was often unable to com-
municate his analysis of the situation. Indeed, in November
1990 the White House actually admitted that there had been
a failure of communication over the Gulf War and the
purposes for which large numbers of American troops were
deployed there.

However, it was noticeable in the Gulf crisis of 1990 that
the President took care to emphasize the collaborative nature
of American intervention and to maintain the sense of
collective international action in the Gulf. And, although
keen to preserve the prerogatives of the presidency, on
foreign policy Bush maintained a consultative stance which
minimized the possibility of domestic disharmony. The suc-

cessful conclusion of the war greatly enhanced Bush's personal popularity, although it is less clear how this will translate into the conduct of his relations with Congress for the rest of his term or how long the popularity will last. The difficulties of governing a system in which the separation of powers pitted an executive of one party against a legislature controlled by the other were compounded by internal changes within Congress itself over the 1970s and 1980s. The American legislature has experienced a degree of internal decentralization which has often made it hard to frame and pass much needed legislation. At the same time the demands on congressional time for non-law-making activities has increased. Thus, although Congress in the late 1980s surprised many observers with a burst of legislative activity, such activism is difficult to sustain in the long run. Yet efforts to reform the system have proved impossible to implement, essentially because no one has any interest or incentive to alter a system that has been shaped to benefit existing members of Congress. This situation of course presents the United States with a paradox: the body charged with making policy in the general interest often cannot do so because of the extent to which it has given individual members the opportunity to veto policies which conflict with their minority interests. Not surprisingly such a situation generates a degree of hostility and cynicism among the electorate – a cynicism which many observers detected in the 1990 midterm elections.

The apparent abnegation of congressional responsibility for hard public policy choices has also led to rather draconian measures such as the Balanced Budget and Emergency Deficit Control Act of 1985 (Gramm–Rudman–Hollings) and the later (1990) Budget Enforcement Act which are eloquent testimony to the inability of Congress by itself to cut spending programs. The example of Gramm–Rudman–Hollings has been paralleled in other legislation which has sought to make hard decisions automatic. And there is also evidence in states such as California of a willingness to contemplate devices which limit the power of legislators. In 1990, for example, California passed an initiative which restricted its legislators' terms of office to six and eight years. This tactic (which was also used in other states) underlined a desire to impose greater accountability on politicians and to exert greater direct control over public policy. Such developments suggest a certain erosion of trust in the ability of representative institutions to make policy in the majority interest and a damaging decline in the legitimacy of elected officials, a decline that was further exacerbated by such public scandals as that involving five members of Congress in the collapse of America's Savings and Loan companies.

It was not, however, just elected officials whose legitimacy had been damaged during the 1980s. The question of the legitimacy of the country's legal institutions and bureaucracy was raised in stark form by the conservative movement at the beginning of the decade, with profound consequences for constitutional debates. In fact the courts had become an alternative arena for pursuing policy objectives by interest groups as much as by individuals and it seems likely that any president will want to retain a strong policy towards the composition of the nation's judicial system. However, as Bush's first appointment to the Supreme Court (David Souter) shows, there may be little to gain from open confrontation with Congress, if the same results can be achieved by less dramatic judicial policies than those adopted by the Reagan Administration. But, as the 1991 nomination of a conservative black jurist (Clarence Thomas) underlines, Presidents may want to put on the Court individuals whose record and personal attributes inevitably generate controversy.

The problem of the public bureaucracy by contrast is that it is internally divided and liable to compete for power over policy as well as being subject to the manipulation of interest groups. Successive presidents have attempted to reform this key institution of policy implementation but their efforts have thus far had mixed results.

The third section of the book deals with problems of making policy in a system where consensus is difficult to achieve and the legitimacy of major institutions has been contested. Of course the process of making policy for a complex society such as the United States would always be difficult and it is also the case that some of the problems which have appeared on America's public policy agenda – for example drugs and education – have themselves been complex and intractable. Also, the fact that the U.S. is a federal system has important implications for the process by which policy is made and the manner in which it is delivered. However, federalism is not a static concept. It evolved from the 1930s to a system in which the federal government took a good deal of responsibility for supplementing state provision and developed a role as a provider of additional finance to support the urban areas where many of America's most profound social problems could be found. From the 1980s onwards, however, the fiscal ability and political willingness of federal government to use its powers to support the states and the cities declined. As a result two phenomena can be discerned in the 1990s. First, we may expect the states to provide a good deal more initiative in policy-making. On the other hand it must be remembered that the states themselves have limited fiscal resources. Therefore there will be additional pressure on the larger cities which will themselves find it difficult to cope with the problems of social decay – an inability which may in turn be expected to produce further flight from the cities and an exacerbation of the inner cities' financial problems.

The changing pattern of federal politics has a direct effect on the style of domestic policy-making. Joseph Hogan sets his discussion of the handling of American economic policy against the background of institutions with divided responsibility for overall economic policy. Thus, although the most obvious clash in the making of economic policy is likely to be the result of presidential conflicts with Congress over the handling of economic priorities, there are other institutional divisions notably between the presidential responsibilities and those of the Federal Reserve which make the construction of a coherent economic policy difficult. Indeed it is a paradox that the country to which much of the modern world looks for leadership in solving economic problems is itself weakened in macro-economic management by a constitutional structure which distrusts centralized leadership, and a political culture which is hardly receptive to efforts to reform the work of the Founding Fathers. And, while some of the weakness in economic management at the federal level can be countered by state level activity, there is still a gap in policy-making capacity which it is difficult to see being filled in the near future.

The legacy of President Reagan's economic policy to the Bush Administration has been severely felt in the field of social policy. But there are elements of change in social policy-making, even though it is difficult to assess the overall extent of the Bush Administration's commitment to any particular set of values.

Fragmentation and a lack of vision were seen as marked features of Bush's foreign policy, where the collapse of communism in Eastern Europe and the Soviet Union itself cast doubt on the assumptions which had guided American foreign policy since 1945 and certainly removed much of the ideological unity of the conservative movement. American foreign and security policy is therefore likely to be more than ever guided by pragmatic and short-term considerations and by new institutional arrangements in the foreign policy field.

As always with the *Developments* series, the editors try to give the constants of policy-making a contemporary focus by selecting issues and themes which are central to current American debate. Here three have been chosen. Gillian Peele looks at President Bush's handling of civil rights policy. The question of civil rights for minorities is in one sense a constant issue in American politics because of the long-standing political and economic inequalities suffered by black Americans and because the country is so heterogeneous. However, this policy area has become especially controversial in recent years because of the new twist given to issues of equality by the policies of the Reagan Administration. Rodolfo de la Garza also addresses the question of civil rights as he looks at the issue of immigration and Mexicans; both themes have long term implications for the polity and have special significance in a period of a new census (1990). And, in considering a period where yet again Congress and the President had such difficulty in agreeing a budget that many of the federal government's activities were threatened with closure, it is useful to have Stanley Collender's examination of the nature of the deficit.

The final section – whose arguments have already been

mentioned – is a reflective piece by Morris Fiorina on the nature of divided government in the United States. Although not all commentators are agreed about the seriousness of the problem, divided government is a feature of American political life which has implications for the American public policy process and gives American government in the late twentieth century a distinctive character. It also poses intriguing questions about American electoral behavior and policy preferences.

Gillian Peele
Chris Bailey
Bruce Cain

PART ONE

The Sources of Political Change

1

Values, Institutions and Policy Agendas

GILLIAN PEELE

Values are important in the context of any political system because they help to shape the institutions and the policy outputs of that system. In the United States the ideas of equality, democracy, self-government, individual liberty, localism, the protection of property and constitutionalism, as well as arguments over the definition of what is 'truly American', have together provided a core set of values to which reference can be made in political debate (Barone, 1990). These values are not necessarily compatible with each other and many of American public policy dilemmas continue to involve difficult clashes of values. Thus advocates of greater equality (which might be achieved through higher levels of governmental spending on welfare) have had to reckon with a political culture in which the idea of progressive taxation is much more suspect than in many European countries. Similarly, advocates of individual freedom have frequently found that the American political system for all its emphasis on constitutional protection afforded to minorities may offer little comfort to those individuals whose ideas offend the majority.

The way in which clashes of values manifest themselves in public debate will of course vary. Different periods present their own conflicts and the extent to which they involve what Laurence Tribe has called 'clashes of absolutes' will also vary (Tribe, 1990). Slavery clearly came to be a major value

14

conflict in the nineteenth century, although it was but one component of a broader clash of cultural values. And in the late twentieth century, abortion has proved a divisive moral issue of major proportions. The abortion controversy also underlines the extent to which clashes of values are reflected in the language in which an issue is presented and may affect the substantive outcome of the political controversy. Capturing the language is thus a significant part of any political cause. Is abortion an issue about the sanctity of life or is it about the notion of freedom of choice, specifically of women? Similarly should the question of pornography be seen in terms of freedom of speech and the constitutional protection afforded by the First Amendment? Or is it, as many feminists would argue, to be seen in terms of the exploitation of women? (MacKinnon, 1987). Or should it be analyzed in terms of an insidious undermining of traditional family values and Judeao-Christian morality as polemicists such as the Reverend Jerry Falwell (the leader of the now defunct Moral Majority) and the Reverend Donald Wildmon (the spokesman of the American Family Association) have suggested?

Political Institutions and American Values

The interplay of values with political institutions and political actors in the United States has frequently seemed unusual because America – unlike so many European countries – has appeared devoid both of strong ideological divisions and of a clear party system based on differences of political doctrine. But, although parties are not as central in the definition of issues in American political debate as in some other political systems, certain institutions have a key role in framing the United States' political agenda. The president, because he obviously has a national constituency and can highlight an issue, can be central to the making of America's public philosophy (Thompson, 1981). Thus Lyndon Johnson's identification of the poverty issue was essential to the mobilization of the United States behind the Great Society programs. The rhetoric of Ronald Reagan by contrast identified government itself as the problem facing the United States and played that identification back into debates about the proper policies to be pursued on such issues as the environment and welfare reform.

Apart from the president, the Supreme Court also plays a crucial role in enunciating values and exploring the logic of competing preferences for constitutional and legal arrangements. The Supreme Court may interpret the constitution to allow or ban discrimination on grounds of race, may place a heavy emphasis on the value of privacy or may permit flag-burning as a constitutional exercise of freedom of speech. Decisions of the Supreme Court (and indeed of American courts generally) may often reflect the clashes of values within the political system or, as in the case of affirmative action, disagreements about the meanings of values; but a Supreme Court pronouncement will not necessarily settle a contentious issue, as the extensive litigation on affirmative action and abortion underlined (see Chapter 6).

The role of the Supreme Court in the United States is in part a reflection of the extent to which the more political branches of the country's system of government – especially Congress – find it difficult to resolve issues definitively or indeed sometimes find it difficult to pass any legislations on a contentious issue or take a substantial time to frame a successful legislative measure. In some cases an apparent political consensus may also dissipate. Thus the Equal Rights Amendment was stalled in the 1980s, despite an apparently easy passage through Congress and early ratification by a large number of states.

Elected officials and the courts are the major actors in the process of defining what becomes an issue in American politics. But other institutions are also important, especially pressure groups. The agendas of the groups and movements which seek the advance of their policy goals will reflect their strategic sense of how hospitable the climate is to their particular causes and, as has been pointed out, an agenda can be advanced by a variety of factors such as a new administration or constrained by factors such as budgetary limitations or shifts in public opinion (Kingdon, 1984). Thus the growth of the conservative movement in the late 1970s and the advent of the Reagan Administration had the effect of restructuring the environment in which America's interest groups had to operate (Peele, 1984). In addition, of course, the mass media – the press but most importantly television – exercises a significant influence over the structure of the American political agenda.

Party Divisions and American Values

The discussion of American political values in the 1990s presents the observer with something of a paradox. On the one hand, the country's political divisions look more rational than at any time since the Civil War as the result of the ideological sorting out of the party system and the erosion of geographically-based partisan cleavages. Thus, while Southern Democrats to some extent remain more conservative than their fellow Democrats, the sharp divergence over race which had cut through the Democrats in the 1960s is no longer a feature of that party's politics. Similarly, although it would be a mistake to see the Republican Party as free of faction in the 1990s, there was in the 1970s and 1980s a marked decline in the cohesion and strength of liberal Republicanism (Rae, 1989). Both of America's political parties have acquired a sharper ideological identity. The Democrats have emerged as the party of governmental intervention on behalf of the economically disadvantaged and have combined this economic populism with support for individual freedom and liberalism on cultural or 'lifestyle' issues. Thus groups such as the poor, blacks, Latinos, feminists and gay rights activists as well as supporters of a progressive environmentalism are usually all to be found in the Democratic camp. The Republicans, by contrast, have defined themselves in terms of reduced governmental intervention in the economy and lower taxes and have combined this economic liberalism with support for traditional social and moral values. Republicans have thus become the champions both of the economically advantaged and the middle American families.

On the other hand, alongside this apparent simplification

of American political opinion, American politics has fragmented in a number of other ways. To some extent, this fragmentation is the result of the unravelling of the majority Democratic coalition – the decline of the so-called New Deal order (Fraser and Gerstle, 1989). This fracturing of the New Deal coalition has had many implications for American political life; but it reflected primarily the incompatibility of values, and the political agendas derived from them, of the disparate component parts of the coalition. Thus the political values of the segregationist white South collided sharply with the political agenda of blacks and liberals who emphasized integration, equality and civil rights. But the agendas of blacks and the poor also collided with the aspirations of white ethnics – such as the Irish and the Italians – who had hitherto been locked into the Democratic coalition by their perception of themselves as disadvantaged by comparison with 'mainstream' American society. By the 1970s however many of these groups had experienced upward mobility and had little in common with an increasingly vocal black constituency and equally little in common with some of the radical cause groups who advocated alternative lifestyles. Jewish groups and labor unions also found themselves suspicious of those policy preferences – more welfare and such strategies as affirmative action – advocated by blacks and by the more liberal elements of the Democratic Party.

This unravelling of the Democratic coalition created new opportunities for the Republican Party, especially at the presidential level. But, although some observers predicted a Republican majority emerging as a result of these and other electoral changes, they did not lead to anything as well-defined as a realignment. Instead there emerged a new electoral regime in which a weakened Democratic Party faced a somewhat strengthened Republican Party and in which the likelihood of split partisan control at the federal level of government increased.

There were in addition in the 1970s and 1980s other factors operating to decentralize and fracture American politics – most notably the rise of political action committees (PACs), the trends in campaign technology and the decline of support for federal government intervention and the *de facto* transfer of responsibility in many subject areas to the state and local level. Thus not merely did the agendas of interest groups take on a life of their own outside party politics in many policy arenas; but the multiple arenas in which claims were pressed further complicated political debate.

In attempting to assess the significance of political values in the 1990s it is therefore necessary to analyze two rather different phenomena. First, it is important to examine the strength of general political ideas as organized through the party system and the broader conservative and liberal movements. Secondly it is necessary to see how some key groups in the American polity have experienced a shift in their strategic position and to see how far their agendas have changed in response to that shift. Only then can we see what values they advance and how far they are likely to be successful in translating their preferences into public policy. Before attempting either of these tasks however it may be helpful to make some general points about the context in which political values are debated in the 1990s.

Political debate in the United States tends to go in cycles. There have thus been periods in which a progressive reforming liberalism has been dominant and periods in which the public mood has been much more conservative and has sought change which will return the United States to some mythical golden age. Thus in the discussion of the public philosophy of the United States, although a range of values always competes for attention, the emphasis will vary from one period to another as between, for example, an appeal to justice or equality or an appeal to freedom and individualism.

But it should not be assumed that periods can always be seen in terms of the influence of one large idea. Sometimes a period may emphasize not so much the intellectual or aspirational goals of public policy, but a series of practical concerns reflecting the concrete needs of sections of the population. In such circumstances American political discourse will reflect the compromises and accommodations made to suit the needs of the various groups. For the American political system it should be remembered is one where policy-making is a highly competitive process. Thus in addition to arguments about which values and policies are to be preferred, there will also be arguments about the best strategies for advancing a given set of priorities. Should, for example, the federal government be relied upon as the best means of promoting greater equality either by redistributive economic policies or by protecting certain disadvantaged minorities? Have the states any role to play in the process? What if anything may be expected from the Supreme Court? Or should there be less emphasis on the role of government and more on the role of markets in determining the distribution of goods in society?

Such questions transcend the routine battles between the political parties, although they will clearly affect the climate in which the Democrats and Republicans must operate. At various points both Republicans and Democrats have had to struggle against the grain of public opinion. Thus the Republicans from the period of the New Deal to the end of the 1960s found themselves on the defensive because of the increasing support for egalitarian values and governmental intervention to reduce poverty. By contrast, the Democrats have found it hard to forge a public philosophy in the climate of the 1980s when support for egalitarian solutions had eroded and the emphasis in public debate has been on the values of individualism and market incentives as well as on the practicality of policies.

A Value Shift in the 1990s?

Many commentators on American politics were looking to the 1990s for a shift in public values. And there were several reasons why change might have been expected. First, the high-water mark of American conservatism seemed to have passed with the exit of Ronald Reagan from the White House. Perhaps even before 1988 much of ideological coherence of the Reagan presidency had faded, although the symbolism of Reagan's presidency remained strong even at the end of his presidency.

The development of the conservative movement in the United States was a complex process which drew on a number of distinctive features of American society. Central to the philosophy of the conservative movement and the Reagan Administration was a skepticism about the efficacy of governmental intervention in a range of policy arenas and a general desire to reduce the role of public provision and regulation. In addition to the preference for non-governmental solutions to problems, which was shared, for example, with British conservatism under Mrs Thatcher's leadership, there developed an emphasis on the so-called 'social issues' which included opposition to abortion, homosexuality and busing and support for school prayer and the death penalty. Policies based on this powerful mix of preferences were to be advanced by a variety of means including the control of the bureaucracy, judicial appointments and the presidency's direct access to the public.

The effect was to give the Reagan presidency an unusually powerful ideological impetus which, even if it faded over eight years, refocused and clarified American political divisions, giving Republicans and Democrats sharpened identities.

Although George Bush clearly wished to take advantage to some extent of the Reagan ideological legacy, he was also a very different politician. Certainly he was willing to be the beneficiary of the transformation of liberalism into a minority creed; but he also sensed that there had been a switch of mood within the United States – a sentiment which he echoed with his call for a 'kinder gentler America'. Ostensibly this suggested that there should be a greater emphasis on the needs of the community and less insistence on the virtues of individualism. Translated into public policy terms this meant an acknowledgement of the need for a greater governmental involvement in such areas of public policy as drugs (an issue perceived by the U.S. public in 1988 to be the key issue facing America), education and child care.

Those who expected a shift in public philosophy were further encouraged by the fact that President Bush was not naturally one of the conservative movement's 'true believers'. Rather he was a pragmatic politician more accustomed to working within government than to urging its abolition. Moreover, his patrician family background and education distanced him from the new generation of conservative leaders in outlook and values and made him somewhat critical of the excesses of the new and ostentatious wealth associated with the Reagan years.

The Evolution of the Conservative Movement

If George Bush was a very different politician from Ronald Reagan, it was also the case that by 1988 the conservative movement itself had changed. The growth of the American conservative movement – or movement conservatism – was one of the major features of the 1970s. It was a development which occurred largely independently of the Republican Party, although it had a major impact on Republican fortunes and thinking. More remarkably perhaps it had the effect of promoting a much more self-conscious concern with values on the right and broadened the conservative agenda to take on a range of controversial social issues which enabled the Republicans to extend their appeal in sub-cultures whose partisan preference had previously been Democratic.

Much has been written about the different components of the conservative movement. Here it is necessary to highlight the range of different traditions represented within the rightwards shift which occurred in the 1970s and 1980s. The 'neo-conservatives' for example drew on the strongly anti-communist and interventionist tradition of the Democratic Party. Although now associated with the Republicans, many of the neo-conservatives had for most of their lives been Democrats, but were alienated from the Democratic Party in the late 1960s and 1970s by the party's perceived submission to anti-Vietnam war activism and by the effect of the party's capture by minority causes and factions.

Many of the people labelled neo-conservative were journalists or academics and they had a strong interest in the efficacy of public policy. Most of them had a strong interest in the maintenance of social cohesion and community obligations and some were anxious to emphasize the role of religion in sustaining the structure of society. By contrast the emphasis of the free market theorists was much more on individual freedom of choice. An interesting contrast on foreign policy was to emerge from this division under President Bush. The libertarians and free marketeers (represented, for example, by such think-tanks as the Cato Institute) were far less committed to traditional alliances such as NATO than were some of the neo-conservatives (such as Irving Kristol) who had been extensively involved in the fight against communist influence in Europe and were also insistent on the importance of supporting Israel in the Middle East.

There were also divergences on questions of morality and culture. Some, though by no means all, of the neo-conservatives had become extremely critical of permissiveness in relation to sexual mores and of movements such as feminism which threatened established social relationships. These trends were apparent in the pages of neo-conservative journals such as *Commentary*, although *Commentary* had once had a reputation for being extremely radical on artistic issues. By contrast, although not all supporters of the free market were libertarians, some applied the principles of the free market to such issues as pornography and adoption, while others simply advanced the proposition that the government should not interfere in matters of personal morality.

Reaganism, of course, did not represent the extreme free market position. Rather, by combining *laissez faire* economics with traditional morality, it advanced a mix which was politically appealing in a country where cultural divisions have been as significant as economic ones.

One factor in advancing the new right's political salience had been the growing involvement of religious groups in politics. Religion has always had a political significance in the United States. What happened in the 1970s and 1980s, however, was a conjunction of two developments. First, the Roman Catholic Church became politically involved in single issues especially that of abortion. Secondly, there was a mobilization of fundamentalists behind conservative causes. It is true that some of the strength of this movement declined over the 1980s as individual 'televangelists' (especially Jim and Tammy Bakker) were discredited by sexual and financial scandals. But the nuances of the politicization of the churches changed and the strident politicization on the right was paralleled by a more extensive political involvement of all the churches, including a more effective lobbying organization by mainstream denominations which were inclined to embrace liberal rather than conservative positions. It was also the case that the black churches remained active on the left of American politics and that some of the most visible black politicians in America (for example Jesse Jackson) were ordained ministers who combined a radical political message with a populist religious appeal.

In addition to a broad politicization of the churches, there has also been a certain fragmentation as individual church leaders have gone their own way or taken up particular issues. This fragmentation was perhaps to be expected in the general arena of American Protestantism which has always been marked by a high degree of centrifugalism and individualism in its congregations. But it should be noted that there are also very important splits within the more 'organized' and 'hierarchical' churches – the Roman Catholics and the Episcopalians.

Of course, the Conservative movement itself was never monolithic and its internal contradictions emerged sharply at the end of the Reagan Administration. Some of the movement's divisions emerged in the 1988 presidential nomination process. The more pragmatic Republicans viewed George Bush as the most credible candidate but the more ideologically committed preferred either Congressman Jack Kemp, a leading proponent of supply-side economics, or Pat Robertson, a televangelist with political ambitions. The relatively easy victory of George Bush in the 1988 primaries and the November election created a situation in which the conservative movement could not expect to have the same kind of access which it had had under Ronald Reagan. And even if the newly elected President attempted to balance the pragmatists in his Administration with a few conservatives such as John Sununu (as Chief of Staff) William Bennett as Secretary of Education (and briefly as Republican Party Chairman after Lee Atwater became ill) and Jack Kemp (as Secretary of Housing and Urban Development) the 'Bush people' were clearly different from the 'Reagan people'. The conservative movement could not readily identify with the Bush Administration in the way that it had with his predecessor's. The long drawn struggle to reach a budget compromise in 1990 and the abandonment of the 'no new taxes' pledge is likely to create further divisions on the right, although it remains to be seen how damaging this will be in the long run either to Bush himself or to the Republican Party in the light of the popularity acquired by the President at the end of the Gulf war. Initially though, the relationship between presidential and House Republicans was soured by the Republicans' rejection of the Bush budget proposals in 1990 and their partisan preference for Newt Gingrich's leadership rather than that of the White House.

Both the budget morass and the Gulf war highlighted a major difficulty facing American conservatism in the 1990s: the task of defining itself in a highly complex domestic and international situation. Many of the conservative movement's successes in the 1970s and early 1980s were achieved because it was able to portray the liberalism associated with the Democratic Party in the 1960s and 1970s as bankrupt. The conservative movement was initially shaped in reaction to a series of specific events and crises. The perceived policy failures of the Great Society, the changes in social behavior associated with a self-conscious youth movement, and the shock of Vietnam which challenged the idea of American omnipotence all contributed to the conservative *weltanschauung* which dominated the 1980s. However by the end of the 1980s a new set of problems had arisen to trouble the American electorate. And it was not clear that conservatives had any obvious remedy for them.

The question of America's role in the world was especially discomforting for conservatives. The American right in the 1970s and 1980s was united by a strong anti-communism coupled with a hawkishness on defense spending. With the demise of the communist threat not merely was this unifying theme for the right no longer so potent; it was also difficult for the right to agree on the meaning of the changes in the communist bloc or their implications for America's policy *vis-à-vis* such institutions as NATO. For some on the right the important priority was to resist calls for rapid defense reductions. For other conservatives there was skepticism about granting trade concessions to the Soviet Union and general unhappiness about Soviet behavior in the Baltic States and in relation to Jewish emigration to Israel.

On the other hand there were some on the American right who welcomed the changed international situation as an opportunity to reassess America's European commitments and especially the assumption that the United States should continue to be the major contributor to Europe's defense even as the European Community becomes an increasingly effective trade competitor. Especially visible in this debate was the free-market Cato Institute which put forward arguments much more reminiscent of the conservative movement's pre-1945 isolationist past than its more recent cold warrior incarnation.

The extent to which there was a fissure on the right between foreign policy interventionists and isolationists as well as a degree of difficulty in defining American national interests was brought out in the Gulf crisis which confronted President Bush in the middle of 1990. Although the President was able to build an overwhelming degree of bipartisan support for his policies, there were criticisms of the decision to intervene against Iraq. These criticisms came not as might have been expected from Democrats in Congress, but in the early stages from the ranks of the right – from Robert Dornan, a Californian conservative, and from Ted Galen Carpenter (Cato's foreign policy specialist).

To pinpoint divisions in the conservative movement is not to suggest that the conservative movement had become exhausted by the early 1990s. One of the major legacies of the burst of conservative and new right thought and activity in the 1970s and 1980s was an extensive network of institutes, think-tanks and foundations which could provide a support structure for conservative and free market activity at a number of different levels in American politics. This structure alone would ensure that conservatism retained a momentum of its own. What had occurred however was a certain fragmentation and diminution of purpose.

A Revived Liberalism?

The divisions on the American right in the late 1980s have to be set against the background of a highly successful period of growth and activity in the period from the mid-1970s to the mid-1980s. Debates within the Democratic Party and amongst liberals had no such background of achievement. Part of the problem which the Democratic party had in the 1980s was its inability to articulate a comprehensive philosophy either to counter an apparently self-confident conservatism or to rally its own disparate forces. The Democratic Party frequently appeared to be a coalition of minority concerns and special interests with no overarching themes to link such single issues as abortion and civil rights.

There were several attempts to fill this philosophical vacuum in the Democratic camp. Some senior Democrats such as Edward Kennedy seemed content to stay with a set of fairly traditional welfare policies aimed at key Democratic constituencies such as the poor, blacks and labor, or like National Committee chairman Ron Brown expressed a liberal philosophy in opposition to Republican values. Others such as Senator Robb of Virginia attempted a slightly different and more conservative synthesis through the Democratic Leadership Council. Liberal think-tanks such as the Urban League remained active in pressing their own agendas on poverty and related issues. Yet, at the more general level of creating a cohesive intellectual framework for Democrats there was very little in the way of new activity.

However, in 1990 there was an attempt by a group of liberal academics centered in Princeton to stimulate new thinking. These academics founded a scholarly journal called *The American Prospect* with the aim of providing the kind of focus to a liberal revival which the journals *The Public Interest* and *Commentary* provided for critics of liberalism in the 1960s and 1970s. The academics associated with *The American Prospect* (who included sociologists Paul Starr and Christopher Jencks) were inevitably anxious to take advantage of what they saw as a changing mood both in international and domestic affairs.

Economic populism would have been one theme which the

Democrats could have made central to their appeal. The Reagan years had dramatically magnified many inequalities in American society and had seen a new alignment of wealth analogous in some ways to the Gilded Age in American history (Phillips, 1990). Many critics also noted cultural similarities between the vulgarities of the post-Civil War period and an America where wealth (frequently acquired in the 1980s as a result of novel financial transactions such as the sale of junk bonds) coexisted with extremes of poverty and homelessness. The economic shifts of the 1980s favored the service industries rather than manufacturing or agriculture and they favored certain regions of the United States (notably the coasts rather than the interior); but they also favored the elderly against the young, the college educated against those without extensive educational credentials and whites against racial minorities. The most notable feature of the economic shifts of the Reagan years, however, was the extent to which much of middle America lost out as a result of the combination of general movements in the American economy and the Reagan Administration's policies of reducing the level of direct taxation.

Changes in America's international trading position and the growth of foreign ownership both of American companies and American real estate led in the 1980s to calls for protectionism. In the 1988 Democratic primaries only Richard Gephardt forcefully expressed concern about America's competitiveness in the international arena, although Jesse Jackson hammered themes which highlighted the domestic inequalities produced by Reagan's America. Whether populist themes could unite the Democratic Party remains to be seen; certainly Michael Dukakis in 1988 did not play the populist card much to the relief, it seems, of Republican strategists. It is difficult to imagine a scenario in which it will not be used in 1992 regardless of who ultimately wins the Democratic nomination. Even so, the Democratic Party is likely to remain troubled by its need to reconcile the conflicting values of those who might be attracted to the party on economic grounds (but who are conservative on moral and cultural issues) and those who might be attracted to Democratic Party primarily on cultural issues. It is not that such a reconciliation could never be effected; but rather that it is difficult at the level of presidential politics, especially given the eagerness with which Republican advisers will be searching for something to allow them to paint a Democratic candidate as outside the mainstream of American values.

Political Movements and American Values

Political parties are not the only or even the major source of new issue agendas in the United States. Pressure groups and movements also construct their distinct agendas for political debate and may prove the motor of policy change. Although it would clearly be impossible in a chapter of this kind to analyze the whole spectrum of pressure groups in the American system, it may be helpful to review here two movements which have either had a major impact on the values of American political debate or have the potential to do so: feminism and black politics.

The Feminist Movement

The feminist movement had never been a homogeneous one and it is hardly surprising that the 1990s found the women's movement exhibiting a high degree of ideological pluralism – liberal feminism, Marxist feminism, radical feminism, socialist feminism and lesbian separatism. And much of this ideological pluralism was reflected in organizational diversity including, for example, a separate organizational structure for ethnic minority women.

The scholarly analysis and explanation of the origins and impact of changing gender relations on American society flourished in American universities during the 1980s and had produced some interesting subfields. Thus for example, although history and literature were the major beneficiaries of the surge of feminist scholarship, law schools saw a feminist version of the continuing 'critical legal studies' debate. However, ideological fragmentation inevitably weakened the intellectual identity of the feminist movement. And, although feminists could be pleased about the extent to which they had achieved academic recognition, increased specialization and the somewhat arcane nature of some of the debates – for instance that between the post-modernists and the feminists – were liable to isolate feminist theories from the broader public policy concerns of the women's organizations.

The women's political organizations which had developed to advance the interests of female equality had by 1990 been weakened both by the assaults of the new right and by their own internal divisions over priorities. Yet at the same time there was an increased interest in the practical economic and social agenda of the women's movement as such issues as child care came to command the attention of legislators even if the package ultimately passed by Congress in 1990 was less generous than many wanted.

On the most divisive issue of the 1980s, abortion, there were signs that the pro-choice element was capable of resisting the efforts of the right-to-life movement to cut back on the constitutional rights enunciated so controversially in *Roe* v. *Wade*. The idea that the *Webster* decision of 1989 would lead to a tide of restrictive legislation at the state level was not supported by political developments. Indeed in states where the governor had attempted to hasten the movement towards greater restriction on abortion there was resistance and sometimes electoral damage to the pro-life politicians. Thus in Florida, in 1990 Governor Bob Martinez lost to his Democratic opponent partly as a result of his aggressive pro-life stance on abortion.

Although the role of organized feminism had appeared to be in decline in the late 1980s – because the women's movement was inevitably locked into a progressive liberalism that was itself weakened – the issues most central to women were slightly better placed by the end of 1990. Not that Congress was able very much to reflect women's views since after the 1990 elections the Senate had only 2 women members and the House a mere 28.

The major women's organizations had recognized that they would be on the defensive in the conservative climate of the 1980s. The question of the role of women and the family in American life had become central to the symbolic cultural politics of a decade. The issues of abortion and the Equal Rights Amendment were central to the feminist agenda but as politics became polarized between the symbolism of Phyllis Schafly's *Stop ERA* movement and the symbolism of radical feminism, it was difficult for groups such as NOW, which were very much in the tradition of liberal feminism, to be effective. Moreover, the feminist cause suffered from the almost inevitable generation change as the activists of the 1960s aged and were replaced by a new generation of women who took career equality for granted, reproducing a pattern similar to that which occurred when the suffragists were replaced by the flappers after the First World War (Broesamle, 1990). The movement thus suffered a double weakening – the direct attack of critics and the apathy of a new generation of women content to enjoy the benefits of feminist agitation but no longer interested in organizing on behalf of the women's movement.

Partly in response to this changed climate and partly because the policies of the Reagan period had a disproportionate impact on women, the women's organizations concentrated on a different set of issues from those which had absorbed their energies in the 1970s and early 1980s. On such issues as child poverty and child care provision – as well as the question of comparable worth – they were able to make alliances with other like minded pressure groups such as the Children's Defense Fund. Such issues were less divisive than the overarching themes of the 1970s and enabled some outreach to minority groups as well as a degree of bipartisanship. But it was interesting that during the hearings on the nomination of David Souter's nomination for the Supreme Court in 1990 the women's groups had to take the lead in criticizing the nomination and other groups (who had been allies in the Bork struggle) such as the Leadership Conference on Civil Rights had to be persuaded by Edward Kennedy to back such organizations as NOW. However, fear of alienating the women's vote clearly influenced Democrats in the Thomas hearings in 1991.

The Poverty Issue

The debate about the causes of poverty and the most effective methods for coping with it became central to the public policy arguments of the 1980s but they also became central to the women's movement because feminists could give their own interpretation to social trends and the Administration's initiatives.

The Reagan cuts in domestic spending affected the domestic welfare programs designed to provide support for the poorest groups in American society. Women have become a disproportionately large component of America's poor and the number of female-headed households in poverty has risen markedly. In 1960 women headed 24 per cent of all poor households; in 1984 they headed 48 per cent of poor households (Katz, 1989). Although there were both white and ethnic minority poor, blacks and Hispanics in female-headed households were especially likely to find themselves in poverty. Thus in 1987 53.8 per cent of female-headed black families were in poverty and 53 per cent of Hispanic female-headed families.

The causes of women's poverty in the United States are complex but two factors in particular have been crucial. First, the structure of the welfare provisions themselves which divide benefits into entitlements (Social Security and various forms of unemployment insurance) and public assistance programs such as AFDC which have targeted the very poor and appear much more subject to the stigma attached to handouts (Katz, 1989). Apart from the different public attitudes attached to the two kinds of welfare provision, it is much easier to cut the second than the first which in turn means that it is easier to cut programs which are crucial for women. Secondly, there is the fact that the kind of work that women do is usually less well paid than the kind of work for which men are employed, especially in the service sector. (It is also the case, as has become apparent from the comparable worth debate, that women are sometimes paid less than men even when the work is similar.)

Any cuts in domestic welfare spending which hit the poor would therefore have been likely to hit women severely. But it was increasingly likely to hit children too since many of the women in poverty were mothers. And, although this association of women and children in poverty was for some a reflection of the breakdown of traditional family structures, it was politically important since it mitigated the harsher attitudes which had become prevalent in the discussion of welfare policy in the 1980s. The women's movement was able to take advantage of this aspect of poverty. Conservative arguments against liberalism had been honed on what were perceived as the costly excesses of the Great Society's poverty programs and the attitudes which supported welfare benefits. In the 1980s on the conservative side a new consensus had been formed by writers who saw the policies of the past two decades as having created a new dependency politics. Thus theorists such as Charles Murray and Lawrence Mead argued that many of these programs central to alleviating poverty in America were functionally inefficient and morally unjustifiable. The poor were transformed from citizens/victims into a category well known to social historians – the undeserving poor. The Reagan years therefore saw both a shift in public attitudes towards the poor and a change in the nature of welfare policies as a result of financial cut-backs. The restructuring of welfare through the Family Support Act of 1988 reflected a conservative view of the conditions under which welfare should be given and, more controversially, a conception of citizenship that was based on the idea of the obligations of citizenship rather than its rights.

Although many of the women's groups might have preferred to respond to these attacks in the language of equality and the overarching themes of progressive liberalism, it was recognized that such a response was unlikely to be successful. However, if the response was framed in terms of concrete issues such as children's poverty and child care, not only was the climate for such issues likely to be more favorable but alliances could be made with other groups to advance legislation.

Blacks

The role which black Americans play in American politics has been shaped by three factors. First, although there have been attempts to transform the black vote into an independent or swing vote in order to enhance its strategic leverage, the blacks have since the New Deal been part of the Democratic coalition. Secondly, blacks have advanced a distinctive and fairly stable issue agenda at least since the Second World War (Walters, 1988). Thirdly, since the 1960s, the growth in the number of black elected officials has provided the community with a leadership cadre capable of operating within the context of America's political institutions.

Two main clusters of issues continued to dominate black politics in the 1980s and seem likely to remain central to the politics of the 1990s. First there were the issues associated with the distinctive position of blacks in American society. Although it could be argued that legal discrimination on grounds of race had been eliminated from American life, the black community was still concerned about discrimination in employment, housing and education. Moreover there was the perception among blacks that many of the achievements of the 1960s were endangered by an increasingly conservative climate. Certainly, the Reagan years saw remedies such as affirmative action subject to attack so that civil rights issues remained on the black agenda in the 1980s (see Chapter 13). In addition to civil rights, however, blacks were increasingly concerned with developing their political muscle and by securing national visibility for black politicians, enhancing black political legitimacy.

However, the second major issue cluster on the black agenda was the economic position of blacks and the promotion of policies designed to tackle the poverty in which a substantial (though not the whole) of America's black community found itself.

The leadership offered to blacks in the 1980s sometimes seemed problematic. Although the 1980s had seen black politicians become more visible, they were arguably less united in their goals and strategies. In 1984 (as in 1988) Jesse Jackson's presidential campaign had the effect of providing a symbolic focus for much of black America; but Jackson's style and his policy orientation made a number of traditional allies nervous. Civil rights groups trying to defend affirmative action in a cold Reaganite climate were fearful about his call to boycott firms that did not hire enough minority em-

ployees. Liberals and Jewish groups were offended both by
Jackson's racist remarks about 'Hymietown' and by his association with Louis Farrakand, the Black Muslim.

Over the period 1984–90 Jackson's politics moved towards
the mainstream; but it is not clear how welcome his charisma-
tic presence was to other successful black politicians such as
Douglas Wilder (the first black Governor of Virginia and who
by 1991 was being discussed as a possible presidential conten-
der) or Mayor David Dinkins of New York. Coleman Young
the Mayor of Detroit did not endorse Jackson in the 1988
primaries.

Nor indeed were Jesse Jackson's politics particularly compatible with those of the black congressional caucus. By the
1990s black members of the House had begun to reap the
fruits of seniority so that individuals such as William Gray
acquired power on key committees and within the Democratic Party as a whole. In a climate of budgetary constraint black
politicians would tend to act cautiously and settle for small if
unspectacular gains.

The lessons of the 1990 elections for blacks were hard to
read. Although Jesse Helms was returned for the Republicans in North Carolina in an election where the fact that the
Democratic candidate was black had inevitably made race an
issue, the outcome was in doubt until the very end. Similarly,
although a populist Democrat in Massachusetts, John Silber,
had apparently refused to make any special appeal for black
votes, the election was in fact won by the more liberal
Republican William Weld.

Conclusions

Despite the apparent ideological promise of the 'Reagan
revolution', the last years of the Reagan Administration and
the early years of the Bush Administration have seen a
fragmentation of American politics. At the same time, many
pressure groups have learned to adapt to a more conservative
environment and have adapted to the politics of realism.
Institutional developments have further fractured the policy
processes and blurred the clashes of values in the American

system. Indeed one is struck by the unwillingness of American institutions to resolve value conflicts as the Supreme Court hands such issues as abortion back to the states and Congress passes questions about distinguishing between obscenity and art back to the courts. Such an environment fits the style of the Bush Administration quite well. The costs in terms of policy-making and democratic legitimacy have yet to be assessed.

2

The American Electoral System

BRUCE CAIN

American electoral trends are rarely simple. A generalization about voting in one area of the country or among a particular subset of the population may not apply elsewhere or to everyone. For years, political scientists tempered their most significant pronouncements about voting in America with the phrase 'except in the south'. In the 1990s, they may need even more face-saving caveats.

The American electorate, which has always been diverse by comparative standards, has become even more varied in recent years. As a consequence of new immigration patterns, Latinos and Asians are among the fastest growing groups in the country; and in certain states such as California, non-whites are likely to constitute a majority of the population (although not a majority of the voters) by the early twenty-first century. As the electorate has grown more demographically diverse, the number of politically salient issues and distinct interests have multiplied, making the landscape of American electoral politics more complex than ever.

The expression of demographic diversity in American politics is shaped by the electoral rules of the game. Single member, simple plurality rules narrow the number of truly competitive parties in the U.S. and force interest groups to enter more broadly-based electoral coalitions than they might otherwise be inclined to join. In addition, the U.S. federal structure gives American elections a distinctive twist. Because elections for the numerous local, state and federal offices are conducted under widely varying rules and procedures, even common voting trends can have very different local and regional manifestations. The decentralization of the American electoral system also means that candidates from a particular political party can do well at one level of elected office but not at another. Consider the case of the Republicans, who have held the presidency for all but four of the last twenty years, but neither the Congress (with the exception of the Senate for six years only) nor a majority of the state legislatures during the same period. The problem of divided government is considered in greater detail in Chapter 15. The procedural feature which makes it possible is that the American ballot offers the voter many separate decisions at different times during the electoral cycle. In any given presidential election year, a voter may have to cast a ballot for a President, a U.S Senator, a Member of the House, a number of state-wide officials, state legislators, local and county officials, judges, and, increasingly, various bond and initiative measures. Many governors, mayors and local government officials are elected during the so-called off-years. Aside from the fact that the contemporary American voter sometimes feels overwhelmed by all these choices, frequent elections and the long American ballot create the procedural opportunities for complex and contradictory electoral outcomes.

Despite the complications of demographic diversity and ballot complexity, it is possible to find some common themes in U.S. elections in recent years. The most important is that there has been a general trend towards electoral fracture and dealignment in the American electorate since 1964. Electoral coalitions are less firmly grounded along traditional party lines, and other factors – for example, race, ethnicity, incumbency, special interests, etc. – shape electoral outcomes to a greater degree than they did in the immediate post-1945 period. The pace and direction of these changes have been at least partly affected by institutional factors. Consequently, much of the current controversy over how to reform the political system is often implicitly about what the electorate should look like in the future. Ought the trend towards fracture be reversed by reinvigorating political parties? Ought it to be encouraged by giving more legal and formal recognition to group representation? Or should it be pushed to some individualistic extreme in which voters are divorced from either their group or partisan identities?

The Fracturing of the American Electorate

A large electorate will inevitably have innumerable potential cleavages. Race, religion, ethnicity, region, gender, language and occupation are but a few of the interests that can and do divide American voters. Catholics, manual workers, blacks, southerners and Jews have traditionally supported the Democratic party while protestants, whites and the middle class have usually lined up with the Republicans (Campbell *et al.* 1960; Lazarsfeld *et al.*, 1968). Many of these same group identities and partisan alignments persist today, although some (such as religious differences in partisan support) are considerably weaker than they used to be. Two important differences between electoral groups in earlier eras and the contemporary one are first that the number of politically relevant interests have multiplied, and secondly, that they are less well linked to established party structures than before. In this sense, the American electorate has moved closer to the Madisonian/pluralist ideal of a large, extended Republic with numerous, flexible electoral interests and away from a system simplified by stable party factions.

The manifestations of this trend towards electoral fracture are numerous, but four are particularly salient. First, and most importantly, party – which has never been as strong in the U. S. as in Great Britain – is an even less important factor than it used to be in the decisions of many American voters. Voters are now less inclined to identify with either of the two major parties than in the past (Rusk and Norpoth, 1982; Wattenberg, 1984). The percentage of major party identifiers has dropped from 80 per cent in 1940 to 70 per cent in 1980, and the number of independents now stands at close to a third of the electorate. The decline of partisanship has been particularly strong among younger, white, well-educated voters.

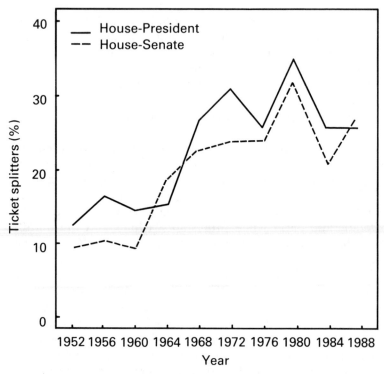

FIGURE 2.1   *Ticket-splitters in American elections, 1952–88*

Related to the trend of weakened partisanship is the
decline in straight ticket voting. A voter is said to have voted a
straight ticket when he or she chooses candidates from the
same party for all the offices on the ballot. A ticket-splitter is
an individual who votes for a candidate of one party for one
office and a candidate of a different party for another office.
Figure 2.1 plots the percentages of individuals over time who
split their vote between House-President and House-Senate
races. As it shows, the trend in the data is generally upward
until 1980, when it levels off at a little over 20 per cent for
both kinds of ticket splitting.

In addition, presidential coat-tails (the degree to which the
president's popularity helps carry congressional races for his
party) have declined, and split election results in congressional districts have become more common (that is seats in

which one party wins the presidential race but loses the congressional race). House and presidential outcomes differed in only 3.2 per cent of the seats in 1920, but by as much as 44 per cent in 1972 and 32 per cent in 1980. As a consequence, the U.S. has had divided control at both the federal and state levels. Nationally, the Republican party has done better in recent presidential contests and less well in congressional races; and, at the state level, about one-half of all gubernatorial–state legislative elections have resulted in divided party control.

In addition to weakened party ties, other factors may account for divided party control at the state and national levels. One speculation is that voters deliberately select candidates from both parties in order to obtain a more balanced policy mix (McCue, 1984). A voter who wants, for instance, to check the free spending ways of a Congress controlled by the Democratic party without endorsing a conservative, Republican agenda might logically choose a Republican presidential candidate to offset voting for a Democratic congressional candidate. Ticket-splitting in this sense is like mixing ideological paints to get the right hue.

Others maintain that the explanation for split-ticket voting is less cognitive and more structural. Some point to widespread and allegedly systematic gerrymandering (the manipulation of district boundaries for partisan gain) as the primary cause. Because, it is argued, congressional redistricting (i.e. the re-drawing of district boundaries after the decennial census) is done by state legislatures, and because these legislatures are predominantly controlled by the Democratic party, congressional boundaries may be biased against the Republican party. The Republican National Committee has pointed out that in a number of states Republican candidates have won a plurality of the state-wide congressional vote, but less than a majority of the congressional seats.

However, social science evidence on the aggregate effects of gerrymandering points in the opposite direction. Several recent studies indicate that there is little or no systematic bias in the ways district boundaries are drawn (Ferejohn, 1977). Even if such evidence were to be uncovered, it is not clear that anything can be done about it. The Supreme Court ruled in a 1986 partisan gerrymandering case involving Indiana's congressional districts that it would not intervene to correct any alleged biases in redistricting unless there was evidence of extreme gerrymandering intended to perpetuate the political exclusion of a particular party or group (*Davis* v. *Bandemer*).

Finally, the strategic decisions of candidates, local parties and consultants may also play a role in causing ticket-splitting. Congressional and local legislative candidates can specifically tailor their campaign statements and subsequent actions in office to the ideological requirements of their districts while those running for state-wide or national office must appeal broadly across a more diverse electorate. If, as some maintain, the Democratic coalition is more heterogeneous than the Republican, then the Democrats will do better at the district level than they will nationally or statewide because their candidates can match their public policy positions more closely to the median preferences of their district constituents. This explanation, however, only helps to account for situations in which the Republicans control the executive branch and Democrats the legislative branch, but not situations in which the electoral advantages of the two parties are reversed.

All of these explanations of ticket-splitting are plausible to some degree, and the empirical task of sorting them out has proven difficult so far. The important point for present purposes is that with the exception of the least likely explanation (systematic partisan gerrymandering), the probable causes of ticket-splitting are at least peripherally related to the weakness of U.S. political parties. If American political parties had greater power over the nomination and funding of candidates, and if the partisan loyalties of voters were stronger, ticket-splitting would be less prevalent, as is the case in Great Britain and most Commonwealth countries.

A crucial question, of course, is does ticket-splitting matter? As Fiorina discusses in Chapter 15 ticket-splitting has made it more difficult for either party to impose its values on policies; but this of course may be exactly what ticket-splitters hope to achieve. Just as importantly, however, the prevalence of ticket-splitting voters seems to have stripped away any residual sense of collective responsibility individual legislators might have had for unpopular policies by their party when in power. The theme of recent congressional elections has been 'every one for themselves' when times are tough, a tactic which makes the connection between policy mandate and voting behavior more tenuous than ever. As will be discussed later, this has led some to advocate measures designed to strengthen American political parties in order to bring back 'collective responsibility'.

In addition to ticket-splitting, a second manifestation of electoral fracture is the increased importance of incumbency and the so-called 'personal vote' (Fenno, 1978). Incumbency is certainly not a new factor in American politics. As compared to the personal vote in other political systems, such as the British, it has traditionally played a more significant role in American legislative elections. But, in recent years, incumbent re-election rates have hovered between 90–94 per cent for the House, over 90 per cent for state legislatures, and between 64 per cent (1976) and 93 per cent (1982) in U.S. Senate elections. The ability of incumbents to get re-elected is reflected in the decline of competitive seats (seats in which the incumbent gets less than 60 per cent of the vote). The percentage of such districts ranged between 33 and 59 per cent from 1850 to 1898, between 10.6 and 36.5 per cent from 1900 to 1948, but only between 10.8 and 23.8 per cent from 1950 to 1980.

What accounts for the power of incumbency in the U.S.? First, as with ticket-splitting, the personal vote will be greater as party ties weaken. Political systems employing single member districts provide representatives with the incentive to carve out an electoral identity that is distinct from that of the party or its leaders. In Britain, the personal vote is measurable, but highly circumscribed by national party forces (Cain *et al.*, 1987). The weakening of partisanship is both a cause and effect of a more powerful incumbency influence. It is a cause in the sense that as incumbents campaign on their personal achievements rather than their party ties *per se*, voters are encouraged to think in less partisan terms about their voting choices. It is also an effect in the sense that the institutional power of parties limits the effectiveness of a personal vote strategy.

Beyond the anemic state of American parties, other factors have contributed to the power of incumbency in American elections. The comparative advantage that incumbents have over challengers in raising money is certainly one of these. Unlike the British system, campaign expenditures are not limited in the U.S. An attempt to regulate campaign expenditures more stringently after the Watergate scandals was subsequently derailed by a 1976 Supreme Court decision (*Buckley* v. *Valeo*) in which the Court equated the right to spend money on a candidate's campaign with the right to free speech. As a result, only voluntary expenditure limitations in exchange for public funding are constitutional, while limitations on independent spending (that is money spent on behalf of a candidate but without his or her control) and limitations on personal spending (the candidate's own money) were held to be unconstitutional. The parts of campaign finance reform the Court left alone (public disclosure requirements and contribution limits) are woefully inadequate to the task of regulating money. Total campaign costs have risen at every level, and the fund-raising advantage of incumbents over challengers has in no way lessened.

In addition, elections have become more technology-driven and media dominated (Sabato, 1989). Polls to assess the relative strengths and weaknesses of candidates, mailings targeted to specific classes of voters, 'diminished universe' get-out-the-vote drives that concentrate upon the so-called 'frequent voters', and thirty-second television and radio political advertisements have become the standard tools of modern camapigns. Candidates now rely heavily upon computer technology and professional expertise, and both are expensive. Those who can afford the means of re-election have a considerable advantage over those who cannot.

Consequently, it is relevant that incumbents raise more money and earlier in the electoral cycle than do challengers. The principal reason for this is the strategic behavior of special interest political action committees (PACs), which heavily favor incumbents over challengers and give money in the off-years as well as during the election years (Jacobson, 1987a). On top of all the other difficulties that would-be challengers confront when they consider running against an incumbent, challengers are typically at an enormous fundraising disadvantage before the campaign even commences. In recent years, amassing a large reserve of campaign funds in the year preceding re-election has become a common method for trying to discourage strong challengers.

The difficulties that challengers face raising money and the unavailability of funds for them from key sources (such as special interest PACs) undoubtedly dampens electoral competition; but there is some disagreement as to whether discrepancies in campaign expenditures *per se* disadvantage challengers. Attempts to measure the impact of money spent in congressional campaigns indicate that the marginal effect of a dollar spent by a challenger seems to be greater than that spent by an incumbent, and that the latter hits the point of diminishing returns faster than the former (Jacobson, 1978). In other words, the critical question may not be how much money an incumbent spends, but rather how much the challenger can raise. The important point, however, is that whether it is because incumbents raise more money or because challengers do not raise enough, the prevailing patterns of campaign finance clearly favor incumbents.

An edge in fund-raising, however, is only one of several advantages incumbents enjoy over challengers. Unlike the British Member of Parliament, American Congressmen and state or local officials have other important resources at their disposal. The British MP who seeks to establish a personal vote labors with a minimum of staff support (usually a part-time secretary and perhaps a party agent). By contrast, Congressman typically have a dozen or so more staff, including casework and project specialists who work full time to enhance the visibility and reputation of their members. Some state legislators and city council members in large urban areas also have large support staff to assist them. In addition, public subsidies for constituent communications, free media exposure and publicity funded trips back to the district have increased in recent years.

Consequently, incumbents begin the election cycle with substantial advantages in name recognition and reputation.

Ratings of incumbents are highly favorable even when opinions of the Congress or government generally are not (Cain *et al.*, 1984). Mayhew, in his seminal work on the so-called 'electoral connection', argued that congressional incumbents have used their activities in office to maximize their chances of re-election (Mayhew, 1974). In particular, casework and project work have proliferated, allowing incumbents to claim credit for things that benefit constituents directly while avoiding controversial position-taking. In this way, holding office *per se* has become the incumbent's most valuable re-election asset.

Strong incumbency effects reinforce the parochialism of American elections. American public opinion naturally inclines towards policy myopia, with voters reacting most emotionally to matters that directly affect their own interests. Thus, so-called pocket-book issues such as inflation, taxes, and personal experience with unemployment will usually have more impact upon voting decisions than will, say, the details of the INF agreement. Moreover, voters often apply simple retrospective decision criteria – for example, am I better or worse off economically than I was last year and is the government to blame – when evaluating candidates (Key, 1966; Fiorina, 1981). To be sure, knowledge and electoral sophistication vary greatly in the American electorate; but, on average, voters are more likely to choose by simple policy criteria than by elaborate ideologies (Converse, 1966a; 1966b).

Candidates can intentionally or unintentionally reinforce the policy myopia of public opinion by the particular campaign strategies they select. A skillful candidate can use campaign literature and the media to influence the relative salience of issues and the way in which issues are framed. A candidate, for instance, who wants a toxic dump site to be the central issue of his or her campaign can try to direct as much free media attention to the issue as possible by holding press conferences at the dump site, issuing a constant stream of press releases on the subject, or by targeting computer generated mailings to the voters who are statistically most likely to care about the issue.

Fear of the unknown and the uncontrollable leads incumbents to employ campaign strategies and representation styles that emphasize noncontroversial, parochial achievements. The Congressman or local official who stresses what he or she has done for the district as a whole, or for particular individuals and groups in the district, is implicitly focusing attention away from national, state or regional issues and conditions and towards an arena over which he or she has more control. Targeted mailings encourage voters to think of certain issues or events as more critical than others. Personalized campaigns encourage voters to distinguish between the responsibility that individual incumbents (as opposed to their parties) share for particular policies, thereby shielding individual legislators from the electoral consequences of unpopular outcomes they cannot easily control. The incumbent's goal is to frame electoral issues in a manner that minimizes risk to him or her; but the unintended byproduct of this strategy may be to reinforce electoral disaggregation.

A third manifestation of electoral fracture is the re-emergence of racial and ethnic issues in American politics. Race and ethnicity also figured prominently in nineteenth-century American electoral politics. The arrival of Catholic immigrants from Ireland and Italy and later of Jewish immigrants from Eastern Europe spurred the formation of the so-called 'ethno-cultural' cleavage (Kleppner, 1970; Kleppner *et al.*, 1981). White protestants were pitted against inner-city, ethnic minorities over issues that in the present day have a familiar ring – such as bilingual education, restrictions on the flow of immigrants, crime and the associated social costs of absorbing large numbers of poor foreigners. These older ethnic partisan loyalties eroded after the New Deal, partly as a consequence of upward social mobility and partly as a reaction to the perception that the Democratic Party had swung too far in the direction of protecting disadvantaged nonwhite groups such as blacks and Latinos (Greeley, 1972; Nie *et al.*, 1976).

Racial and Ethnic Division in the American Electorate

The signs of renewed racial and ethnic division are well

TABLE 2.1   *Presidential vote by race and ethnicity*

	1980		1984		1988	
	Democrat	Republican	Democrat	Republican	Democrat	Republican
White	36	55	35	64	40	59
Black	85	11	89	9	86	12
Latino	56	35	61	37	69	30

Cell entries are the percentage in each racial and ethnic category who voted for the Democratic or Republican Presidential candidate in a given year.

Source: Stanley, M. and Richard G. Niemi (1990) *Vital Statistics*, 2nd edition, Washington, CQ Press.

documented. Over 90 per cent of America's black voters and nearly two-thirds of all Latinos (with the exception of the Cubans) consistently support the Democratic party versus only one third of white voters (see Table 2.1). Some observers have argued that the Democratic party will continue to lose white voters unless it shifts its orientation. Accordingly, after the Mondale defeat in 1984, the new Chairman of the Democratic National Committee, Paul Kirk, abolished racial and gender caucuses in an effort to weaken the party's image as ideologically extreme. For similar reasons, Michael Dukakis kept a safe distance from Jesse Jackson during his 1988 Presidential campaign, hoping to win back the so-called Reagan Democrats.

Apart from racial division across party lines, there is also much evidence of racially polarized voting within the Democratic party itself. The 1988 Democratic primary was a particularly salient example of this. Jesse Jackson managed to win a fairly consistent 12 per cent of the white vote throughout the 1988 primaries, but the threat that he might take the nomination played an important role in consolidating Dukakis' victory (Cain *et al.*, 1989). Super-Tuesday (the date in March when the southern states held their primaries) propelled Jackson into the position of a front-runner and altered the strategic calculus of white Democratic voters in New York and Pennsylvania. A number of Gore supporters switched their support to Dukakis after Super-Tuesday, because they believed that Dukakis had the best chance of defeating

Jackson. The racial division in the New York primary was particularly sharp for several reasons – including a history of tensions between blacks and Jews in New York dating back to the late sixties; Jackson's much publicized remarks about New York being 'Hymietown'; his position on the Middle East and, to no small extent, the provocative role that Mayor Ed Koch played during the primary campaign.

A number of highly publicized races at the state and local level have also manifested racial polarization. In Chicago, for instance, Mayor Richard Daley's death split the city between non-white voters who supported Harold Washington and white voters who supported Ed Vrodoliak. Washington won, but the city remained sharply divided along racial lines until Washington's death in 1986. In California, the 1982 gubernatorial race between Los Angeles Mayor Tom Bradley, a black, and state Attorney-General George Deukmejian, a white, ended in a narrow victory for the Republican caused by widescale Democratic defections in key rural and white suburban areas of the state. Bradley supporters charged that the Republicans used subtle racist campaign advertisements evoking white voter fears of ghetto crime.

All of this has occurred in spite of, or perhaps because of, substantial progress in the lessening of legal discrimination against racial and ethnic minorities in the U.S. (see Chapter 13). Civil rights legislation in the 1960s aimed to eliminate bias in job hiring, school admissions, representation and economic opportunities. But it also provoked resentment in the white community about the advantages that affirmative action, busing and poverty programs conferred on blacks. At the same time, the gap in income and living standards between blacks and whites has increased for all but a small group of blacks (Wilson, 1987). Government poverty programs, critics charge, have perhaps benefited the black middle class, but have done little to help the 'truly disadvantaged'. Black families continue to have the highest rate of family separation, and unemployment remains obscenely high among young black males. Issues surrounding black poverty have not disappeared.

The rising numbers of other non-white disadvantaged populations have also contributed to the renewed political salience of race and ethnicity. The Latino community in particular has grown dramatically during the last two decades. Lured by the prospect of jobs in the U.S. and propelled by poverty in Mexico and Central America, legal and illegal immigration has burgeoned (see Chapter 14). Latinos have sought to win political influence with political and legal strategies patterned after the black civil rights movement (O'Connor and Epstein, 1984). The Mexican–American Legal Defense Fund (MALDEF) – like its black counterpart, the National Association for the Advancement of Colored People – has effectively used the legal system to expand voting rights for Latinos. The Southwest Voter Registration project, based in Texas, has attempted to register and mobilize potential Latino voters throughout the southwest.

But does the re-emergence of racial and ethnic issues necessarily lead to increased electoral fractionalization? In the nineteenth century, immigrants voted along ethnic lines but also within party lines. The Democratic party was able to forge electoral coalitions between immigrant groups and other working class voters. By comparison, contemporary minorities have an uneasy relationship with the established political parties and pursue more of a special interest strategy, looking out for the interests of their particular group. Even though black voters have been historically very loyal to the Democratic party in the post-war period, a number of black leaders now argue that the Democratic party has taken them for granted and have urged black voters to act more like swing voters in order to regain political influence. Blacks and Latinos have also used the courts to force the Democratic party in various states to redistrict boundaries to create seats that minority candidates can win, claiming that Anglo-Democrats cannot best represent the interests of their communities.

Why then has the new racial and ethnic politics exerted a centrifugal rather than a centripetal influence on U.S. politics? First, despite the common loyalty of blacks and Latinos to the Democratic party, there are actually important differences in the interests of their respective populations. They have in common relatively low average levels of education, income and social status, and so, on a number of standard welfare and social service issues, blacks and Latinos have shared policy views that are on average distinguishable from those of the white middle class. In addition, because they often live in poor neighborhoods besieged by crime, drugs and bad schools, they face similar problems at the local level. In Los Angeles, for instance, several black-Latino neighborhood groups have come together to deal with local crime issues co-operatively.

At the same time, blacks and Latinos also have different political interests. During the debate over immigration reform, some black leaders in states such as Florida and California suggested that the flow of undocumented aliens into the U.S. took jobs away from the native-born blacks. On this issue, as Professor de la Garza points out, the position of blacks is closer to that of second and third generation Latinos, who have a similar concern about unchecked immigration from the south. The social service needs of the two communities are also not identical. In one study of social service usage in California, Latinos were found to be less likely than blacks to make use of programs for the elderly and children, because their family structures were still strong (Shastri, 1986).

One last and obviously important difference between the two communities is that the vast majority of blacks are native-born whereas many Latinos are not. As a consequence, the Latino community has linguistic and cultural concerns that are not widely shared in the black community. For instance, Latinos and recently-arrived Asians have an interest in supporting bilingual education and bilingual ballot programs. While blacks do not generally oppose bilingualism, it is not a high political priority for them. It is possible, therefore, that cultural, linguistic, and religious differences (most blacks are Protestants and most Latinos are Catholics) may cause some problems for a durable black–Latino alliance in the future.

Contributing to the politically centrifugal influence of demographic change is the racial and ethnic diversity of the new immigrant groups *per se*. While it is common in the U.S. to refer to Latinos as a single political group, it is important to remember that this term actually embraces a number of different nationalities. A majority of Latinos in the U.S. are Mexican in origin, but the Cubans in Florida, the Puerto Ricans in the northeast, and the Central and South Americans in California are also growing in numbers and do not always have the same perspective as the Mexican–Americans on policies. The Cubans and Central Americans, for instance, are generally more conservative than the Mexican–Americans on foreign policy issues and more inclined to vote for Republican party candidates.

The same can be said of the Asian groups. There are a number of different Asian nationalities immigrating into the U.S. – Koreans, Chinese, Filipinos, Cambodians, Vietnamese – and they bring with them various languages, religions and, in some cases, histories of mutual antagonisms. In addition, some Asian–Americans such as the Filipinos are themselves divided by political controversies in their country of origin. Overall, Asian–Americans tend to be fairly conservative politically, but there are discernible ideological differences between the various Asian–American nationalities. For instance, Koreans, many of whom are first generation, are on average more supportive of bilingual education programs than the Japanese, most of whom are native-born (Cain *et al.*, 1986).

In short, one reason why minority groups are behaving more like special interest groups with less commitment to broadly-based coalitional strategies is that there is an enormous diversity of interests and opinions within and between their respective communities. The majority of immigrants in the nineteenth century were white and European. With the termination of racially-based immigration quotas in the mid-sixties, the stock of contemporary immigrants became more racially and ethnically diverse. This may take coalition-building marginally more difficult.

However, there is also an important structural reason why contemporary minority groups act more like special interest groups than loyal party followers; namely, the political system itself has changed dramatically since the nineteenth century. Incoming groups must adapt to the strategic political environment that they find themselves in. In the nineteenth century, the laws governing naturalization and political participation were not nearly as stringent as they are today. Irish immigrants could be taken off the boat and become political participants immediately, whereas immigrants must now go through a lengthier, more bureaucratized, process of naturalization and registration. Door-to-door mobilization by ward bosses and patronage in return for votes are now relics of the political past. One effect of these institutional changes is the participation gap – the gap between the percentage of a minority group's share of the population and its share of the electorate and office-holders. To take an example, Latinos constituted 19 per cent of California's population in 1980 but only 9 per cent of its electorate. Large disparities of this sort have contributed to the widespread perception that minorities are inadequately represented in the American political system.

It is particularly galling to minority leaders when the gap in minority participation is sometimes attributed to widespread apathy among non-whites. High rates of noncitizenship and of persons under the age of 18 are two major sources of the participation gap. In fact, as Table 2.2 shows, black participation rates in recent years have actually come closer to white participation rates. When blacks of a given education and income level are compared with whites of the same level, black individuals are more likely to have a higher rate of participation.

TABLE 2.2 *Citizen voting by race and ethnicity*

	1972	1974	1976	1978	1980	1982	1984	1986	1988
White	65	46	61	47	61	50	61	47	59
Black	52	34	49	37	51	43	56	43	52
Latino	38	23	32	24	30	25	33	24	29

Cell entries are the percent of citizens in each racial/ethnic category who voted in a given year.
Source: Stanley, H. and Richard G. Niemi (1990) *op cit.*

Secondly, as discussed earlier, contemporary minority groups must compete in a political environment that favors those with money and the ability to use high technology campaign methods. A successful challenge to a Congressional seat can cost a half a million dollars or more, and the expense

of state-wide races in large industrialized states like California and New York (where many immigrants have settled) is
much higher still. Many of the states experiencing high
population growth have frozen the size of their representative institutions so that the number of constituents represented in a district has risen dramatically. To take a most
extreme example, the size of a county Board of Supervisors
seat in Los Angeles has reached 1.7 million people. As the
size of districts expands, the aggregate cost of financing
campaigns for those seats also rises even when the per capita
costs stay fixed (which, of course, is not the case).

Big cities also have large and expensive media markets.
Door-to-door campaigning and canvassing have been replaced by media buys and targeted 'hit pieces', which are less
labor intensive and more capital intensive. Poor minority
communities often lack the base of middle class contributors
needed to finance such efforts. In the past sympathetic
wealthy individuals from outside the district could be
counted on to provide the necessary funds, but campaign
reform, at the federal level at least, has limited the amount of
money that any individual, group or even party can give to a
specific candidate and has not in most instances provided
public financing as a substitute. The effect of post-Watergate
campaign finance reforms at the federal level at least has
been to empower those with access to a wide base of 100 to
500 dollar donors. Unfortunately, not too many first generation, lower income and lower middle class minority individuals can make contributions of that size.

Finally, and related to what has been said so far, the
weakness of political parties puts the burden of organizing
political action on minority communities themselves. When
the major political parties can no longer raise and control the
distribution of campaign money, when incumbency is overwhelmingly strong, and when the methods of modern campaigning are highly personalized, it is only natural for
minority incumbents to run campaigns that appeal somewhat
parochially to their own communities rather than to broader
party agenda. In the absence of party money, minority
incumbents must use their positions on critical state legislative and congressional committees to extract campaign funds

from special interests (as do white incumbents) in order to finance their own campaigns or to promote those of their allies. Successful minority incumbents, in other words, learn to play the game of American politics like other incumbents.

The political environment, therefore, may be encouraging racial and ethnic minority groups to take a more special interest orientation. Moreover, the election of minorities to office has affected policy-making in various ways. In addition to providing voices for a more progressive legislative agenda, minority representatives have pushed for a wider distribution of state contracts and employment opportunities, more affirmative action programs and more responsiveness on the part of federal, state and local bureaucracies to the needs of minority constituents. If jobs and city patronage were the glue that held urban machines together in the nineteenth century, it may be that city contracts, commission appointments and affirmative action policies are the closest equivalent in the modern period – they are both a product of minority political participation and a reinforcement of racial and ethnic identity.

Institutional Fracture

Paralleling the behavioral fracture of the American electorate, there has been much tinkering with the rules and procedures governing representation in the U.S. The central thrust of these changes has been to reinforce the behavioral trends already noted here – further weakening political parties, enhancing the role of special interest groups and giving greater representational voice to minorities. It would be wrong to characterize this institutional trend as self-consciously chosen. Rather, it has evolved incrementally without much thought about the philosophical issues implicit in institutional reform.

A good example of recent institutional tinkering is the case of campaign finance reform. Since the nineteenth century, the U.S. has had federal regulations governing the funding of elections. However, the experience with Richard Nixon's re-election campaign prompted a wave of new legislation to curb the influence of money over elections. At the national level in the early 1970s, Congress passed a series of measures that created two systems of campaign financing – a congressional system with contribution limits and disclosure laws and a presidential system with voluntary expenditure limits and public financing. A number of states and local communities followed suit with their own regulations.

In retrospect, this legislation had several major problems. First, as discussed earlier, parts of the act were ruled unconstitutional by the Supreme Court in its landmark 1976 decision, *Buckley* v. *Valeo*. The Court ruled that contribution limits were constitutionally permissible but that expenditure limits were not, because the act of giving money to a candidate which he or she then spent for election purposes was not directly related to free speech whereas the money spent by the candidate to get elected was. Candidate expenditure limits would only be constitutional if they were voluntarily accepted as part of an agreement for receiving public funding, but not otherwise. In short, stringent campaign finance regulation such as is found in Great Britain ran foul of the constitution's First Amendment tradition. Lacking the constitutional right to limit campaign expenditures, reform laws passed in the early 1970s could not effectively control either the rising level of total campaign costs nor significantly limit the influence of monied interests on elections. The real costs of elections continue to rise, and the influence of special interest money has in no way lessened.

The second problem with these reforms is that they brought unintended effects. Leaving aside the issue of how much the Court derailed the reform effect and how much of what happened subsequently could have been correctly anticipated, the simple fact is that the laws passed after 1972 led to a proliferation of political action committees. Consider the case of congressional elections. Although contributions by individuals still constitute the largest category of donors (about half of total contributions), the proportion of money given by PACs has risen steadily (from 14 per cent in 1972 to 37 per cent in 1984), and the share from party sources has dropped (Jacobson, 1987). This is partly because the reform groups like Common Cause who pushed hardest for these changes tend to regard political parties as just another interest group with no special redeeming status.

Under the post-reform system, individuals with single issue concerns and groups with special economic interests can contribute within legally specified limits to PACs or to candidates directly. Money from businesses and labor unions dominates off-year contributions. While scholarly work does not reveal a simple correspondence between giving money and getting favorable legislative treatment, it does reveal a general pattern of supporting incumbents over challengers, especially those who have been generally supportive of the industry or who sit on the relevant Congressional policy committees (Wright, 1985).

Tinkering with campaign finance laws is an on-going process. Reform groups such as Common Cause or the League of Women Voters continue to propose further refinements, but there is not much chance of meaningful regulation since the Court is unlikely to reverse its position on the First Amendment status of campaign expenditures in the foreseeable future. These incomplete reforms have reinforced electoral fracture by promoting the proliferation of PACs designed to protect specific economic interests or single issue positions as opposed to the more broadly based party themes. Some reformers have begun to contemplate changes that would give parties a preferred status over PACs and individual donors, but historically American reformers have been very mistrustful of political parties. The reformist ideal is one of individual donors giving small, relatively equal contributions to candidates – large enough to fund the operations of a campaign, but not so large as to create unequal voices in public policy.

It is not clear how one would want to give parties a greater role in campaign finance. Party office-holders are increasingly important sources of party money. Grassroots efforts, although more important in the Republican than the Democratic party, are less significant. The issue of greater party involvement in fund-raising at least implicitly raises the question of which part of the party should have primary responsibility for this task. Intra-party tensions between the party in the legislature, the party in the constituency and the party organization would be brought to the surface if the notion of political parties were given a more prominent status in election finance law.

Another institutional development that has contributed to electoral fracture is the trend away from indirect and representational democracy and towards direct democracy. One much noted example of this is the proliferation of presidential primaries. Since 1968, the number of states selecting presidential delegates by primaries has risen from 17 to 33. The rules of presidential nomination have been altered on several occasions, vacillating between more or less proportional delegate selection criteria. Party regulars and elected officials, despite some recent efforts to reverse the trend, now play a less significant role in presidential elections than they did in the pre-1968 period when party caucuses were more prevalent.

By diminishing the role of the organized party and empowering the primary voter, party reform has increased the importance of personal candidate organizations, political consultants and the media. The lesson of past successful primary campaigns has been that aspiring presidential candidates should raise money early, do well at the 'front end' of the primary process, and use the media to the best advantage possible (Orren and Polsby, 1987). How well a candidate does depends not just on the actual results of the previous primary, but also on how the media reports the outcome. Fixated on the so-called 'horse-race' aspects of presidential elections (who is ahead, who is behind and who is catching up), the media can alter the momentum of the campaign by the way that it interprets electoral results. Candidates who exceed the media's prior expectations tend to receive a boost in press coverage, and this then leads to more money and electoral support. A victory is not always a benefit, and a defeat is not always a loss. The media and public opinion have replaced party activists and elected officials as the major brokers of the presidential selection process.

Another example of the populist push in American government is the recent increase in the number of referendums and initiatives on state and local ballots. First introduced in South Dakota in 1898, twenty-three states now provide for some form of initiative, and all but four states provide for either the initiative, referendum or recall of elected officials in at least some units of local government. The numbers of statewide initiatives placed on the ballot across the country have risen dramatically in recent years; there were only 85 in the period between 1960–1969, 120 between 1970–79, and 191 between 1980–87.

The trend is most pronounced in California where 181 measures began the petition gathering process in the 1970s (surpassing the total for the previous four decades) (Lee, 1985). At any one time in California, it is possible to find constitutional amendments proposed by the legislature or by direct petition, bond measures, statutes bypassing the legislature, referendums on legislative statutes, or amendments to laws originally passed as initiatives. These measures have served as vehicles for tax cuts, campaign finance reform, money for roads, hospitals and prisons, and even insurance regulation. The latter illustrates the complexity of the choices voters face. In 1988, Californians had to decide between five different and contradictory insurance measures, each containing pages of fine print and complex, unreadable, technical insurance jargon. Even hard core election junkies felt overwhelmed.

To make matters worse, many of the measures placed on the ballot tend to be hastily drafted, forcing the courts to sort out what is constitutional from what is unconstitutional, and what is truly intended by ambiguous or sloppy wording from what is not. When two contradictory measures pass, it is up to the courts to decide how the two fit together. Adding to all of these concerns, initiatives have become the focus of frenetic entrepreneurial activity. Because the Court has equated spending on initiatives with direct free speech, and because an initiative campaign can be a money-making activity, some measures serve as fund-raising vehicles for promoting individual candidacies or for raising money outside the limits for direct candidate contributions. Ironically, there is now the feeling that direct democracy mechanisms, which were originally invented to offset the influence of special interests upon the state legislatures, are primarily used to promote the very interests they were meant to curb (Magleby *et al.*, 1982).

A third important institutional change affecting representation in the U.S. is the greater legal recognition given to minority representation as the result of the Voting Rights Act. The Voting Rights Act of 1965 was originally written to increase black voter participation in the south (Thernstrom, 1987). As the result of voter intimidation and the discriminatory use of poll taxes and literacy tests, blacks had effectively been denied the franchise in many southern states. The Voting Rights Act made these institutional devices illegal, causing an immediate surge in black registration in the first few years after its passage. The law has subsequently been extended to cover areas outside the south, other protected classes (e.g. Latinos) and other potentially discriminatory institutional devices such as at-large elections and gerrymandered districts.

This has been a difficult area for the Supreme Court to deal with. On the one hand, it has stated repeatedly that there is no constitutional right to proportional representation; but it has upheld the vote dilution portions of the Voting Rights Act in its 1986 decision in *Thornburg* v. *Gingles*. Critics of the law say that in its much amended incarnation, the Voting Rights Act has created a special right of representation for certain subgroups of the electorate but not others (Thernstrom, 1987). Supporters claim that preventing the dilution of the votes of groups with a history of discrimination against them is a natural extension of the idea that everyone has the equal right to an equal vote.

Whichever interpretation one gives to the Voting Rights Act, few would deny its importance in boosting minority representation in the U.S. The number of black and Latino office-holders has increased measurably since the mid-sixties, and most are elected in districts which contain a majority of non-white voters. When there is evidence of racial polarization in the voting within a given area, and if the institutional arrangements or district lines serve to prevent the election of a minority representative, the Court can declare them to be in violation of the Voting Rights Act. While the Supreme Court does not define this as a right to elect a black or Latino official *per se*, it does claim that racial and ethnic communities have the right to elect a representative of their own choice. It is the local activists who are more likely to interpret this as a right to elect a minority representative *per se*.

Unfortunately, the narrow interpretation the Court has given the Voting Rights Act discounts the claims of areas with mixed black–Latino neighborhoods. To win a claim under the Voting Rights Act, groups must have sufficient size and political coherence by themselves to elect an official of their own choice. This has the effect of encouraging minority groups to pursue separate rather than coalitional strategies for enhancing representation.

Conclusion

Americans are divided about which direction they would like their electoral system to develop. As discussed earlier, the implicit ideal of many middle class reformers is individualistic: individual voters should have an equally weighted say in the outcome of elections with as little mediation by parties or other organizations as possible. Although their reforms have in fact empowered special interests, this was unintended. It was never the intent of campaign finance reform to make corporate PACs more powerful. That was simply an unforeseen by-product of their attempt to lessen individual inequities caused by differences in wealth and property. This approach tends to emphasize formal or legal equality over equality in actual political power.

A second way of thinking about political fracture is group oriented. The most explicit defense of group-oriented approaches to representation is made by racial and ethnic minorities who are acutely conscious of the importance of resource inequalities in determining actual political power as opposed to formal equality – differences in the money that can be given by some individuals to finance campaigns; in the time individuals can devote to politics; or in the relative sizes of various voting blocs. Group organization is a way to overcome individual resource and informational disadvantages. The views of certain racial and ethnic group leaders aside, there is generally in the U.S. less support for representation for sectoral or functional groups than in many

European countries. The nearest to a widely accepted group ideal is pluralism; but it emphasizes temporary and fluid coalitions as opposed to permanent corporatist arrangements. The position with the least support in America is for strengthened party representation. Despite the enthusiasm of the political science community and the presence of a few scattered citizen efforts, the plea for stronger parties falls for the most part on deaf ears. It is unlikely that parties will be reinvigorated in the near future. The individualistic perspective in particular is the most strongly embedded in the American reform tradition, and thus future electoral reforms are likely to follow in the same path. The prognosis for the immediate future is for more fracture along present lines.

3

American Political Parties

DANIEL HAYS LOWENSTEIN

The past quarter century has been a time of considerable institutional change in the American party system. In part, change has been instigated by two self-conscious reform movements.

The first of these, in the tradition of American Progressivism, has achieved considerable success in democratizing party processes and reducing the domination of traditional party organizations. These successes, however, have not had the political consequences many of the Progressive reformers hoped for, and there is considerable controversy whether the overall effects on the political system have been beneficial.

The Progressive reformers were concerned primarily with internal party processes. In contrast, the second movement for change, known as the party renewal movement, seeks to enhance the role of parties in their dealings with other political institutions. The party renewal movement has used constitutional litigation to increase the legal autonomy of parties, and has been cheered by substantial growth of the national party bureaucracies, though the latter development has been caused by the dynamics of party competition rather than by reform efforts.

Partly stimulated by the party renewal movement, there has been extensive debate over whether the parties have become stronger or weaker during the past quarter century. Much of this debate stems from failure to bear in mind the manifold nature of parties and the variety of functions they perform. As this Chapter demonstrates, the parties are getting stronger in some respects and weaker in others.

Weakness and Strength

An assessment of party strength or weakness must recognize that parties are manifold entities. American political scientists customarily speak of three essential loci of the major parties: the party in the electorate, the party in or seeking elective office, and the party organization (Sabato, 1988; Sorauf and Beck, 1988). A case has been made for party weakness and decline in all three areas, but in each instance the case for weakness is contestable.

The Party in the Electorate

Decline of the party in the electorate generally refers to a reduction in the salience of party as a determinant of the individual's voting decision. The party system in the electorate is strong when voter decisions are made on the basis of evaluation of party performance or party program. By definition, where there is a strong party system voters are relatively indifferent to the qualifications, opinions, and performance of the particular candidates for partisan office. Weakening of the parties and the party system in the electorate occurs when more voters make individualized voting decisions, either ignoring party affiliation altogether or, more likely, reducing the threshold above which candidate characteristics will override party as a basis for voting (Cain *et al.*, 1984).

The extent to which such a weakening has occurred is considered by Bruce Cain in Chapter 2. It may be said here that the split-ticket voting that has resulted in one party controlling the presidency and both houses of Congress for only four out of the last twenty years provides some evidence of a weak party system in the electorate. The conclusion that the party system has been weakening is further supported by survey evidence showing significant decline in party identification, although the greatest change has been a reduction in the intensity of partisan leaning rather than an outright abandonment of partisan preference (Epstein, 1986, pp. 256–263).

Despite these developments, the party label remains an important voting cue, especially in contests that attract little visibility, such as state legislative elections (Ranney, 1975, p. 128). One indicator of the continuing significance of the party cue for voters is the chronic and peculiarly American furor over partisan gerrymandering in the legislative districting process, which would dissipate if politicians could not predict with at least tolerable accuracy the partisan leanings of voters in particular areas (Grofman, 1990; Symposium, 1985; Cain, 1984).

The Party in Government

The American Constitution establishes a highly decentralized governmental structure. Vertically, the federal system divides governmental power between the national and state governments, and within the states power is further divided between the state government, cities, counties, and innumerable specialized units of local government, ranging from school districts to mosquito abatement districts. Horizontally, the system of separation of powers divides authority among the executive, legislative, and judicial branches. Within the legislative branch, power is further decentralized by the division of Congress into two houses of nearly equivalent influence. Virtually the same system of separation of powers exists in each state, though authority within local units of government is often more unified.

The fragmentation of government authority creates both a need for and a barrier to unified party government. Only a cohesive party, many observers believe, can bring about co-ordination of the activities and decisions of officers in separate branches and levels of government. Yet, the fact that these officers are elected separately, at different times, for different terms and from different constituencies, works against party unity. Candidates feel greater pressure to respond to the current demands, opinions, and interests of the particular constituency in which they are seeking election or re-election than to adhere to a party platform, even if the platform serves broader and more enduring values.

The weakness of American parties in government is often highlighted by contrasting the American system to the British Parliament, in which highly disciplined parties ordinarily act with nearly perfect unanimity. In American legislatures, votes usually are cast as the individual members' consciences or individual calculations of political self-interest dictate. The comparison could be misleading, since the party discipline in the British Parliament is rarely matched in any other democratic country, but cross-national studies have found the degree of party cohesiveness in legislative voting in the United States Congress to be substantially below the average for national legislatures in a large number of democracies (Harmel and Janda, 1982, pp. 75–80).

An exclusive focus on roll call voting, however, may lead to an exaggerated sense of the decline of party strength in American legislatures. An important area in which parties remain of central importance is the organization of legislative chambers. In Congress, the majority party in each chamber selects the leadership. In addition, the chair and a majority of the members of each committee come from the majority party. These and similar structural features give the leadership of the majority party significant power to manage the legislature, even when the absence of party loyalty prevents the leadership from having its way on particular legislation.

The virtually absolute sway of the majority party over legislative organization assures that partisan alignment in the Congress matters to individual members and to the country. In many state legislatures, party control is even greater than in Congress (Epstein, 1986, p. 113). The power of the majority to organize each chamber is a bedrock of strength of the American party system, easily taken for granted, and therefore underrated, because it has been so stable and so pervasive.

Party Organization

Over the past century, the most controversial aspect of

American parties has often been the party organization. The main reason for the controversy surrounding party organization has been its identification, at least in the public mind, with the political machine. Raymond Wolfinger has defined machine politics as 'the manipulation of certain incentives to partisan political participation: favoritism based on political criteria in personnel decisions, contracting, and administration of the laws' (Wolfinger, 1972, p. 374). For much of the nineteenth and the first third of the twentieth centuries, political machines, especially in big cities, were the most salient feature of American politics.

The early twentieth century was marked by concerted efforts to revise political procedures to the detriment of machine politicians. Business leaders were prominent among a group of reformers who sought to weaken or eliminate the machines by reducing the significance of parties in the political system (Thelen, 1981). Their greatest impact was at the local level, and the ideas they represented retain some currency. A strong and growing majority of local jurisdictions in the United States – more than three-quarters by the 1970s – use non-partisan ballots in their elections (Sabato, 1988, p. 226).

A second group, the Progressive reformers, were relatively indifferent to partisanship *per se*, but they were hostile to the machines. These reformers promoted a number of institutional changes, the most important being the direct primary. Instead of candidates being nominated by a caucus or convention that typically was dominated by party leaders, in a direct primary they are nominated by popular vote. The direct primary is now used almost universally in partisan elections at the state and local level.

The introduction of the direct primary in the early part of the twentieth century did not bring an immediate end to the political machine in the U.S. For one thing, adoption of the direct primary was gradual, not becoming virtually ubiquitous until the 1960s and 1970s. Even where the direct primary was in place, old-line political organizations sometimes were able to dictate primary results, thereby retaining effective control of the nomination process.

Nevertheless, a number of long-term factors worked

together with the direct primary to make the sustenance of an old-fashioned political machine more difficult. These included gradual breaking up of ethnic neighborhoods in most large cities; increasing affluence; increasing provision by the government of services and benefits previously supplied by the machines; declining interparty competition in many cities following the 1932 Roosevelt victory and ensuing Democratic dominance; the spread of civil service laws, reducing the ability of party machines to rely on patronage as an incentive for support; higher education levels; and increasing use of the broadcast media and computerized mailing techniques for the dissemination of political messages (Ladd, 1981, pp. 85–86; Schlesinger, 1981, p. 119; Ceaser, 1982, p. 6; Schlesinger, 1985, p. 1160).

Despite these factors, as of the early 1970s, the Democratic Party in just under half the states was primarily 'organized' as opposed to 'volunteer'. Not all the organized parties could be described as political machines, but most of them depended on 'a significant number of tangible, divisible rewards ... to guarantee [a] large aggregate of reliable party workers' (Shafer, 1983, pp. 281–282). Nevertheless, the machine has declined steadily (Epstein, 1986, pp. 141–143). Today, the professional party organization, exercising political power and maintaining itself by dispensing particularized benefits to its supporters, is entirely absent from much and probably most of the U.S., and can be described as dominant only in a few places.

In a setting in which the nomination of candidates is performed by the party in the electorate, at least three functions seem possible for a meaningful party organization. The old-fashioned professional party served a brokerage function, facilitating the exchange of political power and various economic and other particularistic benefits (Merton, 1968, pp. 124–136). The second possible function is ideological. The party organization may provide a vehicle for activists to pursue their ideological objectives by seeking to influence, first, the party program, and secondly, government policy by helping party candidates who are committed to the party program get elected. Volunteer party organizations exercised some influence, especially in California and

Wisconsin, in the 1950s and 1960s, but they have dwindled (Epstein, 1986, p. 145). In recent decades ideologically motivated political activists have tended to work either in single-issue organizations or directly for candidates, rather than in party organizations. The third possible function, which has emerged only recently, is for the party organization to serve as a secretariat, providing essentially technical services to party candidates.

Because of the decline of the professional organizations and the failure of volunteer organizations to replace them in an effective manner, by the late 1970s most observers agreed that American party organizations were in a state of serious and, possibly, irreversible decline. However, developments were already under way that have seemed to some more recent commentators to mark a resurgence of the party organizations.

The new developments differed between the two major parties, though they had the common effect of tending to nationalize the party organizations. In the Democratic Party, the nationalizing effect was manifested by the seizure and exercise of control by the national party over certain activities of the state party organizations. In the Republican Party, nationalization occurred because the party at the national level began to exercise the function of a secretariat.

The building of party organization at the national level in the Republican Party had its immediate origin in adversity. The new development is usually dated from the election of William Brock as chairman of the Republican National Committee (RNC) in January 1977. The Watergate scandal of a few years earlier had brought hard times to the Republicans well beyond the narrow victory of Democrat Jimmy Carter over incumbent President Gerald Ford in the 1976 election. At the beginning of 1977, the Republicans held only a third of the seats in Congress, 12 governorships, and control of both houses of four state legislatures.

Brock's plan was to restore Republican fortunes by turning the RNC into an effective service organization to help Republican candidates. An essential prerequisite was to compile resources, which meant raising money. Traditionally, American parties at the national level had been funded primarily by a relatively small number of large individual contributors. However, the adoption in 1974 of amendments to the Federal Election Campaign Act imposed limits on the amounts individuals could contribute, and in the post-Watergate period, traditional 'fat cats' were reluctant to invest in the Republican Party.

In the 1960s and early 1970s, certain presidential candidates – primarily Barry Goldwater in 1964 and Democrat George McGovern in 1972 – had raised substantial sums in small contributions from large numbers of individuals. Beginning in the 1970s, even before Brock's term as RNC chairman, the Republicans, using new computerized mailing techniques, began to build a similar base of contributors to the party.

After a slow start, the Republican Party's investment in direct mail began to pay dividends. In 1974, the Republican Party at the national level raised a total of $6.3 million. By 1980 it raised $37 million, with about three-quarters of this total coming from direct mail solicitation. More than two million people were on the list of active contributors. During the 1985–1986 election cycle, the RNC raised a total of nearly $84 million, about $77 million of which was contributed by individuals, mostly through direct mail. Together with two other Republican national fundraising arms, the National Republican Senatorial Committee and the National Republican Congressional Committee, the RNC raised a total of over $250 million during the 1985–1986 cycle (Reichley, 1985, pp. 187–188; Sorauf, 1988, pp. 127–149).

Almost as significant as the amounts of money raised by the Republican Party at the national level were the uses to which the money was put. Although most of the money raised by the senatorial and congressional campaign committees went directly into the campaigns of Republican candidates, the main emphasis of the RNC was party-building. A complex organizational structure was established, including regional political directors, organizational directors, regional finance directors, a data processing network, and various organizational and policy task forces (Bibby, 1980).

Although party-building by the Democratic Party began later and has progressed less dramatically than in the Republican Party, the Democrats at the beginning of the 1990s are far better organized nationally than in any earlier period. Because of their control of the House of Representatives and aggressive use of that control in support of fundraising from business groups with vital stakes in national legislation, the Democratic congressional campaign fundraising committees were able to compete fairly successfully with the Republicans (Drew, 1983; Jackson, 1988). However, when Charles Mannatt assumed office as chairman of the Democratic National Committee (DNC) in 1981, the national party was at a low ebb. Electorally, it had lost the presidency and, for the first time in over a quarter of a century, control of the Senate. Financially, it still had not paid large debts dating back to the 1968 election, and had not begun to build a mass fundraising base to replace the 'fat cats' whose ability to contribute had been limited by the campaign finance legislation of the 1970s.

Under Mannatt's leadership, the Democrats began to build a direct mail fundraising program. Partly because Democrats tend to be less affluent than Republicans, and partly because in the 1980s, the Democratic Party was not driven by the sense of mission that many Republicans felt under the leadership of Ronald Reagan, the Democratic program was not as successful as that of the Republicans. By the 1983–1984 election cycle, the DNC was able to raise $46 million, less than half the amount raised by its Republican counterpart (Sorauf, 1988, p. 146). Still, this was sufficient to sustain a staff and services to Democratic candidates beyond anything that had existed in the past.

In the second half of the 1980s there were signs that growth in mass-based fundraising by each of the party national committees was levelling off or beginning to decline (Sorauf, 1988, p. 146). It is possible that, over time, resistance to direct mail appeals will increase and that the surge in national fundraising will prove a temporary phenomenon. For the time being, the existence of a significant secretariat in both the DNC and the RNC, with a marked superiority in size in the latter, will continue as a feature of the American party system.

In summary, the decline of the old style party machines at the state and local level has been partially balanced by the growth of party bureaucracies at the national level. In a reversal from the old era in which the national parties were little more than confederations of state organizations, the state organizations now draw much of their support from the newly vitalized national parties. According to Larry Sabato, the state parties now are 'chartered chapters of Washington-based groups' but with national assistance many of them 'are organizationally stronger than at any time in their history' (Sabato, 1988, p. 90).

Of equal importance to the centralization of American party organizations is the shift in their role. However useful the new party secretariats may be to party candidates in election campaigns, the new parties are service organizations, not governing bodies. Where the benefits provided by the party organization to a candidate are great, there should be potential for the organization to exercise influence over the candidate's actions when he or she assumes office. To date, however, there is little evidence that the party organizations have exercised this kind of influence to any great extent.

Nor is such influence probable in the near future. The new party secretariats have defined their mission as the election of the maximum number of party candidates, not the imposition of party discipline. So motivated, they are not likely to urge a party legislator to sacrifice district support to further broad party policies. Even if the party organization did make such attempts, under present circumstances they would be unlikely to succeed. So long as the personal appeal of the candidate is an important determinant of a large number of votes, most legislators are likely to 'vote their districts', even if this could mean the withholding of party campaign services, which for the most part can be purchased if necessary from private consulting firms.

Progressive Party Reform

Progressivism as a more or less organized political movement dwindled and died with the entry of the United States into the First World War. When a moderately left of center movement was restored to power during the Depression of the 1930s, it came under the new label of 'liberalism', and under the leadership of Franklin Roosevelt it emphasized substantive programs rather than procedural reform. During the 1950s, a new generation of liberal reformers, working primarily within the Democratic Party, began to struggle against the party machines that still dominated many local governments, and in doing so brought a new focus on party processes (Wilson, 1966). Their professed goals included making the parties more accessible to ordinary voters, though in practice this might mean voters with the time, the verbal and other political skills, and the motivation to pursue party activism in an effective manner.

These same goals, inherited from the Progressive movement of the early twentieth century, drove the national party reform movement of the late 1960s and 1970s. The movement was largely limited to the Democratic Party, though its fruits affected the Republicans as well. The presidential nominating process was the site of its major focus and its major effects.

Candidates for President and Vice-President were nominated by the parties at national conventions held during the summer of each presidential election year. The method of selecting delegates for these conventions was largely left up to the states, although the 1964 Democratic convention established rules prohibiting racial discrimination in the selection of delegates. By the late 1960s, although most states were using the direct primary for the nomination of candidates for state and local partisan offices, only a minority of states were using primaries to select presidential nominating delegations. Under the system that then prevailed, a candidate for president could enter primaries in selected states in order to demonstrate popular support, but could not win the nomination without the support of numerous delegations controlled by professional party leaders within the states.

This system was brought to an abrupt end in both parties as the result of the disruption and controversy that attended the 1968 Democratic National Convention in Chicago. Opponents of Hubert Humphrey, the eventual nominee, asserted that the delegate selection procedures in many states had denied them their fair share of delegates. In an effort at mollification, Humphrey permitted the convention to create a commission to recommend reformed delegate selection rules for the 1972 convention.

The commission, known as the McGovern–Fraser Commission, recommended a large number of changes, substantially all of which were approved by the Democratic National Committee and placed in force for the 1972 convention. The most important had the following effects. First, whether the state used a primary or a caucus procedure, the procedure had to be open to all registered Democrats and held at a time and in a manner that would permit each participant to vote for a specific presidential candidate. Previously, in many states, delegates or those empowered to name the delegates were selected long before the presidential campaign began, or otherwise in a manner calculated to discourage participation by anyone but supporters of the dominant party organization. Secondly, the allotment of delegates to the presidential candidates within a state must be at least roughly proportional to the support for the candidates expressed by voters in a primary or by participants in caucuses. This requirement was not fully implemented in 1972, but thereafter states were prohibited from using winner-take-all procedures. Third, the demographic makeup of the delegation, especially with respect to race and sex, but also with respect to characteristics such as age and income, must not depart excessively from the population of the state. By 1980 the Democratic convention required that each delegation include equal numbers of men and women.

The supporters of the reforms wanted to open the nominating process to wider participation, but did not foresee the extent to which this would occur, as they assumed that most of the non-primary states would adopt a caucus procedure under the new rules, and that caucuses would be attended only by political activists, albeit a wider range of activists than had participated under the old procedures. Once the new rules were in place, it became easier for a state to comply with the many technical requirements by adopting a primary than by using caucuses. Furthermore, a caucus procedure resulted in a state convention that was not likely to be dominated by the existing state organization and that would then be in a position to alter the governance of the state party. Accordingly, many states reacted to the new reforms by conducting presidential primaries. By 1976, a considerable majority of the states were choosing delegates in primary elections. Even in states that declined to conduct primaries, candidates have often conducted aggressive campaigns to enlist supporters and urge them to attend the caucuses. The result is that the dynamics of delegate contests in caucus states are not as different from primaries as had been assumed when the reforms were adopted.

The rules recommended by the McGovern–Fraser Commission and approved by the DNC directly affected only the Democratic Party. The Republican National Committee recommended to the states that participatory procedures be adopted and that delegations be demographically representative, but specifically declined to impose these or other major requirements on Republican state organizations (Bibby, 1980). Nevertheless, many state laws adopted to comply with the new Democratic rules were applied to both parties. This might not have been the case if Republicans had strongly resisted. But there was not much strong opposition to the more open procedures in the Republican Party, and many party leaders may have feared that for a state to hold a Democratic but not a Republican presidential primary would have been detrimental to the Republican cause among the electorate.

The demographic requirements for the delegates were not effected by state law, and therefore did not directly affect the Republicans. The Democrats enforced the requirements of racial and gender proportionality with rigor. Between 1968 and 1984, the percentage of black delegates to the Democratic conventions increased from 5 to 18 per cent, and for women the increase was from 13 to 50 per cent. For the Republicans in the same period, black representation at the conventions increased only from 2 to 4 per cent, but the increase in representation for women almost matched the Democrats, as female delegates increased from 16 to 44 per cent. Democratic delegates under the age of 30 increased from 3 to 22 per cent from 1968 to 1972, but gradually declined to the level of 8 per cent in 1984 (Sorauf and Beck, 1988, p. 336).

The successful implementation of the McGovern–Fraser reforms has been regarded by many as a centralizing development in the American party system, comparable to the centralizing effects of the growth of the national party bureaucracies. The significance of the centralization is said to be heightened by the fact that in the cases *Cousins* v. *Wigoda* (1975) and *Democratic Party* v. *Wisconsin ex rel. LaFollette* (1981), the U.S. Supreme Court upheld the right of the national conventions to seat the delegates they chose despite the contrary wishes of state party organizations, or the contrary dictates of state laws. Certainly, the imposition of such major changes on the structure of the Democratic National Convention by a national decision-making process was unprecedented in the history of the American convention system.

Aside from the intra-party institutional significance of the reforms, they coincided with and are at least partially responsible for significant changes in the dynamics of the process of electing a president. Until 1968, primary victories could give a boost to a presidential candidacy, but the nomination could not be obtained without the support of state party leaders at the convention, who would take into account the primary outcomes together with anything else bearing on the acceptability and electability of the competing candidates. Since 1972, presidential nominations have been determined, not merely influenced, by primary elections and by open caucuses that resemble primaries.

The party reforms have been criticized widely on both practical and theoretical grounds. The major practical criticism has been that by largely eliminating any element of peer review from a process that has become almost entirely plebiscitary, the reforms are likely to produce weak candidates and ineffective presidents. It is true, as Nelson Polsby has argued, that to succeed in office, presidents must be able to earn the co-operation of political leaders of the sort whose support previously was necessary to win a party nomination but are now largely bypassed (Polsby, 1983). Still, the assumption that the new system was likely to produce ineffective presidents may have been an over-reaction to the failings of the Carter Administration. Ronald Reagan, nominated by the Republicans under the same plebiscitary system, was a strong president. Nor is it necessarily the case that party professionals will select a stronger candidate than the party electorate in primaries and caucuses. Since the reforms were adopted, no candidate for a contested nomination more plainly has enjoyed the overwhelming support of the professional party leadership than Walter Mondale, who won the Democratic nomination in 1984. Yet Mondale suffered the most disastrous electoral defeat of any candidate during the same period.

Whatever the deficiencies of the plebiscitary system as a method of nominating presidential candidates, the party reforms are not entirely responsible for the conversion to that system. The intense national press coverage of the nomination contests and the 'horse race' focus on who is leading on a daily or weekly basis are at least equally responsible. Indeed, these forces were affecting the system even before the reforms were adopted.

Nor is rule manipulation a likely means of returning to the past. Beginning with the 1984 conventions, the parties responded to criticism of the plebiscitary system by setting aside a percentage of delegate slots for elective and party office-holders, who would be seated by reason of their positions and not by reason of commitment to one of the presidential contenders. The theory underlying this change was that a decisive victor, if any, in the primaries ought to be nominated, but that if the outcome in the primaries was relatively even, the nominee should be decided through a deliberative process in which party leaders would have the decisive voice, rather than by the mere arithmetic of the primary and caucus returns. The theory did not work in 1984, because the great majority of the 'uncommitted' delegates in fact had publicly committed themselves to Mondale before the primaries began. In 1988, many of the ex-officio delegates were uncommitted in fact as well as in theory, so that a decision-making convention rather than a ratifying convention seemed a genuine possibility. Until Michael Dukakis was established as the obvious nominee, the prospect of a 'brokered convention' appeared to most Democratic politicians as disastrous. They feared that the nomination inevitably would appear to be the result of back-room deals and boss manipulation. Thus, when a deliberative process that had seemed beneficial in the abstract became a realistic possibility, those most directly affected were convinced that it was a throwback to an unacceptable past.

A theoretical objection to the party reforms contends that the reformers were inconsistent in demanding that presidential nominating delegations be both democratically representative in that they should reflect the choices of broad-based participation by party adherents, and demographically representative (Shafer, 1983; Reichley, 1985). The argument is that a free democratic process may select a delegation that is not demographically representative, in which case one but not both forms of representativeness is possible.

'Representation' as Hanna Pitkin made clear, is used to mean many things (Pitkin, 1967). In one conception, which she called 'descriptive representation', the representative is qualified for the position by virtue of being 'like' the represented group in whatever respects are deemed pertinent. The requirement of demographic representativeness is based on this conception of representation.

The central issue between the reformers and their critics turns on a different theoretical question, the so-called Burkean debate, stemming from Edmund Burke's assertion that a representative should be guided by his or her own opinion of what will best serve the public interest, even when that opinion conflicts with the views of the representative's constituents (Burke, 1854). In demanding that voters be able to express an effective preference for a specific presidential candidate, the reformers were taking an anti-Burkean position with respect to the presidential nomination, while their critics, who prefer a deliberative convention with an element of peer review, take the Burkean side.

There is no fundamental inconsistency in the reformers' embrace of both the demographic and the anti-Burkean conceptions of representation. The reforms are based on the correct assumption that almost invariably the only concern most voters will have about potential delegates is the presidential candidate they support. It is consistent to favor the democratic selection of delegates according to this single criterion, and to favor leaving the actual selection of delegates to a centralized organization (either that of the presidential candidate or of the state party), who can be required to prepare a slate meeting the demographic requirements.

No more than their Progressive forebears did the party reformers of the 1960s and 1970s place the party system at the center of their thinking about the political process. They opposed 'boss rule' and favored an open, participatory process. Beyond that they had little to say about the role parties should play in politics, and their Progressive orientation provided no criteria by which to evaluate the strength or weakness of the party system as a whole. They were largely successful in altering the process to suit their objectives. Having done so, the movement largely dissipated and its adherents turned their attention either to substantive issues or to other aspects of the political system, especially the system of campaign finance.

In a different sense, the Progressive reformers may have been less successful in accomplishing their objectives. The original impetus for the reforms came from frustration with the events that led up to the nomination of Hubert Humphrey in 1968. There is no reason to doubt the sincerity of most of the reformers in urging a nomination process consistent with Progressive ideals of participatory democracy, but no doubt many reformers hoped the implementation of these ideals would lead to the nomination and election of more liberal candidates. They expected new caucus procedures to open the process enough to permit participation by liberal activists, but failed to foresee that the new rules would lead to a drastic increase in primaries and to a conversion even of caucuses into processes that resembled primaries.

The Republicans have won four of the five presidential elections since the reforms went into effect, and the Democratic candidates nominated (McGovern, Carter, Mondale and Dukakis) do not point to domination of the process by the liberal wing or any other faction of the Democratic Party. In terms of their substantive ideological goals, some of the reformers may have hoped to open up the Democratic nomination procedures 'enough' but not 'too much' to assure increased influence for liberal activists. The result, from that point of view, was that the process opened up 'too much'.

Party Renewal

The Progressive vision of a democratic process in which all citizens form their views independently and express them directly through the ballot and other participatory processes with a minimum of mediation by party leaders is widely held by the American people. An opposing strain of thought, prominent in political writing though reflected only to a limited extent in the working political culture, has sometimes been termed the doctrine of responsible party government.

This doctrine rejects the Progesssive idea that individuals can form their political opinions independently and convert majority views into government policy without the assistance of intermediary groups, especially political parties. For adherents to the doctrine of responsible party government it is unrealistic to expect the majority of citizens, who must concentrate most of their daily efforts on their private affairs, to be well informed and to hold considered opinions on most political issues. Accordingly, processes that ostensibly implement the Progressive ideal often result in domination by narrowly based special interests, who have much greater time and resources than the general public to articulate policy views and press them upon public officials.

The doctrine of responsible party government maintains that democratic processes centered on political parties can avoid these difficulties by simplifying the voter's choice. It is unreasonable to expect most citizens to have particular opinions on a large number of constantly changing political issues; but it is not unreasonable to expect them to choose between two parties, either by evaluating their contrasting programs in broad, general terms, or by evaluating their performance when they are in office. Strong parties will not be immune to the demands of special interests, but they will be better positioned to balance these demands against competing interests than are individual candidates in a system in which parties play a less central role. Those who seek to strengthen political parties in order to move closer to a system of responsible party government have referred to their efforts as the party renewal movement.

To date, the party renewal movement has had a limited impact. Belief in the legitimacy of parties and the dangers of far-reaching party decline probably has become more widespread among intellectual leaders since the early 1970s. Occasionally, this shift in sentiment has been reflected in institutional change, most importantly in amendments adopted in 1979 to the federal campaign finance laws, permitting far more extensive participation in national election campaigns by parties at all levels than had been permitted under the 1974 amendments. In addition, the ideas of the party renewal movement probably influenced the setting aside of a percentage of delegate slots at the national convention for party leaders although, as we have seen, the practical effects of this change have been less than its proponents had hoped.

The public as a whole has yet to be persuaded of the virtues of party government. This was illustrated in 1986 when the California electorate reaffirmed its belief in nonpartisan local elections by approving an amendment to the state constitution prohibiting parties from endorsing candidates in those elections. The party renewal movement had such little faith in public support for its position that the argument submitted to voters in opposition to this amendment failed to urge the desirability of party government, and instead claimed that the prohibition violated freedom of speech. Supporters of the amendment argued against bossism (California Secretary of State, 1986, pp. 26–27).

The party renewal movement's greatest successes have been in litigation. One of the movement's goals has been to win a degree of autonomy for party organizations from regulation by state law (Lawson, 1987). The United States Supreme Court in the cases *Tashjian* v. *Republican Party of Connecticut* (1986) and *Eu* v. *San Francisco County Democratic Central Committee* (1989) has given parties the right to determine eligibility to vote in party primaries, to endorse candidates in primaries, and to control their own governing structures, despite state regulations to the contrary. These victories have had their costs. While the party renewal movement emphasizes the special role parties play in a democracy, the judicial decisions extending autonomy from state regulation have been based on the premise that the parties are indistinguishable from other interest groups, and therefore have the same right of association that other private groups enjoy. Furthermore, the matters on which the parties have won autonomy are of too limited significance to affect the overall position of the parties in the political system. It is true that the Supreme Court's logic could be extended with little difficulty to strike down laws requiring that party nominations be determined by direct primary elections (Gottlieb, 1982). Nevertheless, the likelihood that the Supreme Court will press its logic to that extent is small, and the likelihood that in the present era many state parties would exercise an option to do away with primaries is even smaller.

The emphasis of the party renewal movement on litigation is syptomatic of two important causes for the movement's indifferent success to date. First, litigation is a recourse that bypasses the ordinary political process, with its demand for influencing public opinion. To a large degree, the party renewal movement has limited its writings to learned journals and its political struggles to arenas, such as the courts, where mass persuasion is unnecessary. Over the long run, this is a disastrous strategy. Serious institutional movement toward responsible party government will not occur if the people do not want it.

The doctrine of responsible party government is a powerful one. It will not and probably should not displace the competing Progressive vision of democracy, but its criticisms of Progressivism are trenchant, and American government would be more effective if the public philosophy contained a greater recognition of the need in a democracy for institutional leadership. It may be that there is little the party renewal movement could do to alter public opinion. The imagination of the general public is unlikely to be stirred by the issue of responsible party government in the abstract. If public attitudes change, it is likely to be the result of intensified support for *parties*, not directly for the party *system*. Still, it would be well to place the issues of responsible party government before the public so that in times of intensified political activity, the chance of such activity expressing itself by means of party-building will be enhanced. This means the party renewal movement should now be pressing as aggressively as possible institutional changes that would increase the role of parties in government and that would be espoused on precisely that ground, even if there is little likelihood of early success. A good choice would be a campaign to restore partisanship to local elections.

Second, the party renewal litigation reflects the movement's tendency to assume that strengthening parties means first and foremost strengthening party organizations. This tendency is rarely challenged, and therefore it usually is not defended explicitly. Nevertheless, it has led the movement to focus on institutional changes that are likely to have trivial effects and that in any event may do little to further the goals of responsible party government.

Party renewalists have cheered the increased strength of the party national committees resulting from increased control over state parties and greatly expanded secretariats. Yet these developments do little or nothing to enhance party government. Although the party renewalists applaud in the abstract the seemingly enhanced authority won by the DNC in the course of implementing the presidential nomination reforms, they generally deplore the Progressive orientation of these reforms on the ground that they weaken the ability of the 'party' to select a candidate, meaning by 'party' the party organization. Their enthusiasm for the conversion of the national committees into active service organizations is less ambivalent. But the content of the service and assistance candidates receive from the national parties is no different from what they receive from private campaign consultants, whose emergence in the last few decades typically is regarded by party renewalists as a negative development. The goal of the national parties' secretariats is to elect their candidates, and the tactics they recommend are no more party-oriented or less candidate-oriented than the tactics recommended by private consultants.

The crucial elements for responsible party government are only tangentially related to the strength, weakness or nature of party organizations. What is needed is an increased sense in the electorate that voting decisions should be made on the basis of party rather than individual candidate characteristics, and a corresponding sense among elected officials that their ability to retain office will depend on how their party is judged.

Since the keystone of responsible party government is located in the minds of voters, there is no easy institutional tinkering that is guaranteed to bring it about. Larger party bureaucracies might be expected to accompany responsible party government, but they probably are not necessary and certainly are not sufficient to bring it about. The institutional measures that have the best chance to succeed involve not the party organizations but the party in government. Supporters of the party government should support measures to strengthen the hand of party leadership in Congress and the state legislatures and, especially in the states, to centralize executive authority. They should resist measures that will weaken governmental party leadership, above all the legislative term limits that were adopted in 1990 in Oklahoma, California, and Colorado, and that are likely to be promoted aggressively elsewhere in the next few years. Public financing of election campaigns, a measure needed for reasons not directly related to party renewal, should be distributed by party legislative leaders and a substantial portion reserved for 'generic' advertising – advertising that urges electoral support of a party rather than for individual candidates (Lowenstein, 1990).

Conclusion

The past quarter century has been a time of considerable change in the American party system, but probably not, on balance, a time of marked decline or resurgence. The bedrock strengths of the party system are the continuing organization of Congress and the state legislatures along party lines, and the continuing structuring of most ballot choices at the state and federal levels by party.

In the electorate, party remains an important voting determinant, though probably less important than a quarter of a century ago. A long-term decline in party voting cohesiveness in Congress may have levelled off, if not reversed. The most dramatic shifts have come in the party organizations. The decline of the locally based machine-type organization has continued. In both parties there has been a reversal of the relations between the national and state levels, with the national parties now enjoying the greater resources and, at least on matters affecting the national conventions, legal authority in the event of conflict.

Two concerted efforts to alter the institutional workings of parties have occurred during this period. The efforts of Progressive reformers to render the presidential nominating process more participatory have succeeded, though the most important mechanism, the extension of presidential primaries, was not the one they anticipated. Criticism of the new nominating process is widespread and diverse. To the extent the criticism is based on the reduced quality of the nominees, comparison of the pre- and post-reform eras does not lead to a conclusive verdict. In any event, the reforms may have done no more than accelerated the coming of a plebiscitary nominating process.

The party renewalists have had some influence on elite opinion and considerable success in constitutional litigation, but have had little effect on broad public attitudes or the actual workings of the party system. Their fortunes are unlikely to improve unless they seek more aggressively to place issues of party government on the public agenda, and shift their focus from the party organizations to the party in office.

PART TWO

The Governmental System

4

Presidential Leadership

COLIN CAMPBELL

American presidents serve as head of government for the most powerful nation in the world. As if this were not enough, they enjoy a level of prestige denied the heads of government in other systems. By virtue of being head of state they stand as a symbol of national integrity and unity. Only French presidents even come close to rivalling their U.S. counterparts in embodying both executive authority over the government and the standing derived from being the symbol of the nation.

The generosity of the American constitution towards the president falls short of unambiguous affirmation. Through the separation of powers between the executive and legislative branches, the Founding Fathers made it difficult for presidents to achieve unity of purpose between their administrations and Congress. The increasingly recurrent tendency of Americans to split their support so that they give one party the presidency and the other control of one or both houses of Congress has deepened this ambiguity. With dismay bordering on alarm, some scholars have emphasized the dysfunctions of such divided government (Sundquist, 1986). In some quarters the belief has emerged that only a series of constitutional amendments can revive the presidency to the point where incumbents can actually re-establish national purpose and direction.

Such views conflict with more conventional assessments of the state of the presidency, which range from counsel to leave well enough alone to celebrations of the genius of the institution. Those coming from the former school of thought have championed the view that experimentalism with the presidency should be avoided. They have observed that the strength of the presidency waxes and wanes according to the character of incumbents. Those who oppose experimentalism with the presidency have noted that Americans at their core reveal a strong monarchical tendency; and they point to Dwight Eisenhower and Richard Nixon as examples of presidents who abused their prerogatives in opposite ways (Neustadt, 1976). Eisenhower exploited the prestige of the office by avoiding situations and commitments which would place his standing at risk. Nixon's imperial presidency, on the other hand, seriously depleted public faith in the office.

Recent studies of Eisenhower have taken strong exception to the view that he hid behind the trappings of office. According to this revisionist view, the dual roles of presidents as heads of government and state require them to balance astutely the inspirational and operational dimensions of their office (Greenstein, 1982). Eisenhower often chose to disguise his effectiveness as a political leader in order to maintain the generality of his appeal.

No comparable revisionist process has yet overtaken assessments of the Nixon presidency. Indeed the Watergate affair ensured that even those most favorable to his style of government will have to wait for some time before revisionists find merit in Nixon's interpretation of the prerogatives of the presidency. However, just as the revisionist view of Eisenhower was winning credence among political scientists, Ronald Reagan emerged as a president whose management style exhibited a new mix of qualities.

Reagan seemed self-consciously to distort the traditional blend of inspiration and executive leadership so that the former appeared to have inundated the latter. The significance of Reagan's appeal has been interpreted very differently by observers. Some have traced a gradual drift in presidential leadership away from executive leadership with its emphasis on developing and nurturing bargaining relationships with Congress, the bureaucracy and outside interests. Instead presidential leadership, they would suggest, has shifted towards 'going public' by direct appeals to the electorate over the heads of institutionalized participants in the policy arena (Kernell, 1986). A president who leans too far in favor of going public runs the risk of placing the country on a permanent campaign footing. Such a situation would ultimately undermine the capacity of the president and Congress to grapple with the real-life issues that face the nation. Some observers, however, underline the inherent risks of going public and conclude that, even under Reagan, the approach did not work the wonders which some commentators have attributed to the tactic (Edwards, 1989).

Reagan and the Decline of Policy Competence

Ronald Reagan's election in 1980 posed a serious challenge to those who argued that an administration's success depends substantially on the capacity of the incumbent president to manage the executive branch. Reagan's record as Governor of California suggested that, unlike his presidential predecessor Jimmy Carter, he would not get involved in factual and administrative detail while in office. In the first term of the presidency Reagan fulfilled this prediction and indeed, if anything, he applied himself less rigorously to the micro-management of the presidency than had been anticipated. However, Reagan won a landslide victory in his 1984 re-election bid and it became clear that the nation would absolve him of his detached management style especially since the recovery of the economy had begun to match his upbeat rhetoric (Kiewiet and Rivers, 1985).

During 1986 and 1987 the mounting evidence of the Iran–Contra inquiries pointed to a degree of negligence on Reagan's part in his constitutional duty to oversee the activities of his cabinet secretaries and aides. However, after a precipitous fall from an extremely high level of popularity (over 68 per cent) Reagan's approval ratings during 1987 rarely dipped below 50 per cent (Ceaser, 1988). Moreover, general approval of Reagan may have had effects beyond his presidency. Preliminary analysis of the 1988 election suggests that public support for Reagan's ideas, if not his approach to administration, helped to turn the contest in part into a referendum on his policies (Farah and Klein, 1989).

In the light of Reagan's successes, some commentators have called for a radical change in the criteria for evaluating presidential performance. Some have even promoted the argument that the Reagan Administration does not represent an aberration but is part of a more general trend (Moe, 1985). Such observers believe that recent presidents gradually have eroded the institutionalized dimensions to the presidency. They have noted for instance that Richard Nixon's dramatic increase of the number of political appointees in the previously career-oriented Office of Management and Budget complemented this process and fitted into 'a larger pattern of institutional development', extending that pattern in ways which 'while sometimes excessive and historically unwise, were consistent both with its historical trajectory and the institutional forces behind it' (Moe, 1985, p. 258).

At the heart of such analyses lie deep reservations about the degree to which any president can enhance his performance by improving his ability to tap the neutral competence of the state apparatus. Over the past few decades, several observers have asserted that presidents could improve their effectiveness as presidential leaders by regularizing cabinet level consultations and tapping more permanent officials to provide staff support for such co-ordinative councils (Fenno, 1959; Hess, 1976; Porter, 1980; Salamon, 1982; Campbell, 1986). On the other hand those advancing the 'deinstitutionalization thesis' assume that incumbents seek to engage such resources and utilise such strategies only in a vague manner (Moe, 1985). What presidents really strive for is responsive competence. That is, they strive above all else to maintain their political support. They do not lose much sleep worrying about whether they have embraced the 'objectively' correct solution to a problem. Therefore presidents' managerial strategies will center on the centralization of decisions in the White House and the politicization of the bureaucracy. Both strategies will bolster a president's capacity to circumvent established organizations and vested interests or – to use Kernell's term – 'go public'.

Scholars whose work preceded analyses based on the

deinstitutionalization thesis had already detected among recent presidents a proclivity for focusing on responsive competence in their administrative strategies. These scholars had warned of the dysfunctional aspects of such a focus and had, for example, underlined the fact that presidents cannot override permanent officialdom by fiat alone (Cronin, 1980). Bureaucracy by its nature serves up 'complexity, diversity, jurisdictional disputes, and recalcitrance'. True executive leadership masters and redirects these factors.

Some students of the presidency have in fact called for a blending of an engagement of the state apparatus with attention to political appeal in what is termed 'policy competence' (Campbell, 1986). Responsive competence should not overshadow neutral competence to the point where the presidency loses its capacity to maintain long-term legitimacy. Inundation by responsive competence makes it difficult for incumbents to associate the presidency convincingly with policies oriented towards the national interest rather than opportunistic moves seeking to optimize short term political support. Some scholars have taken this critique of the deinstitutionalization process a step further and attacked the centralization of power in a White House and the politicization of the bureaucracy as the 'managerial presidency' (Hess, 1988). As used by skeptics of the desirability of such developments, the term denotes a 'failed concept'; and they view episodes such as the Iran–Contra affair, Watergate and indeed the Vietnam war as examples of the weaknesses inherent in such an approach to the presidency.

Even the most benevolent treatment at the hands of revisionists will probably conclude that neither Jimmy Carter nor Ronald Reagan achieved policy competence. Jimmy Carter so buried himself in governmental detail that he seemed totally to lose sight of how to achieve the measure of responsive competence necessary to stand a chance of re-election. Reagan, on the other hand, incanted his conservative message at all the correct times, thereby maintaining his political support. Two especially brilliant Reagan performances occurred in the falls of 1982 and 1983. In 1982 Reagan exhorted the public to 'stay the course', notwithstanding the fact that the economy had slumped deeply into recession.

The outcome was a congressional election result involving substantially fewer Republican losses than most observers had anticipated. In 1983 Reagan, in a national address following the bombing of the US marines in Lebanon and the invasion of Grenada, deftly associated both events with Soviet aggression. Regarding the former he adeptly finessed a disaster which would have presented itself under Carter as a tragic humiliation of the United States. Reagan was then able to use that event to justify the Grenadan invasion and to vindicate his 'evil empires' rhetoric.

Reagan worked in broad strokes emphasizing simple themes which did not have to cohere. As a conservative ideologue he sought simultaneously to pronounce upon the central triad of his beliefs about government: the need to cut both taxes and spending programs and greatly to increase defense expenditure. This volatile cocktail was the source of the current American struggle with the deficit, an unfavorable balance of trade and the status of a debtor nation. It also fostered conspicuous consumption rather than industrial renewal; a deepening of the gap between social provision in the U.S. and that available in most other advanced democracies; and an unparalleled profligacy in the Pentagon.

Yet for all the weaknesses which critics can identify in Reagan's policies, it is also the case that Reagan must be given credit for setting up during his first term one of the most effective White House staffs of any president since Roosevelt. In addition it has to be acknowledged that the Administration's system of cabinet-level councils established a new benchmark for the use of such bodies by presidents.

Those who advised Reagan on the organization of his Administration demonstrated a sound grasp of the ways in which the often conflicting goals of responsive and neutral competence might be reconciled. However not even flawless design can compensate for negligence on the part of the pilot. Only churlish observers noted this during the first term. In the second term rough weather and a change of crew forced the Administration off automatic pilot and revealed that Reagan must have been asleep for most of the previous segment of the journey. To ascertain why things went wrong, particularly in the second term, the fit between

Reagan's personality and the organization of the White House must be examined.

Managerial Style and Administrative Organization in the White House

Reagan had an exceptionally bold agenda based on an unashamedly minimalist view of the proper sphere of the federal government. Even in the one area which he believed should expand, defense, he resolutely deflected pressures towards involving himself directly in disputes between program priorities. On the rare occasions in which he actually did adjudicate differences over defense budget proposals, he also invariably decided in favor of the besieged program. As one OMB career official remarked ruefully:

> the biggest hawk in the Administration happens to be the President himself. So, when the issue goes that far, the outcome is predictable. (Campbell, 1986, p. 70)

Notwithstanding his attitude to government and his detachment from detail, Reagan by all accounts relished being president. But presidents do not achieve policy competence simply by narrowing the national agenda and stressing commitments which mandate specific departments to assume a clear lead. As he prepared to take office, Reagan did heed those close to him who urged careful attention to organizational matters. He accepted two innovations in his administrative structure – the modified 'spokes-in-a-wheel' White House and a series of cabinet councils responsible for various fields of domestic policy.

The organization of the White House has proved a headache for most presidents. The two most obvious formats – a hierarchical structure with a strong chief of staff and a 'spokes-in-a-wheel' system in which all assistants to the president enjoy equal authority and access to the president – have both proved deficient if pursued to excess. For instance, the hierarchical nature of the Nixon White House clearly contributed to the aura of the imperial presidency which added fuel to the nation's response to Watergate. By contrast Jimmy Carter's refusal until the summer of 1979 to appoint a chief of staff exacerbated the sense that his presidency lacked direction.

Reagan could not opt for a pure 'spokes-in-a-wheel' format because that model requires a president with energy, immense intellectual curiosity and perceptiveness to run properly. On the other hand to opt for a strong chief of staff risked two dangers. If Reagan chose a true loyalist as chief of staff (someone, for example, in the mold of Edwin Meese) he would leave himself vulnerable to the accusation even from Republicans that he had made his Administration subject to radical conservatism. But if he appointed an operative known for his efficient management, such a person would conjure up images of H.R. Haldeman's relationship with Nixon, especially since Reagan's inattention to detail had already made knowledgeable observers skeptical about his aptitude for the presidency.

The Reagan White House

The compromise which Reagan endorsed was in many respects brilliant. It installed a triumvirate with James Baker, Edwin Meese and Michael Deaver each heading White House clusters (Schieffer and Gates, 1989). Baker, the Chief of Staff, bore responsibility for what became known as the 'implementation side' of the White House. This area included the assistants to the president for intergovernmental affairs, legislative affairs, public liaison personnel and the Counsel to the President. Meese belonged to the cabinet and took the title 'Counsellor to the President'. He oversaw cabinet administration, the Office of Policy Development and – until William Clark replaced Richard Allen as Assistant to the President for National Security affairs – the National Security Council staff. Michael Deaver, the deputy Chief of Staff, supervised the working of offices responsible for travel preparations, scheduling and special support services. More importantly, Deaver became the principal custodian of Reagan's image and day-to-day coverage in the media.

This triumvirate, consisting of one Washington insider

(Baker) and two loyal Reagan aides from California (Meese and Deaver), provided everything that Carter's White House had lacked – namely someone who knew the town and how to make the trains run on time there, an ideological conscience and a political operative with a sense for how to get and maintain media attention. The triumvirate became 'the big four' when Clark took over as National Security Adviser and would not settle for reporting to Meese and not belonging to the cabinet. Even with a fourth member, the modified spokes-in-a-wheel format operated extremely effectively. It maintained this high level of performance, moreover, in spite of a steady flow of press stories reporting its imminent demise.

The members of 'the big four' attributed the format's success to the recognition by the original triumvirate of the necessity of setting aside differences and pulling together in the wake of the assassination attempt in the early days of the Administration. As one member put it:

> It is hard work for all of us to make it work . . . one of the things that changed this whole chemistry in here was the shooting itself; . . . it forced us to work closely together and we learned how to. (Campbell, 1986, p. 102.)

In addition to coming up with a workable adaptation of the spokes-in-a-wheel approach, Reagan's top aides recognized that any team must have group dynamics. This stood in sharp contrast to Carter's senior people who seemed to take pains to avoid any semblance of formalized decision processes. Even though the President engaged himself only selectively, White House aides maintained the lines of communication through regularized channels – especially routine breakfast meetings prior to presidential briefings.

The Cabinet Councils

The idea for Reagan's complex array of cabinet councils came after Meese and Baker reconciled competing views of how the Cabinet should function. When Governor of California, Reagan had created a supercabinet system in which cabinet secretaries dealt with the over-arching policy issues emanating from large sectors of government without involving themselves in operational details of day-to-day management of specialized agencies. Meese wanted to reorganize the federal bureaucracy according to this design – an idea which Nixon in fact had pushed in 1971. He also believed that the Administration would operate better as a team if Cabinet regularly considered issues which fell between departmental mandates in such a way that each cabinet secretary would freely comment on contentious matters independent of their expertise or their responsibilities. Baker doubted that the Administration could pull off a wholesale reorganization of the federal bureaucracy. He also argued that the magnitude and diversity of the federal government did not lend itself to a system whereby every cabinet secretary should find it possible to weigh in on every presidential issue.

Baker had been a strong supporter of the Economic Policy Board (EPB) – a cabinet committee which had greatly facilitated economic decision-making when Baker served as Under-Secretary of Commerce in the Ford Administration. He believed that the EPB model could be extended to other policy areas. Rather than moving immediately toward super-departments, the administration should first attempt to integrate issues within policy clusters through cabinet councils.

Eventually seven such groups emerged – Economic Affairs; Commerce and Trade; Federalism and Health and Human Resources; Natural Resources and Environment; Food and Agriculture; Legal Policy; and Management and Administration. The President nominally chaired all of these committees. However, most of them functioned with acting chairmen until they reached the point where they could present issues to the President. As a result Reagan only attended about one third of cabinet council meetings. On the foreign policy side, the National Security Council (a statutory body since 1947) functioned only as such when the President chaired it. On other occasions the NSC would meet in Senior Interagency Groups (SIGs) which were chaired by the cabinet level head of the department with the major issue on the agenda. For example the Secretary of Defense would chair SIGs concerning the development of new weapons systems.

The cabinet council process undoubtedly contributed to the relative harmony of the Reagan first term. However there were other factors which contributed to co-ordination. At the outset the budget decisions made by the Administration – largely under the auspices of David Stockman – severely constrained the options available for cabinet secretaries. The budget decisions left little leeway for the types of policy innovation which would ordinarily lead to disputes between departments. Further the Administration's tight screening of political appointees assured a higher level of consensus on potential areas of conflict within and between departments than would normally prevail.

The Administration probably did not require as many as seven cabinet committees on the domestic policy side. Indeed, only the cabinet councils on Economic Affairs and Commerce and Trade handled very heavy workloads. The others tended to meet sporadically. They also did not resolve a great many of the really difficult issues which the Administration faced. That is the White House had to step in and impose solutions to some problems upon which cabinet councils had become deadlocked. Indeed, the White House kept the most sensitive matters out of cabinet councils.

Nonetheless, the system helped immensely in keeping many issues out of the Oval Office or delayed their entry there until cabinet secretaries had already resolved most of the outstanding questions. In the words of one White House aide not entirely enamoured of the system, this workload reduction function did mean that cabinet councils – or at least the busy ones – paid for themselves:

> [The system] works extremely well on issues that are, on a scale of zero to ten in terms of the President's political interest, ranging to about six or seven level. When you get things that are really close to the guts of the Administration, it becomes essential for the President's staff to mount an effort to get around the council process. That's when we really need to get deeply involved; ... beat the drum and figure out how to get it through the Hill. (Campbell, 1986, p. 75).

Interestingly the Reagan Administration employed highly routinized procedures during the first term for dealing with matters whose difficulty exceeded the cabinet councils' capacity for reconciliation of differences. It did this through two committees internal to the White House. The first, the Legislative Strategy Group, included Baker, Meese, Deaver, the Assistant to the President for legislative affairs, other White House officials whose participation seemed appropriate to the occasion, and the cabinet secretaries directly responsible for the issue at hand. Under the chairmanship of Baker, this group both tackled the most bitterly fought disputes in the Administration and reviewed the recommendations of cabinet councils from the standpoint of how readily they would win congressional approval.

The second body, the Budget Review Board, consisted of a similar constellation of White House aides under the chairmanship of David Stockman, the budget director. Each budget season it would engage in dialogues with individual secretaries. These encounters were designed to convince the agency heads that they should be good citizens and 'give at the office' rather than press the resource demands of their departments. This device helped keep the pressure on domestic expenditure. However, as has already been suggested, it barely touched defense budgets.

The Onset of the 'Regan' Administration

From the standpoint of organization, the Reagan Administration clearly took another path during the second term from that followed prior to 1985. This turn of events occurred partially because of changes in the President himself. But it also derived from the style of James Baker's replacement as Chief of Staff, Donald Regan. To no small degree, the first half of Reagan's second term became the Regan Administration.

Despite the predictions of the media the triumvirate, which again replaced 'the big four' after William Clark was replaced by Robert McFarlane as National Security Adviser, never fell apart. Instead it burned out. When the Reagan landslide victory in 1984 seemed to secure for the President a continuation of his policies, Baker, Meese and Deaver all took the opportunity to bow out of the White House. Baker and Meese assumed key cabinet posts; Deaver went on to pursue a lobbying career in the private sector – a path that in his case ended in ignominy.

It had become clear at the end of the first term that Reagan himself was losing energy and interest to the point where his engagement had become minimal. This partially explains why Donald Regan who had been Secretary of the Treasury ended up as Chief of Staff. Baker wanted to leave the White House. However, moderates feared that arch-conservative Republicans might use his departure as an opportunity to install one of their own (for example Jeane Kirkpatrick) as Baker's replacement.

The idea of a Baker–Regan switch – which the two had dreamt up in consultation with Deaver – provided a perfect escape from the mounting political predicament. Most importantly, Reagan took no role in its development (Schieffer and Gates, 1989). In fact, Deaver informed him of the deal after it had been agreed by both parties. This bizarre example of a president simply being informed of a *fait accompli* concerning one of his central prerogatives – the approval of personal advisers – proved to be a harbinger of how the Administration would run during the second term.

It has been argued earlier that the modified 'spokes-in-a-wheel' format suited Reagan perfectly. By limiting the number of aides with whom he had regular contact, it allowed him to remain semi-detached from office. By exposing him to the advice of more than one person, it permitted him to avoid the charge that he had abdicated key presidential tasks to a single person who acted as his surrogate. The appointment of a strong Chief of Staff immediately raised suspicions that the President was going to 'let Regan be Reagan' for the exercise of vast areas of presidential authority. One White House official, anticipating a sharp contrast between the operating styles of Baker and Regan commented on the difference between the two in the *New York Times* soon after the swap:

Baker was a lawyer, a negotiator, a chief of staff who tried to make the case of his client through negotiation. Under

Baker there wasn't a hierarchy – there were three or four senior partners with access to the President. Don [Regan] will eliminate parallel sources of access; as a businessman by nature he operates in a hierarchical manner rather than a negotiating manner. He seems like an uncharacteristic person for the job. (Weinraub, 1986.)

Regan trimmed the White House hierarchy so as to optimize his strategic position as Chief of Staff. He downgraded several 'Assistant to the President' posts to 'Deputy assistant'. He squeezed out three assistants, Robert McFarlane, Edward Rollins (political and governmental affairs) and Max Friedersdorf (congressional relations), after his first year. And he also neutralized two key surviving aides – John Svahn (policy development) and Patrick Buchanan (communication).

The poor fit between Reagan's dwindling interest in the routine aspects of the presidency and Regan's domineering style had all sorts of deleterious effects on the way in which the Administration operated during the second term. However, none of these rivals in gravity the well documented Iran–Contra Affair in which both the President and the Chief of Staff displayed a near-total absence of policy competence. Regarding Reagan, the Tower Commission observed that the President's management style was to put the responsibility for policy review and implementation onto the shoulders of his advisers. However, even in such circumstances, the Report noted, the President should have ensured that the National Security system did not fail. But the President did not 'force his policy to undergo the most critical review of which the NSC participants and the process were capable'. Nor did he insist upon accountability and performance review (President's Special Review Board, 1987, pp. 79–80).

The Commission did not however absolve Donald Regan from responsibility. 'More than almost any Chief of Staff of recent memory', it noted, Regan had 'asserted personal control over the White House staff and sought to extend this to the National Security Adviser'. Regan was personally active in national security affairs and attended almost all of the relevant meetings so that he 'as much as anyone should have insisted that any orderly process be observed'. As a result, Regan in the Commission's view, 'must bear primary responsibility for the chaos that descended on the White House' (President's Special Review Board, 1987, p. 81).

Thus over two Reagan Administrations, the management of the presidency had gone from careful preparedness and well-structured organization to a situation in which policy control was lost and the executive branch was in disarray. This odyssey left a curious legacy for the Bush Administration.

The Bush Presidency

Bush came to office pledged to usher in 'a kinder, gentler' America. He could not achieve such a goal, however, simply by presenting himself as embodying these qualities. He had in addition to emphasize that there would be a better gearbox in his Administration to give greater direction to his presidency. He had to devise a method of providing a greater level of consistency between the presidential rhetoric and concern for those affected by the policies emanating from the White House.

One major problem for the Bush Administration in promoting a new issue agenda was the legacy of the 1988 election campaign. Bush aides had discovered a startling fact in May 1988. For each voter who liked Bush, another disliked him. On the other hand, five voters registered positive views of Democrat Michael Dukakis for every one who saw him in an unfavorable light. The Bush team had to take dramatic action to offset this imbalance. Once the campaign got underway, they astutely shifted the 'negatives' to Dukakis. Perhaps the most aggressive Bush strategy was the subliminal appeal to racial prejudice in the frequent recitation of the facts of the Willie Horton case in which a furloughed (paroled) black prisoner raped a woman. The visual component of this assault consisted of a TV commercial in which a predominantly black group of inmates was passing through a revolving gate.

Bush's victory through a negative campaign was not cost-free. The fact that it had failed to convey any personal or national vision meant that Bush's presidency began without a mandate and from the beginning faced bitter opposition from Congress. Some political commentators saw the style of Bush's campaign and such personal decisions as the selection of Dan Quayle as running-mate as reflective of a fundamental character flaw in the president – a 'readiness to sacrifice the future for temporary political advantage' (Broder, 1988).

Bush knew that the 1988 campaign tactics had hurt his image, despite an astute post-election campaign to persuade the public that he possessed statesmanlike qualities which could now emerge (Campbell, 1991). Bush's inauguration speech in January 1991 offered Congress the prospect of compromise and conciliation even if it lacked clarity and vision. But when Bush's first budget proposals were unveiled, they antagonized Congress because there were no commitments to defense cuts beyond the next fiscal year and because they included a package of social policy 'add-ons' which required unacceptable cuts in other social programs to finance them.

The unsuccessful nomination of John Tower as Defense Secretary offered further insights into Bush's presidential character. Although Bush had been warned against making the nomination, the President remained loyal to Tower even after it had become clear that the Senate would not confirm him because of widespread allegations of personal misconduct by Tower, which included heavy drinking.

Such loyalty as Bush displayed in the Tower episode may be admirable in private life; but the drawn-out Senate hearings delayed the appointment of a Secretary of Defense, though Bush's second nominee – Dick Cheney – was well-regarded. Since asserting political control of the Pentagon bureaucracy was one of the most important challenges facing the Bush presidency, the episode underlined a puzzling set of priorities. Indeed in the early fight over the Tower nomination Bush accidentally raised the specter of President Carter – a president more interested in proving points than getting on with the project of governance. Bush also thereby suggested that he was not easily able to achieve the first element of policy competence – responsiveness to political reality.

The presidential image which Bush wished to convey to the public was that, in contrast to Ronald Reagan's detached and passive style, he would be an active and hands-on manager, involved in the substance of policy-making. In organizing the White House, Bush ignored the counsel of James Baker who had urged the President-elect to adopt a Reagan-style triumvirate. Instead he chose John Sununu to be his Chief of Staff. Observers considered Sununu (the Governor of New Hampshire, who helped capture the primary in that state) highly likely to operate in a hierarchial manner. And Bush's implicit choice of this model convinced many observers that his administration would function more decisively than the Reagan Administration. A Republican senator, quoted in the *International Herald Tribune* of 21 November 1988, waxed eloquently that Bush had 'shown he's the boss in no uncertain terms' and that, whatever might be thought of Sununu or his lack of Washington experience, Bush had to be given credit for showing this kind of 'independence and determination'.

Although Sununu was to become a highly controversial political figure by the summer of 1991, the initial opinions about his suitability for the role of Chief of Staff varied. Some Bush aides questioned whether he had the capacity to delegate or to work as part of a diverse team. Some outside observers suggested that Sununu had an imperious bent. For example, his opponent in the 1986 gubernatorial race in New Hampshire suggested that Sununu's character might make it difficult for him to work as a consultative Chief of Staff, noting that Sununu did not need help to find answers but would reach a decision 'in three minutes flat and stick with it' (Pichirallo, 1988).

Many observers also thought that Sununu's personality was a contributing factor in Robert Teeter's decision not to join the White House staff. Teeter had been Bush's pollster and political strategist in the 1988 election and, although he gave personal reasons for declining to serve in the Bush Administration, it was likely that he had little wish to work closely with Sununu. The fact that Teeter would not come on board dismayed many senior Republicans, who regretted the absence of anyone with Teeter's experience or ability to handle presidential communications.

The previous hierarchical chief of staff (Donald Regan) had downgraded the level of many key White House posts and had been quick to fill vacancies with people who owed their career advancement to his patronage. Sununu has not used his powers of patronage so decisively but he has limited the number of White House units headed by full-fledged Assistants to the President. Indeed there were 9 fewer officials at this rank at the beginning of the Bush Administration than there had been in the Reagan Administration.

Sununu may simply have been attempting to prevent the seemingly inevitable expansion of the White House staff and to simplify the complexity of White House organization. But there was also a determination by the Bush Administration to create the image of a low-profile White House staff which went with a more activist approach to governing and greater reliance on senior members of the cabinet such as James Baker and Nicholas Brady, who were also close friends of the President. Thus, as a January 1989 article in the *Wall Street Journal* indicated, Bush – in contrast to Reagan – sought a White House that would simply flesh out his initiatives and would not rely so much on senior advisers to resolve difficulties within his administration or need them to prod the president into action (Seib, 1989).

Despite Sununu's efforts to trim the organizational structure of the White House, the Bush Administration saw most of the units which had existed under the Reagan Administration surviving in some form. The pattern first established by Sununu at the White House was relatively systematized. A meeting with senior staff each morning at 7.30 a.m. would be followed by a meeting at which the President was briefed on national security developments by the CIA and by Brent Scowcroft (the Assistant to the President for National Security). Sununu would then have a private session with the President to plan the day's agenda and would meet again with him at 4.45 p.m. to assess the day's events. Senior Staff would in addition have a weekly review of events each Friday.

Like President Bush, Sununu has adopted an inflexible management style which has emphasized informality and

face-to-face encounters. Sununu has been open to staffers
and has encouraged personal interchange to build a sense of
cohesion in the White House. But Sununu's role – like that of
any Chief of Staff – can be dangerous for a president and the
internal harmony of an administration. A Chief of Staff who
makes himself the sole or even the major channel of information to the President and who decides when ideas may be
presented to a President runs the risk of antagonizing other
advisers. Such advisers may feel alienated if they are frequently excluded from decisions on matters which overlap
with their responsibilities. He also runs the risk of denying
the President adequate direct exposure to his aides and to
their exchanges on the merits of various initiatives, exchanges which might leave the President with a sense of his
aides' abilities and the reasoning behind their policy positions.

With respect to formal consultative mechanisms the Bush
Administration has kept essentially the same structure which
operated under Reagan. Sununu chairs the Legislative
Strategy Group, but the precise importance of this committee
under Bush is not yet clear. During the preparation of Bush's
first budget, the Chief of Staff; the Assistant to the President
for economic and domestic policy, Roger Porter; the Treasury Secretary, Brady; the director of OMB, Richard Darman
and the chairman of the Council of Economic Advisors,
Michael Boskin, met as often as two or three times a day with
the president.

The National Security Council, the only cabinet-level committee mandated by law, has met regularly. However, its
performance was unimpressive in the first test of crisis
management – the October 1989 coup attempt against
General Noriega of Panama. Confronted by the contrast
between Bush's tough rhetoric on Noriega and the disarray
of the Administration when presented with the opportunity
to seize him, the press asked the President whether there had
been a breakdown of communications. Senior members of
the Administration made it known privately that the Panama
crisis had exposed serious flaws in Bush's policy-making style.
In particular it had highlighted the dangers of relying on
informal contacts with key members of the cabinet and with a

small number of aides. The degree of internal dissatisfaction with the decision-making process led Sununu to hold an enquiry into the way the machinery had actually worked during the crisis. However this led to such a cacophony of voices within the Administration that President Bush was moved to issue a strict order to prevent aides second-guessing the Administration's handling of the coup attempt. The problem, as one well-placed official revealed in the *Washington Post* shortly afterwards, was Bush's unstructured style:

> For ten months they've had this collegial, informal atmosphere ... They took in the facts as they needed them. They shut out the bureaucracy. The flow of information ... should have been more organized. There should have been a central collection point. There never was a point where someone said: 'Let's call a meeting.' That's not the kind of thing you do if it's just the boys. You just say 'Let's go in and talk.' (Hoffman, 1989)

In retrospect it might seem that Bush's indecisiveness during the coup attempt ultimately did not matter. After all, the December 1989 invasion of Panama resulted in Noriega's overthrow and eventual capture. Since the U.S. defeat in Vietnam, any U.S. military accomplishment – no matter how tiny the conquered nation – provides a surge in presidential popularity. Yet any scholarly assessment of presidential performance must go beyond an incumbent's support in the polls. Bush's handling of Panama suggests that he can turn very mean when embarrassed. It hardly mattered to the American public that the invasion may have violated international law and certainly brought death and destruction in vast disproportion to the specific incidents which served as Bush's immediate justification for his action.

The Economic Policy Council and the Domestic Policy Council – unlike policy councils on the domestic side at the beginning of Reagan's first term – have taken a long time to get into full swing. The delays were to a large extent the result of difficulties that the Administration has encountered in staffing sub-cabinet level positions in the departments. To be effective such councils require working groups of sub-cabinet officials which can prepare issues for cabinet level review.

If Bush truly has underutilized the structural apparatus available through the NSC and the cabinet councils, he has also neglected the benefits he could have reaped from the excellent selections he made for his assistants for national security and for economic and domestic policy. The respective incumbents, Brent Scowcroft and Roger Porter, bring long experience and strong reputations for even-handed brokerage to their positions. Scowcroft previously held his position under Gerald Ford. And Porter has worked apprenticeships in the same field under Ford and Reagan. This experience gives him unrivaled credentials for the assumption of the top economic and domestic policy position in the White House.

Organizational Stress

Any administration, no matter how well organized and staffed initially, will show some signs of stress – sometimes to a point which threatens the President's political effectiveness. However the Bush Administration seems to be an example of one which exhibited signs of stress relatively early in the term.

It appears that fluidity rather than hierarchy has so far prevailed in White House dynamics. Bush has apparently become involved in a fair amount of presidential minutiae – a trait which prompted one Republican strategist to remark in the *New York Times* on 19 March 1989 that Bush was in a sense 'doing his own staff work' and not staying within 'carefully defined channels' (Boyd, 1989).

Such a pattern, if it becomes established in the White House, can put the Chief of Staff in an untenable situation since people will tend to blame him, even if he has failed to achieve the kind of hierarchical command which would enable him to have a hand in all the major decisions emanating from the White House.

This tends to take the satisfaction out of being a lightning-rod Chief of Staff. Strong chiefs of staff draw blame away from the President but they also imbibe the heady wine of making things happen. On several occasions Sununu took the brunt of criticism leveled at the administration for major failures of the White House machinery. An early example occurred when Richard Darman, the Director of OMB, and Nicholas Brady, the Treasury Secretary, proposed a tax on deposits in bank accounts, ostensibly in order to provide funding to rescue the ailing savings and loans companies. The hostile public reaction caused the Administration to back down quickly. Sununu himself put the error down to a failure of communication on the Administration's part and suggested that its goals need to be set out more clearly both to Congress and the general public. However one administration official made some pointed remarks about the lessons Sununu could learn about his own performance from the aborted tax proposal:

> . . . he still has a few things to learn about Washington. The first is that when you've got an idea floating that may not fly, you keep it out of the White House. That's why you have a Secretary of Treasury or head of OMB. (Weinraub, 1989.)

Another occasion when Sununu was criticized occurred after Bush's first one hundred days in office. To mark the event Bush went on a four-day barnstorming trip which fell flat in that it attracted very little media attention. Considerable dissension arose in the White House over the failed trip. However Sununu refused this time to accept blame. In fact he shifted responsibility to aides for 'grousing' to the media.

Senior Republican strategists outside the White House noted that the episode reinforced their earlier concern about how well the White House would handle the media without an experienced communications operative such as Robert Teeter, having to rely largely on Sununu.

Congressional Relations

The Bush White House's handling of congressional relations was arguably another area in which Sununu overestimated his ability to get by with low-profile staff. Sununu himself was escaping blame for the state of executive–legislative relations until the summer of 1989. At one stage he had to make a special trip to Congress to soothe the Republican caucus. A week before he had offended the party's leadership by berating them about the need for greater loyalty to the President. He ran into a further spate of trouble in the fall when he began to give versions of the President's wishes with respect to specific pieces of legislation even though those versions contrasted sharply with what department and agency heads had requested from Congress. Subsequent assessments, on into the spring of 1990, of the heightened tension between the White House and Congress suggested that Sununu's interventions amounted to last minute efforts to compensate for the inadequate staff work of an inexperienced congressional relations office. However the antics of both Sununu and budget director Richard Darman during the summer and fall of 1990 left no doubt that Bush's indulgence of his 'bad cap' aides was undermining his credibility in the struggle with Congress over resolution of the budget crisis.

At first sight, the behavior of C. Boyden Gray during the early months of the Administration suggested that Sununu would have to share the role of being the lightning rod of the Administration. Gray, who as Counsel to the President serves as the White House's chief lawyer, had stumbled into the midst of several early Administration crises. In fact he had contributed more than his part to nullifying the original plan that Bush's White House would distinguish itself from Reagan's by the degree to which staffers assumed a low profile. Gray is the heir to a multimillion dollar tobacco fortune. He worked for eight years in Bush's vice-presidential office. He has a passionate interest in substituting grain alcohol fuel for gasoline. Observers have suggested that the relationship between President Bush and Gray stems principally from their very similar patrician backgrounds. As Lee Atwater remarked, in an interview with the *Washington Post*, President Bush has 'developed a confidence and trust level with Boyden that's not going to be shaken'.

Gray has frequently caused problems for the Administration, acting as a loose cannon in the conduct of negotiations.

Early on Gray gave a private briefing to Republican senators on the FBI report on the original Bush nominee for Defense Secretary (John Tower). This infuriated Senator Sam Nunn (D-Ga) to the point where it became impossible to gain his support for the Tower nomination. As chairman of the Senate Armed Services Committee, Nunn believed that the private briefing revealed more than a simple lack of follow-through in Bush's inaugural commitment to bipartisanship. It also suggested that the President was not going to take the congressional leadership into his full confidence.

Gray also embarrassed the President by his conduct of his own financial affairs. As White House counsel, Gray was responsible for compliance with 'conflict of interest legislation', yet he retained chairmanship of his family's communications company and only after extensive press criticism did he resign the post and put his assets into a blind trust. His reluctance to comply with the law raised serious questions about how faithfully the Administration would enforce the ethics provisions of the federal government.

Subsequently Gray's behavior cast doubt on the Administration's intention not to let aides compete for power with cabinet secretaries. Gray twice locked horns with no less a personage than James Baker. On the first occasion, Gray, who was no doubt reeling from his own embarrassment over continued involvement in his family business, took Baker to task for holding shares in Chemical Bank. He maintained that, since Chemical had some $4 billion in outstanding Third World loans, Baker's investment constituted a conflict of interest. One mutual friend of the President's and the Secretary's noted that Baker, normally the picture of gentility, was 'wild' with anger because Gray had implicitly questioned his integrity.

Other confrontations between Gray and Baker occurred early in the Administration. In late March when Baker had successfully negotiated an agreement with the congressional leadership which would allow aid to the Contras in Nicaragua to expire after November 1989 unless four congressional committees wrote letters approving continued support. Gray argued within the White House that this arrangement would impinge upon presidential powers. After failing to arouse a sympathetic hearing among his White House colleagues, Gray went public by giving an interview to the *New York Times*. Baker shot back that the policy did not violate presidential prerogatives and furthermore had won the approval of a higher White House official than Gray. The next day the President and the Chief of Staff had a private session with Gray in which they made it clear that he was not to go public in this way in the future. One White House official quoted in the *Washington Post* put the Administration frustrations with Gray graphically:

> We carefully work out something with congressional support – a hell of an accomplishment, a very positive thing, in only the first two months – and what happens but we have somebody out of personal pique [raising questions].

After this episode Gray kept a low profile. However he played a key role in representing conservative interests on issues concerning both environmental protection and civil rights.

The Gulf War

Bush's handling of the Iraqi invasion of Kuwait in August 1990 will almost certainly loom as the paramount test of his presidential leadership. From the outset, the agility with which Bush put together the coalition in support of forcing the Iraqis out of Kuwait earned him high marks for skill at international brokerage. However, three defects in Bush's response raise questions about his effectiveness in handling the crisis.

First, Bush continued the pattern of relying almost exclusively on a small group of trusted advisers in attempting to resolve the crisis. This contributed to the speed with which he committed U.S. forces and maneuvered in the international community to obtain military and financial assistance and support for sanctions against Iraq. However, Bush's decisiveness foreclosed other options. Most important, the amassing of the huge military force pretty well preordained that it would have to be used. Otherwise, Bush would have exposed himself to attack for succumbing to the 'Vietnam syndrome'.

As the reality of the devastation of Iraq and Kuwait sinks in, many observers have asked if such massive use of force was in fact necessary.

Second, Bush's tendency to personalize struggles with adversaries led to the needless inflammation of the crisis. On occasion, for instance when he likened Saddam Hussein to Hitler, it even exacerbated the difficulties he had encountered in selling his policy to Congress and the American people. This proved especially the case during October and November 1990, when the electorate began to read across from his indecisiveness on the budget issue to some of his zigzags on his objectives in the Gulf.

Third, Bush's inability to articulate his long-term objectives has revealed itself in the aftermath of the war. While he did finally rally the nation around the promise of a new world order, we see now that this vision was largely illusory – especially for Kurds and Shiites who took Bush's rhetorical flourishes about getting rid of Saddam Hussein seriously. Indeed analysts should look very closely at what produced the swing toward support of the President once the air attacks began in January 1991. They might well discover that the superlative briefings and videos provided by the military – not the speeches of the President – produced the immense rally effect which bloated Bush's approval ratings to unprecedented heights.

Conclusion

The difficulty of reconciling the roles of head of state and head of government is one of the enduring problems of the American presidency. It has been argued that presidents who strive for policy competence stand the best chance of achieving an appropriate blend of the two presidential functions. In order to achieve optimal integration of their roles, presidents must understand themselves. And they must take care to organize their administrations in ways which will complement their personalities.

Reagan during his first team benefited from a stroke of genius. The administrative format urged upon him by James

Baker consisted of a modified 'spokes-in-a-wheel' White House and a system of cabinet councils. We are just beginning to get a clear picture of Bush's managerial style. However, given what we do know about his character and the experience of his Administration so far, it is probable that Bush would have benefited even more than Reagan from using a modified 'spokes-in-a-wheel' format for his organization of the White House. For, contrary to the initial fears about Sununu's preference for a hierarchical White House, it appears that Sununu has not established a discipline within the White House and Bush has accordingly had to tolerate a degree of confusion and dissension within the Administration's inner ranks. Equally, the range of policy misfires, from the first Panama coup to the repeal of the Medicare surtax, suggests that the Administration's ability to engage the state apparatus has operated less than perfectly. Yet it remains to be seen how far these administrative weaknesses will be corrected as the Bush presidency progresses and indeed how far they translate into electoral opinion, which is long on general support but short on endorsements of his handling of specific issues. Certainly the crisis in the Persian Gulf proved a severe test of Bush's abilities. At first blush he came through with flying colors. However, sober second thoughts might reduce his mark from a 'first' to a 'second' – even a 'lower second'. In the meantime the verdict on the leadership given by the Bush presidency in both domestic policy and foreign affairs must remain a mixed one.

5

Congress and Legislative Activism

CHRISTOPHER J. BAILEY

In a burst of legislative activism that confounded many of its critics, Congress in the late 1980s and early 1990s reasserted its policymaking prerogatives. Taking advantage of a vacuum in presidential policymaking during the last two years of the Reagan Administration, Democratic leaders of the 100th Congress (1987–88) forced through legislation which addressed, among other things, the problems of welfare reform, housing, the homeless, and civil rights. Jim Wright, then the Speaker of the House of Representatives, even began to challenge presidential prerogatives in foreign policy by offering his own solution to the stalemate in Nicaragua. Emboldened by such success, Democratic leaders were unwilling to cede the initiative to President Bush, who they believed had been elected without a clear mandate of his own, and as a result continued to pursue their own agenda in the 101st Congress (1989–90). Before adjourning in the early hours of 28 October 1990, the 101st Congress managed to grind out an impressive stack of laws that redirected U.S. policy in fiscal matters, pollution control and immigration. The 102nd Congress also showed signs of continued legislative activism when the House passed a Civil Rights Bill, which was opposed by President Bush, in June 1991.

The legislative activism of the 100th Congress and the 101st Congress surprised most observers. Congress, like legislatures throughout the western world, has had trouble adapting to the twentieth century. Rising public expectations about the role of government have led to demands for action which Congress has all too often seemed incapable of meeting. Ostensibly unable both to assimilate vast amounts of information and to formulate policy responses to the problems confronting Americans, Congress has tended to rely upon the executive branch for legislative initiatives. Unlike the British Parliament, however, which has ceded almost all of its policy-making authority to the executive, Congress has remained an important actor in the American political system. Protected by provisions of the Constitution which reserve certain powers to Congress and guarantee members a power base which is independent of the executive branch, the legislature of the United States has managed to retain both power and independence.

Although Congress has retained the *capacity* to act, periods of legislative activism since 1932 have been rare. Presidents Eisenhower and Nixon both had to confront at different times a Congress that was eager and able to assert its own policy priorities rather than relying simply on presidential initiatives; but such occasions have been the exception rather than the rule. In the past it has proved difficult for the leadership to maintain the control and discipline necessary to enact a systematic programme over a long period of time. Whether the legislative activism of the 100th and 101st Congresses can be sustained for very long is, therefore, open to debate, and raises a number of interesting questions about congressional competence.

First, there has been considerable debate as to whether members of Congress possess either the incentive or the expertise necessary to formulate effective public policy. Critics often point out that Representatives and Senators appear to devote more attention to securing their re-election through the provision of constituency services than crafting public policy. Secondly, even if members of Congress are interested in formulating policy, it is not clear that congressional procedures facilitate the enactment of such policies into law. The procedures of the House of Representatives and the Senate often appear to be slow, cumbersome, and replete with veto points. Finally, if there are question marks over the ability of Congress both to formulate and enact policy then the old debate over the proper role for a legislature in a modern system of government becomes pertinent. After all, Congress is now over two hundred years old and the type of society for which it was designed has long since passed.

Constituency Attentiveness

The relationship between the individual Representative or Senator and his or her constituency is central both to an understanding of the role of Congress in the U.S. political system, and any explanation of congressional behavior. Not only does the relationship legitimize Congress's role as a legislature and give some substance to the claim of 'government by the people', but pressure from constituents also helps shape the actions of members of Congress. Individual members have to determine what proportion of their limited time and resources they wish to devote to constituency service, and the perceived views of their constituents will have an influence on how they cast their votes. Both factors will have an impact on congressional policy-making. More time and resources devoted to constituency service means less time and resources can be devoted to policy-making, and concern for the perceived views of constituents will effect the content of policy.

Emphasis on Constituency Service

Members of Congress have always paid attention to the interests of their constituents. However, the need for members of Congress to be aware of and responsive to the demands of their constituents has become increasingly important in recent years as a consequence both of changes in the electoral environment and an opening of congressional procedures. Rule changes during the 1970s, which were designed to bring 'government into the sunshine' by opening committee and subcommittee hearings to the public, mean that a detailed record of a legislator's activities may be kept by any interest group or PAC. That record may then be exploited through television advertising or other forms of grass-roots lobbying either to discredit or credit a member in his constituency. More intense media coverage of Congress has also resulted in greater publicity for many representatives and senators. The result of these developments has been to undermine the control that members of Congress possess over the flow of information to their constituents about their activities.

The possibility of losing control over this flow of information poses an electoral threat to members of Congress. With a better-educated, more self-reliant electorate no longer relying so heavily upon party labels as voting cues, continued electoral success depends to a large extent on how well the individual Representative or Senator can control the image that voters have of his record. Defeat at the polls can follow all too quickly if a member of Congress loses control of his or her image. To minimize such a danger, members of Congress have increasingly devoted more attention and resources to their constituencies.

In many respects, Representatives are better positioned to control their image than Senators. With smaller constituencies, Representatives are able to maintain tight control over their districts, establish a role as ombudsmen and providers of services, and thus insulate themselves from external political forces. In contrast, Senators who typically serve large geographical and numerical constituencies find controlling the flow of information to constituents is an inherently more difficult task. Previously such control was not deemed necessary. The longer terms of Senators, together with larger constituencies with a greater heterogeneity of interests which tend to check and balance one another, facilitated a degree of freedom from constituency pressures. Only with the approach of the next election would Senators turn their attention to the voters. The defeat of a large number of Senators during the late 1970s, however, served to accentuate constituency attentiveness. Many of those defeated were perceived to have ignored their home states, and this lesson has not been lost on their successors. Senators now pay more attention to their constituencies. As Senator Dale Bumpers

(D.–Ark.) noted in 1982:

> The Founding Fathers gave Senators six year terms so they could be statesmen for at least four years and not respond to every whim and caprice. Now a Senator in his first year knows any vote could hurt him five years later. So senators behave like House members. They are running constantly.

Senators, like representatives, have sought to control their image far more tightly in recent years.

The move towards the increased preoccupation with constituency matters can be seen in many aspects of Congress's operations. Perhaps the most obvious indicator of the greater attention paid to constituents, however, is the volume of mail sent out by congressional offices using the franking privilege (the right to send free mail to constituents). In 1980 511.3 million items of franked mail were distributed by members of Congress. By the end of the decade the volume of mail had increased to approximately one billion items. This volume of mail is the equivalent of four letters for every man, woman, and child in the United States. Of this mail, the Post Office has estimated that approximately 90 per cent are unsolicited items which provide favorable reports of the legislator's activities. In addition to mass mailings, both the Senate and the House have established their own radio and television studios where programs can be produced very cheaply. These programs are then distributed to national and local radio and television studios. As with the franking privilege, these facilities are generally used by members of Congress to advertise their activities. In other words, they are a tool for self-promotion.

Underpinning the ability of members of Congress to adverise their activities has been a considerable expansion in the computer facilities available to them (Frantzich, 1982). On the whole, Representatives and Senators have used their computers to keep track of an ever increasing volume of incoming mail. Generated initially by Watergate and then by the grass-roots lobbying techniques of PACs such as the National Conservative Political Action Committee, the level of incoming mail has almost quadrupled since 1973. In 1983, for example, 153 million items of mail came into the House compared, with a mere 40 million items ten years earlier. In most congressional offices this mail is coded according to factors such as sender, subject and location. The computer is then often used to formulate a reply by choosing from a selection of pre-written paragraphs stored in its memory. Computers can also be used to generate mass mailings. With computerized lists these mailings can be targeted at different groups or even individualized.

To reinforce the effect of mass mailings, members of Congress have been spending an increasing proportion of their time in their constituencies. In 1970 Representatives spent an average of fifteen weeks each year in their districts. By the late 1980s the amount of time that Representatives spend in their constituencies had risen to just over twenty-five weeks. In short, Representatives are now spending just under half of the year in their constituencies rather than in Washington DC. Although not quite so pronounced, a similar trend can be observed among Senators. To accommodate such changes, the legislative schedules of the Senate and House of Representatives have been structured to allow members to spend time with their constituents without jeopardizing their legislative interests. The House commonly schedules legislative business on a Tuesday-to-Thursday basis in order to allow Representatives to spend long weekends with their constituents. Similarly, the Senate adopted in 1988 a 'three week-one week' schedule. During every month, the Senate is in session for three weeks and off for one week.

To maintain a presence in their constituencies while they themselves are on Capitol Hill, members have also increasingly diverted staff and resources to their local offices (Johannes, 1984). In 1972 approximately 22.5 per cent of House staff were based in district offices, and 12.5 per cent of Senate staff were based in state offices. By the late 1980s these figures had risen to 40.9 per cent and 34.2 per cent respectively. The main function of these staff is to provide a source of assistance for constituents. The result has been an increase in the amount of casework being undertaken by members of Congress and their staff. In fact, many members now behave much like ombudsmen. They deal with requests from constituents to sort out problems with the bureaucracy, to give information about government publications or benefits, or just to provide general advice. Provision of such services, it is argued, brings electoral benefits to the individual Representative or Senator: greater visibility and a favorable rating (Cain *et al.* 1987).

In recent years considerable concern has been expressed about the way that members conduct casework. Two criticisms, in particular, have been made. First, critics contend that some constituents receive more service than others. Constituents who have previously made contributions to the member's campaign fund are more likely to have their problems dealt with than those who have not. Secondly, critics contend that the distinction between legitimate actions on behalf of a constituent and improper 'arm twisting' of federal bureaucrats is frequently blurred. Both criticisms were brought into stark relief in the so-called 'Keating Five' scandal. In the Autumn of 1989 Senators Alan Cranston (D.–Calif.), Dennis DeConcini (D.–Ariz), John Glenn (D.–Ohio), John McCain (R.–Ariz.), and Donald Riegle (D.–Mich.) were accused of improperly intervening with federal thrift regulators on behalf of Charles Keating, chairman of Lincoln Savings and Loan. Keating had previously made large contributions to each of the Senators' campaign funds. After a fourteen-month inquiry into the scandal, the Senate Ethics Committee in March 1991 found that there was substantial evidence of wrongdoing by Senator Cranston and issued mild reproofs to the other four.

The 'Keating Five' scandal raised important questions about the propriety of certain forms of constituency service. More generally, the increasing proportion of time and resources being devoted to constituency services by both Senators and Representatives places a question mark over the capacity of Congress to craft effective public policy. Senator Richard Shelby (D.–Ala.) alluded to this problem in a statement made in 1987:

Many freshmen view their role differently than 25 years ago, when a Senator was only a legislator. Now a Senator is also a grantsman, an ombudsman, and a caseworker, and cannot ignore [these activities]. When we are asked by our constituents to help, we can't say we don't have time because we are focusing on national and international issues.

Policy-making is time-consuming. It requires time to identify a problem, to design an appropriate response, and to persuade others that such a response is the best available. What the statistics about the emphasis on the provision of constituency services suggest is that time for policy-making is a rare commodity in Congress.

The Parochial Congress

In addition to structuring the workload patterns of Congress, the attentiveness that members display towards their constituencies affects their policy choices. There has been considerable debate, however, as to whether such attentiveness to constituency concerns is beneficial or detrimental to the policy-making process. On the one hand, it is argued that members of Congress are responsive to the demands of their constituents. They are aware of the problems and concerns of their constituents and attempt to produce appropriate policies (Eulau and Karps, 1977). On the other hand, it is frequently argued that members of Congress are too responsive to these demands. The suggestion is that parochial concerns all too often take precedence over national concerns (Fiorina, 1980).

The benefits to policy-making which accrue from an attentiveness to constituency are a heightened capacity for identifying the issues that concern people. Previously considerable doubt was expressed about the importance of constituency considerations in influencing the policy choices of Senators and Representatives. Studies carried out during the 1960s and early 1970s revealed that voters generally knew little of their member's voting record, and only rarely offered any kind of guidance on how to cast a particular vote (Miller and Stokes, 1963). The communications gap between legislators and their constituents, however, has been reduced by advances in technology during the 1970s and 1980s. Members of Congress now use opinion polls and election returns to assess the views of constituents. In this way, Representatives and Senators are able to gain a more accurate perception of the views of their constituents than had previously been the case.

Advances in technology have also been supplemented by changes in congressional practices. The fact that members of Congress are spending more time outside Washington, and have diverted more staff to their local offices, means that they are more likely to be aware of the particular problems and difficulties facing their constituents. As a result, they are in a position to order their policy-making priorities in a way which corresponds closely to their perceptions of the desires of the people they are elected to represent. The legislation passed by the 100th and 101st Congresses, for example, addressed many of the issues which successive opinion polls had identified as of most concern to the American people. In four years (1987–90) Congress enacted measures designed to improve highways and mass transit systems, to bolster elementary and secondary education, to help clean up the environment, to fight drugs, and to extend civil rights to disabled Americans. Almost the last act of the 101st Congress was the passage of a comprehensive Clean Air Act which was designed to reduce pollution in the United States.

Although not denying that certain benefits might result from an attentiveness to constituency concerns, many critics would argue that all too often the result of such attentiveness is a parochialism which is detrimental to policy-making. In their concern to look after the interests of their constituents members frequently neglect or act counter to the interests of the country as a whole. As one influential observer has noted:

> ... individual members of Congress are overwhelmingly influenced by the parochial interests of their particular districts and by special interest lobbies, and that incoherent national policies are often the result. (Olsen, 1982, p. 50.)

The parochialism of Congress, for example, is often cited as a means of explaining the impasse which appears to exist over the budget deficit of the United States. A former Director of the OMB, David Stockman, has complained that:

> The fact is, politicians can be a menace. They never stop inventing illicit enterprises of government that bleed the national economy. Their social uplift and porkbarrel is wasteful; it reduces our collective welfare and wealth. The politicians rarely look around. Two years and one Congressional District is the scope of their horizon. (Stockman, 1986, p. 15.)

Not only do members of Congress appear unwilling to make the hard political choices which are deemed necessary to resolve a national problem, but their actions often seem to make the matter worse.

Evidence to support the view that members are either unwilling to make hard political choices or else tend to initiate a course of action which makes matters worse can be found in the response of Congress to the budget deficit. The difficulties experienced by Congress in its attempts to find a solution to the problem of the budget deficit are indicative of the obstacles facing the legislature when it tries to address national issues. Not only are there problems in collecting and assimilating information on such a complex subject, but the concern shown by individual Senators and Representatives for the welfare of their constituents makes it extremely difficult to find agreement for a national policy. Parochial interests tend to take precedence over national interests. After all, the size of the national debt is a meaningless abstraction to most constituents; the level of welfare payments and the size of the tax bill are not. The Fiscal 1988 budget package, for example, was 3296 pages long, weighed 43 pounds, and contained provision after provision authorizing spending on various projects. It was criticized by President Reagan in his State of Union address of 25 January 1988 for catering to local concerns and special interests by providing funds for items such as 'cranberry, blueberry, and crawfish research'. In an era of budget deficits such blatant pork-barreling seemed to many to be irresponsible. Concern about the tax bill also led Congress to reject an agreement negotiated between congressional leaders and President Bush in 1990 that would have cut public spending and raised taxes on the middle classes. Agreement was only reached on the Fiscal 1991 budget when President Bush agreed to increase the taxes on the rich rather than the middle classes.

The record of the 100th and 101st Congresses reveals very clearly both the benefits and problems which result from congressional parochialism. Representatives and Senators are in a good position to identify the issues which most concern their constituents. The way that they respond to such issues, however, is also determined by parochial concerns. Wherever possible the preferred course of action is distributive policy (Lowi, 1964; 1972). By transferring resources from the public treasury to constituents, distributive policies have obvious attractions for members of Congress. Distributive policies are so attractive to members, in fact, that Congress bears most of the responsibility for the growth of the federal government in the twentieth century (Fiorina, 1977; Moe and Miller, 1983; Colie, 1988). When difficult decisions have to be made the preferred course of action is nondecision-making (Bachrach and Baratz, 1970). If a decision is likely to alienate an important section of a constituency it is best not to make such a decision. As one observer has noted:

> A United States congressman has two principal functions: to make laws and to keep laws from being made. The first of these he and his colleagues perform only with sweat, patience and a remarkable skill in the handling of creaking machinery; but the second they perform daily, with ease and infinite variety. (Bendiner, 1964, p. 15.)

In short, parochialism not only determines congressional priorities, but also determines the way in which those priorities are to be addressed. This means that the priorities of Congress in the early 1990s are likely to be those issues which currently preoccupy the American people: drugs, homelessness, health care, and the environment. It also means that Congress is most likely to address these problems through distributive policies.

Strengthening Congressional Capacity

Being able both to identify the problems preoccupying the American people and to find the time to consider responses to such problems, provides no guarantee that Congress will actually be able to arrive at either the most appropriate solution to the problem, or indeed, arrive at any solution at all. Two difficulties, in particular, are frequently mentioned. First, to translate a demand for policy into a well-conceived legislative proposal requires considerable espertise about a subject. Many critics contend that members are generalists who simply lack the information and knowledge necessary to craft coherent policy responses to the problems facing the United States (Toffler, 1980). Secondly, to gain the enactment of a legislative proposal requires an ability to overcome opposition to a policy. Many critics argue that the procedures of the House and Senate are replete with multiple veto points which makes the leadership necessary to enact legislation very difficult to sustain over a long period of time (Sundquist, 1981; Kingdon, 1984).

Doubts about the capacity of Congress to play a meaningful role in the policy-making process reached a peak during the early 1970s as the Vietnam War and Watergate ended the illusion that the presidency could be relied upon to be a benign actor in the political system (Rieselbach, 1986). The result was a series of reforms designed to improve Congress's capacity to make policy and challenge presidential leadership. In an effort to reduce Congress's reliance upon the President for information, and at the same time enhance congressional expertise, Representatives and Senators voted to provide themselves with greater resources. The number of staff that members were able to employ rose dramatically, the position of existing support agencies was strengthened, and an Office of Technology Assessment (OTA) and a Congressional Budget Office (CBO) created. At the same time, a series of procedural changes designed to facilitate the enactment of legislation were introduced. Reforms weakened the power of committee chairmen, enhanced the authority of the party leadership, and attempted to streamline floor procedures. The effect of such changes, however, was not exactly as envisaged. More resources may have improved expertise, but they also created problems of management. The authority of the party leadership may have been strengthened, but the weakening of the dominance of the committee chairmen fragmented power in Congress. In short, the reforms of the 1970s generated almost as many problems as they had sought to overcome.

The Increase in Resources

The 1970s saw a dramatic increase in the amount of resources available to members of Congress. Both the desire to assert Congress's authority in the wake of Vietnam and Watergate, and an influx of new members who were anxious to make an immediate impact on policy, fuelled an unprecedented growth in the number of staff working in the House of Representatives and the Senate. Between 1972 and 1980 the number of personal staff working for individual members rose from 7706 to 11 117, and the number of staff working for committees of the House of Senate rose from 1661 to 3108. In the same period, the number of people working for the Congressional Support Agencies increased from 5221 to 6412. Although part of this increase may be accounted for by the creation of the OTA in 1972 and the CBO in 1974, the number of staff working for the Congressional Research Service (CRS) and the General Accounting Office (GAO) also grew. In 1972 the CRS had employed 479 staff, and the GAO had employed 4742 staff. By 1980, these two agencies were employing 868 and 5196 staff respectively. In total, the number of personal staff, committee staff, and staff working in the Congressional Support Agencies rose from 14 588 in 1972 to 20 637 in 1980. Since 1980, however, the rate at which the number of staff working in Congress has increased has slowed down. In 1986 there were 11 694 personal staff working for individual representatives and senators, 3029 staff working for committees, and 6244 staff working for the Congressional Support Agencies. The total number of staff working in Congress in 1986 was 20 967.

On the positive side, the expansion of congressional resources over the last two decades has meant that members of

Congress are able to gather more information about specific issues. The budget forecasts of the CBO, for example, are widely regarded as more accurate than those of the OMB, and have helped to legitimize Congress's frequent rejection of presidential budgetary proposals. Such an improvement in the quality of information, however, has been achieved at considerable cost. Financially, the increases in staff have contributed to an explosion in congressional costs. In 1960 it had cost approximately $129 million to run Congress. By 1989 this figure had risen to $1.8 billion, with the Library of Congress alone costing $199 million. In 1990, the cost of running Congress broke the $2 billion barrier. Increased staff have also brought about a change in the individual member of Congress's role from that of someone who weighs, deliberates, and debates public policy to that of a chief executive running what might be regarded as a 'legislative enterprise' (Salisbury and Shepsle, 1981). Representatives and Senators must ensure that these 'enterprises' are run efficiently, that activities are co-ordinated, and that personnel problems are solved. All of which adds to the workload of individual members.

The bureaucratization of Congress, in short, has generated many of the same problems that accompanied the bureaucratization of the presidency. Just as the growth of the Executive Office of the President (EOP) has created managerial problems that a modern president must resolve, so the increase in congressional staff over the last two decades has created similar problems for members of Congress. Ironically, a development which was supposed to have improved Congress's capacity to play a meaningful role in the policy-making process may have had the opposite affect (Malbin, 1979). Although increases in staff mean that Senators and Representatives may now have access to the information and expertise necessary to craft coherent policy, the changing demands of the job brought about by such increases in staff mean that members have less time to consider and evaluate the information provided by their staff.

Strengthening the Political Parties

In addition to generating a demand for more resources, the desire to assert Congress's authority in the wake of Vietnam and Watergate also led to demands for changes in congressional procedures. Acting upon the belief that the presidency had grown in power because of congressional impotence, Representatives and Senators introduced a series of procedural changes designed to facilitate the enactment of legislation by strengthening the party leadership. In 1974 the Democratic Caucus in the House of Representatives gave the Speaker the power to refer bills to committees jointly and sequentially and to create *ad hoc* committees to expedite business. In 1975 the Caucus made the Speaker chairman of the party's Steering and Policy Committee, and gave this group the power to determine Democratic committee assignments. The Caucus also gave the Speaker the power to nominate members of the Rules Committee and to choose its chairman. In the Senate a modest proposal was accepted in 1977 which gave the leadership new controls over bill referrals and scheduling. Care must be taken, however, when assessing the affect of these changes. Although the rule changes of the 1970s increased the resources available to the Speaker, other reforms during this period served to fragment power and enhance individual prerogatives.

The problem facing party leaders in both the Senate and the House of Representatives has been to find some means of exercising control over institutions in which leadership is regarded with great suspicion. Leaders are expected to promote party unity, and work to further the legislative goals of members of their party, but are given few resources to perform such tasks. Party unity in Congress is difficult to sustain, and the control that party leaders have over the legislative process is undermined by the prerogatives afforded to committees, subcommittees, and individual members.

In most western democracies the ability of party leaders to control the legislative process is predicated upon the support of a unified political party. Party cohesion in Britain is particularly strong. In the House of Commons the percentage of divisions in which 90 per cent of the Conservative Party has voted against 90 per cent of the Labour Party has been over 94 per cent for most of the twentieth century. Although party unity in Congress is evident on procedural questions of organizing the two chambers, the general levels of party cohesion found in the House of Commons have only been approached in the House of Representatives at the beginning of the twentieth century. Under Speaker Joseph Cannon, the level of party cohesion in the House reached an all time high when 90 per cent of Republicans voted against 90 per cent of Democrats on 64.4 per cent of the total number of roll calls in the 58th Congress (1903–4). Even if party cohesion is redefined to mean those votes where a majority of Republicans vote against a majority of Democrats, the proportion of roll call votes displaying clear party divisions has rarely risen above 50 per cent in either the House or the Senate (see Table 5.1).

TABLE 5.1   *Votes in Congress showing party unity, 92nd to 101st Congresses (per cent)*

Congress	Senate	House
92nd (1971–72)	39	33
93rd (1973–74)	42	36
94th (1975–76)	43	42
95th (1977–78)	43	38
96th (1979–80)	46	43
97th (1981–82)	45	36
98th (1983–84)	42	52
99th (1985–86)	51	59
100th (1987–88)	47	53
101st (1989–90)	44	52

Note: Table indicates the percentage of all votes on which a majority of voting Democrats opposed a majority of voting Republicans.
Sources: *Congressional Quarterly Almanacs* (various years).

The low levels of partisan voting in Congress can be explained by a relative lack of party homogeneity, and an almost complete absence of mechanisms for enforcing party discipline. As both the Republican Party and the Democratic Party in Congress have tended to encompass a variety of different interests, achieving a consensus which will unite the various elements of the parties is difficult in itself. Any difficulty is compounded, however, by the absence of any devices to enforce unity. Part of the reason why party unity is so high in the British House of Commons lies with the sanctions that the party leadership can impose upon an errant member: promotion to a position of government is wholly dependent upon the leadership, and withdrawal of party support from a member will usually mean his or her defeat in the next general election. Neither of these sanctions is available to leaders in Congress. The party organization has little control over electoral success, and although party leaders do possess some influence over the process by which freshmen are assigned to committees, the operation of the seniority system means that, thereafter, promotion within Congress is largely automatic.

Party leaders have sought to compensate for their lack of control over promotion within Congress by creating posts within the party hierarchy which they can then use both to reward supporters and to inculcate junior members with party norms. In the House, Tip O'Neill (D.–Mass.), who was Speaker from 1976 to 1986, adopted a leadership style which has been termed 'leadership by inclusion' (Sinclair, 1981). He expanded the Democratic whip system to include a number of deputy, at-large, regional and assistant whips in an attempt to broaden the leadership structure. Beginning in the 95th Congress (1977–78) Speaker O'Neill also began to supplement the whip system by appointing *task forces* to deal with controversial measures. On one level, the purpose of these task forces was to collect information and seek commitments to vote for a specific measure. On another level, they were used to bring junior members into the decision-making process in the hope of making them more responsive to the demands of the party. In the Senate, Robert Byrd (D.–W.Va.), the minority leader from 1981 to 1986, used task forces in a slightly different way. In 1981 he appointed nine task forces to develop party policy. He also created the Democratic Leadership Council to prepare the party for the elections of 1982. More recently, one of the first actions of George Mitchell (D.–Me.), following his election as majority leader in 1988, was to cede power to others. In an important break from Democratic tradition, he adopted a pattern of leadership very similar to that of the Republicans in the Senate when he gave up the chairmanship of both the Democratic Steering Committee and the Democratic Policy Committee. The move was a calculated attempt to broaden the Democratic leadership structure in the Senate.

The creation of more posts within the party hierarchies has had little effect on the cohesion of parties within both the House of Representatives and the Senate. Legislative coalitions still have to be built on an issue to issue basis, and attempts to construct unified party positions across a wide range of issues have met with little success. The political parties are too heterogeneous and their leaders too lacking in institutional power to forge unified party positions except on an issue to issue basis. Partisanship is low in Congress, in short, because it is at odds with the political environment in which Representatives and Senators operate.

Low levels of partisanship severely limit the ability of the party leaders to control the legislative process. Without the cement provided by unified parties, it is difficult to hold together the various stages of the legislative process over a sustained period of time. A decentralized legislative process where committee, subcommittee, and individual prerogatives are stressed is the result. Committees and subcommittees process legislation in their own time, and individual Representatives and Senators feel free to pursue their own objectives on the floor. Amending activity on the floor of the House and Senate, in fact, increased dramatically in the late 1970s and early 1980s as the prestige of committees faded and the policy expertise of individual members increased as a result of the explosion in staff resources (Smith, 1989).

Party leaders have little control over the way that committees and subcommittees process legislation. In the House, the increased use of multiple referrals, or sending bills to more than one committee for consideration, has provided an opportunity for the Speaker to become involved in legislation before it reaches the floor both by setting time limits on each committee's consideration of the bill, and using the Rules Committee to iron out any differences in each committee's version of the bill. In general, however, the party leaders of both chambers are wary of infringing upon the rights of the committees. Leadership at this stage of the legislative process had tended to rely upon persuasion and cajolery, with party leaders forced to use blandishments and enticements to get committees to process legislation.

The greatest opportunity for party leaders, particularly in the House of Representatives, to control the legislative process occurs when bills are reported out of the committees. Speakers have increasingly used their control over the Rules Committee, derived from their right to appoint its Democratic members, to control the flow of legislation to the floor. Speakers have also relied upon the Rules Committee to control the recent surge in amending activity. Speaker O'Neill began using this technique to bring some order to the proceedings of the House in the mid-1980s, but the practice grew under Speaker Wright. From the opening of the 100th Congress in January 1987 until September 1987 no fewer than 43 per cent of the bills processed by the Rules Committee were given restricted rules which severely limited or prohibited amendments. A decade earlier, only 12 per cent of all rules dealt with by the Rules Committee had been given such rules (Bach and Smith, 1988). Party leaders in the Senate have no mechanism like the Rules Committee to control both the flow of legislation to the floor and amending activity. Senate leaders, have instead been forced to rely upon unanimous consent agreements to control the debate and amendment of legislation. Like the 'rules' issued by the Rules Committee, unanimous consent agreements have become more restrictive in recent years, but ultimately, the type of restrictions that Senate leaders are able to obtain is limited by the need to secure unanimity for an agreement.

The difficulties experienced by party leaders in controlling the legislative process raises serious doubts over the likelihood of a sustained period of legislative activism. Legislative activism not only requires time and expertise, but also needs a leadership able to overcome the many potential veto points in the congressional policy process. In the past, such leadership has proved possible in the short run, but impossible to sustain in the long run. Doubts about Congress's ability to sustain a period of legislative activism, however, raise important questions about the role of Congress in the American system of government. A legislature that apparently finds it difficult to legislate is a strange institution.

The Role of Congress

Although the activism of the 100th and 101st Congresses provide some evidence that Congress is not quite the 'broken branch' that some observers had once feared, there is still considerable dissatisfaction about congressional performance both within and outside the institution (Clark, 1964; Davidson *et al.*, 1969). Despite all the efforts of the reform movement of the 1970s, Congress is still regarded as being slow, cumbersome, and inefficient. An increase in resources has created as many new problems as it has solved, procedural reforms have fragmented power, and attempts to strengthen the authority of the leadership have been unsuccessful. Continued dissatisfaction about performance, however, has not resulted in any sustained movement for further reforms. Both the House of Representatives and the Senate have periodically established committees to review their operations, but little has been done to act upon their recommendations. In the late 1970s both the Obey Commission and the Patterson Committee recommended significant changes in the committee system of the House but to no avail. Similarly, the changes recommended in the Senate's procedures by the Pearson–Ribicoff Report in 1982 and the Quayle Committee in 1985 were also shelved. On 20 September 1988, the Rules Committee of the Senate approved a report urging a number of reforms to reduce procedural delays in the chamber. Among the report's proposals were plans to introduce better procedures for dealing with non-controversial bills, to restrict debate on procedural motions, and to establish a two year budget cycle. As with earlier attempts at reform, though, no further action on these proposals was taken. Efficiency-oriented reforms which seek to restrict individual prerogatives simply have no sizable constituency in either the House or the Senate (Bailey, 1988a).

To a certain extent there is little that is new in most complaints about congressional efficiency. Concern about the performance of Congress is almost as old as the institution itself. In *Democracy in America*, first published in 1835, Alexis de Tocqueville declared that: 'The laws of the American democracy are frequently defective or incomplete' (de Tocqueville, 1945, p. 246). Just over half a century later, Lord Bryce in his book *The American Commonwealth* echoed such criticisms when he wrote '... the legislation ... which the House turns out is scanty in quantity and generally mediocre in quality. What is more, the House tends to avoid all really grave and pressing questions ... seldom meeting them in the face or reaching a decision which makes an advance' (Bryce, 1988, p. 193). Even Woodrow Wilson concluded that: 'Only a very small part of [Congress's] most important work can be done well; the system provides for the rest of it done miserably, and the whole of it taken together done at haphazard' (Wilson, 1914, pp. 113–114).

If complaints about the performance of Congress have been fairly commonplace, what is new is a growing sense that Congress is not just inefficient, but rather, is incapable of meeting the demands of modern American society. Such concerns pose very real questions about the proper place for a legislature in a modern system of government. At issue is not merely a question of procedures, but more significantly, a question of fundamental design. Critics contend that Congress was designed at a time when government involvement in social or economic affairs was minimal, if not nonexistent (Blondel, 1973). For the Founding Fathers, laws which dealt with issues such as welfare, education, and health were inconceivable. Instead the purpose of most legislation was to regulate the private relationships between individuals. Statutes, on the whole, covered such issues as property rights, individual rights, and family law. As the nineteenth and twentieth centuries have progressed, however, Congress has been called upon to regulate social and economic matters as well as private relationships. That there should be doubt as to Congress's capacity to perform such a task well given its original design, critics argue, should come as no surprise. Such critics believe that only the executive is capable of meeting the policy demands of the American people, and that consequently, the role of Congress should be limited to legitimizing decisions made elsewhere (Lippman, 1955). In effect, the suggestion is that Congress should abandon its legislative function (Huntington, 1973).

Although not going so far as to suggest that Congress should abandon its legislative function, recent discussions on constitutional reform have sought to find means of encouraging the emergence of parliamentary government in the United States (Cutler, 1980; Sundquist, 1986). The main thrust of these discussions is that reforms should be enacted which would enable a president to form a government. Among the changes usually advocated as being necessary to achieve such an end are plans to allow members of Congress to serve in the president's cabinet; to require voters to cast their vote for a slate which would combine each party's candidates for the Presidency, Vice-Presidency, Senate and House of Representatives; and to establish simultaneous terms of office for presidents and members of Congress. By lengthening the term of office for a Representative to four years and for a Senator to eight years, advocates of constitutional reform believe that the parochialism of Congress would also be reduced. As with the proposals for procedural reforms within Congress, however, such constitutional reforms are unlikely to be enacted in the foreseeable future. Once again, there is simply no sizable constituency in Congress for reforms of this sort.

The suggestion that parliamentary government is necessary in the United States is opposed by those who believe that Congress still has an important role to play in the policy-making process. While conceding that the nature of legislation has changed over the last two hundred years, supporters of Congress contend that this does not necessarily mean that Congress is inherently incapable of meeting the demands of the late twentieth century. They argue that the case presented by proponents of the executive supremacy model does not rest upon a question of fundamental design, but rather, upon a particular notion of what Congress should be doing. In other words, Congress is criticized because it fails to act in the way thought necessary by the critics. From this it follows that suggestions that Congress is incapable of serving the nation rest upon a set of assumptions about both the nature of the demands of the American people and the best way that they can be met. Proponents of the legislative supremacy model, however, contend that the only way that the demands of the American people may be identified and articulated is through the aggregation of local issues which occurs in Congress. They argue that Congress remains as suited to deal with the tribulations of the 1990s as it was to deal with the problems of the 1790s. If it acts slowly or not at all that is because solutions to America's problems are complex or else that no consensus exists in the country as to the best way to proceed (Ornstein, 1981, p. 382).

Determining what the ideal role of Congress should be in American government is extraordinarily problematic, not least because there is no agreement on how to evaluate congressional performance. Measuring the output of Congress is relatively simple, and can be achieved by counting the number of bills passed, the number of hearings held, the number of newsletters sent to constituents, and so forth. Evaluating such output is not so easy. The problem is to distinguish *outcomes* from *outputs* (Cooper and Brady, 1981, p. 999). Most accounts agree that members of Congress serve their constituencies well, but differ as to their assessment of the effectiveness of congressional policymaking (Bailey, 1989; Shepsle, 1989). Such accounts are supported by evidence which shows that Americans tend to rate individual members of Congress higher than the institution (Fenno, 1975; Parker and Davidson, 1979). Whatever the validity of such arguments, however, there can be no doubt that Congress remains an important actor in the American political system. Its activities matter, and have a direct impact on both domestic and foreign policy.

6

Constitutional Legitimacy and the Supreme Court

RICHARD HODDER-WILLIAMS

Introduction

De Tocqueville's observation more than 150 years ago that 'scarcely any political question arises in the United States that is not resolved, sooner or later, into a judicial question' is an exaggeration, but an understandable one. Because Americans litigate with enthusiasm, most divisive issues *do* receive an airing in the courts. And, precisely because they are divisive, any resolution is likely to call forth both praise and criticism. For the critics, whether conservative or liberal, the fact that an unelected and unaccountable body – and very possibly only five of that body's nine members – has negated a law passed by a duly elected legislature or a regulation promulgated by a duly appointed executive officer is particularly galling. The curiosity in a culture so aggressively democratic in its rhetoric (although perhaps not in its actions) is that these moments of public passion do not occur continuously, but only irregularly (Nagel, 1965; Pritchett, 1961; Murphy, 1962; Schmidhauser and Berg, 1972). The Supreme Court's legitimacy, therefore, must be considerable.

In the late 1980s, however, some commentators began to question whether this legitimacy could survive. It had, in a sense, been something of a confidence trick in the first place. There was no escaping the fact that individual Justices, employing their own judgment and philosophies, decided cases which had significant political consequences, but were not accountable for those important decisions. The sophisticated arguments which buttressed this use of judicial power had little currency in popular discourse when contrasted with the simple, if crude, principle of electoral accountability. However, so long as the Court gave the appearance that its judgments were indeed impersonal and objective conclusions of technical judicial processes, its sanctity as guardian of the revered Constitution could endure. Its legitimacy, in the sense that the People accept its judgements as authoritative and its role as proper, could then be assured.

However, three developments threatened the survival of this myth. First was the division in partisan support of the legislative and executive branches which meant that there was no dominant political consensus in Washington about the right judgements of the Court. Second was the increasingly open way in which partisan interest groups used litigation as part of their overall political strategies and thus embroiled the Court in some of the most contested controversies of the day. Third was the extent to which the Reagan Administration set out publicly to influence the judicial branch as a whole and the Supreme Court's jurisprudence in particular. These developments appeared to pose a very real threat to the mythic role of the Supreme Court as the impartial guardian of the Constitution and thus offered a challenge to its legitimacy.

The bitter controversy which arose over President Reagan's nomination of Robert Bork to a vacancy on the Court epitomized the extent to which it had been drawn into the political arena. The Bork nomination thus brought into stark relief the central problem about the Supreme Court and American democracy. Because it lacks the obvious legitimacy of electoral accountability, it must clothe itself in a legitimacy derived from the symbolic status of the Constitution and its own reputation for being *above* politics; it must discover the law, not create it. Of course, the latter requirement is impossible. The trick is to establish the illusion that the Court is neither the plaything of politicians nor a home for politicians in judicial clothes. The Bork nomination – and both sides must share the blame – went some way to destroying that essential illusion.

The Problems of Divided Partisan Control

For the vast majority of the United States' history, objections to the Court's rulings have been the laments of minorities and have hardly had an impact on the Court's high reputation. One reason for this has been the simple fact that, for the most part, the Court has reflected the political majority in Washington (Dahl, 1957). So long as one of the major parties has tended to control both executive and legislative branches for long periods at a time, the appointment process (nomination by the President and confirmation by the Senate) should inexorably place on the Court Justices reflecting that dominant party's judicial philosophy. And this is what has generally happened. But the fit has not always been exact. Presidents of the same party can have differing judicial philosophies: nominations can be made for geographical or symbolic reasons rather than on grounds of jurisprudential conformity; Justices can themselves shift their positions in the security of their independence; issues may come onto the Court's agenda which were not anticipated (Pritchett, 1954; Abraham, 1985; Tribe, 1985). The general rule is that the Supreme Court has traditionally legitimized national government action and has marched in step with presidents and their party support in the Congress (but see Funston, 1975; Casper, 1976; Adamany and Grossman, 1983).

However the most dramatic moments in relationships between the Court and the wider political community have coincided with a new political majority in Washington. Political realignments – such as occurred in the 1860s, the 1890s and the 1930s – were hastened by Court decisions which highlighted the new lines of cleavage (Lasser, 1985). During such periods, when a new majority is emerging, the Court may be out of line with the more political branches and both Congress and the President may inveigh against its supposed undemocratic challenges to the presumed will of the majority.

The elections of 1968 ushered in a new era in which there

was no consistent Washington majority. Bifurcated politics, in which Americans elected members of Congress to represent their parochial interests and Presidents to reflect their more metaphysical needs, prevailed (Shafer, 1988). The consequence was that, for the most part, a Republican President faced a Democratic Congress. The consensus of the 1960s, which had favored the administrative state, a positive push for enhanced civil rights, and an emphasis on equality, broke apart. Defenders could still be found in Congress; but the primary support for that consensus now lay within the Supreme Court.

When Ronald Reagan was elected President, he brought with him to Washington advisers and supporters who openly opposed that liberal view of the state. The Republican platform reflected many of the party's most visible publicists in its rejection of a range of social policies rooted in Supreme Court decisions: affirmative action, busing, the rigid separation of church and state, the right to an abortion, clear constitutional rights for suspects, the predominance of central power over state authority (thus weakening the federal principle), and the propriety of judges enforcing their substantive views of the Fourteenth Amendment.

The Supreme Court thus became a major battle ground in the political struggle between a rejuvenated conservatism and a defensive liberalism. The struggle was conducted on several levels and in different forms. Both of Reagan's Solicitors–General, who are responsible for an administration's litigating policy, tried to persuade the Supreme Court that its precedents in the sensitive areas of abortion and other social issues were erroneous (Caplan, 1987). Members of the Administration, most notably Bradford Reynolds, head of the civil rights division of the Justice Department, and Edwin Meese III, Attorney-General for much of Reagan's second term, tried to sway public thinking by using public occasions to express criticism of the Court's jurisprudence (Meese, 1985; Meese, 1986–7; Reynolds, 1982; Reynolds, 1983).

The most effective way, however, of transforming the Court's judicial philosophy would have been to replace liberal members of the Supreme Court with more conservative appointees. The opportunity for Reagan to do so did not occur for some years, for his first appointments did little to alter the balance of the Court. Sandra Day O'Connor was a shade more supportive of the Reagan agenda than Potter Stewart, whom she replaced (Witt, 1986). The elevation of William Rehnquist to the Chief Justiceship in place of Warren Burger altered the Court's dominant ideology hardly at all, although it ensured a more intellectually confident leadership of the conservative cause; and his replacement by Antonin Scalia made little difference in this respect either; both were moderately solid supporters of the President's agenda (Brisbin, 1990). The critical point occurred in the summer of 1987 when Lewis Powell retired (Hodder-Williams, 1988).

The extraordinary passions that surrounded the nomination of Judge Bork illustrate the importance attached to the Supreme Court as a political institution by those individuals and groups competing for power and influence in Washington (Bronner, 1989; McGuigan and Weyrich, 1990; Pertschuk and Schaetzel, 1990). Conservatives hoped that it would provide the opportunity to place upon the Court somebody who would provide the fifth vote in favour of the jurisprudential changes they so ardently sought. Liberals, by the same token, feared that it would provide a dangerous threat to the preservation of those liberal principles which the Reagan victories in 1980 and 1984 had by themselves been unable to reverse. The unresolved tensions between a legislative branch which at heart supported the precedents of the Warren and Burger Courts and an executive branch determined to cut back on those precedents were to fuel a bitter struggle over the nomination.

Never before did so many interest groups raise so much money to play so great a public role in a nomination to the Court. The comfortable convention that presidents were entitled to place upon the Court whomever they chose, provided a minimum level of intellectual standing and moral probity was reached, was shattered. It had already been weakened in 1968, when conservatives who were ideologically opposed to the Warren Court blocked Johnson's nomination of Abe Fortas; in 1971 when liberals wreaked their revenge by voting down Nixon's nomination of Clement

Hainesworth; and in 1986 when a large minority in the Senate voted against the elevation of Rehnquist from an Associate Justiceship to the Chief Justiceship. These precedents encouraged many Senators to exercise their constitutional duty 'to advise and consent' to presidential nominations with the kind of partisan and policy concern that their predecessors in the nineteenth century had shown.

The openness of the policy debate placed considerable strain upon the Court as an institution. Its high standing in the nation and the legitimacy granted to it in the exercise of its undoubted power depends upon the survival of the myth of independence and impartiality. A public seminar (and the committee hearings on the nomination of Judge Bork were a public seminar) could too easily lay such a myth bare, especially if it stressed not only the substantive consequences of Supreme Court decisions but also their dependence upon the unpredictability of casual vacancies and the ensuing nominees' jurisprudence. There was a danger, therefore, that an open struggle over Bork's nomination might weaken the popular sense of the Court's objectivity and lack of political partisanship. If people's rights depended so obviously upon a single nomination, then these rights could not be secure and the Court's power was laid embarrassingly naked. The success of the civil rights lobby in blocking Bork's nomination ultimately resulted in an appointment which, in the public arena of media politics at least, seemed less partisan, less crudely politically inspired. After the fiasco of offering and then withdrawing Judge Ginsburg's name, Reagan nominated Judge Anthony Kennedy, whose professional qualifications for the Court were orthodox and less controversial. That his votes have been very similar to what Robert Bork's advocates hoped their nominee would cast is ironic, but beside the point.

The Bork nomination is like the eruption that makes awfully visible the pressures beneath the earth's crust. After the eruption, there is peace above ground; but the pressures beneath continue. The tensions which gave rise to that special event have not gone away. The new Court reflects only part of the Washington majority. Still alive and active remains a Democratic Congress with its supporting cast of liberal interest groups, most of whom have a vested interest in the precedents established by the Warren and Burger Courts and the resources, both political and judicial, to defend them. How public the argument becomes between those who defend the Court's precedents and those who attack them will determine how far the Court can preserve its remarkable degree of legitimacy. There were signs in the 1989 and 1990 Terms that the Justices themselves were aware of the danger; certainly the opportunity to carve out quite new constitutional principles, and thus reinvigorate the partisan debate, was passed up.

When President Bush was presented with his first opportunity to nominate a Justice, he was also offered a chance to shift the central jurisprudence of the Court most definitely in a conservative direction. The resignation of Justice William Brennan, the doyen of the liberal wing and an exceptional influence within the Court itself, removed much of the liberal intellectual leadership. The resignation of Thurgood Marshall in 1991 gave President Bush his second nomination to the Court. Bush, however, clearly sought deliberately to reduce the conflicts around his nomination. Bork had been a lightning rod, the archangel of conservative hopes and the satan of liberal fears. David Souter, bookish and unknown, could raise few passions. His public life gave little indication of his private views and less evidence on which to build a sustained and believable attack. His confirmation recalled the more traditional, and less partisan, Senate review of potential Justices. The passions associated with Bork's nomination may thus come to be seen as the sort of aberrant behavior which does occur from time to time when a weakened president openly, and unwisely, challenges a resurgent and ideologically opposed Senate by nominating somebody who symbolizes the very differences which fuel the executive–legislative frictions of the day. The jurisprudence of those nominated since then has unquestionably been conservative. But the Senate has confirmed them all, even Clarence Thomas, whose positions on abortion and affirmative action were thought to be similar to Bork's and whose confirmation hearings were marked by allegations of personal unsuitability.

There is, of course, an intrinsic tension between the republican ethos of the United States political system and respect for a written, limiting Constitution complete with a Bill of Rights. In simple American mythology, legitimacy must flow from the consent of the governed, acting through their elected representatives, both in the individual states and in the federal government. At the same time, however, there is the paradoxical assumption that the Constitution may shield the individual, however unpopular, from certain laws and regulations passed by those same elected representatives. The Supreme Court, playing the role of the Constitution's final arbiter, has in the nation's fourth quarter been increasingly called upon to decide when elected officials have overstepped the line and denied individuals their constitutionally protected rights. Inevitably, this has required it from time to time to deny to elected authorities the full fruits of their electoral victories and to elevate above them the interests of a single person or group (see *West Virginia State Board of Education* v. *Barnette*, 1943). In a sense, therefore, a minority can, in a very unrepublican manner, prevail against the majority. Taking the long view, however, over the two centuries of United States existence the consequences of this intrinsic tension have normally been accepted as the necessary and acceptable price of limited, constitutional government.

The occasions on which a minority has been pitched against the authority of elected politicians have only become relatively common in recent years. This is due in part to the new ideology of state responsibility for citizen welfare which has legitimized an almost exponential growth in the laws and regulations affecting social and economic life. Increased state activity inevitably impinges upon individual autonomy. It was also due to the addition of the Fourteenth Amendment to the Constitution, which established constitutional limitations on the actions of state officials and which, in the last fifty years, has been interpreted as making applicable against the individual states most of the provisions of the 1791 Bill of Rights (Abraham, 1972, pp. 29–88), although that had originally been conceived as a limitation on the federal government alone (*Barron* v. *Baltimore*, 1833).

Once the Roosevelt Court had given its constitutional

blessing to extraordinarily wide Congressional power to regulate the national economy and through those regulations much of social behavior, too (*United States* v. *Darby Lumber Co.*, 1942; *Wickard* v. *Filburn*, 1943), the Court's agenda came to be dominated by the claims of individuals that their constitutional rights had been abridged. These claims tended to bring the Court initially into conflict with some of the states, rather than with the federal government. It is important to recollect that the national law-making majority in the 1960s, when so many of the path breaking decisions in this area were made, broadly sympathized with the Court's new jurisprudence. After all, this was the time of the 1964 Civil Rights Act, the 1965 Voting Rights Act and the 1968 Open Housing Act.

In the 1970s and 1980s, party fragmentation in Washington and the emphasis on individual rights against state governments contrived to place the Supreme Court in a very difficult position. Consistent Democrat majorities in the Congress, despite the fluctuating significance of a conservative coalition, placed on the statute book a mass of legislation which granted individual Americans new rights (which often antagonized vocal vested interests) and easier access to the Courts to claim those rights (Chayes, 1982–3). It would have been possible for the Congress to have reduced the sort of access to the courts which it had provided, for example, in much of the environmental protection legislation; but it did not choose to do so. Hence, cases were regularly, and properly, litigated in the federal courts calling into question the actions of the Environmental Protection Agency.

By contrast, Republican presidents were regularly supported by politicians and intellectuals who disliked the new rights (gender equality, voting rights, affirmative action, abortion) and the ease with which individuals could bypass the political process through litigation on behalf of whole classes of people, as was happening in cases involving the environment. The new Republican presidential majority found considerable support precisely from those who objected to the extension of rights, either on grounds of substance (as with abortion) or on the general grounds of local autonomy.

Although the center of political gravity within the Democratic coalition shifted during the 1980s, much of the party's liberal wing still survived with strong bases in industrial America and in the South, although now among black Americans. With Democrats holding a majority of governorships and remaining in control of the Congress throughout the last forty years, there have been eloquent voices, backed by both position and resources, to protect the Court from attack. Much of the United States, therefore, remains supportive of most of the major constitutional innovations of the Warren and Burger Courts (Marshall, 1989).

Interest Groups, Policy Preferences and the Use of the Supreme Court

The power of the Supreme Court lies in its now virtually unchallenged authority, set forth in *Marbury* v. *Madison*, to say what the Constitution means. This is, however, not the end of the matter, for the American political process relentlessly tests each Supreme Court decision, spawning further litigation or generating legislation which goes some way to nullify a court decision (Fisher, 1988). But this is to take the medium term view. In the short term, it is the apparent finality of a Supreme Court decision which generates political responses. Different interpretations of the Constitution will necessarily produce different outcomes, favoring some people while disfavoring others. And the issues involved frequently go to the very heart of the interests of important and well-supported groups. It matters deeply to major sections of the American people – to businessmen or churchmen or blacks or women or fundamentalist Christians or labor unions as the case may be – how the Supreme Court applies the Constitution to the facts before it.

It should come as no surprise, therefore, that interest groups have regularly participated in litigation. This is associated most readily with the activities of the NAACP and the American Civil Liberties Union (ACLU), but they are very far from being the only groups to operate in this way

(Kluger, 1975; Epstein, 1985; Walker, 1990). Business recognized way back in the nineteenth century that victories in the judicial branch could be of enormous value, since triumphs there applied the Court's ruling across the whole country, binding each individual state to the new interpretation of the supreme law of the land (Vose, 1972). Populist governments eager to restrain the combines in some states could thus be thwarted by success at the level of the Supreme Court. It was this recognition of the nation-wide applicability of the Court's rulings which encouraged the NAACP in its litigation strategy, especially when it was clear that victory was unlikely even in the national legislature, let alone in the states of the deep South.

The appreciation of the logic of a litigation strategy has become widespread over the last fifty years, partly because the NAACP's successes showed how it could be used by those unable to marshall a majority in Washington. Litigation also became more necessary as a strategy to challenge increased governmental regulation. The judicial process allows a variety of types of involvement and interest groups choose as seems most appropriate to them. Few actually initiate lawsuits. These are still, for the most part, generated by an individual's conviction that his, or her, rights have been unlawfully abridged (Irons, 1988). Thereafter interest groups can assist such a plaintiff with their expertise, their money, and their contacts.

This assistance ranges from the filing of a brief *amicus curiae* (that is, a brief technically designed to assist the Justices on an abstruse point of law as a 'friend of the court', but actually designed to persuade the Justices that the law and the facts point in the direction desired by the interest groups writing the brief) (Krislov, 1962–3), through advising the plaintiffs on the writing of their briefs, to the complete funding and supervision of the case itself. The extent to which groups are involved differs from case to case, but it is now exceedingly rare for any case to reach the Supreme Court without a number of interest groups getting involved. In the first major affirmative action case, *The Regents of the University of California* v. *Bakke* (1978), more than 50 such briefs were filed.

One of the growth areas in Washington recently has been the public law firm (Aron, 1989). A glance through the Washington DC telephone directory will show an enormous number of associations, organizations and firms whose primary purpose is lobbying or providing information and expertise on specialized topics. The civil rights lobby, for example, is well supported by a wide range of small organizations, themselves staffed by committed researchers and lawyers. They stretch from the relatively non-partisan such as the Lawyers' Committee for Civil Rights under Law to more overly partisan such as the Alliance for Justice or People for the American Way. This is also increasingly true of the business community and those espousing a conservative social agenda. The Washington Legal Foundation has been extremely active in promoting conservative causes and attacking liberal positions, as has the Free Congress Research and Education Foundation. The states and local governments have also established a well-funded office in Washington to assist them in the preparation of briefs and argument for the Supreme Court. Litigation before the federal courts is now a major industry, to which large numbers of Americans commit money and time.

It is also the case that the Supreme Court itself, almost of necessity, encourages this development. Since 1890, when it first began to have some control over the cases it actually hears, the Court has increasingly come to control its own docket. Now, with a handful of exceptions, it can decide for itself which 150 or so cases of the 4500 appealed to it will be heard. In effect, all appeals must now seek its discretionary *writ of certiorari*, the legal formula for inviting parties in a lower court to inform the Supreme Court of their case's details. The criteria for this choice, a major exercise of power, are not clear and are not shared in their entirety by all the Justices (they certainly disagree on occasions about which cases to take); but there is a general acceptance that the cases granted review must raise important questions which would affect more than the interests of the two parties involved in the litigation itself. This requirement of a general interest characteristic is an invitation to groups to indicate the importance of any case of concern to them and the direction in which they would like the Court to go.

Group involvement in litigation goes further, however. Groups soon become deeply committed to cases with which they have been involved and whose results they have spent much energy on procuring. The Court then becomes a friend, or a foe, as the case may be, an institution to be praised or vilified. Because so much psychic energy, not to mention money, is devoted to litigation, the results take on a special significance. They become benchmarks not only of a group's success but of a Justice's reputation. Justices then become political assets to those whose political aims their judicial decisions advance and the interest groups thus watch the White House with care, and sometimes trepidation, whenever vacancies on the Court occur. Given the pivotal fifth vote which Powell had regularly cast to uphold the right to an abortion, the constitutionality of most affirmative action programs and the wall of separation between church and state, it is scarcely surprising that groups became so involved in the Bork nomination.

Litigation can therefore be seen as part of the system of interest group politics which characterizes American government. It is another mediating mechanism and another of the multiple points of access in the endless pluralist competition between groups. In short, it is *used* by actors in the American system as a political institution and forces the judiciary to make hard choices in difficult cases. Inevitably the results in such cases will satisfy some and dismay others.

To what extent then are courts to be seen as active participants in the political process rather than, as Justice Robert Jackson suggested, essentially passive instruments (Jackson, 1955)? Certainly one of the most forcefully expressed criticisms of the Court in the late twentieth century has stemmed from its practice of regulating public facilities. Thus judges like Frank Johnson in Alabama (who spent a decade trying to reform the state prison facilities to conform to the Eighth Amendment) or John Garrity who oversaw the restructuring of the Boston school system were castigated for undertaking tasks which were properly the responsibility of the political branches. In an ideal world, of course, politicians and administrators – rather than courts – would have responsibility for the organization of prisons, schools and mental health facilities. But the reality of American politics has meant that elective officials have frequently been taken to court by citizens who claim their constitutional rights have been eroded. As a result judges have been drawn into such disputes (Cooper, 1988).

What is striking is not the activism of district judges but their restraint. The facts behind many of the major cases are squalid and reveal a refusal by officials to abide by initial judgements. Thus in *Swann* v. *Charlotte-Mecklenburg County Board of Education* (1970), for example, a Republican court judge was faced with a choice between allowing a school board to persist in its defiance of his order to desegregate a dual school system and fashioning an equitable remedy himself (Schwartz, 1986). In *Finney* v. *Hutto* (1977) Arizona district judges were faced with a similar problem when, despite allowing local authorities a good deal of latitude to reform prison conditions deemed incompatible with the Eighth Amendment's prohibition of 'cruel and unusual punishments' and despite several promptings, the authorities failed to act. Only then did the judge intervene to set a deadline for the implementation of the reforms. In these cases, judges find themselves forced to intervene in the detailed organization of public services as a result of efforts by other agencies to circumvent their decisions.

The point therefore is that any useful and meaningful discussion of the Supreme Court's role in American public life must situate it realistically in the political system of which it is part. For excellent prudential reasons, interest groups will use the courts, among other institutions, to forward their interests. The courts are thus virtually forced to become political, a position thrust upon them still further by the terms of much congressional legislation (Hodder-Williams, 1990). By the same token, when a judgement has been made on a case properly before them, the judges must ensure that their decrees are complied with. If they are not, then judges must either abdicate from their duty to see that justice (as expressed through parts of the Constitution) is carried out or themselves intervene to frame programs which would provide relief to successful plaintiffs. To argue that judges do not know what they are doing in specialist areas like penitentiary or educational systems is, once again, to step away from reality into an imaginary world of knowledgable politicians concerned only to advance the public interest and cloistered judges unsullied by the sordid facts of real life. Politicians are frequently less saintly; and judges not only have political experience themselves, mix in Washington social circles and take a lively interest in the world around them, but they also normally employ experts to advise them on remedial actions.

The Reagan Administration and Attempts to Influence the Judicial Branch

It is often forgotten that the party which appears most often before the Supreme Court is the United States itself. It should not be surprising. The Supreme Court, after all, is the highest appellate court of the *federal* court system, in which disputes over federal legislation and the exercise of the national government's discretionary authority are raised and resolved. The bread and butter of the lower courts is national business. Federal statutes and executive branch action do raise constitutional issues, it is true, but most of the litigation revolves around questions of statutory interpretation. The few disputes which gain high visibility, over the legislative veto or the special prosecutor for instance, are the exceptions (*INS* v. *Chadha*, 1983; *Morrison* v. *Olson*, 1988). The only cases which reach the Supreme Court from the states are constitutional cases. Few are actually heard (less than 2 per cent of those seeking writs of *certiorari* on average in the 1970s and 1980s), but several of those which are granted *certiorari* make the headlines.

The United States government, of whatever hue, takes very seriously its position as chief litigator. Since the 1870 Judiciary Act, which established the post of Solicitor–General within the Justice Department, there has been a single member of the Administration responsible for the federal government's litigation. For the most part, this involves the careful screening of cases in the Appeal Courts to ensure that the particular ones chosen for appeal to the Supreme Court are likely to be accepted by that Court and also provide a good set of facts for a statutory or constitutional question of general significance to be resolved (Horowitz, 1977). In this sense, the Solicitor–General, who is an officer of the Supreme Court, acts as a 'Tenth Justice' by winnowing the very large number of potentially reviewable cases to a manageable number of good cases. Justices have appreciated this and have granted *certiorari* to the appeals by the United States at an extraordinarily high rate, when compared to their niggardly acceptance of cases appealed by other parties.

The Solicitor–General, however, can also play a still more creative role. In cases to which the United States is not a party (mainly the cases originating in the states), he may file an *amicus curiae* brief, setting out the Administration's position on the issues raised by the litigation, even though the United States has no direct interest in the case. The Solicitor–General, then, can act in a way very similar to the interest groups which have already been discussed. Initially, such briefs tended to be factual, providing for the Supreme Court data which the executive branch was best able to collect and collate. Over the years, this informative function, although it has by no means died, has given way to a more overtly lobbying function and the Administration of the day can present arguments in favor of its own political preferences. In the Eisenhower years, several briefs were filed to encourage the Court to move in a liberal direction over civil rights (Huston, 1968); in the Kennedy years, Archibald Cox was persuaded by Robert Kennedy to lend the Administration's authority to the principle of 'one man, one vote, one value' established in *Reynolds* v. *Sims* (Navasky, 1971, pp. 314–366). Under Carter, too, the *amicus* brief was employed to stress the Administration's support for several liberal lines of decision (O'Connor, 1983). In the Nixon and Ford years, too, Solicitors–General intervened selectively, filing briefs more frequently in suspects' rights cases, for example, than their Democratic predecessors (O'Connor, 1983; Segal, 1988). Compare, for instance, Wade McCree, Carter's Solicitor–General and Robert Bork, Nixon's Solicitor–General. McCree presented 'pro-rights' briefs in 79 per cent of all his

amicus interventions and in 43 per cent of the criminal cases
in which he participated, while Bork's figures were 40 and 0
per cent respectively. Thus the use of the *amicus* brief in the
two Reagan Administrations was not entirely new, as Solicitor–General Fried was often at pains to point out, but the
number and tenor of the briefs were unparallelled.

Unfortunately from President Reagan's point of view, the
independence of the judiciary prevented him from directly
influencing its actions on many of the issues close to the
hearts of his vocal supporters. But he could, and did,
intervene indirectly. The Solicitor–General was a primary
weapon, clearly and sometimes quite aggressively pushing
for the reversal or the cutting back of existing precedents.
While previous Administrations had also used the courts to
advance their own agendas, they had not done so by chal-
lenging the decisions of the Supreme Court, with the exception of the segregatory precedent enshrined in *Plessy* v.
Ferguson, (1896) on the constitutional grounds that the presidential duty to see that the laws be faithfully executed
prevented this and on the prudential grounds that a political
system in which the Constitution played so major a role, both
real and symbolic, required that the Constitution, and those
who elucidated it authoritatively, should not become political
footballs. Not all their supporters always agreed, but presidents generally limited expression of their criticism of the
Court to the privacy of their friends. Reagan, and those close
to him, did not.

The Administration aimed to affect the Court in a second
way, acting through the public arena to influence public
opinion. There were several aspects to this strategy. Speeches
were one. Meese, Reagan's controversial Attorney-General,
deliberately chose some public occasions to attack the Court's
jurisprudence; William Bradford Reynolds also used opportunities before public audiences to express his disquiet at its
jurisprudence; both Rex Lee and Charles Fried likewise were
prepared to give interviews and make speeches to publicise
their conception of the Constitution far more frequently than
their predecessors had done. Actions by officials within the
Justice Department, through acts of omission as well as
commission, used the discretionary power of any executive

branch department to dampen the full thrust of judicial opinions through cautious application (Selig, 1985). Lobbying the Congress for constitutional amendments or for legislation which would limit the Court's appellate powers were also indications of the Administration's determination to use its political resources to challenge and, it hoped, chip away at the Court's prestige and support (Fisher, 1988, pp. 201–30).

These strategies were not as successful as the power exercised by the President in his responsibility to nominate men and women to the lower federal courts. From early in 1981, the Justice Department had among its staff a number of committed opponents of the dominant jurisprudence of the Court. These political appointees were anxious to use the nomination power to ensure that the 'right' judges were put on the courts. It was not new for an Administration to take very seriously this duty; but no Administration had devoted so much time and care to the scrutiny of potential candidates. Given the pluralist nature of American politics and the non-monolithic nature of American parties, this supervision could not, and did not, fill the federal judiciary with clones of Fein or Meese. But it did ensure, broadly, that the courts were increasingly being staffed by people who shared the Administration's dislike of past practices and in some notable cases, especially at the Courts of Appeal level, this began to filter through into judgements (Schwartz, H., 1988; O'Brien, 1988; 'note', 1986–7). The civil rights lobby, for one, began increasingly to pursue their aims through litigation in some state courts rather than through the federal courts which had, in the three decades before Reagan's first inauguration, been their friends.

The high priority given to the judicial branch by the Reagan Administration is a new development in American politics. Given the nature of the conservative agenda, it is not a surprising development. But it has qualitatively altered the relationship between the Supreme Court and the American public. Whereas attacks on the Court in the earlier periods could be presented as the tactics of a few frustrated politicians protecting vested interests (e.g. southern segregationists against *Brown* or rural legislators against *Reynolds*), this would no longer do. It was the President of the United States himself, representing the American people as a whole, supported by men and women close to him and obviously enjoying his favor, who was now attacking the Court. Seen this way, the Bork nomination then became merely one logical step in a campaign to alter the Court, akin to Franklin Roosevelt's court-packing plan of 1937. The driving force was a narrow political vision of what was required of the Court; the Administration's relations with the judicial branch were policy driven and ideologically motivated. In 1937, many Americans who were broadly on the side of Roosevelt and the New Deal reacted negatively to such an attack. They felt that the Court had erred, but they also felt that a direct onslaught upon it, although it might have short-term benefits, would in the long term weaken the standing of the Court, disparage its legitimacy, and thus damage perhaps irrevocably one subtle part of the complex constitutional structure which preserved American democracy. In the 1980s, there were fewer people who took this larger view.

The New Debate over Jurisprudence

The Supreme Court is a political institution to the extent that it authoritatively allocates power and resources; but it is also a moral institution to the extent that it represents some of America's highest ideals and stands for 'Equal Justice under Law' where the crudities of politics are supposed to have no place. Its power is thus real and symbolic at the same time. Not surprisingly, therefore, the arguments about its performance have a confusing melange of the real and the symbolic, the political and the moral. It is often difficult to disentangle the two and even protagonists cannot be certain which is the real family of arguments in which they believe.

Critics of the Court have always, and still do, come from the ranks of those who object to what the Court has done. Put starkly, they disapprove of the decisions. It was the segregationists who most objected to *Brown*, church-goers who inveighed against *Engel* and *Schempp*, 'hangers and floggers' who resented the cases limiting law enforcement officers' freedom of action, and so on. Dislike of decisions is the father of action. But, because the Supreme Court is also in American mythology a moral body, it is uncomfortable to accuse it of being merely political (although some do) lest its idealized role as discoverer of law and justice is destroyed and a rival ideal, the subjective exerciser of naked power, takes its place. Hence, articulate critics of the Court complain about its procedures and methods, about the perception of its role and its disjunction from history. By locating criticism in the higher reaches of jurisprudence, they are less easily accused of being self-serving. This was as true of the liberals in the 1930s as it is true of the conservatives in the 1980s. Certainly, this decade has seen a large outgrowth of theoretical writings on the Court which challenge many of the assumptions on which its majority had based their votes.

The philosophical attack on the Court has both a negative aspect and a positive one. The negative arguments deplore what the Court has done, accusing it of exceeding its true function as impartial arbiter between the claims of two rival parties each with a recognizable stake in the outcome of an issue. They challenge the Court for even considering an array of issues which, they assert, are not amenable to judicial solutions and should not be resolved through the judicial process. There is some truth in this argument (for surely on occasions the Court has been relaxed on questions of standing and justiciability), but it tends to ignore the realist argument that, if, for example, individuals claim that their treatment in prison is 'cruel and unusual', they are entitled to a judgement on that claim.

Furthermore, so the indictment goes, a majority of the Justices have simply misconstrued the Constitution. Edwin Meese, at one extreme, questioned the whole line of cases, stretching back more than fifty years, which have effectively incorporated most of the Bill of Rights into the Fourteenth Amendment's 'due process' clause (Meese, 1985). Others have queried the extent to which the Court, since the 1940s, has seen itself peculiarly as the guardian of individual rights; they argue that, where a claimed right comes into conflict with a law of regulation properly enacted, the presumption of constitutionality must lie with the elected officials rather than the individual. Similarly, the principle of federalism is held to grant to the individual states a very wide discretion to exercise their authority; hence, it is argued, federal laws which constrain their exercise of power or judgements which lay upon the states uniform practices (e.g. on what counts as pornography) are improper derogations from an essential feature of the United States political structure.

These positions are entirely defensible; but they are far from proven. The negative approach to any jurisprudence is the easy way. It is not difficult to challenge the complex theories which defenders of the liberal jurisprudence have put forward by questioning their historical foundations and arguing that their defenses are not grounded in incontrovertible logic or clear exposition of intent from the days of the Founding Fathers. The truth is that history is muddied, that the generations who established the Constitution and were responsible for the major Amendments, especially the Fourteenth, were politicians rather than legal philosophers and consciously left much unclear, and that the passage of time has produced sets of facts and conditions that the Founding Fathers never conceived of and for which the Constitution was not designed.

Critics of the Warren and Burger Courts, many of whom were very close to the Reagan Administration, did have a positive line as well. They sought the answer to the difficult question 'By what principles should a Justice decide hard cases?' and found it in the words, assumptions and practices of the Founding Fathers. For them, the key phrase was 'original intent'. But the emphasis placed upon those in Philadelphia is itself too time-bound. It is arguable, for instance, that ideas and principles accepted *before* that date retained their significance thereafter. Two examples come to mind, each highly disputed. A philosophy of natural rights and limited government underpinned the whole exercise of devising a national constitution which ensured that the compact between people and government did not destroy the fundamental and pre-existing belief that government action was not necessarily legitimate just because a government wields power through an electoral mandate (Corwin, 1981; Jaffa, 1981). Some of the Justices, too, held that certain rights predated the Bill of Rights. Arthur Goldberg was perhaps the most explicit exponent of this view; why, otherwise, he asked rhetorically, would the Ninth Amendment, which presupposes that there are rights not enumerated in the earlier amendments and in the body of the Constitution, have been included? (*Griswold* v. *Connecticut*, 1965). A natural law philosophy in the United States and the common law tradition both suggest that judge-made law is not unwelcome and that governments, however democratically based, are nevertheless limited.

The debate over original intent, devoted essentially to the late eighteenth century and largely ignoring the Fathers or later Amendments, was certainly given a new life during the Reagan Administration. It had an immediate attraction, for it acknowledged the special position of past heroes while relegating contemporary judges to the technical role of discovering the intentions. It was easy to shift from the philosophical debate about appropriate principles to the political debate about illegitimate power by implying that the Court's majority was improperly substituting its conception of good policy for the Founders' considered views on the political process.

Here, too, the Bork nomination brought a current debate among the elite into the public arena. The hearings spent much time discussing the normative question of the Court's proper role and, in particular, the rival stereotypes of 'original intent' and 'the evolving constitution'. It was a remarkable piece of public education. But the public is rarely at home on the intellectual level of abstract theorising. 'Where's the Beef?' was a question which undermined more than presidential hopefuls; it brought the argument about Bork's nomination back to the real world by focusing on the actual consequences of the rival judicial philosophies. If original intent meant no affirmative action and the right to outlaw abortions, few liberals were prepared to buy such a philosophy. Among conservatives, with a handful of exceptions, the philosophy of original intent provided a high minded defense of policies they espoused for their own sakes.

Conclusion

The last half century has seen a radical change in the Supreme Court's docket. This is, of course, immediately evident by a rapid glance at numbers alone. In the 1953 Term, the first year of Earl Warren's Chief Justiceship and the year in which so much of the Justices' time was spent in fashioning a unanimous court for *Brown*, 1293 cases were disposed of and 78 full opinons of the Court issued (13 of which were *per curiam*). By the 1969 Term, when Warren Burger began his Chief Justiceship, the numbers had risen to 3357 and 94 (11 *per curiam*) respectively. The apparently inexorable increase continued so that, by the 1979 Term, 3812 cases were disposed of and 149 full opinions (17 *per curiam*) handed down. After a slight easing of the pressure in the mid-1980s, the numbers began to rise again, so that the Court disposed of 4806 cases in the 1988 Term and issued 143 opinions (10 *per curiam*). Clearly, then, by one measurement, the American people see the Court as a legitimate route through which to advance their interests. There is some indication that an increasingly self-abnegating attitude is developing within the Court; for the first time in memory, it decided at one of its weekly Conferences in November 1989 not to grant a single writ of *certiorari*.

Quantity is one thing, quality another. Here there have been three important changes and they are closely interrelated. The Congress has itself passed a great many laws which have spawned extremely complex litigation; the Civil Rights Acts, Voting Rights Acts, and Social Security Acts are only the worst offenders. Federal courts have then been pulled into the political arena by the national legislators whose laws not only provide statutory encouragement for disaffected individuals to litigate and demand interpretation but also deal with issues which deeply divide Americans. The result has been that litigation has increasingly come to reflect political conflicts about general principles fought out over public law issues in the judicial branch rather than the 'traditional' controversy between individual private parties with a precise bone of contention between them. The conflict is the greater because the laws do not represent a majoritarian consensus; divided control of the legislative and executive branches encourages the supporters of each to turn to the courts to consolidate legislative victories or to seek change after legislative defeats.

Second, many of the major issues of the 1980s involve disputes which can to a singular degree be translated into judicial questions. The rise of 'rights' as a major source of political conflict has provided political energy to draw the courts into the political process. Republican principles, of course, put a premium on the legitimacy of the people's representatives, but their liberal roots also include a healthy suspicion of government. The enduring, and unresolved, tension in American political ideology between elective accountability and individual protection against government has always existed, but in the 1980s it increased in saliency and thrust the Court into a well nigh impossible position. On the one hand, some societal forces had come to see it as the bastion of individual rights and a liberal bulwark in an increasingly conservative culture. On the other hand, other societal forces, newly encouraged by Republican political successes and strengthened by a shift in the center of elite ideological gravity toward a more critical appraisal of the 1960s liberalism, had come to see it as an undemocratic obstruction to a newly emerging conservative majority. Hence, the Court was enmeshed in the center of a national battle between left and right in which many of the central bones of contention were those very issues for which the Court uniquely was held responsible.

Third, the competition between the old but declining majority, comfortable with the Court's civil rights record, and a new conservative challenge growing in confidence but highly critical of the Court's civil rights record, had reached a new pitch of intensity. For many of the most articulate and committed members of the 'New Right', the revolution was infuriatingly incomplete. Handsome victories in presidential races had been matched by a triumph in the 1980 Senatorial races. But this did not represent a realignment. The Congress remained obstinately Democratic; state governments refused to shift decisively with the conservative tide; the Senate reverted to Democratic control in 1986; the Supreme

Court continued to erect a solid wall between church and state, to uphold the constitutionality of abortions, busing and affirmative action, and generally to exercise its judicial power. Frustration and disappointment heightened conservatives' determination to control the judicial branch. Like their nationalist predecessors in 1801, they too sought to extend their influence long into the future through judges who serve not for a fixed term but for life. The Bork nomination thus took a central position in this strategy.

The passions involved in the struggle for the philosophical, and hence, substantive, heart of the judicial branch burst into public denunciations. Meese's head-on attack on the jurisprudence of leading members of the Court in 1985 was deliberately arranged for the annual gathering of the prestigious American Bar Association. This frontal attack sparked off a remarkable, and highly publicized, response from the Supreme Court. Brennan, in particular, challenged Meese's assumptions; but so did Stevens (Brennan, 1986; Stevens, 1986). And both White and Rehnquist, to some extent in coded language, added their voices to the criticism. This entry into the political arena, almost without precedent, inevitably provided grist for the conservative commentators' mill; the *Wall Street Journal*, for example, reprimanded Brennan and Stevens for 'acting like politicians, setting policy, instead of like honest interpreters of the Constitution'. But one person's honest interpreter is another's misguided judge.

At one level, the argument appears to be a philosophical one about the proper role of the courts in a democratic system. In my left corner, as it were, are those who argue that limited government necessitates a powerful judicial branch, that the protection of individual rights is a high national priority and also requires a powerful judicial branch, and that elected politicians, either through moral weakness or the limitations inherent in accountability to mass electorates, are not always to be trusted. In my right corner, then, are those who argue that the primary democratic principle is electoral accountability, that governments have rights which are to be limited only in clearly egregious circumstances, and that the role of the judiciary is to be self-restrained because otherwise it in effect legislates, a function for which it lacks both skill and legitimacy.

But, if the argument was merely philosophical, it would remain in the academic backwaters of philosophy and jurisprudence classes. But it is not; both sides have a hidden agenda. Each philosophy leads ineluctably towards different substantive outcomes. The almost precise match between desired outcomes and chosen judicial philosophy suggests that the causal chain may begin with preferred outcomes. The philosophies are, therefore, less benign than they seem; for they essentially offer rationalisations for disparate policy preferences. In short, then, the argument is really about power. However, since the American myth requires that the Court should be a judicial rather than a political body, that argument needs to be clothed in intellectual rhetoric. Thereby hangs its chances of continuing legitimacy.

New appointments to the Court have in part strengthened a new conservative rhetoric and this is reflected in a perceptible shift in the Court's public jurisprudence. Kennedy, who replaced Bork, has been in this conservative majority more often than not and his agreement rates with Rhenquist are very high. There is little doubt that the Court is much readier to give the benefit of the doubt to governments and their agents than it was a few years ago and continues to favor the police position over a suspect's claim. Decisions in the areas of affirmative action and abortion rights (*Richmond* v. *J. A. Croson Co.* and *Webster* v. *Reproductive Health Services*) have been interpreted as signs of Reagan's ultimate success in fashioning the Court to his liking. But what is interesting is that Justice O'Connor, the pivotal fifth vote in these cases (as also in *Allegheny County* v. *American Civil Liberties Union*, which outlawed a Christmas display), has not gone the whole way in repudiating either *Bakke* or *Roe*. Indeed, Rehnquist and White carefully did not overrule *Roe*, when they might have been expected to do so, almost certainly because they knew they could not get O'Connor's vote to do so.

Division and conflict dominate analysis of the Court. Given the fact that normally only the 'hard' and divisive case are taken, the degree of unanimity is striking. In the 1988 Term, over a quarter of cases provoked not a single dissent and unanimous cases covered a wide spectrum of legal issues: there is no right to a jury trial in drunken driving cases; judges cannot throw out prisoners' lawsuits as frivolous;

states cannot ban party endorsements in primary elections; teenage-only dance halls do not violate teenagers' right of free association; land ownership cannot be a prerequisite for membership of a board charged with the reorganization of city and county government. Thus, although the statistics show quite clearly that the Court was firmly dominated by the quintet of Rehnquist, Scalia, Kennedy, White and O'Connor, that block does not always cohere (as the right to burn the American flag case indicated) and, even when it does, it usually holds back from striking out in entirely novel directions. While the arrival of Souter will yet further strengthen that bloc, it is likely that they will ensure that its activism is still kept under control. Precedents may well be cut back; they are less likely to be overruled.

The Rehnquist Court thus stands, at the beginning of the 1990s, in an uncomfortable position. The direct criticism of its predecessor by criticis of the 'right' and the direct action to thwart the Bork nomination by supporters of the 'left' nearly stripped the Court as an institution naked. Rehnquist's task is to re-establish its image, rebuild its impression of disinterested judgement, and refurbish its tarnished reputation among the right without destroying trust among the left. The conditions for this are not propitious. Divided authority in Washington, a lobby culture deeply inured to litigating strategies, and issues of profound and divisive content are ready to exacerbate the position.

But there are signs that there is a growing realization throughout Washington that a Supreme Court without legitimacy, which could conceivably be the legacy of the Reagan years, is not in the American interest. The executive branch dramatically reduced its overt criticism of existing precedents, especially once Bush entered the White House; and the Rehnquist Court has carefully chosen neither to outlaw affirmative action nor to repudiate *Roe* v. *Wade* in either the 1988 or the 1989 Terms. Political calculation has historically been a strength of the Supreme Court. That is the great irony; for it is only by political calculation that the Court can retain the apolitical image upon which its power, authority and legitimacy ultimately depend.

7

Public Bureaucracy in the American Political System

B. GUY PETERS

American government is complex and divided. The public bureaucracy is yet another institution competing for power and resources with others, and is within itself deeply divided. There is no *bureaucracy* in the U.S. federal government; there are rather a set of *bureaucracies*, each with its own interests and its own culture. Most modern Presidents have recognized the divisions within the federal administrative structure, and also recognized the importance of those bureaucracies for making and implementing public policy. They have sought to exert policy control over the career civil service but in the process have generated their own personal bureaucracies (the White House staff, the National Security Council, etc.) and added to the complexity and confusion of government. While George Bush's long experience in Washington predisposes him toward using the career service and the established agencies more than his predecessor did, he must still attempt to put his own stamp on government and fight the continuing battle of the 'administrative presidency'.

Unlike a President, the average American in the street would not think of administrative agencies as central actors in their political system. She might be willing to concede that the bureaucracy does have some impact (usually negative) on how programs actually are implemented; but she would not think that civil servants were central to the overall performance of the public sector. This lack of understanding of the role of bureaucracy is in part due to popular ignorance about the complexities of managing a large modern government, spending over $1 trillion (at the federal level alone) and employing over 4 million people (again, federal only). In larger part, however, the failure to recognize the importance of the civil services reflects the general negative perception of the 'bureaucracy' in American political culture. To most Americans, the desire of George Wallace to throw the bureaucrats and their briefcases into the Potomac River strikes a very responsive chord. The anti-statism of American political culture and political life extends to a negative perception of bureaucrats, and the tendency to think of bureaucracy almost totally in terms of red tape, buck passing, and inflexibility. The bureaucracy is something to be blamed for failure, not recognized for its contributions to making government work at all.

If the general public already had negative attitudes toward the bureaucracy, they found a champion for their views with President Ronald Reagan and his Administration. Reagan came to Washington after campaigning against Washington, big government, and bureaucracy. His Administration explicitly or implicitly treated the career civil service as their enemies, and sought to buffer the Administration's policy commitments against possible tampering by the bureaucracy. It came into office with the stated goal of reducing the size, power, and rewards of the civil service, a commitment embodied in the person of Donald Devine as President Reagan's first Director of the Office of Personnel Management (OPM). This made Devine responsible for the administration of the merit system and virtually all personnel management programs in the federal government, including the Senior Executive Service. The Administration's assessment of the role of the civil service was summed up in the statement of Terry W. Culler, an Associate Director of OPM under Devine, who argued that excellence was not necessary in the public service, only minimal competence. Political pressures made the reappointment of Devine for a second term as Director of OPM impossible and President Bush made positive statements about the civil service during his campaign and avoided the 'bureaucracy bashing' of his predecessor. These changes, however, have done little to change the objective working conditions of the career civil service.

Despite the negative images of bureaucrats held by a large portion of the general population, and the explicit attacks of the Reagan Administration, the civil service remains an important component of governing in Washington, just as it would be in any other national capital. That importance is highlighted somewhat ironically by the amount of time and energy that the Reagan Administration (and, in fairness, a number of Administrations prior to that one) spent in attempting to reform the civil service to fit their own ideas concerning good public administration. It is clear that the bureaucracies control most implementation, and further that the manner of implementation directly influences the outcomes of a policy or program (Pressman and Wildavsky, 1973). In addition to its role in implementing public policies, administrative agencies also have a central role in making policies. Secondary legislation ('regulations') is written by the bureaucracy and, although the law governing this process mandates public disclosure and an opportunity for public reaction, this gives the bureaucracy tremendous power to ramify the meaning of legislation passed by Congress (Gormbey, 1991). The bureaucracy is also responsible for adjudicating the results of their own implementation through trial examiners and appeals procedures. The sheer volume of work undertaken by the federal bureaucracies dwarfs the activities of Congress, the Courts, and even the President and, whether Presidents or citizens like it, most of what happens in government happens through the bureaucracy, or really multiple bureaucracies.

Structure and Performance

Public administration in the United States is substantially more complex and decentralized than is the case for most

European countries. Even if the effects of federalism and the role of state and local governments are ignored, the American administrative system (if it can be called a system) is still very decentralized and permits a great deal of autonomous action by the organizations, and even the individuals, that comprise it. President Reagan and now President Bush have made more political appointments than other recent presidents, but still have not been able to eliminate the autonomy of most agencies. Therefore, to understand how the system functions, it is necessary to understand how individuals and organizations within the public bureaucracy relate to one another, and how they in turn relate to the other institutions of government.

Public Employees

The first question which must be answered about the public bureaucracy in the United States is who the civil servants are, and how is the personnel system in the federal government organized. This is not a simple question. The over 2.8 million civilian employees of the federal government (there are an additional 2 million personnel in the armed forces) are organized in a variety of personnel systems, with different grading systems, different standards, and to some extent different purposes. This fragmentation is some indication of the degree of decentralization in the federal government. The decentralization of their own management system, and the even more decentralized structure of the executive branch of government, also inhibits the capacity of the civil service to function as a unified political force.

The majority of civilian federal employees (just over 50 per cent in 1990) are in the General Schedule, a merit-based personnel system with 18 pay grades (each with ten steps) beginning with very menial occupations (GS–1) and running through some of the top positions in the career civil servants (GS–18). Positions in the civil service are classified according to the requirements to fulfill tasks in a position, the difficulty of the work, and so on and individuals who qualify are then placed into the available positions. The individual may be qualified for a position by taking a test, through formal education, or through a combination of the two. A number of issues have arisen concerning the fairness of testing for minorities, and the applicability of the skills measured in tests to the work to be performed in some jobs. These concerns have led to the suspension of one of the more commonly used classification examinations and its replacement with job specific tests, as well as increased latitude for agencies to hire without written examinations (Horner, 1989). Although the personnel system of the federal government is intended to be strictly a merit system, issues such as affirmative action for minorities and the preferences given to veterans for their prior service demonstrate that it is also a major public institution committed to attaining goals other than simply always hiring the person who scores the best on a test. Despite those caveats, the General Schedule remains a merit system attempting to enforce relatively uniform criteria for public jobs.

On top of the hierarchy of the General Schedule are two other personnel systems. One is the Executive Schedule (ES), which includes most political appointments (although some of those ES positions may be occupied by career civil servants); almost nine thousand positions are available in the Executive Schedule and other executive systems. These jobs are not conceived of as being filled by merit alone, in the usual sense of the term, but are clearly political jobs. Nor are these career jobs, and most occupants spend a period of months rather than years in the positions. The flow of 'in and outers' into and out of the federal government is quite different from recruitment of senior administrators in most industrialized democracies (MacKenzie, 1981). The availability of politically committed personnel should provide vigorous pursuit of policy goals and some political control, but sacrifices continuity and, all too often, substantive expertise in the policy area being administered. Most Presidents have filled some of the executive jobs with career civil servants, but this practice was curtailed during the Reagan Administration. President Bush is using more careerists in ES positions than his predecessor, but he has not used as many careerists as previous presidents.

The second personnel system sitting on top of the General

Schedule is the Senior Executive Service (SES). This 'service' was formed in 1979 as a function of the provisions in the Civil Service Reform Act of 1978, and included a large proportion of civil servants who were then in the senior levels of the General Schedule (GS-15 to 18). There were a number of reasons for creating the SES, but one of the more important was to create a cadre of senior career executives who could serve as a fungible management resource in government (Ingraham and Ban, 1984). This mobility of managers was to be in contrast to the tendency of most civil servants in the United States to spend their entire careers within a single department, or even a single agency. This sometimes prevented deploying the best employees for particular job demands, and produced narrow parochial viewpoints among senior employees. In addition to creating mobility, joining the SES created both opportunities and risks for those managers. The managers were supposed to have the opportunity for substantial bonuses, sabbaticals and more important positions, but ran a greater risk of being fired for poor performance than if they had remained members of the General Schedule system. Finally, the SES was 'Carter's gift to Reagan' because it permitted a larger number of political appointments in nominally civil service positions. The Reagan Administration readily seized that opportunity, and the Bush Administration has continued with political appointments, albeit without the 'political litmus test' that characterized its predecessor. In short, while an important innovation in the American bureaucracy, the SES was not an unmixed blessing to the career managers in government.

Finally, there is everyone else – a variety of other personnel systems that account for almost 45 per cent of total federal employment. The largest personnel system outside the General Schedule is the Postal Pay System which covers over 600 000 employees of the U.S. Postal Service. In addition to that substantial number of workers, the Wage System covers some 400 000 employees working in blue-collar jobs in government. The CIA and the NSA each has its own personnel system to meet the very special needs of their intelligence operations. Several public corporations, such as the Tennessee Valley Authority with over 100 000 employees, also have their own personnel systems. Each of these personnel systems, however, broadly follows the merit principles of the General Schedule, but the divisions within government make a coherent personnel policy that much more difficult to implement.

Organizations

The decentralized and largely unco-ordinated nature of the personnel systems of the federal government are echoed in the structure of the organizations which comprise American government. Whereas many European governments are organized around cabinet ministries which are clearly the dominant actors in the policy process, American cabinet departments are largely holding companies for a number of agencies within them. (Seidman and Gilmour, 1986). These agencies have a legal life of their own, most having been formed by an act of Congress or an Executive Order, and have their own budgets and personnel allocations. The agencies also have their own clientele groups, and their own supporters on congressional committees and subcommittees, and therefore are able to exercise considerable political muscle if they must. As a consequence of this decentralization, the best way to understand the dynamics of public administration in the United States is to look at the agencies and their actions, rather than concentrating on cabinet departments.

Autonomy   As is implied by the above discussion, the system of organization in the United States allows a great deal of autonomy for individual agencies. Having their own legal mandate provides them a basis for independence from their cabinet department, and their ability often to argue their own cases before congressional committees for budget and personnel again loosens their bonds to their nominal superiors at the departmental level. Some agencies, the Public Health Service or the Food and Drug Administration for example, use their professional expertise to insulate themselves from control by often non-professional cabinet secretaries. Others such as the Extension Service in the Department of Agriculture may use their political ties in almost every county in America to exercise autonomous power. While this autonomy of agencies makes the task of the cabinet-level secretary difficult and often frustrating, it does permit entrepreneurship by an agency which has attractive program ideas, and may in the long run enhance the budget, power and prestige of the department.

Not all agencies, however, have an equal capacity to exercise autonomy in their relationships with their own department, with Congress or with their own clients. The differences are in part because of the very high prestige and power of some agencies (the FBI or the Social Security Administration), as contrasted to agencies which have had very checkered histories and hence tend to attract significant legislative oversight (General Services Administration, and for a time NASA). In addition, Congress and the President have chosen to make some organizations that logically might be components of cabinet departments autonomous, hence giving them even greater latitude. For example, NASA might have been a part of the Department of Defense (especially given its early reliance on military personnel and rockets) but was given independent executive status for a variety of reasons. Finally, some cabinet departments – especially Housing and Urban Development – are organized more around their Assistant Secretaries than around agencies, and therefore the central administration of the department has more power within the organization (Peters, 1988). The scandals over Secretary Samuel Pierce's management of HUD demonstrate that this control is not an unmixed blessing. Even with these caveats, however American, the public bureaucracy is extremely decentralized and provides a great deal of autonomy to its component organizations.

Links to the Outside A large portion of the strength of bureaucratic agencies comes from their links to outside organizations. In particular, the agencies have links both to Congress and to the relevant interest groups in their policy area. This contact is facilitated because Congress is itself almost as fragmented and decentralized as the constellation of executive agencies and therefore the agencies can do business with friendly and specialized committees and sub-committees to facilitate both their appropriations and their legislation. Likewise, the universe of pressure groups surrounding government provides no shortage of interested parties; indeed the difficulty for most bureaus has become limiting participation rather than finding any groups who are interested.

The standard means of describing the relationship among the agencies, Congress, and interest groups has been iron triangles, or 'cozy little triangles' (Freeman, 1965; McConnell, 1966). These characterizations implied that there was a close, symbiotic relationship between a single agency, one congressional committee or subcommittee, and one interest group. This arrangement limited the range of advice and information offered to Congress and tended to produce a monolithic view of good policy in that policy domain. For a variety of reasons, these triangles have become much less cozy than they were, and one commentator has characterized them recently as 'big, sloppy hexagons' (Jones, 1982). A less flamboyant name for the phenomenon is 'policy communities' (Jordan, 1981). The concept of the policy community is that there is a number of interest groups which may have a relationship to the bureaucratic agency and to its programs. In particular, consumer groups and client groups have come to challenge the domination of producer interest groups and their close relations to the agencies. Government agencies typically must now listen to a wider range of policy advice, although they may still continue to have favorite organizations and favorite points of view within that broader universe of advice.

If the advice being provided an agency – and Congress – is now more diverse than it had been, the congressional committee system still tends to be receptive to the appeals of the agencies they are supposed to oversee. The most common pattern found in committees and subcommittees is for Congressmen whose constituents have an interest in a program to be members of the committees that exercise oversight for the agency. It is difficult for a Congressman to be very harsh with, or cut the budget of, an agency that is providing a large volume of services to his or her constituents. The fragmentation of congressional decisionmaking into a large number of committees and subcommittees, each granted substantial powers over its own set of programs and agencies, allows the fragmentation of the public bureaucracy into many public bureaucracies to be translated into a great deal of autonomy and power.

Although the agencies look to Congress and interest groups for the resources (financial and political) to fulfill their missions, many are also connected closely to other actors. Many federal programs must be implemented through state and local governments, and still others depend upon non-governmental actors to implement their programs. In some policy areas the same type of restrictive arrangements – referred to as 'picket-fence federalism' – that had characterized the relationships with interest groups also mark intergovernmental relationships. Specialized officials in all three levels of government are linked together and insulated from external political forces by their expertise – county health officials, state health officials and administrators in the Department of Health and Human Services work closely together in isolation from mayors, governors and the cabinet secretary. A major difference, however, is that in these cases the federal agency is usually the source of funds, and hence is the sponsor rather than the supplicant, but there is still mutual dependence.

The Policy Rule of the Bureaucracy

The demands on modern government make it virtually impossible for a legislature to make all the rules needed by a society. In part this is because of the volume of rules needed, but it is also a consequence of the technical information required for some of those rules. A legislature may know that it wants to outlaw carcinogens in the workplace but would have to rely on a technically qualified bureaucracy to identify those chemicals and their toxic levels. Likewise, it is impossible for the regular court system to cope with all the adjudications which must be made, and for the same two reasons: volume and complexity. These problems within the political institutions of government put the public bureaucracy in the position of being the only institution that readily can fulfill these needs for the society and the government.

The sheer volume of the rule-making and adjudication activities of the federal bureaucracy are immense. In an average year, the federal bureaucracy makes thousands of rules (regulations, not including thousands more interpretative and informal rules), while Congress may pass only several hundred laws – some of which are private bills of little policy consequence. In 1986, the SSA alone heard several hundred thousand appeals against its own decisions, and the Veterans Administration close to another 100 000 appeals. In that same year only a few thousand cases were heard in the regular federal court system (Mashaw, 1983). While many of the rules being made by the bureaucracy are narrow and technical, and many of the cases being heard involve relatively little money, they are of great importance to the parties involved and must be processed. Without the bureaucracy, it seems likely that the entire system of government might grind to a halt.

The rule-making and rule adjudication activities of federal administrative agencies are rather closely regulated by the Administrative Procedures Act of 1946 (APA) and its amendments (such as the Freedom of Information Act). (Freedman, 1978). The provisions of this Act are too detailed to present here, but some basic principles of administrative law for the United States can be extracted from the Act. The first would be the importance of participation and openness. For example, in administrative rule-making the act prescribes access for the public. This participation can be either through written 'notice and comment' (informal rule-making) or through testimony (formal rule-making). The courts have tended to expand the requirements for evidence in rule-making and have produced 'hybrid rule-making' with greater formality than informal rule-making (Gormley, 1989). Few private citizens are sufficiently interested to comment on proposed regulations on their own, but many interest groups monitor religiously the *Federal Register* which contains all notices of proposed rule-making activity, and are prepared to react to any rule-making efforts which affect them. Likewise, administrative adjudications, even if informal, permit the affected parties to present their case in a reasonably open forum and to be heard, if not always satisfied. In short, the APA does make rule-making a public activity and prevents the bureaucracy from doing all of its work without taking the wishes of the public – at least the organized public – into account. Further, the Freedom of Information Act permits citizens to find out just what the agencies have done, either in rule-making or in applying the rules to particular individual cases (Peters, 1989).

A second principle which emerges from the APA, as it has been implemented, is that administrative agencies do have a great deal of discretion when they act. The public does have to be heard, and the actions taken by the agencies must be related specifically to an act of Congress or an Executive Order. Beyond that, however, the agencies are free to exercise their own discretion so long as that does not produce outcomes which are 'arbitrary and capricous'. So long as the agency decision-makers have some evidence or logic to justify their decisions, they are able to make the decision they think is correct. They can do so even if the preponderance of evidence offered by citizens is in contradiction to the final rule issued.

The requirement that decisions reached by an agency must not be arbitrary leads to a final general principle about administrative law in the United States. This is that the activities of administrative agencies ultimately are judged in reference to general standards of constitutionality. The right of citizens to participate is a requirement for procedural due process in decision-making, while the requirement that the resulting decisions appear reasonable is a statement of substantive due process. Although there must be a substantive legal or constitutional question, the results of administrative actions can be appealed into the federal court system. Thus, although the procedures for making or adjudicating laws may not be the ones which most citizens would expect, they do not abdicate any of their basic rights as citizens when their cases are being considered in the bureaucracy.

The public bureaucracy in the United States is an important actor – some would argue the dominant actor – in policy-making. Its autonomy, its fragmentation and the fragmentation of political institutions which might control it, make enforcing accountability difficult. In addition, the administrative agencies are closely linked with outside interest groups and to subnational governments, all of which increases their power. The bureaucracy is not, however, without constraint. Some of that constraint comes from the values held by individuals within the agencies, and their commitment to public service and more particularly to service to their own clients. Another important restraint is the role of legal requirements and doctrines that make the bureaucracy conform to basic constitutional standards. Despite its power and importance, the bureaucracy is rarely able to act without reference to laws, or to act in a totally arbitrary manner. Americans are generally very dubious about their bureaucracy and its power, and have managed to develop a legal system to control or at least publicize most of the possible excesses of a modern bureaucracy.

The Reagan Years

It is easy to write in a detached, academic fashion that the federal bureaucracy has not run amok. But to many participants in the real world of politics, who have come to Washington expecting to change the world – or at least change a corner of it – and to control an area of public policy, it may appear that the bureaucracy is firmly in control. This was certainly the perception that most people in the Reagan Administration had when they began, and many of them left Washington with the same impression. Few people in the Reagan Administration regarded the public bureaucracy as their allies and friends, and as a consequence a number of actions were taken during those eight years that were directed at reducing the power, prestige and emoluments of the career civil service.

The Personnel System

One component of the attacks of the Reagan Administration on the bureaucracy was directed at the personnel system.

The several merit systems in the U.S. began with the Pendelton Act in 1883, and over time the merit system has come to play a central role in the management of the civil service, and to be a shibboleth for defenders of the existing personnel system. Even for public employees not explicitly covered by the merit system, some of its central principles defining personnel policy have structured their working lives. In particular, concepts about how pay and perquisites should be determined for the public sector, and concepts of the political role of the civil service, have an impact on the nature of public employment generally.

Pay and Perquisites   The principle of comparability between public and private pay scales has been central to pay determination for the civil service (Hartman, 1984). The basic assumption has been that people doing a job in government should receive approximately the same pay as those working in the private sector. The principle of comparability was adopted both out of a sense of fairness, and out of a perceived need to be able to recruit the 'best and brightest' into government. Even before the 1980s the comparability principle was facing a number of challenges, but those problems were exacerbated during the eight years of the Reagan Administration.

One barrier to ensuring comparability of compensation in the federal executive is that Congress does not want anyone other than the President, the Vice-President, Cabinet Secretaries, and Supreme Court Justices to make more than its members do. This congressional reluctance to be paid less than executive branch officials would not in principle be a barrier to comparability if there were not strong political pressures (seen very clearly in January 1989 and to lesser extent again in November 1989) to restrict raises in congressional pay. With congressional pay not increasing as rapidly as inflation or as wages in the private sector, the principle of pay comparability – especially for top executive and managerial positions – has been eroding. By 1987, average compensation for employees in the federal government was over 25 per cent lower than for comparable positions in the private sector, and the salaries for senior executives was much farther behind the private sector.

In addition to underpaying top managers, the pay cap and resultant salary compression imposed because of a failure to increase congressional salaries makes motivation in the civil service more difficult. Compensation rates for the service as a whole have continued to increase (albeit not in line with wage rates in the economy as a whole), but employees reach a point at which they can go no higher because congressional salaries have not been increased. Many people at different grades and with different levels of responsibility may be paid the same amount. Monetary rewards are not the only things that motivate civil servants, but they do not hurt either. Under current arrangements federal managers have been denied one of their tools to motivate and reward employees, This loss, in turn, has produced significant problems in recruitment and retention of the most capable employees and prospective employees.

One way around the pay ceilings described above has been 'special rate' pay for certain professional employees needed in government, such as engineers, lawyers and physicians. Even the top of the federal pay schedule does not come close to paying these professionals what they might be able to earn in the private economy, and therefore if government is to be able to hire any competent people in these categories they have had to create special pay schedules for, by 1988, over 100 000 employees (Levine, 1988). In addition, because pay rates for the federal government are national, federal pay for some jobs (secretaries, for example) in large metropolitan areas are not at all competitive with the private market and some special pay arrangements have had to be made for these employees.

While these special arrangements do solve short-term problems, they also undermine some basic principles of the merit system and the classification system for jobs in government. The civil service may cease to be a single service (which some critics would actually welcome) and become more of a reflection of the private labor market. The federal government has, for example, begun to experiment with pay systems not based on a classification system. Instead, facility managers would be given a personnel budget and then told to hire the people needed and find some way to make the costs match the requirements of the job. Also, the increasing emphasis on pay for performance in the public sector tends to erode the principles of the classification system for pay determination.

The Reagan Administration certainly was no advocate of increased compensation for federal employees. Early in his Administration, President Reagan first proposed a 5 per cent reduction in federal pay, and then argued that federal pay should be 94 per cent of the pay for comparable jobs in the private sector – that 6 per cent difference reflecting his (if no one else's) valuation of the inflation-proofed pension and other benefits then offered to government employees (Peters, 1986). Terry Culler from OPM argued that government should not pay workers enough to buy excellence in its employees; government was sufficiently unimportant to get by with workers who were minimally competent. His idea appeared to be that anyone who was really competent would not want to work for government in the first place – the real action was in the private sector. The Reagan Administration also funded only a fraction of the bonuses envisaged as a means of rewarding excellence in the SES, and therefore one means of evading the pay cap imposed by congressional salaries was largely eliminated. President Reagan did propose salary increases in some of the eight years he was in office, but these rarely matched other wage increases in the economy, and he also could be reasonably certain that Congress would not fully fund the proposed increases. In short, the Reagan Administration did little to help fill the pocketbook of the average federal employee.

Although the valuation of benefits proposed by President Reagan was not shared by everyone, federal benefits had been an important attraction for the workforce. These too were to some degree undermined under Reagan. In particular, the federal pension system, which had been a frequent target of critics of the federal bureaucracy, was made portable so that employees were no longer tied to government but could receive benefits if they retired after leaving government. This obviously made it easier for the best civil servants to leave government, taking their training and experience with them.

The Reagan Administration did not behave as the friend of federal employees along several other dimensions. One was its attitude toward public employee unionization, reflected in its strong reaction to the strike by air traffic controllers in 1981. The Administration was willing to bear some criticism and some disruption in air traffic to enforce its commitment to the principle that federal employees could not legally strike. The reaction to the strike, and a variety of other actions, were attempts to weaken the labor movement in the federal government although in reality the effect may have been the opposite; union membership by the federal employees has continued to increase slightly as a percentage of all employees. Some appear to believe that unions may be needed to replace the declining protection and influence of the merit system for federal employees.

A final way in which the Reagan Administration undertook to reduce the position of the career civil service was through increasing politicization of management in government. As noted above, the Civil Service Reform Act of 1978 permitted a President to make political appointments to the SES; up to 10 per cent of the generalist positions in the SES could be filled by political appointment, and during the Reagan Administration that full 10 per cent was utilized (Newland, 1983). The Administration was also very certain that the individuals who were appointed to those positions, and indeed to any other positions, were 'true believers' in the conservative mission of the Administration. Finally, the Reagan Administration was very careful about where it placed its political appointees. Many were placed further down in agency hierarchies than might normally have been the case, with the opportunity to then use them to bypass career agency heads (Ingraham, 1987). The careerists may have responsibility for management, but could be kept in the dark on policy initiatives. More than previous administrations, there was substantial tension – over policy and over a variety of other matters – during the Reagan years between the political appointees and the career civil servants; over half of respondents to a survey of career executives reported that relationships between political and career officials were a detriment to good management.

The overt politicization of the civil service by the Reagan

Administration may have produced some less overt politicization of another sort. It became abundantly clear that this
Administration was not about to benefit the civil service and
its policy and career goals. While some civil servants went
with the wind and adopted more conservative goals, others
attempted to fight back. This fighting back to some degree
could be done by resistance and delay in implementing rules
that the civil servants did not like, but there has been a
movement to allow greater political activity by civil servants.
The Hatch Act restricts the political activity of civil servants
to voting and little else, and whether for partisan reasons or
simply for human rights reasons, there has been a growing
movement to repeal or amend that Act so that civil servants
can participate more openly in politics.

The Private Sector as Exemplar

In addition to direct assaults on the pay and organizational
power of the civil service, the Reagan Administration also
undertook – almost certainly consciously – to undermine the
position of the civil service by its use of the private sector and
its management styles as the exemplar of good management.
Although many individuals in the Administration noted their
own difficulties in managing in government because of
requirements like the merit system, contracting laws, freedom of information and the like, they often assumed that if
government would only run itself like a private business, then
all of its problems would be solved. This belief in private
sector management was embodied in *Reform '88*, an effort
shortly after Reagan took office in 1981 to reform federal
operations. This program had ten objectives, including such
things as improving cash management, reducing the size of
the workforce, and reducing paperwork. Although less visible than the Grace Commission (see below) this program
probably generated greater real improvement in federal
management. Going along with the view that the private
sector could do things better than government, the Administration sought to remove as many programs as possible from

the public sector and give them to the private sector. It was clear in all this activity that for this Administration the private sector was the exemplar of all that was good. This belief is mirrored in the programs of the British Conservative Government such as the Financial Management Initiative and Next Steps which also mimic management in the private sector.

One of the ways in which public sector management was to be improved by the Reagan Administration was to have private sector executives review the operations of government and propose ways of correcting defects, again using the private sector as the exemplar of how it should be done. In 1982, the President's Private Sector Survey on Cost Control was established, under the leadership of businessman J. Peter Grace. Using the format developed for state and local governments, a team of over 2000 business executives loaned by their employers descended on Washington and began to examine the operations of the federal government. Working for a period of 18 months, the Grace Commission produced almost 2500 recommendations for cost savings in the federal government. They calculated that these proposals could save the federal government almost one-third of its total budget. Again, there is a British equivalent – the Rayner scrutinies – although in Britain other civil servants rather than private sector managers were involved.

Analyses of the Grace Commission's proposals were largely negative, even those evaluations made by organizations, such as the GAO, which have a commitment of their own to saving money in government. Many of the recommendations did assume that government was just like a private business, and did not recognize that there were legal and even ethical criteria which prevented the government from operating in the way that these businessmen thought would be most efficient. Some of the recommendations of the Grace Commission concerned the civil service, and advocated changes in the (allegedly overgenerous) pension system and other employee benefits. Subsequent analysis pointed out that the attacks on the civil service may not have been justified, and that the benefits offered by Grace's own company were substantially more generous than those available to federal employees. A relatively small number of the recommendations of the Grace Commission have been implemented (very few having to do with personnel administration), but the exercise was an example of the perception that good business techniques could 'fix' government (Goodsell, 1984). In addition, some of the attacks on the civil service – probably most importantly the notion that benefits are excessive – remain alive in the demonology of the critics of the public sector.

Utilizing the Private Sector

Another of the programs for reducing the power and influence of the civil service, although the Grace Commission itself had many recommendations in this area, has been the movement toward privatization of government services. Privatization has been a common remedy for the ills of government in almost all countries – including some very poor ones in the Third World (Savas, 1987). In the United States, however, the process began with relatively small public sector ownership of assets, so that the emphasis has been on contracting out services and on deregulation. There have been some major privatizations of assets, e.g. the 'fire sale' of Western lands under James Watt as Secretary of the Interior and the sale of ConRail, but these sales have been less significant than finding ways to deliver services that cost less, or at least that make the federal government's share of the cost less apparent. In fairness, it should be pointed out that interest in contracting out and deregulation as means of enhancing the role of the private sector began prior to the Reagan Administration, with both President Ford and President Carter, but these policies gained greater prominence during the Reagan years.

Privatization through contracting out programs is less dramatic than selling off assets, but can still have a profound effect on government and society. To date the proposals to privatize have been more dramatic than the actual privatizations. If, however, moving programs out of the federal government to state and local governments are included in the enumeration of all the loads that have been shed, then the federal government has been able to reduce its role in the economy and society (Nathan and Doolittle, 1987). Many changes in the regulatory regime of federal agencies were subtle, and some involved more changes in emphasis (for example, in anti-trust regulation not assuming that any virtual monopoly was necessarily illegal) than termination of programs. The sum of the activity, however, was a smaller and less intrusive federal government. The reduction of the federal role, in turn, has meant not only a smaller role for the federal civil service, but also the undermining of a number of years of patient policy development on the part of civil servants in some of the agencies.

One critic of the actions of the Reagan Administration has written of the 'war on the bureaucracy' (Comarow, 1981–2). The language may be somewhat hyperbolic, but the basic point appears valid. The eight years of the Reagan Adminis-tration represented a major attack on the status of the public bureaucracy in the federal government. Some actions in the second term, such as the appointment of Constance Horner as Director of the OPM, mitigated some of the effects of these attacks, but the civil service left to President Bush is not in as good condition as that President Reagan inherited.

A Civil Service for the Year 2000?

Morale in the civil service in the aftermath of the Reagan years is very low, and this is affecting the performance of many public employees and is causing many of the best of them to depart for the private sector. The notion of some in the Administration that anyone who had the capability to work in the private sector would work there is becoming a self-fulfilling hypothesis. This low morale, and flight of many of the more qualified from government does not auger well for the future of the federal government, especially as the requirements for technical expertise and competence in-crease rather than decrease.

Morale, Recruitment and Retention

The extent to which morale has been diminished in the

federal civil service, especially in the top of the service can be seen in the responses to a questionnaire organized by the Federal Executive Institute Alumni Association in 1985. The responses from members of the SES indicate much lower morale than has been indicated in earlier studies. Perhaps particularly telling is that of those who gave an answer, almost 60 per cent said that they would not encourage a young person to consider a career in government. The respondents also pointed to declining morale in their agencies, and declining opportunities for themselves. In short, the working life of senior career managers in the federal government had been made much less desirable than it once was, and many were considering leaving.

Not only are many considering leaving, many *are* leaving the civil service. Since the formation of the SES, an average of over 10 per cent of the positions have been vacated each year. One of the virtues of the civil service has been its continuity, and its consequent ability to advise and, even protect, newly arrived political executives. That ability is being diminished year by year, so that the civil service which remains is less experienced and seemingly less professional. In addition to economic problems, the limited evidence available indicates that many members of the SES were leaving the civil service because of some disgruntlement with their career prospects and their ability to have any influence over policy. The 'best and brightest' who once flocked to government are now flocking away, taking experience and training and commitment with them.

The evidence is that those career civil servants who are leaving government are not being replaced in the manner in which they once might have been. The 'public service' is no longer the respected career that it once was, and surveys of students – even students in schools of public policy and administration – indicate that relatively few are attracted to a lifetime career in government. If a difficulty in attracting new recruits to government jobs is true in general, it is especially true for professional and technical graduates who find their economic opportunities in government severely constrained. In the long run most positions in the civil service will be filled, but almost certainly not with the calibre of personnel that had vacated the positions.

Hopes for the Future

Despite all the assaults on the federal civil service, there are some causes for optimism. One hopeful sign is that President Bush and his Administration do not appear to have the contempt for the civil service that so many political appointees under Reagan manifested. George Bush is less of an outsider to Washington than was Ronald Reagan, and has had much greater experience in working with career civil servants. While his Administration and the bureaucracy may not always be in agreement of policy initiatives, there should be a greater basis of understanding and perhaps mutual respect than there has been in the past eight years. In fact, George Bush even managed to say a few positive things about the civil service during the course of what was in other ways a very negative campaign (on both sides). In addition, the first years of his presidency showed somewhat greater respect for the advice being offered by the bureaucracy. The pragmatism of much of the Administration permits the career civil service to have greater impact than in the more ideological Reagan years. Further, the slowness in which he filled many of the available executive positions allowed the career civil servants to reassert some control after being shunted aside during the Reagan years.

Another hopeful sign for the future of the civil service has been the recognition that something has been going wrong with the career service, and that something must be done if the federal government is to maintain acceptable levels of performance. The recognition of the problems, and the proposals for remedying them, came rather naturally first from the civil service, its professional organizations, and academic organizations concerned with public administration (Stahl and McGurrin, 1986). The concern has, however, spread more broadly within the public affairs community, and has produced a number of reports and task forces. The most notable of these is the Volcker Commission – more properly the National Commission on the Public Service. This Commission, chaired by the former Chairman of the Federal Reserve Board and composed of a number of distinguished public servants, has made numerous detailed recommendations to strengthen the public service and restore its vitality. Not the least of these recommendations has been a proposal to increase pay in federal jobs by 25 per cent immediately, and then review an additional 25 per cent increase for many positions. Although it is far from clear if all of these proposals can be implemented, at least a number of influential and distinguished public figures are now on record in support of preserving and strengthening the civil service. The reform of congressional pay in 1990, for example, has allowed more room for increases in civil service pay.

Even with all of these hopeful signs, some serious damage has been done to the civil service. A large number of experienced and qualified public servants have left government. Virtually a decade of potential recruitment has been lost as public service has been denigrated and its compensation reduced drastically in real terms. Rectifying the pay problem will require money that a conservative administration may be unwilling to spend. Once out, the genie of politicization of the civil service may be impossible to return to its bottle, and all presidents may now utilize all the levers at their disposal to gain control of, or bypass, the civil service. The 'quiet crisis' afflicting the public service has now been recognized, identified, and shouted about but remedying the problem may take much longer.

PART THREE
Public Policy

8

The Changing Federal Balance

DESMOND S. KING

States' rights have historically held an important place in the U.S. political culture. The neglect before the 1950s by the federal government of discrimination against blacks in the southern states illustrates the power of this doctrine. However, from the 1930s and the birth of the 'modern presidency' during Roosevelt's incumbency, states' rights have been eroded. The 'modern presidency' included a significantly expanded legislative role for the president and the establishment of executive agencies institutionalizing the president's powers. During the Roosevelt Administration the role of the federal government in federal–state relations was enlarged through New Deal programs implemented in response to the Great Depression. National administrative institutions were established and federal grants-in-aid to state and local governments increased: trends which assured that the Roosevelt presidency left an enduring mark on the U.S. political system (Beer, 1978; Polenberg, 1966). The New Federalism policies pursued by the Reagan Administration were designed to reverse this enlarged federal government role to enhance the policy freedom of state governments and to reduce federal grants-in-aid.

The substantial growth in federal grants from the 1950s (rising from 4 per cent of federal expenditures in 1954 to

15.2 per cent in 1979, falling to 9.5 per cent in 1987), the expansion of federal regulatory policy, the strengthening of local government through the provision of direct federal grants, and the civil rights decisions of the Supreme Court collectively weakened the political role of the states in the federal system. By the late 1970s some scholars characterized state and local governments as fiscally dependent upon federal funds (Fossett, 1983; Wirth, 1985). The 'modern presidency' had also resulted in the centralization of political authority and policy-making in Washington DC at the expense of the states. This judgement ignored, however, the key role of the states' laws and codes and their role in implementing public policy (Treadway, 1985). For instance, since the foundation of the welfare state in the Social Security Act of 1935, the states have held discretionary powers with which to set eligibility criteria and benefit levels – thus Alabama awards $118 per month to a one-parent family of three on Aid to Families with Dependent Children (AFDC) whereas California provides $663.

This chapter examines the impact of the Reagan Administration upon the federal system. It begins with a discussion of theoretical approaches to federalism and then identifies and assesses the main objectives of Reagan's New Federalism. It is argued that the Reagan Administration succeeded in increasing the power of the states by reducing federal grants but that in other respects centralization of authority did not decline during this era. The former success did, however, modify the incentive structure of the national, state and local governments within the federal system.

Approaches to Federalism

Scholars of federalism distinguish between two principal approaches: dualist and co-operative federalism. Dualists emphasize the constitutional division of responsibilities between the two levels of the U.S. polity noting that the federal government holds exclusive powers to coin money, conduct foreign relations, regulate commerce with foreign nations and among states and to declare war, while the states retain exclusive power to establish local governments, regulate commerce within a state, implement measures for public health, safety and morals, and to conduct elections. On the other hand, the Constitution explicitly denies the federal government the power to tax articles imported from one state to another or to violate the Bill of Rights, while the states may not tax imports or exports, coin money, or enter into treaties. Dualists stress the delineation between the federal and state governments' respective activities implied by this constitutional division of powers and responsibilities. The constitutional source for this view is Article I, Section 8 and the Tenth Amendment, which together are taken as establishing the equality of the federal and state governments. The conservative political implications of this dualist approach are plain: the federal government's role is one which should be constrained, and states' rights are highly valued.

Co-operativists are less rigid about the division of powers and responsibilities between the federal and state governments. Under this view the Constitution is based on a contract between the American people. The constitutional base for this interpretation is the 'elastic clause' of Article I, Section 8 which accords to Congress the power 'to make all laws which shall be necessary and proper for carrying into execution the foregoing powers, and all other powers vested by this Constitution in the government of the United States, or in any department or officer thereof'. It implies a liberal, activist interpretation of the federal government's role in part because of the failings of the states.

Co-operative federalism is implied by the growth of the federal grants-in-aids and regulation since 1945. Dualism describes nineteenth-century federal relations more accurately. This view is confirmed by the decisions of the Supreme Court which until the mid-1930s upheld the states' powers over the federal government (Walker, 1989). The Court's stance towards states' rights has changed since the 1930s as its decisions upheld the Fourth to Eighth Amendments, and forced desegregation and voting rights. Subsequent federal legislation – the CRA (1964) and the VRA (1965) – was opposed (unsuccessfully) for its ending of dualist federalism.

Advocates of co-operative federalism justified setting federal voting requirements with the Fifteenth Amendment. Complementing the Supreme Court's decision-making and the resultant legislation was the growth of federal grants and regulations peaking in 1978. To understand this complex interdependent federal system Reagan and Sanzone propose the notion of 'permissive federalism' according to which 'there is a sharing of power and authority between the national and state governments, but . . . the state's share rests upon the permissiveness of the national government' (Reagan and Sanzone, 1981, p. 175).

There are alternative models of federalism, many developed during the early 1980s to account for the post-war growth of the national government's role in the system. For instance, Paul Peterson analyzed the distinct responsibilities and resources of each tier – federal, state, local – of government terming them 'structural characteristics' (Peterson, 1981). The federal government is responsible for policies redistributing social resources and economic development while local governments are structurally constrained to focus upon policies enhancing their local economy. Different responsibilities result in alternative interests for each level of government within the federal system: 'where the national policy is developmental, local and national goals will overlap and the policy will be executed with a good deal of co-operation and mutual accommodation' (*op. cit.* p. 82). But conflicts can also occur: '. . . where the central government is pursuing a more redistributive objective, its goals are likely to conflict with those of local governments. The national interest in equity will conflict with the local interest in efficiently developing its local economy. As a result the process of implementing the national program will be considerably more complicated' (*op. cit.* pp. 82–3). The different emphasis placed upon developmental and redistributive policies gives the federal, state, and local governments separate interests in Peterson's framework.

Gurr and King (1987) focus upon the national government's interest in its relationship with cities. Gurr and King argue that for the national government well-defined interests – maintaining its legitimacy and revenue supply – inform this relationship. These primary national interests are complemented by expedient interests, tasks assumed by the national government to meet short-term crises – notably the urban riots of the 1960s – though they frequently became absorbed into the first category. It was just this sort of process, the permanent acquisition of expanded federal government responsibilities, which alarmed the Reagan Administration and stimulated the New Federalism agenda. Federal and city government officials differ in their priorities since for the former not all cities are of equal importance whereas 'it follows from the spatial and political location of local officials ... that they are more concerned with the maintenance of essential urban services, and the economic wellbeing of their *city* than are national officials, who are interested more in the aggregate wellbeing of the urban city than of individual cities' (Gurr and King, 1987, p. 42).

These two political economy models of federalism provide a more thorough account of the national government's role within the expanded post-war federal system, and explain how this expansion modified each tier's incentive structure. It is important that the distinct interests of different government tiers within the federal system be recognized. However, two qualifications about these approaches are warranted. First, the role of the federal government, measured in federal grants-in-aid, was reduced under the Reagan Administration. Second, and as part consequence of the first point, greater attention must be accorded the interests and activities of state and local governments within the federal system. State governments have been strengthened and professionalized since the 1960s, and as a consequence, state legislators and governors have the capacity to formulate and pursue policy innovations (Sabato, 1978). Between 1979 and 1988 the number of professional full-time staff employed in state legislatures rose by 64 per cent from 8346 to 13 755 (Weberg, 1988). Professionalism and institutionalization enabled many state governments vigorously to respond to Reagan's New Federalism.

President Reagan and the New Federalism

In his Inaugural Address, President Reagan observed that 'all of us need to be reminded that the Federal government did not create the states; the states created the federal government'. These observations revealed Reagan's sympathy for a dualist conception of federalism and his policies can best be seen as intended to restore such a model. Reagan was unhappy with the growth of the federal government and of its responsibilities, and was sceptical of co-operative federalism. Further he declared that:

> It is my intention to curb the size and influence of the Federal establishment and to demand recognition of the distinction between the powers granted to the Federal government and those reserved to the states or to the people.

Not only should the states have the power to initiate those policies they wished, but they should also be responsible for their funding. The Reagan Administration objected also to the dominant role of the Supreme Court and federal bureaucracies in federal relations. A Domestic Policy Council report in 1986, *The Status of Federalism in America*, maintained that 'for more than 50 years, Congress, the Supreme Court, and federal agencies have been subverting state sovereignty'.

The reform of federalism was a high priority for the President and his first State of the Union Address included a section, titled 'New Federalism', devoted to this reform initiative. He made the following proposals.

Federal Welfare Programs

Included in these reforms was an ambitious proposal to 'swap' welfare responsibilities between the federal and state governments. Under this 'single broad stroke' as Reagan termed it, the state governments would assume complete responsibility for food stamps and AFDC programs while the federal government funded Medicaid (Conlan, 1988). Unlike the other elements of Reagan's New Federalism this proposal received little congressional support and was opposed by the state governors through their organization, the National Governors' Association (NGA).

Federal Grants

President Reagan's New Federalism included two objectives for reform of the grant system. First, he sought to reduce federal grants-in-aid to state and local governments. If these governments wished to continue federally funded programs they would have to use their own resources to do so. Second, Reagan wanted to replace, by merger, categorical grants (those awarded by a higher government to be used for a specific purpose) with block grants (those awarded by a higher government to be used within a broad activity, for example, urban renewal).

In these aims the Reagan Administration enjoyed considerable success. In the ten years from 1978 to 1988 grants-in-aid fell by 25 per cent, and as a percentage of state-local revenues federal monies fell by 22 per cent (Walker, 1989; ACIR, 1988). General revenue sharing (grants which included few details about their use other than for legitimate government activity) was ended in 1986 at which time it amounted to $4.6 billion. The bulk of these cuts occurred in fiscal years 1982 and 1983 when support amongst members of Congress for the Reagan Administration was at its greatest.

In the Omnibus Budget Reconciliation Act of 1981 60 federal programs were ended, and another 77 were merged into nine new block grants. These were: Elementary and Secondary Education; Community Services; Low Income Home Energy Assistance; Community Development for Small Cities; Preventive Health and Health Service; Alcohol, Drug Abuse and Mental Health; Child and Maternal Health Services; Social Services; Primary Care. Significantly, block grants gave greater power to the state governments at the expense of the local governments, a deliberate intention of the Reagan reforms.

As a consequence of the reduction in federal aid and the 1982–3 recession most states increased taxes either on property, sales, or income. Initially they made little effort to replace federal programs ended by the Reagan policies but sought simply to maintain basic services; in subsequent years as their revenues stabilized some state governments did use their resources to renew programs. Those state and local governments which were careful to have separated federal funds from their own resources suffered less since they used the former source for funding non-essential services. Some local governments could not afford this strategy, however, as they were highly dependent upon federal aid. Consequently cuts in services provided for the poorest residents were not uncommon. As Peterson has stated:

> the type of cuts made in the first term were the easiest ones for the city governments to handle ... The fact that city budgets escaped relatively unscathed from the first term of federal policy reform reflects, to a significant degree, the ability of city governments to pass on the effects of program reductions directly to program beneficiaries (Peterson, 1986, p. 35).

Reforming Federal Regulatory Policy

As an advocate of the free market and an opponent of government intervention Reagan was naturally hostile to extensive federal regulation. In a speech setting out the Administration's economic policies Reagan focused upon regulation alluding to the 'federal regulation burden' – 'ineffective targeting, wasteful administrative overhead'. He maintained that these undesirable attributes could 'be eliminated by shifting the resources and decision-making authority to local and state governments. This will also consolidate programs which are scattered throughout the Federal bureaucracy, bringing government closer to the people and saving $23.9 billion over the next five years'.

Federal regulations were tackled through executive orders. In February 1981 Reagan issued Executive Order 12291 instructing federal agencies to design and implement regulations as cost-effectively as possible. Executive Order 12612, issued in October 1987, restricted the power of federal departments and regulatory agencies to review the activities of state and local governments. The Executive Order instructs these national agencies to 'recognize the distinction between problems of national scope (which may justify federal action) and problems that are merely common to the states (which will not justify federal action because individual states, acting individually or together, can effectively deal with them)'. In addition national agencies should 'refrain, to the maximum extent possible, from establishing uniform, national standards for programs and, when possible, defer to the states to establish standards'. The aim of these executive orders is to privilege state over federal standards apart from when a 'federal law expressly authorizes issuance of preemptive regulations'.

Institutionally, the Reagan Administration tightened the federal regulatory system. In Executive Order 12498 the Office of Information and Regulatory Affairs (OIRA) was established within the OMB to evaluate new regulations proposed by federal departments or regulatory agencies. This new office provided an institutional center to the regulatory process. Federal agencies were obliged to submit any proposed regulation to OIRA together with a justification and a cost assessment.

To evaluate existing regulations Reagan established a Presidential Task Force on Regulatory Relief in February 1981, chaired by Vice-President George Bush. The Task Force was ended in 1983 after issuing a final report in which the Force's members calculated they would save $150 billion in the ensuing ten years for those governments relieved from earlier regulations (Harris and Milkis, 1989).

Many local governments welcomed Reagan's executive orders and the Report of his Task Force having felt restricted by existing federal regulations. For small units of government many federal regulations such as those issued by the Environmental Protection Agency were costly to implement.

Not all of the Reagan Administration's regulatory policy was intended to reduce the federal role. The intellectual ideas of the 'New Right' which influenced President Reagan and his Administration not only advocated the free market but a willingness to use a strong state when necessary (King,

1987; Peele, 1984). Thus although the thrust of Reagan's policies appeared to end regulations, in fact, numerous new ones were introduced such as that raising the minimum drinking age and others for trucking and national product liability insurance (Conlan, 1988). The Reagan Administration emphasized regulatory relief in social programs but was prepared to regulate other activities when judged necessary.

Reforming Urban Policy

The Reagan Administration opposed an interventionist federal urban policy. Reagan appointed Samuel Pierce as Secretary of Housing and Urban Development (HUD) and subsequent evidence has revealed Pierce took a lax view of his position. HUD was the subject of several investigations and the source of much scandal.

Three principles informed the Reagan Administration's urban policy, enunciated by HUD representative June Koch: 'to create the right economic climate for stable urban growth, strengthen state and local governments, and stimulate public and private co-operation to improve social and physical conditions' (Joint Economic Committee, 1984, p. 4). Reagan believed that urban economies could be revived as a side-benefit of national economic growth. Local governments should work to forge partnerships with local businesses and to design policy frameworks which would facilitate business investment. Furthermore, the federal government's role – both as a provider of grants to cities and as a regulator – should be restricted if not entirely ended. Thus general revenue sharing was reduced and then terminated while urban direct action grants (UDAGs) were cut from $675 million in 1980 to $215 million in 1988 and then abolished. By replacing categorical with block grants the Reagan Administration increased the power of the states over local governments since they gave the states discretion about what local programs to fund and also 'removed most of the regulatory or administrative rules limiting states' choices about how to implement grant-supported programs' (Peterson, 1984, p. 229).

Reflecting New Right principles the Reagan Administration's policies were free market oriented. Reagan argued further that government intervention could not succeed in a market economy since it countered natural market forces. The President's 1982 National Urban Policy judged most existing federal urban programs a failure and, consistent with the Administration's New Federalism, called for giving 'maximum feasible responsibility for urban matters to states and through them to their local governments' (HUD, 1982, p. 46; Wolman, 1990).

Granting 'maximum feasible responsibility' to local governments devolves policy responsibility to them. Under the New Federalism local governments were strongly encouraged to implement their own economic development plans based on public–private partnerships and the attraction of private investors to their locality. One popular strategy for achieving these ends is the use of enterprise zones – that is designated districts within which tax breaks and regulatory relief are accorded investors. Over 200 cities established enterprise zones during the Reagan Administration but the latter's efforts to persuade Congress to enact them nationally failed.

The poor treatment of cities during the Reagan Administration stemmed from their declining electoral significance and the weakness of representatives from urban districts within the Congress. Evidence of the former is provided by the decline in the state share of the presidential vote located in large cities: in 1952 41 per cent of Illinois' share of the presidential vote was concentrated in Chicago; by 1984 this figure had dropped to 24 per cent. The reduction and then termination of UDAGs and general revenue sharing modified the incentive structure for members of the Congress from urban districts by reducing the federal funds for which to lobby.

The Administration's approach to cities and urban policy did not go uncriticized by Congress. In hearings in 1984 the Governor of Maryland, Harry Hughes, was critical of the Administration's citation of Baltimore as an example of its policy:

... the renaissance of downtown Baltimore began long before this national administration developed any urban

policy . . . Unfortunately the urban policy of this administration actually poses a threat to continued development in
Baltimore because of its proposed thrust against the use of
industrial development bonds. (Subcommittee on Investment, Jobs and Prices, 1984, p. 25.)

The Reagan Administration was suspicious of big cities and
their representatives, believing them to be the bastions of
Democratic support and too dependent upon federal grants.
The two objectives of reducing the federal government's role
and empowering the state governments combined to weaken
the power of local governments and their representatives in
Washington DC. It changed also the institutional incentives
which had structured local governments' behavior within the
federal system since the 1950s.

Federal Housing Policy

The Reagan Administration was determined to cut markedly
federal funding of public housing construction even though
historically this source was the most important for housing
(Caves, 1989). From 1981 to 1986 the federal government's
subsidies for low-income housing production were reduced
by approximately 60 per cent. The budget of HUD, itself,
was cut from $35.7 billion in fiscal 1980 to $14 billion in 1987.
The result of these reductions in funding was a dramatic fall
in the production of new public housing. In the 1970s the
federal government funded 200 000 units of public housing
annually. In 1986 the federal government funded 27 000
units (Dukakis, 1987).

President Reagan did not just want to reduce federal
funding of public housing. He wished also to implement a
new policy based on New Right free market principles. He
established a Commission on Housing whose report recommended the substitution of housing grants with vouchers.
This recommendation was accepted and in 1983 15 000
vouchers were distributed on a demonstration basis, a figure
expanded to 90 000 in fiscal year 1985. Needy tenants receive
a voucher for housing and they can either rent a unit at
exactly the voucher's value, below the voucher's value and

receive the excess, or above the voucher's value and add the difference. President Bush's HUD Secretary, Jack Kemp, is a supporter of housing voucher schemes and they have continued.

Housing vouchers do not tackle the fundamental problem facing local governments: the shortage of affordable rental units appropriate for persons with low incomes. The market system has been unable to generate sufficient housing of the appropriate sort in the appropriate quantity to dissipate the homeless problem. According to Swanstrom 'in large metropolitan areas, many households simply cannot find affordable housing at the bottom of the rental market' (Swanstrom, 1989, p. 81). The extent of the housing problem facing local governments is demonstrated by the number of homeless Americans. Since this is a politically charged issue there are varying estimations of their numbers. One study undertaken by HUD in 1984 estimated the number as 350 000 but this report was much criticized, and a subsequent survey by the National Coalition for the Homeless in November 1988 settled upon 3.5 million. The homeless population is composed of both unemployed persons together with their families and former mental patients or substance addicts released under the community care policy of deinstitutionalization. The size of the problem is recorded by housing waiting lists in large cities: in 1987 there were 44 000 on the list in Chicago, 60 000 in Miami, 200 000 in New York City, 23 000 in Philadelphia, and 13 000 in Washington DC. Local governments lack the resources to build appropriate and sufficient public housing.

Tax and Economic Policy

The final element of Reagan's New Federalism is the least direct. Both Reagan's macroeconomic policy and his major tax reform in 1986 had significant consequences for state and local governments and should be analyzed as part of the New Federalism.

The Reagan Administration's macroeconomic policy – strongly influenced by supply-side economics – dictated budgetary cuts in non-defense spending and reductions in taxes. The former cuts, introduced in the Omnibus Budget Reconciliation and Economic Recovery Tax Acts of 1981, fell most sharply upon social programs, and not only created a fiscal framework for the Reagan Administration's policies (including New Federalism) but had their primary effect at the state and local levels (Conlan, 1988). Since social programs were distributed through these sub-national governments their budgets were reduced and many of the persons losing benefits looked to them for alternative assistance.

The Tax Reform Act of 1985 introduced far-reaching changes for local governments. The Act drew a distinction between public and private use bonds, and restricted tax exemption to the former sort. Included within the new definition of public use were expenditures upon bridges and roads, but excluded were housing, development or convention centers. Tax exemption on a public bond was reduced to 10 per cent for private contractors. As a consequence of these changes the number of municipal bonds issued dropped significantly from $201 billion in 1985 to $100 billion in 1987 as investor demand declined. Local governments must compete with corporations in the financial markets without being able to offer extensive tax exemption benefits. Since issuing tax exempt bonds was the primary source of revenue for financing capital projects these modifications have been important.

The New Federalism and the New State Policy Role

The New Right principles influencing the Reagan Administration imply a reduced government role and increased reliance upon market forces. These tenets were extended to state and local governments who, in consequence, became much more entrepreneurial – one scholar has characterized them as 'entrepreneurial states' (Eisinger, 1988). Both state and local governments have designed and implemented a range of measures intended to foster economic development within their respective economies.

Local governments have been the more modest. They have been most active in forging public–private partnerships as the basis for economic regeneration particularly of derelict inner city areas. Economic development has been a vital component of city governments' economic strategy and almost all cities have established a department or agency responsible for this policy (Feagin and Gilderblomm, 1989; Stone and Sanders, 1987). In this activity the cities have been strongly encouraged by HUD whose 1986 pamphlet *The Entrepreneurial City* is self-explanatory.

It is the states which have the resources and power to make the greatest presence in economic development. In this activity they have been strongly encouraged by the National Governor's Association, which in 1987 published *Making America Work: Productive People, Productive Policies*. In the first part, 'Jobs, Growth, and Competitiveness', the NGA identified four priorities for national economic policy – a lower deficit, productivity rises, fair trade relations, and lowered inter-state inequalities – and urged the state governments to be more productive and efficient.

In pursuit of these aims the states have implemented public–private partnerships, encouraged investors to locate in their jurisdictions and assisted local businesses. A variety of state agencies have been formed to realize economic development, including the Texas Economic Development Commission, the Department of Economic and Community Development in Maryland, and the Innovative Finance Corporation and State Technology Council in New York (Piccigallo, 1988). Established in 1985 the Massachusetts Centers of Excellence Corporation fosters industry–education partnerships and promotes the use of new technologies. It is funded by the Massachusetts legislature. The same state's Bay State Skills Corporation is intended to improve the supply of skilled workers available for industry.

All states offer a range of supply-side incentives such as reduced taxes and regulatory relief for fixed periods to attract investment. However, the fact that all states offer such incentives reduces their effectiveness, and some states have developed demand-side strategies in which they concentrate upon building up their resources such as the concentration of highly-skilled workers and new-technology based industries (King, 1990). The success of Route 128 in Massachusetts and the Silicon Valley area in California are examples of this latter strategy. Such demand-side policies have been adopted in response to two key restraints limiting state economic policies: the internationalization of investment whereby U.S. corporations will happily invest in third world countries for cheaper labor costs than in parts of the U.S.; and the widespread availability of supply-side investment incentive packages which has produced considerable competition between states vying for a fixed amount of mobile capital.

State Welfare Policy

In October of the last year of Reagan's presidency the Congress passed, and Reagan signed, the Family Support Act: the first major reform of the welfare system since the Social Security Act of 1935 (King, 1991). One key element of the new Act was the introduction in federal policy of a work or training requirement for the receipt of welfare payments – a requirement to be established in state welfare programs from October 1990. This important modification of the welfare system built on measures implemented by the state governments in the preceding seven years. The reduction in federal aid and the linkage drawn explicitly by the NGA between welfare and economic prosperity resulted in the state governments designing and implementing work–welfare programs. The thrust of these programs – implemented in half the states by 1988 – was to provide persons receiving benefits with exposure to work or training skills which would facilitate their transition to full-time employment. The then New Jersey Governor Thomas Kean argued with others that the U.S.'s tightening labor market required those in receipt of benefits to acquire skills appropriate for joining the workforce. The design of programs which would meet this imperative was facilitated by the Omnibus Budget Reconciliation Act (OBRA) of 1981 which empowered the states to introduce on a demonstration basis discretionary work requirements in exchange for distributing benefits. Some of these experiments – such as those in Massachusetts (Employment Training Choices, ET), California (Greater Avenues to Independence, GAIN) and Georgia (Positive

Employment and Community Help Program, PEACH) – were judged successful and were used as models for the 1988 federal Act.

Using the opening provided by OBRA half the states had by 1984 formulated work–welfare programs combining one or more of the following options: work incentive programs; job search (eight-week period for AFDC applicants and recipients to search for employment); and the Community Work Experience Programs (CWEP), whereby AFDC recipients perform community work – commonly termed 'workfare' (Ellwood, 1988; King, 1991; Mead, 1985; Murray, 1984). Measures linking work–welfare schemes had been encouraged by laws before the 1980s such as the 1962 Community Work and Training Programs and the Work Incentive Program of 1967 (WIN). These programs were specifically concerned with fostering skills amongst those receiving relief. The 1981 OBRA clause, however, was intended by the Reagan Administration to be a punitive measure to discourage seeking of welfare – hence its characterization as 'workfare' by Administration critics.

By integrating work and welfare policy the work–welfare option initiated in 1981 by OBRA marked a significant shift in federal welfare policy, one consolidated in the Family Support Act of 1988. Not all the states responded to the 1981 option, and those that did, responded in different ways. Oklahoma and South Dakota founded state-wide workfare programs, but other states, for example Mississippi, considered such schemes unnecessary given their low AFDC benefit levels. Work–welfare programs were established in selective counties only in California, Ohio, New York, and Washington states (Nathan and Doolittle, 1987). That a general trend to establish work–welfare schemes existed was clear by 1986: 'the historic lack of priority and visibility on work–welfare issues has now clearly changed' (Nightingale and Burbridge, 1987, p. 63).

The NGA's views on welfare reform on the basis of these state experiments and their assessment of the U.S.'s economic needs were outlined by an executive committee chaired by Bill Clinton of Arkansas. The committee's report, 'Job-Oriented Welfare Reform', was published in February 1987, and subsequently embraced by the White House and leading congressional reformers, notably Senator Daniel Moynihan. The Governors' proposals emphasized the importance of linking work opportunities to welfare programs:

> the Governors' aim in proposing a welfare reform plan is to turn what is now primarily a payments system with a minor work component into a system that is first and foremost a jobs system, backed up by an income assistance component ... The Governors recommend that all employable welfare recipients must participate in an education, job training, or placement program and accept a suitable job when it is offered. (NGA, 1987a, pp. 1–2.)

The Governors wished to end welfare dependency by providing recipients with work skills appropriate to the current labor market. These proposals were influential in the debates preceding the Family Support Act of 1988.

Conclusion

The Empowered States and Persistent Center

The first general thesis is that the Reagan Administration's New Federalism has produced one fundamental longterm modification to the federal system. His policy of reducing federal grants-in-aid and relaxing federal regulations have provided an opportunity for the state governments to assume a revitalized role within the federal system, an opportunity exploited by the professionalized state legislatures and NGA. At the same time the power of local governments in the federal system has been weakened by the termination of direct federal aid and the increased use of categorical grants.

This revised state role must be qualified in at least two ways. First, the changes achieved in the grants system have not been extended to judicial rulings. The Supreme Court retains its considerable capacity to issue judgements which apply nationally. Second, the federal government has maintained its national power to regulate, and indeed, the establishment of OIRA has strengthened not weakened the institutional capacity of the presidency. As two commentators observe, the Reagan Administration's 'commitment to centralize review processes and to clamp down on the expansion of regulatory authority far surpasses that of previous administration's' (Harris and Milkis, 1989, p. 103). Paradoxically, the Administration committed to removing the federal government's presence in the regulatory system has in some ways increased its power.

The outcome of these trends – reduced grants but national judicial rulings and regulatory power – is qualified co-operativism. Certainly, the perceived policy role of the states, the severing of the direct federal–local grant system and loosening of some federal regulations has enabled the states to achieve a new force within the federal system. The budget deficit legacy of the Reagan Administration has accentuated these trends by limiting federal policy initiatives and obliging the states to devise and implement their own programs. But the modern federal system is a vast interlocking set of relations between tiers of government which is impossible to disband in one eight-year Administration.

Institutional Incentives and the New Federalism

These developments have implications for the institutional incentives structuring state and local government participation in the federal system. First, state governments now receive a substantial portion of federal funds as block not categorical grants. This change reduces the need for state governments to lobby Washington DC for assistance for specific programs, and the budget deficit precludes any significant increases in aid. What the state governments do have to lobby about are federal regulations.

Second, local governments must now focus upon their state governments since it is these who are responsible for allocating federal block grants. This development has reduced significantly the need to maintain an extensive presence in Washington DC. The lobbying system build up by local governments during the 1970s to tap funds such as those provided in general revenue sharing and UDAG grants is now largely redundant.

Finally, there are implications for theories of federalism. First, theorists must not be excessively influenced by trends in federal grants-in-aid since these contract as well as expand. This process of expansion and contraction must be integrated into analyses of the interests of different tiers of government within the federal system as these interests will change over time. Secondly, theorists must appreciate that the division of policy responsibilities by level of government is now more flexible than in earlier periods. The reduced federal role and the strengthened state policy-making institutions means that the scope of initiatives at these levels has changed. For instance, in the absence of expanding federal policy, state governments may decide to pursue redistributive measures as well as developmental policies. Such modifications to the type of policy pursued by different tiers of government will influence the politics of federalism and future federal relations.

9

Economic Policy

JOSEPH HOGAN

The origins of postwar economic policy and the institutional structures for making economic policy in the United States can be traced back to President Franklin Delano Roosevelt's efforts to revive the American economy during the 'Great Depression'. The collapse of the economy in the late 1920s and its devastating impact upon society was a condition that demanded action, but there were no structures or leaders in place for meeting this demand before Roosevelt took office as President in 1933. In the course of his first Administration he effected a series of dramatic reforms in the management of the economy. The Securities and Exchange Commission was established to regulate the securities market, the Federal Deposit Insurance Corporation was set up to guarantee bank deposits, unemployment compensation was enacted, minimum wage laws were passed, numerous public works programs were established to provide temporary relief for many unemployed people, and social security transfer payments were provided for the first time to the elderly. A vast salvaging operation was thereby begun to reform the management of the economy in order to promote economic recovery.

Roosevelt's reforms were not part of any planned approach to get the economy moving again, but instead simply represented a willingness to experiment with new kinds of social and economic policies and structures in order to rescue American capitalism. While these prewar policies might have been conceived as temporary, however, the demands created by global armed conflict required further and more extensive management of the economy by the federal government. The result of these unplanned developments from the 'Great Depression' through the Second World War was the creation of a substantial and permanent network of federal governmental institutions for managing the economy, and the evolution of a set of broad and quite widely accepted economic policy objectives that supported extensive and sustained macroeconomic management.

These developments comprise the Roosevelt legacy. At the center of this legacy was the idea that government should be concerned with the promotion of aggregate demand within a policy framework that emphasized the need for an activist fiscal policy to offset the instability of private spending. An activist fiscal policy was effected by using the federal government's budget – its taxing, spending, and borrowing powers – to promote economic growth and employment. The Roosevelt legacy also included governmental regulation of selected sectors of the economy. The form of regulation adopted was certainly not punitive in nature as it involved protecting sectors, such as agriculture, from free competition in order to plan demand and stabilize the economy. These innovations, taken together, marked the demise of the hegemony of private capitalism over the economy in the United States (Stein, 1985). The policies put in place by President Roosevelt proved surprisingly durable, lasting until the climate of ideas changed in the 1970s and the 1980s in favor first of monetarism, second to the inactivism of the rational expectations school, and third to supply-side economics. The institutional legacy proved to be even more durable.

The Institutional Structure of Economic Policy-making

The shape and nature of economic policy-making is heavily influenced by three institutional factors. First, the federal nature of the United States divides power between the national government in Washington DC and the state governments. This division has encouraged conflict between the different levels of government and has made it difficult for federal law-makers to impart cohesion to any area of public policy, Second, the 'separation of powers' divides power between the three branches of the federal government. This clearly promotes rivalry between the branches, particularly between Congress and the president, and there is very little to oblige them to act in harmony. Third, unlike the United Kingdom and most other Western countries, the United States has a Central Bank – the Federal Reserve Bank – which possesses real and independent powers, and is prepared to exercise them in conflict with federal policy-makers.

As a result of these three factors, the power to make economic policy is, at least in principle, much dispersed between powerful rivals and thus there is much scope and, given the real desire of each institution to protect its constitutional grants of power, incentive for conflict. This is especially true for fiscal policy-making where there are a series of separate presidential and congressional procedures that are required to interact sequentially to agree a federal budget, a federal tax regime, and other policies for regulating the economy. In practice, the opportunity for conflict between the executive and legislative branches over such important policy issues is great. Divided government thus inhibits efficient and cohesive policy-making.

President Roosevelt responded to this problem by expanding the capacity of the presidency to manage the economy, mainly by increasing its staff and, in 1939, establishing the Executive Office of the President (EOP), within which there were organized a number of specialist economic units. The most important development involved transferring the Bureau of Budget from the Treasury to the EOP. The Bureau, now called the Office of Management and Budget (OMB), prepares the president's budget and is his main instrument for imposing his fiscal policies upon the many departments and agencies that comprise the executive branch. The Treasury Department under Roosevelt took responsibility for managing the tax system, for leading on foreign economic policy, for conducting relations with the International Monetary Fund, and – through the issuing of Treasury Bills – is also responsible for managing the government's debt. A third advisory body to the president on economic affairs, also located within the EOP, is the Council of Economic Advisers (CEA), which was created by the Employment Act of 1946. The CEA analyzes the consequences of economic policy proposals and helps initiate policies desired by the president. In particular, it takes the lead in determining the economic assumptions upon which the president's budgetary and economic goals are built (Berman, 1979; Clifford, 1965; Norton, 1977).

The OMB, the CEA, and the Treasury are the president's economic 'troika'. In the past the 'troika' used to meet regularly to formulate and adjust the president's economic policies. In recent years, however, the OMB has come to play a much more dominant role, and the 'troika' has met less often. Once the president's fiscal proposals are folded into his annual budget proposals and submitted to Congress, the first stage of federal policy-making is completed. The second stage involves congressional examination of the president's budget proposals. This process is both very complicated and time-consuming. It involves parceling out various components of the president's budget for consideration by just about every committee in Congress, and it has to occur, in near duplicate form, in both the House of Representatives and the Senate.

This complex structure for fiscal policy-making creates multiple opportunities for Congress both to resist and to revise, often radically, the president's proposals. Because each chamber possesses substantive and independent law-making powers, there is ample scope for conflict not only between the president and Congress, but also between both chambers of Congress over fiscal policy-making. The absence of strong, coherent parties in Congress only adds to the confusion. As a result, fiscal policy-making in the United States has great potential for conflict, is at best time-consuming, and at worst non-existent (Schick, 1983).

Determining and managing the monetary component of federal economic policy is also a complicated process because it requires the president, his advisors, and Congress to co-ordinate monetary objectives with a central bank which possesses genuine and independent powers. The Federal

Reserve Bank is organized into twelve districts and there are two main decision-making forums. The first, the Federal Reserve Board, is composed of seven members appointed by the president for fourteen year terms (the person designated Chairman holds office for four years at a time on appointment by the president and with the consent of the Senate). The Board exercises exclusive jurisdiction over many factors concerning bank regulation and also sets the discount rate. The second, the Federal Open Market Committee (FOMC) consists of the seven board members and five of the presidents of the district banks. The FOMC is the most important forum for monetary policy decisions. It makes decisions about how to try to influence interest rates, the money supply, and ultimately, inflation and economic growth. At the same time, like all central banks, the Federal Reserve can act as a lender of last resort to forestall national liquidity crises and financial panics (Bach, 1971; Woolley, 1984).

The degree of independence of central banks is always a relative matter, but there is not much doubt that the 'Fed' lies at the freer end of the spectrum. Its decisions do not have to be ratified by the president. Appointments once made cannot be undone. Most importantly, it has proved willing and able in practice to back its own judgement against the wishes of the president when it has felt this to be necessary.

The fragmentation of economic power and the legitimation of conflict in economic affairs in the U.S. creates the potential for an exceptionally confused and anarchic form of policy. In practice the degree of cohesion or confusion has changed over time and is somewhat different with respect to micro policy, fiscal policy and monetary policy.

Micro policy, being by its nature more decentralized and often having a legislative component, has been most subject to the bargaining process of Congress. It is also variable on a state by state basis and even locality by locality. As a result, it can be argued that 'there is no federal industrial or regional strategy worth the name, and training and manpower policies are more ameliorative *ad hoc* measures than true labor market strategies' (McKay, 1985, p. 283). This does not mean that the U.S. has no micro policy. There are over one hundred different independent establishments, government corporations, boards and commissions each writing regulations designed to constrain the actions of private and public organizations. Equally, it does not mean that there have been no changes in the thrust of micro policy: in the 1970s and 1980s, for example, there has been the growth of consumer and environmental concerns which U.S. lobbyists have used with skill, but neither this network nor the policies adopted have been strongly influenced by a central leadership.

There is therefore nothing in the U.S. directly comparable with the growth of interest in indicative planning from the center such as occurred in France and Britain in the 1960s nor any attempt to increase co-ordination either nationally or locally that is comparable to the role played by MITI in Japan. In fact the one consistent theme of U.S. micro policy has been the extent to which compared to other countries, planning and co-ordination *between firms* has not been on the agenda – although some authors, writing when ideas of indicative planning were at their height, suggest that the U.S. compensated for this by having large firms and extensive planning *within* them (Galbraith, 1967; Shonfield, 1965). This is not to conclude that there are no attempts to adopt a central approach to micro policy, the main point is to recognize that these attempts fail. Proposals made by Democratic congressmen from the 'smokestack' areas in the northern and eastern United States during the recession of 1981–3 to promote industrial policies to counteract economic contraction were readily rebuffed by Republican congressmen and the Reagan Administration as foolishly trying to use government to pick winners in the marketplace. The U.S. approach to price and wage policies exhibits the same point. Such policies were used rather infrequently and, even when they were, they took the form primarily of either direct legislative controls or of confrontations with one or two large firms. There is nothing comparable to European corporatism, because corporatism was neither an option desired in the U.S., nor, it could be argued, one readily available. The experience of the only serious attempt made recently at corporatist policy-making – Jimmy Carter's Accord with the AFL–CIO indicates that corporatism is floated only when presidents face a crisis.

Confusion and crisis over fiscal policy, in contrast, was significantly muted during the first two decades of the postwar era as both the executive and legislative branches shared something close to a consensus on the goals and instruments of economic policy. As a result, it was only when the U.S. economy was heavily disturbed, partly by its own fiscal actions and partly by external shocks, that the real difficulties in running a 'rational' fiscal policy in the U.S. came to the fore. Such difficulties would thrust the burden of economic stabilization onto monetary policy. Here the problem would prove to be less one of fragmentation, and more the difficulty of achieving multiple objectives via a single instrument.

Postwar Economic Policy

Avoiding another economic collapse comparable to the 1930s was – and, indeed, still is – the prime objective of postwar economic policy. For much of the period this objective was pursued by making periodic adjustments to control aggregate demand. The main policy debate concerned the relative potency of monetary and fiscal policy instruments. There was a heavy emphasis on leading with fiscal policy in the late 1940s, with a shift to an intermediate view that incorporated both monetary and fiscal policy in the late 1950s and early 1960s to a greater tendency after 1968 to doubt the potency of fiscal policy and assign a strong causal role for monetary changes as initiating fluctuations in aggregate demand growth. During the 1970s the case for the monetarists weakened because supply shocks and the resulting inflation in prices undermined support for their claim that money should grow at a constant rate, and gave greater credence to using changes in taxes and subsidies to counteract the effect of supply shocks on inflation. The Reagan Administration eschewed fiscal manipulation and led with the so-called 'supply-side' cuts in personal and business taxes to promote economic growth.

The first two decades of the postwar era revealed a significant continuity in the choice of economic policy objectives and instruments. There were partisan tilts over this period, with Republican administrations favoring monetary and tax instruments while Democratic administrations relied more on fiscal instruments. But these differences are overshadowed by what is accurately regarded as a postwar consensus on economic policy. This consensus ran, however, into extremely rough waters in the mid-1960s.

The accession of Lyndon B. Johnson to the presidency marked the zenith of the activist view of fiscal policy, with increased public expenditures and frequent changes in income tax rates as the central policy tools for managing the economy. Monetary policy, at least at first, was relegated to maintaining a low and stable level of long-term interest rates. The problem was that Lyndon Johnson wanted to do everything almost at once. The tax cuts of 1964 were therefore followed virtually immediately by the 'Great Society' initiative with federal programs expanded to cover the poor, the elderly, the cities, the rural areas and, in order to build support for another round of fiscal activism, the middle class as well. At the same time he extended and accelerated U.S. involvement in Vietnam. More butter *and* more guns were Johnson's requirements.

While the tax cuts of 1964 were seen as a triumph for compensatory finance, the compensation in the opposite direction, as the economy started to overheat in 1966, proved to be a fresh and more difficult battle. Tax cuts were one thing, tax increases another. Thus, although inflation accelerated fairly continuously after 1965 and although, as early as 1966, the Joint Economic Committee recommended a tax surcharge, Johnson did not send a legislative proposal to Congress until August 1967. Even then, the battle between President and Congress was not resolved until well into 1968 when a ten per cent tax surcharge was combined with a mandatory reduction in federal expenditures.

As the economy deteriorated, the consensus about the role of fiscal policy began to fall apart. Amongst economists the issue at first was whether fiscal policy was as important as some of the Keynesians supposed – was not monetary policy equally powerful, or more powerful? Later it became the much larger question of whether demand management policy did anything at all in the long run to real output. More importantly, the U.S. found itself facing simultaneously both unemployment and inflation, which led to the demise of the postwar consensus on the management of the economy. It was this persistent problem of stagflation which bedevilled the presidencies of Nixon, Ford, and Carter, and which led eventually to the supply-side economics of Reagan.

President Nixon inherited in 1969 a stubbornly inflationary economy. During the first two years of his presidency he pursued the traditional, essentially conservative approach adopted by past Republican presidents to tackling inflation. This involved tightening tax and spending policies to accumulate a small budget surplus. In addition, the Nixon Administration restrained the supply of money. The Administration recognized that tackling inflation meant accepting some increase in unemployment, but believed that by pursuing fiscal policies that sought moderate disinflation they could restrain the rise of unemployment. President Nixon was, unsurprisingly, criticized strongly by congressional Democrats for pursuing disinflation at the expense of a rise in unemployment. This criticism mounted during the summer of 1970, when the Administration's economic policy was charged with the responsibility for creating a recession. Faced with the onset of recession Nixon changed course.

On 15 August 1971 President Nixon announced his 'New Economic Policy'. The centerpiece consisted of a 90-day wage and price freeze, along with the creation of a Pay Board and Price Commission to lead the drive against inflation. At the same time, the Administration adopted a stimulative fiscal policy, which involved increasing public expenditure in the second half of the year and reducing taxes. The Federal Reserve Board also supported this switch to a stimulative fiscal policy by expanding the money supply. The final component of Richard Nixon's new economic initiative involved abandoning the policy of converting dollars into gold on demand at a price of one ounce of gold for $35, mainly because the amount of foreign-held dollars outstanding had become far larger than the value of the U.S. gold stock at that price. The federal government thus adopted a free, floating exchange rate instead of a fixed one for the dollar. The package achieved good initial results. In the early part of 1972, real output rose strongly, unemployment began to fall, and inflation did move down. In the longer term, the package was much less successful. The wage and price controls did not usher in a period of disinflation. Instead the controls appeared to set a floor rather than a ceiling on wages and prices, which therefore encouraged inflation. The advent of the two 'supply shocks' in 1973 in the form of an explosion in world food prices due to crop failures and the rise in petroleum prices because of the OPEC cartel were special and unforeseen factors that further complicated the situation. The Administration soon found that it was boxed into controls: their mere existence seemed to encourage the public to anticipate that there would be a rise in inflation once controls were abandoned. To deal with this expectation the Administration had extended the controls several times beyond the initial 90-day period expiring on 30 April 1974. Sustained and chronic inflation and a sharp reduction in consumer spending pushed the economy into recession again in late 1973.

The problems faced by the Ford and Carter Administrations, and the policies they used, were essentially a continuation of those of Nixon – only more so. Unemployment and inflation were both high at the same time, and policy oscillated between giving priority to the cure of one and then the other. Ford, faced with high inflation in 1974, resolved to pursue fiscal and monetary restraint, but with the knock-on effect of the oil price rise and the world recession still coming through, he found himself, at first, with both more inflation and more unemployment. However, by 1977, the persistently high level of unemployment was associated with a decline in inflation and President Carter announced in early 1977 that his prime economic objective was fighting unemployment rather than inflation. He stated his intention was to reduce unemployment from 7.9 per cent in January 1977 to a 'full-employment' target of 4.9 per cent. To do so he proposed a major increase in fiscal expenditures to stimulate the economy. Carter also proposed a package of tax cuts and sought to increase the money supply. This switch to a stimulative fiscal and monetary regime did produce a significant recovery, but it was also followed by further inflationary pressures. In particular, the second OPEC oil supply shock between 1978 and 1979 escalated inflation to record levels. As measured by the consumer price index, inflation reached 13.3 per cent from December 1978 to December 1979. The unemployment rate also moved upwards at the same time.

This escalation of the 'misery index' in 1979 signalled the demise of liberal activism in Democratic economic policy, and led to a major change of course as the Carter Administration made fighting inflation – first by monetary means – its prime economic objective. In this respect, the Democratic Administration bought Republican policies, effecting a new postwar policy consensus that was again fashioned by an economic crisis. Paul Volcker, the chairman of the Federal Reserve Board, with the support of the Carter Administration, took the lead in crafting and implementing the war on inflation. On 6 October 1979 he announced, on behalf of the Federal Reserve, a change in procedures in which more attention would be paid to controlling bank reserves and less to controlling interest rates. The move signalled a sterner determination to check inflation. The money supply had been rising rapidly and had clearly fuelled inflation. The foreign exchange value of the dollar had also fallen to a low level, which had upset foreign central bankers, and led them to emphasize the need to fight inflation. Volcker's move was thus widely supported. The effect was immediate. U.S. Treasury Bill rates rose sharply and, following this 'credit crunch', the economy slowed down in early 1980. Carter did not, however, rely solely on monetary policy in the fight against inflation. In his January 1980 *Economic Report* he proposed a four-point economic program for tackling inflation. The fiscal component sought to reduce the federal budget deficit by restraining the growth in federal expenditures. The budget deficit, estimated at $40 billion in fiscal 1980, was set to become a small surplus by fiscal 1982 (Stein, 1985).

The attempts made by both Gerald Ford and Jimmy Carter to use restrictive fiscal policies in order to tackle inflation were, however, at odds with both the predominant policy orientation and the economic policy-making structures in Congress. Congressional liberals in the Kennedy–Johnson era had reformed congressional policy-making to make the legislature both more open and more accommodating to pressures for increased federal spending. There was greater participation in the legislative process by public pressure groups, who used their access to expand existing spending programs and to advocate new ones. At the same time congressmen realized that satisfied claimants were likely to re-elect their representatives and consequently made many spending programs, particularly those with the most recipients, more secure through the passage of legislation that mandated spending on federal welfare and other benefit programs irrespective of how the economy was performing. Distributive budgeting boomed at the very time when the economy no longer yielded a 'growth dividend' to finance enlarged federal expenditures. In the first half of the 1970s the cost of social insurance and retirement programs doubled in real terms. Increased spending on electorally popular domestic policies had been financed at the expense of progressive reductions in defense spending and by growth in the federal deficit. Budget deficits averaged about 3 per cent of GNP during the second half of the 1970s, which was twice the percentage of the previous decade.

As the 1970s drew to a close it was thus evident that both ends of Pennsylvania Avenue were seriously divided over the objectives and instruments of economic policy. Successive presidents had made fighting inflation their prime economic objective, and had pursued this policy by seeking fiscal and monetary restraint. Achieving monetary restraint was the more practical objective since it involved only obtaining the support of the Federal Reserve, which in fact often pursued monetary restraint in advance and independent of the presidency. By comparison, Congress had pursued accommodative spending strategies, rejecting presidential requests for spending constraint. The contradictory mix of periodic monetary restraint and loose fiscal policies was undesirable. In order to restrict spending as part of any attack on the unusually high rates of inflation in the late 1970s, it was clear that a president had also to solve the dilemma of how to wrest political control of the institutions of federal budgeting from Congress (Fisher, 1975; Mann and Ornstein, 1981).

When President Reagan took office in the beginning of 1981 unemployment stood at more than 7 per cent, consumer prices had risen by 24 per cent over the previous two years, interest rates were high and volatile, and productivity rates were lagging well behind America's competitors. The Reagan Administration came to office committed to adopting 'supply-side' policies for tackling simultaneously all these economic problems – or so they claimed. Supply-side economics asserts that the weight of government expenditures and the resulting tax burden acts as a drag on economic growth. Its supporters claim that by lowering government expenditures and taxes, and by reducing regulation of the economy, energies in the marketplace will be unleashed to bring about a surge in private economic activity.

Reagan's initial economic policy took the form of a four-point program. The first three parts of this program – tax cuts, reduced growth in federal spending, and regulatory relief – were intended to provide greater incentives for individuals, corporations and businesses to work, save, and invest. The fourth, slower growth in the money supply, was designed to lower inflation. The President's advisers soon encountered difficulties with the fiscal component of this economic plan. David Stockman, the Director of the OMB, found that the plan to cut taxes deeply and to increase sharply the Pentagon's budget would widen the gap between revenue and expenditure, and thus lead to even greater budget deficits. At Stockman's request, the President agreed at the last minute in the process of executive budgeting to incorporate a series of further reductions in federal spending. In the event, Stockman managed to cut spending by $49 billion over fiscal 1981–2. But even cuts of this unprecedented magnitude were insufficient to produce the balanced budget Reagan had promised for 1984. The 'solution' was found in the form of the 'magic asterisk' ploy under which Reagan's first budget incorporated 'unidentified spending reductions' amounting to $74 billion over the 1983–4 fiscal years (Greenstein, 1983; Stockman, 1986).

What actually happened to the economy was a further slow

down, and then a fall in output beginning in the second half of 1981 and continuing through 1982. Thereafter there was a dramatic recovery with the economy growing by 3.6 per cent and 6.8 per cent in 1983 and 1984 respectively, followed by a further expansion at nearly 3 per cent per year in the subsequent three years. At the same time inflation slowed sharply from 1981 to 1983 and then stayed at a low level thereafter. These developments, together with the growth of employment and a great expansion in the number of new small firms, were hailed by the Reagan Administration as evidence of the success of its supply-side policies. Whether this is the whole truth is highly doubtful. There are three main counter arguments.

First, Reagan did not balance the budget by 1984. On the contrary, a combination of deep tax cuts, sharply increased defense spending, and 'hoped for' but unattainable expenditure reductions, produced a rapidly rising deficit. Admittedly, the Reagan Administration did achieve reductions in domestic expenditures planned for 1982–4, but these amounted to only $130 billion against the $200 billion proposed. Moreover, at the same time, Congress passed much larger tax cuts: for the period 1981–7 the President had requested cuts of about $300 billion, whereas the actual cuts were approximately $1 trillion.

Secondly, conventional theory explains what happened perfectly well. The 'Fed' was able and willing to implement the monetary part of the package and so interest rates were pushed to record levels in 1981. Then, following a crisis of Mexican debt in mid-1982, monetary policy was substantially relaxed. A similar argument can be made for fiscal policy. To see this the deficit must be adjusted for three factors: (a) declines in output and employment which raise the deficit even though tax rates are unchanged; (b) the effects of inflation; and (c) interest rate changes which alter the real value of the stock of government debt outstanding. Eisner (1986) shows that adjusted for these effects fiscal policy was tight in 1981 and then had the biggest expansion on record. In short, with both monetary and fiscal policy indicating recession and then recovery it is hardly surprising that this occurred.

Thirdly, falling commodity prices – especially for oil – from 1981 to 1985 allowed all countries to improve their inflation performance over this period. Added to this, the high interest dollar rates in the U.S. began a long speculative upsurge in the dollar, with the result that its rate against the average of all other countries rose by one third from 1980 to 1985. This not only lowered import prices, but also contributed to a huge surge in imports that put U.S. industry under much greater competitive pressure.

In other words, there is no need to resort to supply-side explanations to account for either the output or the inflationary experience of the U.S. in this period. Moreover, if a supply-side change had occurred in this period it ought to have shown itself in improved productivity, higher savings, and improved capital formation. Admittedly, there was some improvement in productivity compared with the years 1973–9. However, productivity still remained below the average for the years before 1973–79, while investment as a percentage of GNP was slightly lower and personal savings fell sharply as a share of disposable income. Moreover, during the years when supply-side benefits are supposed to be evident, the U.S. continued to perform poorly in international comparisons of investment and savings ratios and in the growth of productivity.

Less controversially, there is little doubt that the rapid rise in the deficit and the associated rise in the dollar produced a seriously unbalanced economy. The budget deficit grew from 2.6 per cent of GNP in fiscal 1980 to 4.1 per cent in fiscal 1981 and then to 6.8 per cent in fiscal 1983. The total budget deficit grew from $908 billion in 1980 to just over $2.8 trillion at the end of the Reagan Administration. The combination of demand for credit and a tight monetary regime during the trough of the recession of 1981–3 led to high interest rates. This increased foreign demand for the dollar, which appreciated in face value. Dollar appreciation made U.S. goods more expensive in foreign markets. The high dollar also made foreign imports more cheap and hence more attractive to domestic consumers. The effect was to convert the U.S. from its longstanding position as the world's largest creditor nation in 1982 into the largest debtor nation by 1986. By 1985, the

U.S. had a budget deficit and a balance of payments deficits, each of which was more than 3 per cent of GDP.

The effects of the twin deficits, together with more gradual changes about the role of the U.S. in the world economy, set in train a significant reappraisal of U.S. economic policy. The most obvious outward sign of change was the agreement amongst central bankers to bring down the dollar (the Plaza Accord of 1985), but this was followed later in 1985, by the Baker plan for third world debt, and then in 1986 by Reagan's call for international 'policy co-ordination'. In other words, exchange rates were no longer to be left to the market, and demand management, now at the international level, was firmly back on the economic policy agenda in the United States.

Conclusion

Postwar economic policy in the United States did succeed in preventing another economic contraction on the scale of the Great Depression. Throughout the postwar era, economic activity has been far more stable than in previous periods of modern U.S. history. This much greater level of economic stability must be attributed in significant part to the establishment of transfer payments in the form of unemployment funds and other benefits that work as automatic stabilizers when the economy experiences rough times. Marginal tax rate changes, federal deposit insurance on bank deposits and financial regulation have further helped to stabilize the U.S. economy. The willingness of the Federal Reserve Board to take actions to promote economic growth has also helped.

The postwar consensus on economic policy objectives and macroeconomic instruments contributed greatly to this success. But when the economy in the mid-1960s began to experience persistent problems, the postwar consensus gradually eroded. This consensus had muted the great scope for conflict that is inherent in the constitutional structure of divided government. These conflicts became increasingly evident after Johnson's pursuit of guns and butter had fuelled inflation. This was especially the case in fiscal policy.

Congress over the period 1965–74 increased greatly expenditures on domestic spending, then passed legislation to convert many of these programs into mandatory entitlements,
and next utilized new procedures for budgeting to both
increase its influence over fiscal policy and protect these
spending programs from the retrenchment policies of the
Ford, Carter, and Reagan Administrations. Parallel conflicts
emerged during the late 1960s and for most of the 1970s
between the executive branch, the legislature, and the Federal Reserve Board over monetary policy. These conflicts
regularly cast Congress and the president in favor of quickly
expanding the money supply to deal with troughs in the
business cycle while the Federal Reserve favored a slower
more cautious approach.

The Bush Administration has thus encountered several
enduring forces in its continuing efforts to manage the
economy (see also Chapter 12). First, the machinery for
making economic policy has continued to be fragmented.
The Bush Administration has encountered strong opposition
from the Democratic-controlled Congress to any attempt to
tackle the twin deficits by making major policy changes that
will hurt Democratic voters. The GRH legislation, enacted in
1985, and twice amended since then, in 1989 provided, in the
absence of voluntary agreements between the White House
and Capitol Hill, the main means for lowering the deficit. Its
targets, however, were not reached in Fiscal 1990. But by
stretching out the GRH schedule for reducing the budget
deficit and also by reducing the amount of cuts to be made in
one year, the Bush Administration and Congress were able to
point to sustained reductions in the budget deficit without
having to engage in the bloody, but not particularly profit-
able, budget battles that were such a persistent feature of the
1980s.

Putting U.S. fiscal policy on automatic GRH pilot has
increased reliance upon interest rate adjustments in managing the U.S. economy. Indeed, the Bush Administration has
felt it has only a single policy instrument with which to
manage the economy, and that instrument is mainly under
the control of the Federal Reserve Board. This has made
impossible demands on interest rates to simultaneously con-

trol domestic demand, to achieve equilibrium on the balance of payments, and to avoid a debt crisis. The reliance on one policy instrument has required the Bush Administration and Alan Greenspan to act closely together. There have been strains in this relationship over the pace and level of interest rate adjustments. The failure in 1989 of the Bush Administration and Congress to agree measures to lower the deficit significantly meant that the pressure to seek meaningful reductions in 1990 was more intense. A softening economy led voters to blame the Bush Administration for failing to provide effective budgetary leadership. This perception tilted budgetary leadership towards the Democratic-controlled Congress. The opportunity was quickly taken to enforce tax increases on a President who had proclaimed 'No new taxes' in the 1988 campaign and sharp reductions in defense spending. President Bush achieved significant reductions in domestic spending. Nonetheless, the Bush Administration was clearly dominated by Congress in forming the federal budget in 1990.

The Bush Administration has also faced significant economic constraints externally. The concern about the balance of payments deficits is the most obvious example. Dealing with Japan has become a priority. Much of the current account deficit is the product of Japan's simultaneous penetration of the U.S. market and protection of its domestic market from U.S. penetration. The Bush Administration must persuade the Japanese that it is in their own interest to open their market to American competition. At the same time the Bush Administration will need to make it clear that U.S. industries have to improve their productivity to compete effectively with the Japanese and other foreign competitors.

Clearly, the Bush Administration has already faced great demands in managing the economy. This is the case because its internal policy-making powers are limited, and counter-balanced by the independent policy powers and prerogatives of Congress and the Federal Reserve Board. In addition, the United States needs to make important trade and other economic adjustments with foreign powers whose national interests conflict with those of the United States. The Bush Administration can make valuable forward movements if it seeks incremental and conjoint rather than major policy changes. However, cyclical economic adjustments can always undermine any administration's efforts to manage the economy, and this is especially the case now that the U.S. economy is more interdependent with – and thus vulnerable to – changing world credit and trade flows.

10

Social Welfare Policy

ROBERT X. BROWNING

U.S. social welfare policy is fragmented and multifaceted. These characteristics date back to the origins of the Social Security Act (SSA) of 1935 and have endured through many periods of reform. The lack of a universal or comprehensive social policy is a distinguishing feature of American politics which has been reinforced through federalism and through the underlying work ethic of the U.S. economic system. During the eight years of the Reagan Administration efforts to dismantle, to restructure or to reform existing social programs were only partially successful. One might cynically observe that another president has come and gone, but the basic structure of U.S. social programs remains largely intact (Palmer and Sawhill, 1982; 1984).

U.S. social policy has long been characterized by a two-tiered approach. This division predates the SSA, but the development of that act has certainly reinforced the division. On the one hand, there are social insurance programs; on the other hand, there are public assistance programs. The former, which includes social security, are viewed as earned benefits. The latter are collectively known as welfare and are often popularly derided as 'government giveaways'.

The U.S. social welfare tradition is also a mix of federal, state and private programs (Patterson, 1981; Steiner, 1971). The state has traditionally been viewed as a protector of last resort. Before 1935, virtually all social programs were state programs, with the exception of Veterans' programs. With the enactment of the SSA, certain groups were entitled by virtue of their employment to new federal social programs.

The states, however, were left the responsibility for programs for the poor who did not fit the federal entitled categories. The states, in turn, often looked to private charities, churches, and personal initiative as the first party responsible for providing for the public welfare. Benefits thus varied greatly across states.

The Reagan Administration came into office with a conservative philosophy regarding social programs. From his experience as Governor of the largest state, Reagan campaigned against excessive government spending and often related anecdotes about welfare abuses. Political history, however, had propelled social security to a protected status. Thus, Reagan's campaign further broadened the public's perception that social security was better and different from the welfare programs which went to those who could and should be working.

Efforts at comprehensive reform are rarely successful. Thus, the effects of reform are always seen at the margins. Indeed, the Reagan Administration was always saying that they succeeded in slowing the rate of growth, not in reducing the level of spending. After eight years in office, the effects of the Reagan agenda could be seen. The legacy for the next administration was not so clear. With social security off limits, with a campaign pledge of no new taxes, and with a new president who promised a 'kinder, gentler budget', the agenda for social policy was at the same time constrained and in transition.

The Nature of Social Programs

Social welfare programs in the United States are a mix of federal and state programs of cash and in-kind benefits. Social security constitutes the largest federal program (Derthick, 1979; Witte, 1963). Its enactment was later followed by other titles of the SSA. Medicare provided health insurance for the elderly and Medicaid provided health insurance for the indigent. Insurance programs entitle individuals to benefits based upon earnings or age. When first enacted, only workers were entitled, and benefits varied with lifetime earnings. Patterned after European social insurance, social security was a forced savings designed to protect individuals against loss of earnings due to circumstances beyond their control (Rimlinger, 1971).

Over time, provisions were added to insure workers against disabilities. Benefits were extended to widows and children. Subsequently all elderly people were entitled. Other insurance provisions added to the SSA were disability insurance and health insurance. Initially, workers could not earn any other income while drawing social security. Over time, this provision has been relaxed and the limits raised. Persons over age 70 have no limit on the amount of income they can earn without a reduction in their social security benefits.

While social security expanded, the public assistance programs languished. These were primarily state programs. Federal involvement was limited to matching provisions. Initially, the expectation was that public assistance programs would wither away. To the extent that federal insurance programs entitled specific groups, they did. The public assistance programs initially consisted of four programs: Old Age Assistance, Aid to the Blind, Aid to the Permanently and Totally Disabled, and Aid to Children. Throughout the 1950s as widows, elderly, disabled and dependents of insured workers were entitled under social security, outlays in these programs declined.

One significant group, however, was not part of this trend. These were the intact poor families and single-parent families. Thus the AFDC program, which became synonymous with welfare, grew as the major federal–state cash program for the poor, in 1972, when the proposed Family Assistance Program advocated by White House adviser, Daniel P. Moynihan, failed to be enacted, the other remaining assistance programs were merged in Supplemental Security Income (SSI) (Moynihan, 1973). AFDC remained largely unreformed, unindexed and unpopular.

Thus, the context of social welfare policies in the United

States is one of insurance versus public assistance, federal versus state responsibilities, and public versus private responsibilities. The federal role was defined as taking care of those who had lost their ability to work due to conditions beyond their control. These conditions were primarily age and disability. Beyond these, programs were categorical. If an individual fits within a particular category, including veteran status, he may be eligible for some federal program. If not, they would be expected to rely on private resources, charities or state general assistance.

Patterns of Growth

U.S. social programs have their origin in the New Deal (Browning, 1986). The major growth, however, has occurred in recent decades. This growth has been driven by demographic changes and the indexing of benefits. Statutes which provide benefits to all who meet the qualifications lead to what has been termed uncontrollable spending. That is, Congress cannot limit this spending through the appropriations process. Rather, they have to change the statutes which obligate the spending. This latter process has been facilitated somewhat in recent years through the use of reconciliation process of the Budget Act.

The role of the state and federal government is seen in the ratio of federal to state spending for social programs. The figures in Table 10.1 indicate that in 1950 the federal government spent 81 cents for every dollar spent on social

TABLE 10.1   *State-Federal social welfare comparisons (millions of nominal dollars)*

	Fiscal year 1950	Fiscal year 1960	Fiscal year 1970	Fiscal year 1980	Fiscal year 1986
Federal	10 541.0	24 956.7	77 337.2	302 631.1	472 364.4
State	12 967.3	27 336.6	68 518.5	189 896.7	298 157.5
Ratio	0.81	0.91	1.1	1.6	1.6

Source: Bixby, Ann Kallman (1989) 'Public Social Welfare Expenditures', *Social Security Bulletin*, no. 52, Feb., pp. 29–39.

welfare by state and local governments, and in 1980 the federal government was spending $1.60 for each state and local dollar (Bixby, 1989). Federal expenditures increased thirty-fold during this period, while state and local expenditures increased by a factor of fifteen. This ratio has remained constant from 1980 to 1986.

Within the total spending, there is variation. These varying growth rates are the result of the different emphases which have been placed on social policy by Congress and the president over time. During the 1950s the growth was in cash programs – primarily social security and public assistance. In the 1960s under the Kennedy and Johnson Administrations, in-kind expenditures – education, social services and health – were the dominant growth areas. In the late 1960s and early 1970s under Nixon and Ford, food stamps and manpower programs grew rapidly with a resurgence in cash programs. In recent years spending for other veterans, education, housing, and other programs have slowed. Table 10.2 shows the pattern of some of these changes.

Another result of these different program emphases across time has been the change in the relative share of programs. As Table 10.3 reveals, the percentage of total federal dollars spent on social insurance increased over the last three decades from 20 per cent to over 60 per cent, while veterans' expenditures moved exactly in the opposite direction. All the other program categories show increases in the share of the total except health. While there have been very large increases within these categories, the absolute size of the expenditures for social insurance dwarf the other categories.

Entitling New Groups

Social welfare programs in the United States consist of over 150 distinct programs with different eligibility requirements. These programs are found in four major functional budget categories: (1) income security; (2) health; (3) education, manpower and social services; and (4) veterans' benefits. Within each category there are further subfunction and program classifications. The programs are administered by different federal agencies and are under the jurisdiction of

234

TABLE 10.2 *Federal social welfare expenditures by category (millions of nominal dollars)*

	Fiscal year 1950	Fiscal year 1960	Fiscal year 1970	Fiscal year 1980	Fiscal year 1986
Social Insurance	2103.0	14 307.4	45 245.6	191 162.0	326 588.2
Public Assistance	1103.2	2116.9	9648.6	48 666.5	65 614.8
Veterans	6386.2	5367.3	8951.5	21 253.6	27 072.1
Education	156.7	867.9	5875.8	13 452.2	15 022.4
Health	603.5	1737.1	4775.2	12 702.8	19 925.6
Housing	14.6	143.5	581.6	6608.1	10 164.4
Other	174.0	416.7	2258.9	8785.9	7976.9
Total	10 541.2	24 956.8	77 337.2	302 631.1	472 364.4

Source: Bixby, Ann Kallman (1989) 'Public Social Welfare Expenditures', *Social Security Bulletin*, no. 52, Feb, p. 29–39.

TABLE 10.3   *Federal social welfare expenditures by category (per cent)*

	Fiscal year 1950	Fiscal year 1960	Fiscal year 1970	Fiscal year 1980	Fiscal year 1986
Social Insurance	20.0	57.3	58.5	63.0	69.1
Public Assistance	10.5	8.5	12.5	16.2	13.9
Veterans	60.6	21.5	11.6	7.0	5.7
Education	1.5	3.5	7.6	4.3	3.2
Health	5.7	7.0	6.2	4.4	4.2
Housing	0.1	0.6	1.0	2.2	2.2
Other	1.6	1.7	2.9	2.9	1.7
Total	100.0	100.1	100.3	100.0	100.0

Source: Bixby, Ann Kallman (1989) 'Public Social Welfare Expenditures', *Social Security Bulletin*, no. 52, Feb., pp. 29–39.

different congressional committees thus increasing the problems of co-ordination and limiting comprehensive approaches.

The pattern of growth and expansion of federal programs has been to create benefits for categories of individuals who, through circumstances, birth or environment were unable to support themselves. Cash payments were provided only under the social insurance programs, public assistance and veterans' programs. In all other cases, in-kind benefits were provided. These in-kind benefits were in the form of food, food stamps, housing, housing vouchers, education payments, job training and social services.

There was no universal program and no comprehensive integration of programs. As programs were modified at the margin, people in different situations were entitled for benefits. First widows of deceased workers were entitled to social security benefits. Then children were added. Then children were provided benefits until age 21 if they were still in school. A minimum level social security benefit was added as were payments to persons over age 72 who had not worked long enough to be entitled. A similar pattern is seen in the way that different in-kind programs for varying conditions were added.

The Elderly

One group which has fared well throughout these different political and economic periods has been the elderly. Starting with the changes in the social insurance programs in the 1950s, the elderly became an entitled group. The entitlement of aged people who had not worked enough quarters to receive benefits was a significant departure from the original conditions of social security. After a long struggle, medical insurance (Medicare) was added as another entitlement and important benefit for the elderly. Various other in-kind programs from food to housing were also added throughout the 1960s.

The net effect of these changes was threefold. First, it raised the incomes of many of the elderly to above the poverty line. The cash programs, and primarily social security, were responsible for the change in the poverty status of the elderly. Secondly, it enhanced and encouraged the political power of the elderly. As the elderly became dependent upon these benefits they took an active political interest in their continuation. Politicians such as the late Claude Pepper (D–Fla.) recognized and responded to this political power. Thirdly, it contributed to the privileged position of social security as a U.S. social welfare program. The social security phenomenon is discussed below.

In-kind Growth

Table 10.4 shows federal expenditures for the major social programs. Health expenditures in the Medicare and Medicaid programs continue to grow rapidly. After periods of expansion, spending for social services, food stamps, child nutrition and other public assistance programs have slowed. For a few categories, such as the original anti-poverty programs (OEO), expenditures have actually declined. In the 1960s, new programs such as food stamps, aid to elementary and secondary education, social services were enacted. Many of these programs were greatly expanded in the early 1970s. In the late 1970s and early 1980s, these in-kind expansions were scaled back.

TABLE 10.4 *Spending for major federal social welfare programs (millions of nominal dollars)*

	Fiscal year 1950	Fiscal year 1960	Fiscal year 1970	Fiscal year 1980	Fiscal year 1986
Social Insurance					
Social security	784.1	11 032.1	36 835.4	152 110.4	271 980.0
Medicare	0	0	7149.2	34 991.5	75 902.6
Public Assistance					
Cash and WIN	1097.2	1857.7	4465.3	7234.8	9573.3
Medicaid	0	199.8	2607.1	14 550.2	24 826.2
Social services	0	0	522.0	1757.1	2003.0
SSI	0	0	0	6439.8	10 316.6
Food stamps	0	0	577.0	9083.3	12 397.0
Other	6.0	59.4	9601.3	6688.6	6498.7
Public housing	14.5	143.5	459.9	5246.9	9530.9
Child nutrition	121.2	306.1	710.9	4209.3	4588.2
OEO/ACTION	0	0	752.8	2302.7	504.5
Other	27.6	32.9	181.3	1210.8	1290.0
Elem. & sec. education	47.1	441.9	2968.8	7429.6	7472.1
Higher education	48.5	293.1	2154.6	4467.5	6070.7

Source: Bixby, Ann Kallman (1989) 'Public Social Welfare Expenditures', *Social Security Bulletin*, no. 52, Feb., pp. 29–39.

The Limits of Reform

Welfare reform has been an elusive goal for executive, congressional, and academic advocates. The lack of a comprehensive policy has been commented on and criticized by many. The categorical eligibility requirements create both gaps in coverage and notches in benefits. A gap arises, for example, from the interdependency of programs which can leave a mother and child without health benefits once they exceed the income eligibility requirements for AFDC. A notch arises from eligibility formulas that result in loss of benefits when income exceeds a certain level.

Welfare in the United States is a panoply of programs from social security, Medicare, Medicaid, food stamps, nutrition, housing and work training programs. These programs are administered by different federal, state and local agencies. Oversight is by different congressional committees. Each program can have different income and eligibility requirements.

President Nixon proposed a comprehensive reform, but his reforms failed to make it through the legislative process. Generally, reforms are criticized by liberals for not going far enough and by conservatives for going too far. The final result of the Nixon initiative was to combine three of the four public assistance programs into one federal–state program, Supplemental Security Income (SSI), AFDC, the primary program benefiting the single-headed poor household, fell out of the reforms. It was to have been replaced with a negative income tax.

This Nixon welfare reform and all others since have been dominated by debate over work requirements. Many states and the federal government have been reluctant to pay cash benefits to households in which a person resided who could work. A provision of AFDC for households with an unemployed parent (AFDC–UP) was enacted in the early 1960s and adopted in only 27 states by 1980. In the U.S. child and family allowances were not the focus of debate, rather the debate always centers around work and training requirements. This debate echoes the basic themes of social welfare policy described earlier.

Proposed reforms in the Carter years also failed to clear these policy hurdles. When Reagan came to office, the agenda was shifting to one of controlling federal spending for domestic programs and emphasizing the need to increase spending for defense because the size of the federal government and the taxes imposed to finance this spending were seen as a detriment to economic growth.

Thus, when Reagan was elected, one might suspect that the window for comprehensive reform was closing. Changes would be expected to come from the 'tireless tinkering' with conditions and requirements for social programs. These types of changes at the margins are found throughout the history of these programs. However, at the end of the Administration, a welfare reform bill was enacted. It was the classic compromise between liberals and conservatives in Congress. Liberals sought expanded benefits and conservatives sought work requirements. The reform basically continues the existing programs, but adds new conditions and benefits.

For example, it mandated benefits to two-parent poor families and provides child care and Medicaid benefits to recipients for a year after they leave the welfare rolls. This addresses the long-standing problem where a recipient loses in-kind benefits when they got a job. Conservatives included provisions requiring participation in job training programs and stronger child support enforcement provisions. Liberals won a provision requiring states to adopt AFDC–UP.

This reform addressed many of the problems long debated by those from both liberal and conservative camps. It was not, however, a comprehensive reform. Rather, it changed the programs along familiar lines. The changes also came during the last year of a conservative Republican Administration. A conservative in the White House with the threat of veto may be in a better position to make compromises with liberal Democrats while placating the conservative flank with other provisions. In contrast, a liberal in the White House may have a harder time placating the left on social policy while compromising with the conservatives.

When President Nixon proposed increases in social spending, the Democrats in the Congress often increased the expenditures over his requests. It is important to understand the implications of divided party government for reforms and social welfare policy. Until Democrats win the presidency or Republicans the Congress, this will continue to be the condition of party control of the U.S. government.

The Reagan Agenda

Ronald Reagan came into office committed to stemming increases in federal social welfare spending. Approximately 75 per cent of the federal budget was termed 'relatively uncontrollable' meaning that spending would continue at that level unless Congress altered existing laws and previous commitments. Spending for social programs consumed over half of the $700 billion budget. To an Administration philosophically opposed to many of these social programs and with its own priorities to increase the defense budget and lower taxes, cuts in social programs were high on the agenda.

In a very early policy document, budget director David Stockman indicated that he knew where he would achieve the social welfare savings. Setting aside social security, which he wrote, 'would be a political disaster to tinker with in the first round', he zeroed in on non-social security entitlements. In the so-called 'Dunkirk' paper of December 1980 he wrote:

> Current expenditures for food stamps, cash assistance, Medicaid, disability, heating assistance, WIC [Women, Infant, and Children Food Program], school lunches, and unemployment compensation, amount to $100 billion. A carefully tailored package to reduce eligibility, overlap, and abuse should be developed for these areas – with potential savings of $10–20 billion. (Greider, 1981.)

The 1981 OBRA did implement cuts in many of these programs. The importance of this bill was that it changed many existing laws and altered many statutory eligibility criteria for *de facto* entitlement programs. In fiscal year 1982 budget savings of $35.2 billion were projected from the cuts made in seventeen federal programs. These cuts primarily altered the liberalized eligibility requirements and benefit adjustments enacted in the 1970–6 period. For programs such as Pell grants for education, CETA job training, WIC, energy assistance and Title XX services a cap was placed on total expenditures to reduce program costs. Federal program contributions to Medicaid and school nutrition programs were reduced. Eligibility was restricted for food stamps and school lunches while benefits for AFDC recipients were reduced. Two programs, CETA public work jobs and the social security minimum benefit, were eliminated.

Throughout this debate, the Administration emphasized its support for the safety net – those programs targeted at those who 'rely on government for their very existence'. These programs were identified as social security, Medicare, Veterans' pensions and compensation, SSI, Head Start, summer jobs for disadvantaged youths and free school lunches and breakfasts. This emphasis reinforced the concept of a federal welfare commitment to the elderly, the veterans, and the destitute. Those who were barely above the poverty line, or who were only above the poverty line by virtue of the federal in-kind benefits they received, would bear the brunt of the cuts in non-social security entitlements. While seeking to end benefits to those who could pay, the Reagan cuts fell hardest on the working poor.

Most important from the standpoint of this analysis is to understand that the priorities of the Reagan Administration were not targeted primarily at War on Poverty programs, but at the expansion of the welfare state realized in the post-Johnson years. Most of these eligibility changes and new programs were enacted during the Nixon and Ford presidencies. Nixon had already done battle with the War on Poverty, and the original OEO programs had been modified and placed under new auspices. The increases in program benefits of the safety net program were also enacted in the post-Johnson years. Although the poor, and especially the elderly poor, have benefits from these increases, the bulk of the safety net programs (social security, Medicare and veterans' benefits) are not specifically targeted at the poor.

Originally the public assistance categories were expected to wither away. As more of the elderly and disabled were insured under social security provisions and assisted further by in-kind services, these categories did dwindle and the economic well-being of recipients improved. The same phenomenon did not occur with the public assistance program commonly thought of as welfare – AFDC. This program grew rather than shrunk. It was also dependent upon states to implement federal changes and raise benefits. This did not readily occur in many states.

The Social Security Issue

Political history made social security a protected program. The program was originally enacted during the Roosevelt presidency. His successor, Harry Truman, proposed expansions including health insurance. When Eisenhower was elected in 1952 as the first Republican to follow Roosevelt, there was much speculation about whether Eisenhower would adhere to the Republican positions opposing the program. He signaled early on that he would not. Over the succeeding years, social security grew to be a popular, 'earned' program with politicians and the public. Many academic conservatives, however, continued to take positions opposed to the program on free market principles.

Ronald Reagan came to office out of the conservative or Goldwater wing of the Republican party. By this time, social security was so established a program, that support for social security was a litmus test for any politician. Presidential candidates would in practice have to pledge that they would oppose any reductions in social security.

At the same time, the financing and benefit structure of social security required attention. Since the issue of reducing benefits was so controversial, it could not be addressed through the normal legislative channels. A bipartisan commission with executive and legislative appointees was created to address future deficits in the social security trust fund arising from the projected retirements in the next century. A series of reforms were enacted which would guarantee the solvency of the trust fund. This political solution illustrated how social security had become such a sensitive political issue that no politician wanted to be on the record as proposing cuts in social security.

Even then the issue of social security did not disappear. The rising federal budget deficit and the newly projected surpluses in the social security trust opened the possibility that social security funds could be 'borrowed' to offset the budget deficit. Early in the next century, these funds are needed to meet the retirement payments for the large baby boom population. In the short run, however, more will be paid in than paid out.

The controversy over social security will not go away. In part, the problem arises from the historical development of social security as an earned program into which workers are paying into throughout their lives. As social security administrators, presidents and the Congress increased benefits over the years, often exceeding inflation, they contributed to a set of expectations about the program. Any changes in the program after expectations are created are difficult to enact because these changes are portrayed as reductions in earned benefits.

The social security notch issue is an excellent example of this problem. When Congress indexed social security benefits for inflation in 1972, they actually double indexed them by indexing both the wages and the benefits in the formula. By the time this was corrected in the reforms of 1977, some retirees were already benefiting from this over-indexing. Rather than reducing their benefits, Congress put the revision in effect for future retirees. Thus a notch was created, in that persons born between 1917 and 1921 receive lower benefits than those born before. In the last several years, Congress has received a lot of pressure to correct this situation from those called the 'notch babies'. A recent study forecasts that it would cost between \$24 and \$30 billion to correct this differential. This problem illustrates the difficulty in making any changes in social security especially when it makes a significant political group worse off.

Housing Programs

One set of social programs targeted early in the Reagan Administration was federal housing expenditures and subsidies. These programs came under attack because they were not a free market mechanism and because some federally supported housing projects were abandoned as failures. The Administration proposed using vouchers as a way to let the poor obtain housing in the market system. Building new housing units was greatly decreased. The problem, it was argued, was affordability, not availability.

Throughout the Reagan Administration, the number of urban poor homeless people visibly increased. This was viewed by many reporters and politicians as a sign of failed housing policies. Coupled with a growing drug problem in the cities and housing projects, the housing issue was receiving increased attention. At the same time, President Bush appointed an activist Republican congressman and a former presidential aspirant to head HUD. Jack Kemp, an early advocate of supply-side economics, was expected to be very active in the area of housing, drugs, and homelessness. Observers anticipated that he would attempt to fashion a new Republican position on these problems. Thus as we leave the Reagan era, the future of housing programs will be extensively debated. What solutions and mechanisms will be proposed is not yet clear.

Shortly after the Reagan Administration left office, a congressional committee began to uncover a widespread abuse and mismanagement in programs administered by the Department of Housing and Urban Development. These hearings coupled with the agenda of the new department head, Jack Kemp, will undoubtedly discredit much of the Reagan housing record. The investigation uncovered the awarding of housing contracts based upon the political influence of the contractors, rather than the merits of the proposal. The attention on this scandal has limited the ability of Secretary Kemp to fashion his own agenda. Vouchers that enable recipients to purchase housing of choice, rather than financing the construction of subsidized units may be the preferred policy of the Administration.

Increase in Poverty

Throughout the Reagan Administration, poverty increased.

Some of this increase can be attributed to economic effects. Another large part is due to changes in the demographic distribution. Income transfers only partially offset these adverse effects. Table 10.5 shows changes in poverty rates from 1979 to 1982 (Bawden, 1984).

TABLE 10.5   *Changes in poverty, 1979–82*

	1979	1982
All persons	11.7%	15.0%
Young men	12.7	18.5
Prime age men	6.1	9.1
Elderly	14.9	14.3

Source: Gottschalk, Peter and Danziger, Sheldon (1984), 'Macroeconomic Conditions Income Transfers, and the Trend in Poverty', in *The Social Contract Revisited*, D. Lee Bawden, ed. Washington, DC, The Urban Institute.

During this period, poverty increased for all groups except for households headed by the elderly. This is a continuation of a trend of reduction in elderly poverty observed since 1967. During this period a 13.5 per cent reduction in poverty has been observed among the elderly. Transfers, and especially social security, have been largely responsible for this reduction in poverty. Economic and cyclical effects are important factors affecting the poverty level for households headed by young and prime age men (Gottschalk and Danziger, 1984).

The Post-Reagan Period

President Bush pledged that his would be a kinder, gentler presidency. This very statement suggested politically that somehow the Reagan presidency was too harsh and uncaring. Exactly what this means in terms of policy is not clear. Given the size of the federal deficit and Bush's pledge of 'no new taxes', one would not predict that there would be many new domestic spending programs. However, the Democratic Congress was elected with its own perceived mandate. The Congress can be expected to pursue its own domestic program if it did not find Bush's to its liking.

Some directions of this new agenda could be seen in the early months of the Bush Administration. A congressional committee was investigating scandals in the administration of housing programs. The Congress was debating the minimum wage, child care programs, health insurance and tax credits.

Late in 1988, in the middle of the presidential campaign, George Bush broke with the Reagan Administration to support full funding of the reauthorization of the McKinney housing bill. This bill did increase funding for programs to aid the homeless. Part of the housing debate will center on administration and controls. Policy and strategy in the provision of housing for both the poor and the middle class will continue to be debated. There was a strong feeling at the beginning of the Reagan Administration that for all of the money spent on housing, the problem was still acute. At the beginning of the Bush Administration, the same statements are now being repeated. The 1990 census brings attention again to the numbers and the problem of the homeless Americans. Since there is not even agreement on how many homeless there are, there can hardly be an agreement on what programs are needed. Housing policy will continue on the agenda of social policy issues being debated with continued emphasis on private market strategies and incentives.

Social security will continue in its protected status. Any suggested change is labeled by others as a reduction in benefits. Few politicians want to be associated with any proposals which could be perceived as reducing social security. Any future changes will most likely have to come from bipartisan commission established with a specific mandate. Senator Daniel P. Moynihan stoked the political fires by proposing that the social security be taken off-budget. This would prevent the use of social security trust funds to finance federal borrowing, the effect of which would be to force expenditure cuts or a tax increase.

One of fastest growing social expenditures has been health expenditures. One initiative in the Reagan years was catastrophic health insurance. As these supplemental fees for this insurance began to be levied, opposition to this new program grew. It once again illustrates the problem of taxing individuals for collective benefits. Many of the affluent elderly who were required to pay increased fees for this program lobbied Congress to repeal the program. In late 1989, this effort was successful. The Pepper Commission was created to examine the future of the Medicare trust fund. Undoubtedly, this commission will have to recommend changes in the structure of taxes and benefits required to keep the fund solvent, to keep expenditures under control and to satisfy expectations of about the level of benefits.

While welfare programs have always been hotly debated, there is broader support for programs for working families. Congress is expected to pass a child care bill which has gained support from conservatives. Much of the debate has focused on the use of the earned income tax credit. The Senate version makes the existing tax credit refundable and provides a new tax credit for child health insurance premiums paid by low income families. This debate shows the potency of the family issue and moves the U.S. a step closer to family allowances. It once again illustrates the incremental nature of U.S. social policy. The welfare reform and the child care debate are separate. Further, the Earned Income Tax Credit is slowly being increased and strengthened as a component of social welfare. If referred to as a negative income tax to replace all of the categorical programs with one universal cash program, it does not have popular support. Used as an instrument to provide benefits to working families with children, it gains support. In time, it may become an even more important program and a back door into more far-reaching reforms.

Another issue on which the Democratic Congress and the President had a protracted battle was a proposal to raise the minimum wage. Congress has passed an increase which was vetoed by President Bush. After failing to override the veto, the Congress compromised and passed a new bill. This debate divided along party lines. Moreover, it shows how the agenda for social policy takes in many peripheral issues which are debated in terms of their effects on the market. The Reagan and Bush Administrations present the case for relying on economic growth. The Democrats in Congress press for more traditional methods of government intervention.

Social Policy in Transition

U.S. social policy is in transition. Because the Republicans
never controlled both Houses of Congress, there was never a
complete Reagan social policy revolution. There were cuts in
programs and a slowing down of spending for certain social
programs. There was debate within the Democratic Party
about the future of the Democratic social agenda.

George Bush is viewed as a much more pragmatic or
mainstream Republican. Ronald Reagan was much more
ideological. Therefore, the clash over ideas and policy direction is not simply between Democrats and Republicans, but
between Republicans and Republicans. The major social
initiatives may be developed in the housing area by Jack
Kemp. He is ideologically closer to Reagan than to Bush and
will seek to use his position to demonstrate that there is a
social policy based on market principles. Other watchdog
groups on the right, often with support from the Heritage
Foundation, will continue to monitor the Administration's
adherence to conservative principles and to develop papers
on the Republican policy alternatives.

Privatization, or the use of the private sector to implement
and deliver social programs, will continue to be debated. The
housing scandal will cause the Congress to take a closer look
at the administration of these programs. President Bush has
often used the '1000 points of light' metaphor to refer to
solutions that do not originate only from the central government. The parameters of this policy are still not well developed. Certainly, the debate over housing and child care
will emphasize market incentives and tax credits.

Interestingly, discussions on tax credits often bring liberal
and conservatives together. Refundable tax credits constitute
a negative income tax. Once a second refundable tax credit is
enacted for the same group, it is easier to combine them.
Thus, a child care credit with credit for health insurance costs
can then be an instrument for integrating other categorical
benefits. The advantages of lower administrative costs, less
market distortion and uniform eligibility criteria often win
support from a broad enough coalition to enact the legislation. The experience in implementing the 1988 welfare

reform may point to new ways to integrate federal welfare policies through tax credits.

Democrats are also trying to shape their own social policy agenda. The popular success of Reagan's campaign against big government and federal spending caused many Democrats to re-evaluate traditional party positions on social welfare policy. No clear consensus has developed, however, and Democrats are divided. At the same time, interests such as labor, women and blacks, keep the pressure on the party not to abandon their support for social programs. The failure to win the presidency and the failure to agree on a social agenda continues to hamper the Democratic Party's ability to set forward a clear social program.

The future of social policy in the U.S. is limited by the lack of money and consensus. Over the next several years, numerous ideas will be proposed and debated. The limits of the deficit will prevent major initiatives from being proposed or enacted. Strategies using the tax system or marketplace incentives are more likely to gain consensus over federally administered programs, although these programs will also face limits (see Chapter 8). Above all it is the lack of agreement about the extent to which public authority and the government should compensate for adversity which will ensure that U.S. social policy continues to be fragmented and limit the changes that do occur.

11

American Foreign Policy

MILES KAHLER

National debate over America's position in the world opened and closed the 1980s. The decade began with Ronald Reagan's victory over Jimmy Carter, a contest that was widely interpreted as the victory of a muscular and assertive view of America's world role over a more cautious and multilateral approach to American strategy. By the mid-1980s, as a new Soviet leadership hinted at the end of the 'new' Cold War and the Reagan Administration savored a landslide victory in 1984, domestic debate in the United States reopened. Arms control and Central America had already served as Democratic points of attack on the Republican Administration's foreign policies; the new critics levelled a more profound set of arguments against the Reagan foreign policies. Growing budget and trade deficits, coupled with other economic shortcomings, such as slow productivity growth, threatened to undermine the economic pre-eminence on which America's international position rested. Paul Kennedy's analysis of 'imperial overstretch' through the ages was the most visible of these skeptical treatments, but his arguments concerning the ill effects of excessive military spending were echoed by others who focussed more narrowly on the twin deficits and their long-term effects on the American economy (Kennedy, 1987; Friedman, 1988).

The 'declinists' have since spawned 'anti-declinist' responses, arguments that the United States has not declined dramatically in relative international position if one chooses a later benchmark (1960 rather than 1945) and that the American portfolio of power resources remains much broader than any of its possible rivals, whether the economically stagnant Soviet Union or non-nuclear Japan (Huntington, 1988–9; Nye, 1990). The collapse of the Soviet position in Eastern Europe and the promise of a peace dividend rather than continued high levels of military spending have forced both sides of the debate to begin a reassessment of their post-Cold War positions.

Scholarly consideration of the implications of American hegemony and its decline had preceded this more public argument by at least a decade. The shocks of the early 1970s – stagflation, the withdrawal from Vietnam, the end of the Bretton Woods monetary system, OPEC's oil price increase – prompted anxiety over international economic disorder in a world in which the United States was no longer so dominant. Robert Gilpin and Charles Kindleberger argued that an international economy without such a single dominant power risked instability and closure rather than the stable and liberal order established after the Second World War (Gilpin, 1987; Kindleberger, 1973). The balder versions of this theory of hegemonic stability were questioned by those who doubted whether the United States had ever been so dominant or whether its relative position had slipped very far; even more questionable were its predictions of inevitable disorder in the liberal international order. Revised and qualified in ways that attempted to salvage the core of the theory while awarding a greater role to international institutions, hegemonic stability theory captured in more rigorous form the possibilities and consequences of American decline (Keohane, 1984).

Neither the theory of hegemonic stability, which offered an explanation for change in the *international* order, nor the recent declinist debate has explicitly addressed the American *domestic* order that had sustained hegemony in the postwar period. Lurking in these discussions, however, are two contrasting views of the United States and its foreign policy-making in the post-1945 decades. One is an implicit comparison of foreign policy during the 'golden age' of hegemony before the Vietnam War and the rude jolts to the American position in the 1970s. Compared to the divisions of the 1970s and 1980s, the politics of American foreign policy in the 1950s and early 1960s was in this view consensual and coherent. The executive branch was as hegemonic domestically as the United States was internationally. Led by competent presidents who oversaw a unified executive, supported by a deferential Congress and an acquiescent public, foreign policy was little influenced by interest groups, other than those with well-defined and predictable material interests. This unified foreign policy system was the basis for a clearcut strategy of containing communism and expanding the liberal economic order. This nostalgic image of the years from 1947 until 1968 overlooks both the severe partisan division that did occur, particularly during the Truman Administration, and the fact that the Cold War consensus was unusual in the conflict-ridden history of American foreign policy.

When comparing the politics of American foreign policy with the foreign policy of other countries rather than an earlier historical period, a second image of policy-making is often presented and applied, even to the golden age of hegemonic consensus. That model is the 'weak state', a fuzzy concept that attempts to capture those features of American foreign policy-making (and politics) that set the United States apart from many other industrialized countries. Stephen Haggard has nominated four features that are typically included in the notion of the weak American state. Fragmentation is key, particularly the unique sharing of powers between the executive and legislature. That fragmentation extends to the bureaucracy as well, which lacks the internal cohesion and formative institutions of the civil services in such 'strong states' as Japan and France. The weak state is easily penetrated by interest groups, whose activities are widely regarded as a legitimate part of the policy process. Finally, the weak state does not possess a wide array of policy instruments for shaping economy and society: its field of action is therefore limited (Haggard, 1988).

These two images – the post-hegemonic and the weak state – can be combined: a weak state which managed its hegemonic role for twenty years became even weaker with the shocks of Vietnam and economic decline. For the most part, however, the connections between international position and policy process have been left aside; as noted above, the policy process hardly figures in recent debate over changes in the American international position (Mastanduno *et al.*, 1989). In striking contrast to the reassessment that took place during and after the Vietnam War and assigned to an imperial presidency, a servile Congress and an uninvolved public major responsibility for American policy failure, process has not played a leading role in the latest round of American self-examination. The political process by which the United States arrives at its external policies has not figured prominently for two reasons. Most of the explanations advanced for the relative decline of the United States are more closely connected to exogenous changes in the international system (the position of many hegemonic stability theorists) or to domestic policy choices (the declinist view) rather than foreign policy. The political process certainly shapes these outcomes, but the foreign policy process, conventionally defined, does not. Also, many of those who are concerned about the foreign policy process and its effects on the United States position are profoundly pessimistic about the possibilities for changing that process: they are, in the words of Raymond Vernon and Debora Spar, resistant to 'making proposals that ask elephants to fly' (Vernon and Spar, 1989). After many exhortations to change the policy process and little evidence of any change, one detects a note of weariness in those who assess the making of foreign policy in the United States. In evaluating American policy toward the Soviet Union, for example, Joseph Nye draws attention to the costs of a policy 'marked by incoherence and inconsistency', but attributes many of the characteristics of that policy to deeply rooted, even cultural causes, an attribution that severely restricts the possibility for change (Nye, 1984).

Such lack of attention to the institutions of American foreign policy inhibits a sharper examination of the possibilities for American adaptation, to both its putative economic decline and the dramatic systemic changes that have been labeled the end of the Cold War. Imperial overstretch may have its roots in a particular political constellation within American society and that constellation may prove difficult to reorder. A perceived Soviet threat was the basis of executive dominance during the postwar decades and has served as an important lever for presidential influence more recently. A reconsideration of the institutional and political bases of American foreign policy may open the way to estimates of the course of American adaptation in the 1990s. The reconsideration undertaken here will compare the politics of foreign policy during the 1980s with two earlier periods: the era of executive dominance from 1947 until 1968 and the period of Congressional activism in the 1970s. The Reagan Administration believed that its effort to reassert American leadership internationally was linked to re-establishing presidential predominance domestically in the making of foreign policy. Was the Reagan counter-revolution successful or did the institutional trends of the post-Vietnam War era persist? In the attempt to construct an institutional response to this question, attention will center, not on constitutional or legislative provisions (although these are important guides) but rather on the rules of the policy game and the incentives that it presents to key foreign policy makers. Assumptions of 'weakness' in the American state or of peculiarities inherent in foreign as opposed to domestic policy will be avoided unless they are demonstrated. In examining the politics of foreign policy, however, it will soon be apparent that the most significant questions concern the *circumstances* under which particular generalizations apply. Specifically, the process of making foreign policy may vary considerably across time and from issue-area to issue-area (arms control versus trade, for example). This variation bedevils many generalizations about foreign policy-making (such as the 'weak state'), but it also provides an opportunity to tease apart what it is about particular periods and issue-areas that may make the politics of each so often different.

President and Bureaucracy: Conditions for Coherence

In the lore of American foreign policy foibles, executive

branch veterans and State Department diplomats assign principal responsibility for an incoherent foreign policy to the Congress and its unique role in the American political and foreign policy process. As Graham Allison demonstrated in his account of the 1962 Cuban missile crisis, however, even in settings that exclude direct Congressional intervention – such as superpower confrontation with a high risk of nuclear war – the President has often had difficulty in imposing his preferences on players attuned to their own bureaucratic interests and in obtaining implementation from a large national security bureaucracy programmed to follow standard operating procedures (Allison, 1971). A particular facet of bureaucratic politics has plagued recent American administrations: the struggle between White House 'courtiers' and Cabinet 'barons' (Destler *et al.*, 1984). Two figures in particular have contested control of policy – the Assistant for National Security Affairs in the White House and the Secretary of State. Since the elevation of the National Security Assistant position, first under McGeorge Bundy and later under Henry Kissinger, its co-ordinating role has often been subsumed by the desire of the National Security Adviser to be the President's principal foreign affairs adviser and often his principal negotiating agent. Conflict reached its peak during the Carter Administration, when competition between Secretary of State Cyrus Vance and National Security Advisor Zbigniew Brzezinski reflected contrasting policy lines toward the Soviet Union.

White House–State Department competition diminished in the Reagan Administration, in part because of greater ideological homogeneity, in part because the National Security Advisers enjoyed both short tenures and various handicaps in their assertion of a leadership role. Secretary of State George Shultz, on the other hand, held office for more than six years and enjoyed the President's confidence throughout. His principal competition, in the areas of arms control and the use of American military force abroad, came not from the White House, but from the Defense Department. (Bureaucratic politics had little predictive power on the issue of using military force, however, since Shultz tended to support such measures and Defense Secretary Caspar

Weinberger was typically the skeptic.)

The flourishing of bureaucratic politics under Ronald Reagan was hardly surprising: Reagan was a president notably diffident about the details of policy and relaxed about oversight of his subordinates. As a president, however, he did have a number of intensely held ideological convictions and a widely respected ability to convey those convictions to the public through the medium of television. Those instances in which bureaucratic politics were suppressed in the Reagan Administration are of particular interest as anomalies, indicators that when a diffident president devotes attention to an issue and sharpens his preferences before the public, the costs for bureaucratic squabbling rise markedly, and the power of bureaucratic politics as an explanation for American foreign policy declines.

Two such issues were Central America and the Strategic Defense Initiative (SDI or 'Star Wars'). Reagan's anti-Sandinista views were clear in the election campaign of 1980: his victory was celebrated by right-wing political forces in the region. If anything, his views against negotiation and in favor of support for paramilitary measures (the Contras) hardened during his first term. Within the Administration, however, and particularly in the State Department, some attention was given to a compromise with the Nicaraguan government: no support for other revolutionary movements in exchange for American tolerance of the regime. The bureaucratic opponents of this view in the National Security Council, the CIA, and the Defense Department supported a more forceful effort to overthrow the Sandinistas. Their most important ally became the President. In an effort to overcome congressional resistance to the course that his Administration was charting, Reagan gave a speech in March 1983 on El Salvador and another in April before a joint session of Congress, heightening the partisan tone of the policy debate and attempting to mobilize the American public. Equally important, this clear staking of views suppressed bureaucratic resistance to the hardliners within the Administration. As one participant noted, after this point, 'your loyalty to the President was questioned if you suggested there were two ways to skin a cat. ... No one wanted to get in front of a

moving train' (Arnson, 1989, p. 109). Rejection of the negotiation strategy and the President's high-profile commitment
on Central America served to isolate the principal proponent
of that policy, Thomas O. Enders, who eventually left his
State Department post to become an ambassador.

An even more striking example of presidential abilities to
overcome bureaucratic resistance was Reagan's Strategic Defense Initiative. As even skeptical analysts have conceded,
both the manner in which SDI was promulgated and the
concepts underlying it were unprecedented: unlike other
innovations in nuclear weaponry, this was a top-down decision, reflecting 'nothing so much as the mind-set of a single
person – the president who enunciated it on the recommendation of a handful of like-minded political supporters'.
SDI also represented the first time that an American president 'launched and sustained a wholesale public repudiation
of the legitimacy of nuclear weapons as a way to gain support
for an unprecedented buildup of the American nuclear
arsenal and rejection of arms control' (Lakoff and York,
1989; Nolan, 1989).

The hold of SDI on the President derived in part from
Reagan's attachment to the notion of defense – even against
nuclear weapons – and his dislike for the core concept of
MAD (mutual assured destruction). Those simple and
apparently deeply held beliefs – which ran counter to the
postwar mainstream in nuclear weapons policy – legitimated
the ideas of a number of specialists, such as Daniel Graham
and Edward Teller, who had been considered 'minor-league
cranks and strategic superiority nuts'. The manner in which a
small group of advisers – White House staff with no experience in foreign or defense policy, members of the 'kitchen
cabinet', and scientific free-lancers such as Teller – managed
to produce the SDI speech in March 1983 was a case study in
the circumvention of bureaucratic procedures by a president
and a handful of his staff. As Martin Anderson describes, the
SDI speech was part of a conscious strategy *not* to pursue the
traditional route of asking the Defense Department for its
analysis and recommendation, since 'missile defense would
be seen as a new idea, and nothing threatens an entrenched
bureaucracy like a new idea, especially a new idea they have

not thought of themselves' (Anderson, 1988, p. 93). (Reagan did obtain what was taken to be the approval of the Joint Chiefs of Staff in February 1983 just before his announcement of SDI.) It was no accident, however, that those surrounding Reagan in this instance and urging him to pursue a course that broke radically with both postwar nuclear strategy and the advice of most experts were political strategists. After Reagan's March 1983 speech announcing SDI, defense experts discovered that he had tapped into a great unease in the American public about nuclear weapons and the threat of nuclear war:

> It was quickly evident that the popular appeal of the astrodome concept, along with the overwhelming technical complexities associated with space defense, was a deadly combination for opponents. (Nolan, 1989, p. 170.)

Reagan could appear more radically opposed to nuclear weapons than the backers of the nuclear freeze, while at the same time proposing one of the most expensive military programs of his Administration.

After the President's speech, SDI became, like aid to the Contras, a touchstone of loyalty and a litmus test of conservative credentials, within the administration and outside it. Even a longtime hawk such as Paul Nitze could be accused by his bureaucratic opponents in the Defense Department of being 'soft' in his support of Star Wars (Talbott, 1988). In both instances, however, controlling the divisions among bureaucratic barons within the administration imposed costs or failed to produce the outcomes that the President desired. The suppression of bureaucratic checks (a more positive description of bureaucratic politics) in policy toward Central America permitted the emergence of bureaucratic entrepreneurs who pushed illegal maneuvers to circumvent the Administration's policy stalemate with Congress. When the Iran–Contra scandal broke in late 1986, the cabinet barons (Shultz and Weinberger) pled ignorance: quite apart from the secrecy that surrounded Oliver North's operation, even high-ranking figures had learned not to question even the most questionable moves in support of the Contras. This bureaucratic gambit went so far as to contemplate the creation of The Enterprise, 'an attempt to escape Congressional oversight entirely, to construct a CIA outside the American government' (Treverton, 1990, p. 92).

Star Wars did not produce such runaway ambition on the part of its bureaucratic proponents, but it also failed to penetrate all of the organizational recesses of the Defense Department. Following Reagan's speech, protection of the American population against a full-scale nuclear attack became only one of many rationales offered for the program. As the purpose of SDI became fuzzier (in the absence of clear Presidential directives), bureaucratic contests began (Nolan, 1989). Even more crucial, since it spanned most postwar administrations, was the inability of the Reagan Administration or its predecessors to gain access to nuclear planning in the Defense Department that would make any new doctrine a reality. As described by Nolan, repeated failure to exert civilian control in this critical sphere of implementation was pure Allisonian organizational politics:

> The means by which civilians had been excluded from examining [nuclear targeting] plans were often subtle, and not necessarily the result of blatant military subterfuge. For the most part, it was simply the banality of bureaucracy. Targeting is dull stuff, and senior officers and officials have more pressing and interesting things to do than go over technical charts about damage expectancies. (Nolan, 1989, p. 254.)

Only the dogged action of a civilian at the Pentagon managed to insert some civilian oversight into the process, but its future success was highly dependent on the active interest of future presidents and secretaries of defense.

The ability of a president to suppress damaging bureaucratic politics and the costs of that suppression are clearly documented in the Reagan Administration: public engagement on an issue by the President served to bring even cabinet barons into line. George Bush has so far escaped severe bureaucratic haggling during a period of rapid international change by choosing a close friend and political ally as his Secretary of State and a self-effacing manager as his National Security Adviser. With these choices, he has seemed to reverse an apparently inevitable gravitation of power to the White House staff in recent administrations. Given the personal ties between James Baker and Bush, the lead agency in foreign policy has seldom been in doubt. In addition, Bush's personal involvement in foreign policy is perhaps the greatest since Richard Nixon, a product of his career and his Administration's meager domestic agenda. Whether he can establish a degree of bureaucratic tension that will enhance his own influence over policy, rather than slipping into the perils of suppressing bureaucratic dissent witnessed in the Reagan Administration, remains to be seen.

Congress and Foreign Policy: Consolidation or Retreat?

Edward Corwin's oft-cited description of the constitutional provisions governing foreign policy – 'an invitation to struggle for the privilege of directing American foreign policy' – also captures the reality of executive–congressional conflict over foreign policy for much of American history (Corwin, 1957). The Cold War years before the Vietnam conflict were exceptional in the degree to which Congress deferred to the president's management of external relations. The Vietnam War was critical in turning the Congress toward an activism in foreign policy that resembled, though hardly surpassed, earlier periods. Vietnam was not the only change that altered congressional behavior, however: Congress's less deferential stance was supported by a new array of foreign policy interest groups – antiwar activists, ethnic lobbyists, even foreign governments – and by a more skeptical public. The international environment, which heightened American economic vulnerability while lowering the Soviet military threat, also encouraged Congress in its new course: constituents threatened by international competition demanded government action; a declining external threat removed one of the principal levers that a president could use to enforce deference.

As important as these historical contingencies, however,

were internal changes in the legislative institutions that would be far more persistent than memories of Vietnam. The power of individual Congressmen, without regard to seniority, grew: diffusion of power away from committee chairmen and longtime 'insiders' began first in the Senate, as early as the late 1950s; in the House, the process began in the early 1970s but proceeded more rapidly. By the 1980s, the 'inside game' of congressional barons had been transformed into an 'outside game' in which the key foreign affairs and defense committees still played a central role but one that was now more circumscribed by the parent chamber. The power of the members was reinforced by the institutionalization of subcommittees and by the democratization of floor procedures, in particular an increase in recorded votes. The resources available to individual members also increased: staff exploded in numbers and the research capabilities of the Congress in often arcane areas of foreign policy increased substantially. These independent information-gathering mechanisms in turn fed demands for additional information from the executive branch; by the 1980s, for example, the Congress, through its intelligence oversight committees, received nearly every piece of intelligence that found its way to the executive branch (Lindsay, 1991). The result, in the eyes of critics, was an even slower institutional pace. 'We've gone from a Senate where power was concentrated in a few leaders to one where there are 100 different power centers, and you can't accomplish much', stated Senator Daniel Evans (R.–Wash.) (Quoted in Warburg, 1989, p. 104.) Policy entrepreneurship on foreign policy issues exploded in the new environment.

These changes, international and domestic, produced, across issue-areas, a 'revolution' in the congressional role in foreign policy-making:

> The congressional role has grown from that of a relatively minor actor, frequently outspoken but only sporadically consulted, rarely involved in actual decisionmaking and never in policy execution, to that of a player with star billing in the U.S. national security policy-making and sometimes the lead role in U.S. government decisions. (Blechman, 1990, p. 109.)

Although the Reagan Administration came to office hoping for a counter-revolution of executive branch reassertion, the record shows at best a chipping away at congressional gains. The congressional role established in the 1970s was consolidated in the 1980s, even though some of the new institutional levers proved to be unsuccessful in shaping foreign policy. In similar fashion, the individual members seemed unwilling to return very much power to the committees and their chairmen: even Les Aspin, a forceful chairman of the House Armed Services Committee and one who seemed to reflect his party's views, was called to task by the Democratic Caucus on issues of arms control. Reconstructing the old system of deference to the executive branch under these circumstances would be difficult, if not impossible.

The end of deference does not mean predominance, however, nor does congressional activism mean consistent involvement over time. In predicting when Congress is likely to be involved in foreign policy-making and the degree of influence that it is likely to exercise, the incentives that confront individual members (and their leadership) provide on balance a better predictor of congressional behavior than simply focusing on constitutional provisions or on the new instruments that Congress developed in the 1970s. Even more critical is the selection of cases: in much of the analysis of Congress and foreign policy, cases are selected for the controversy that they arouse in Congress. The skewed sample that emerges gives a false impression of the degree and intensity of congressional interest in foreign policy issues.

The simplest approach to modelling congressional behavior after 1968 looks to the electoral connection and the re-election imperative: members of Congress are motivated to intervene in foreign policy issues in order to provide benefits to their constituents or to reflect their views, receiving votes and campaign contributions in exchange. On certain issues, such as trade, the link to the material interests of constituents or interest groups is clear, and the ability of Congress to buffer itself against interest group pressure through strong committee leadership has declined (Destler, 1986). In other cases, the Congress, and particularly the House of Representatives, has reflected shifts in public opinion that were not immediately recognized (or were resisted) by the executive branch. Barry Blechman documents the effects of a fairly rapid rise in public concern about arms control issues in the early 1980s on congressional initiatives in this issue-area. In a few years, public opinion shifted from a dominant preoccupation with military strength to concern over the threat of nuclear war, a concern voiced by a rapidly growing nuclear freeze movement in 1981–2. Democratic arms control proponents were offered the political space to oppose Reagan administration policies; Democratic opponents of the SALT II Treaty, such as Senator John Glenn, rapidly changed course as the electoral implications of freeze sentiments became clear (Blechman, 1990).

In other issue-areas, a strong electoral link to foreign policy behavior is more questionable. A survey of congressional involvement in nuclear weapons development and defense policy suggests that only on the issue of military base closures can one document a strong and persistent connection between district benefits and congressional voting (Lindsay, 1991). Most studies of voting on defense issues indicate that personal ideology or policy views correlate more strongly with congressional votes than district benefits. Of course, teasing apart the Congressman's 'real' views from those espoused by constituents is a nearly impossible task. One can suggest other motivations, however, apart from the purely electoral, that may explain congresssional behavior in this arena: career advancement, within the Congress and outside it, is one reason for choosing to specialize in foreign or defense policy. Les Aspin and Sam Nunn have both achieved greater influence within their respective chambers through specialization in defense; Albert Gore based much of his presidential campaign on his record in proposing novel arms control initiatives.

Within the parameters set by the individual incentives of Congressmen, legislative and governmental norms and institutions do matter in explaining congressional intervention in foreign policy-making. One predictor of congressional activism is a challenge to legislative prerogatives by the executive. The Senate, which had been acquiescent in aid to the Nicaraguan Contras when the House of Representatives had voted repeatedly to cut off that aid, proceeded to vote for ending aid following the mining of Nicaraguan harbors. The offense of the Reagan Administration was less the mining itself than the alleged failure of the CIA to brief the Senate Intelligence Committee on the operation (Treverton, 1990). The Reagan Administration's effort to circumvent the 'narrow' interpretation of the Anti-Ballistic Missile Treaty also brought a storm of senatorial criticism for infringing on the constitutional responsibility of the Senate to give advice and consent to the president on treaties. In each of these cases, substantive (and partisan) motivations were reinforced by concern over an erosion of Congress's role in shaping foreign policy.

In other cases, institutions mattered less. The new institutions so carefully crafted in the 1970s to ensure greater congressional weight in key foreign policy decisions often failed in their purpose. The greatest disappointment was undoubtedly the War Powers Resolution of 1973, hallmark of the new congressional activism, a watershed measure in response to the imperial presidency and the Vietnam War. Designed to guarantee that Congress would be involved in any decision to use American military forces abroad, the War Powers Resolution has been resisted by presidents of both parties, and in nearly every instance of the deployment of American military force since its passage the executive has successfully devised a strategy to avoid meaningful congressional restraints (Warburg, 1989). In only two instances has section 4(a)(1) – which sets ticking the sixty-day clock for use of American military forces – come into play. In one case, that of the *Mayaguez* in 1975, the operation was over before the president's report was submitted; in the second, more contentious case – Lebanon in 1983 – Congress invoked the section by resolution but, as part of the bargain with the Reagan Administration, granted the executive a free hand for eighteen (rather than two) months. Conflict between the branches reached a new peak during the Gulf crisis of 1987, when American warships were dispatched to the region to protect friendly shipping. Despite repeated calls from members of both houses to invoke the War Powers Resolution and an unsuccessful effort to use the courts to force its

invocation, congressional leaders opposed passage of a resolution. Following the lengthy wrangles of that year, 'the law
itself had become an embarrassment to a majority in Congress' (Katzmann, 1990).

The failure of the War Powers Resolution to accomplish its
end can best be understood by examining the political
incentives facing members of Congress during most military
actions overseas. A 'rally round the flag' effect boosts public
support for presidential use of force early in an intervention.
At that moment, when invocation of the resolution would
probably be most useful in clarifying national goals without
necessarily undercutting the president's policies, congressional incentives to invoke the resolution are at their lowest.
As an intervention drags on, the political risks attached to a
resolution loom larger, since Congress could be assailed for
undercutting American positions at a critical juncture. The
War Powers Resolution, in short, has proven a blunt instrument. Although Vietnam-style circumstances have not re-
occurred, American military interventions grew in number
during the 1980s, but they were abbreviated in duration and
not very costly in American lives. In such circumstances,
congressional deference dominated any urge toward
activism.

Other institutional innovations, such as numerous reporting and certification requirements (particularly on human
rights) have also been disappointing in their effects on an
executive determined to assert its policies. Congressional
influence has been exerted more successfully through the use
of traditional instruments that are clearly and constitutionally
designated as part of the legislative power. Chief among
these is the power of the purse, which was put to innovative
use by Congress in shaping arms control policy in the 1980s.
'Costless' executive branch policies (such as failure to intervene against human rights violations) were much harder for
Congress to influence or police. One should not judge
congressional oversight too harshly on the basis of such
episodes as the Iran–Contra scandal, however: as Treverton
suggests, 'if presidents are determined to do something
stupid, they will find someone, somewhere, to do it'
(Treverton, 1990, p. 92). In light of these shortcomings, after

the exaggerated hopes of the 1970s, what influence can Congress exert over foreign policy?

Certainly, unless it is driven by constituency pressures, one should not expect sustained and broad oversight of foreign or defense policy. Typically, Congress picks and chooses its issues on the basis of changes in both international and domestic political settings. Even in domestic policy, Congress often finds it more efficient to use 'fire alarms' rather than 'police patrols': establishing mechanisms for those affected by policies to signify their discontent rather than monitoring bureaucratic behavior (McCubbins and Schwartz, 1984). In foreign policy, those who would ring the fire alarm are often outside the American political system, although even those actors (see below) may be heard in Congress. Rather than the fine-grained oversight often endorsed by critics of Congress, one is more likely to find Congress as 'lobbyist, gadfly, supporter, and arbitrator than as detailed manager of ongoing programs' (Art and Ockenden, 1981).

Congress is also unlikely radically to overhaul foreign policy or to initiate new departures. Congress has forced (at least on paper) the adoption of particular negotiating stances in arms control negotiations and weapons systems that were resisted by the executive; perhaps the most prominent example of congressional initiation was the passage of South African sanctions legislation in 1986 over a presidential veto, the first override on a foreign policy issue since the War Powers Resolution. These instances are exceptional, however: Congress generally exercises a conservative influence on foreign policy, intervening when the executive deviates from existing parameters and doctrine.

Finally, congressional influence is limited by the presence of a centrist bloc in both houses that still defers to the executive in the making of foreign policy. In many of the contests during the last two decades, the president and his opponents in Congress have battled for the loyalty of those centrist members: Central America, the use of military force and arms control are only three examples. Although the incentives for congressional activism in foreign policy have grown, a large number of Congressmen still see political benefit in supporting the president in his conduct of external relations.

Passions and Interests in Foreign Policy

Although the evidence is sketchy, many would argue that foreign policy is now influenced by a far larger number of interest groups than at any time in the past. In some cases, this proliferation of organized interests has resulted from changes in the international environment: the increased openness of the American economy has, for example, fostered a larger array of groups seeking to influence commercial policy. No longer are labor-intensive 'losers', with their substantial electoral clout, the only industries that must be placated. As American competitors moved rapidly into technology-intensive and knowledge-intensive sectors such as semiconductors, those industries also pressed for government support.

Issue-areas that had hardly existed or had seen little interest group activity witnessed such mobilization for the first time. Human rights lobbies created an instant constituency for the populations of nearly all repressive societies in the world: countries as remote from the United States as Somalia or Paraguay could quickly become the object of op-ed articles, letter-writing campaigns and demands for congressional intervention. International monetary policy had traditionally been a closely guarded executive branch sphere: Congress had little interest in it, and economic interest groups shared the general political diffidence. The overvaluation of the dollar during the 1980s rapidly altered the old pattern of exchange rate politics, however. Industries which saw their export markets close and their domestic market threatened as the dollar soared, did not devote all of their attention to commercial policy. Business organizations such as the National Association of Manufacturers became vocal lobbyists in favor of dollar depreciation for the first time, and their unprecedented intervention eventually helped to tilt the Reagan Administration toward a more activist policy to bring the dollar down (Destler and Henning, 1989).

Not only the *number* of interest groups in the foreign policy process, but also the *types* of interests being articulated have marked a break with the recent past. The newcomers to interest group politics were often ideological or 'hot issue' interest groups, driven by ethnic identity, moral passion or concern over America's status in the world. Unlike the older politics of material interests, their injection of ideological concerns into foreign policy-making often made the political brokering of these issues difficult. Many of the new hot issue interest groups reflected and were linked to earlier polarization within the foreign policy elite and to the rise of foreign policy professionals, often attached to ideologically defined think-tanks, who had largely replaced the older and more pragmatic foreign policy establishment that had been weakened by the Vietnam War.

On no issue were the new interest group politics clearer than Central America, in which conservative organizations, often with close ties to the White House, backed military aid to the Contras; and human rights, church, and labor groups opposed the Administration's policies in the region (Arnson, 1989). The rise of first conservative and then liberal interest groups to do battle on arms control and nuclear weapons policy also exemplified the new interest group politics: the Committee on the Present Danger and its less prominent allies had waged a strenuous campaign against Carter Administration Soviet policy in the late 1970s. Within a few years, they confronted a peace movement opposition in the form of the nuclear freeze movement, which focussed its attention on Congress and the passage of the nuclear freeze resolution. Other interest groups bridged domestic and foreign policy: the hot issue of abortion carried over into efforts to influence international population control policy.

A second type of actor in the politics of interest representation also became more prominent in the 1980s: foreign governments. Alarms had been sounded in the wake of the 'Koreagate' scandal concerning efforts by American clients to influence the policies on which they depended so heavily. Despite these warnings, foreign government lobbying, particularly in Congress, became even more overt. Middle East arms sales aroused the parties to the Arab–Israeli conflict, each of which enjoyed excellent access to Congress. The sale of AWACS (airborne warning and control system) planes to Saudi Arabia in 1981 became a battle royal between the

Israeli government and its American allies, particularly AIPAC (American–Israeli Public Affairs Committee) and Saudi Arabia, which had retained skillful lobbyists and had support from major American corporations, including arms manufacturers and oil companies. Israeli Prime Minister Begin lobbied senators directly; a member of the Saudi royal family was given an office on Capitol Hill to further his lobbying efforts. Despite intense opposition from AIPAC and after equally intense Reagan Administration pressure on key senators, the Saudi arms sale was narrowly approved (Jentleson, 1990).

The proliferation of interest groups and the intensity of their engagement derived in part from the expansion of Congress's role in foreign policy-making: Congress had traditionally been the first stop for many interest groups, its larger role and decentralized power structure made it even more attractive as a target. Lobbying did not stop at the legislature, however, in trade and other issue-areas, the executive branch was also assiduously pressured. Despite heightened activity and many complaints about single-issue politics, there is little clear-cut evidence that interest groups were more successful in influencing policy in the 1980s than in earlier periods. A number of limits to interest group influence became apparent during the decade. First, the political style of the new, hot issue interest groups did not mesh well with the institutional norms of Congress and the executive. The nuclear freeze movement did succeed in altering the political incentives facing members of Congress on arms control issues, but the peak of the movement's influence in Congress – the passage of the freeze resolution by the House of Representatives in 1983 – was also marked by divisions within the movement over the need to enter into the decidely less ideological operating procedures of Congress (Waller, 1987). The confrontation between the 'purists' of a mass political movement and the brokers of conventional politics was a familiar one in the history of such groups.

A second limitation to interest group influence might be termed the 'equal and opposite reaction' effect: interest mobilization increasingly affected both sides of an issue. Those supporting Israel now confronted a small but growing

Arab–American lobby, which began to break the virtual monopoly that the Israeli point of view had enjoyed in the media. Powerful corporate interests that had thwarted sanctions against South Africa faced a rapidly growing movement of African–American, church and human rights groups. In trade policy, one of the explanations for the ability of the executive and Congress to restrain legislated protectionism is the emergence of anti-protectionist interest groups to confront those demanding trade restrictions. Often these industries benefited from exports to countries that would be affected by American measures, or their production costs would increase as a result of trade limitations. In 1984 industrial users of copper weighed in against import relief for the U.S. copper industry. Their arguments were particularly compelling in an election year since the fabricating industries had more workers than the copper industry and they were located in states that had more electoral votes (Destler and Odell, 1987). Helen Milner's findings that more internationalized industries would tend to espouse more liberal trade policies suggest that the internationalization of the American economy, while adding to pressures for protection from less competitive industries, would also swell the ranks of anti-protectionists (Milner, 1988).

A final restraint on the power of foreign policy interest groups was the skewing of institutions to favor particular outcomes. Congress in particular attempted to deflect protectionist pressures in order to preserve the core of the liberal trading order and forestall any return to the congressional predominance in trade policy foreseen by the Constitution. Even in the new circumstances of decentralized power within Congress and in the face of intense protectionist pressures stemming from the 1981–2 recession and the overvalued dollar, Congress managed to pass a balanced trade law in 1984. The leadership still controlled enough institutional levers to ensure that legislated protectionism was kept to a minimum (Destler, 1986). Congress also directed protectionist demands to the International Trade Commission, an 'independent' agent of the Congress that reviews complaints of injury by domestic import-competing interests. As Judith Goldstein and Stefanie Ann Lenway argue, 'the ITC became a buffer between Congress and constituents. Congress set legal standards that were open to interpretation by the ITC and could be vetoed by the President.... Even today, the perceived political costs of direct control of trade protectionism remain unacceptably high' (Goldstein and Lenway, 1989). Although Congress remained the principal point of access and its barriers to interest group influence were probably lower because of its own institutional redesign, the liberalizing bias in American trade politics, based on congressional delegation of its tariff-negotiating authority to the executive, remained intact.

Public Opinion and Foreign Policy

Public opinion, like other facets of American foreign policy-making, underwent dramatic change under the polarizing impact of the Vietnam War. William Schneider has documented a split in elite opinion as a result of the war and other changes in American society in the late 1960s and early 1970s. The attentive public, which had been content to follow its national leaders in pursuit of policies of containment and economic liberalism, divided between liberal internationalists, who 'emphasized economic and humanitarian problems over security issues and rejected a hegemonic role for the United States' and conservative internationalists, who used an East–West lens to view the world and emphasized military power and national security (Schneider, 1987). In addition to discovering these tribes of internationalists, Schneider also found that about half of the American public are 'noninternationalists', skeptical of international involvements of all kinds. 'Conservative' and 'liberal' (in the post-1960s meaning of those labels) do not capture the reality of this relatively inattentive portion of the public. The history of American public opinion and foreign policy since 1965 is one in which this noninternationalist near-majority provides both a ballast (its fixation on peace and strength have remained relatively constant) but also an element of volatility. The public has grown far more skeptical and less deferential of its national leadership; the noninternationalist public has emphasized first its concerns with peace (allying with liberals in the Vietnam War era) and then its concerns with military weakness (allying with conservative internationalists in the late 1970s and assuring the election of Ronald Reagan). This volatility has been influenced by the growing importance of television in shaping public attitudes toward foreign affairs: the formerly 'inattentive' audience now absorbs international information whether it wishes to or not through the edited medium of television news. The result: 'an unstable system of competing coalitions in which the mass public swings left or right unpredictably in response to its current fears and concerns. A stable, two-track foreign policy has given way to an erratic alternation' (Schneider, 1987, p. 51).

In many respects, Schneider's model seems to capture the apparently dramatic swings in United States foreign policy stance over two decades, swings that were often greater in the realm of rhetoric than in actual policy change. Nevertheless, the influence of public opinion on foreign policy has long been the subject of scholarly skepticism. It is very difficult to assess how much of public opinion is cause (influencing policy-makers) and how much effect (taking its cues from those same policy-makers). Public attitudes toward military spending and arms control issues may well have been affected by media attention, first to conservative assaults on Carter Administration policies and then to the nuclear freeze movement. The limits of such strategies of influence are indicated by Reagan Administration 'public diplomacy' on Central America, however. Despite an intensive campaign to bring the media into line behind the president's position and effort to mobilize sympathetic political groups to win support for the Contras, public opinion remained consistently opposed to military aid to the Sandinista opponents. Decades of elite support for liberalized trade have not shaken the consistent support of the uninformed public for protectionism (Parry and Kornbluth, 1988).

Perhaps the greatest barrier to a clear influence of public opinion on policy-makers is the often contradictory or ambiguous nature of the public's attitudes. This is particularly the case for the noninternationalist segment of the public, which often demonstrates strong patterns of support for or against a country or issue without endorsing particular means to deal with that problem. Although the public refused to support the Contras, it consistently held that a 'communist' regime in Nicaragua represented a threat to the vital interests of the United States. Public opinion acknowledged a responsibility to help the developing countries, but opposes increased foreign aid by a large margin (Schneider, 1987).

Finally, the conventional wisdom concerning electoral behavior – the key link between public and its representatives – has long held that elections are not determined by foreign policy issues but by judgments regarding economic performance. This finding has always raised one troubling question: why do candidates, particularly presidential candidates, devote so much time to burnishing their international image if their efforts are unrewarded at the polls? Some recent studies indicate that the candidates are right and scholarly wisdom wrong: public attitudes on foreign policy 'have had a strong impact on voting in most of the recent elections and have played at least some role in virtually all presidential elections during the previous thirty-odd years' (Aldrich *et al.*, 1989). On a periodic basis at least, the electoral connection between public opinion and foreign policy can be re-established.

George Bush's handling of foreign policy in an era when many of the old, Cold War cleavages are obsolescent will provide an interesting test of the stability of public opinion. His decision to send troops to defend Saudi Arabia in the wake of Iraq's invasion of Kuwait served to unite elite opinion around a military intervention for the first time in decades. By carefully emphasizing the United Nations and multilateral backing for the intervention, Bush won the support of liberal internationalists who might otherwise have opposed intervention. The less attentive public, however, expressed the same doubts over foreign entanglements that had persisted for two decades. In a *New York Times* poll published on 12 August 1990 after the president's decision was announced, a strong 'rally round the flag' effect was evident. Nevertheless, 42 per cent held 'that the current situation in the Middle East is a lot like Vietnam in the 1960s' and 59 per cent of the sample believed that the intervention was very or somewhat likely to lead to a long war. Although Bush had captured the internationalist elite, the noninternationalists continued to express their strong reservations. Foreign entanglement is still viewed warily by many Americans.

The New Politics of American Foreign Policy

For most of the actors in the making of American foreign policy, the Vietnam War era was a watershed, shifting their roles and changing the process beyond recognition. Despite reassertion of executive leadership by Ronald Reagan and efforts to swing public opinion and Congress behind a conservative internationalist vision of the world, the process was by and large consolidated in the 1980s: the golden age of Cold War consensus was not to be re-established, even by a popular president who could wield the Soviet threat as well as any of his predecessors.

The new politics of foreign policy seems likely to persist, but assessing its record is difficult. At least three criteria may be applied in judging foreign policy success or failure. The first is democratic control: does foreign policy reflect the wishes of the electorate? Is policy under the direction of representative, elected officials? Counter to this criterion is an elitist standard, endorsed by many realists and other skeptics of democratic capabilities in the international sphere: does a foreign policy embody certain (presumably persistent) national interests? Through volatile popular moods and the rise and fall of administrations, are those core interests satisfied? Finally, the criterion of efficiency is dear to specialists in public administration and management. Are national goals accomplished at the lowest cost with the least expenditure of official time? Does a policy emerge at all? How cumbersome is the process by which it emerges?

The realist criterion of national interest is the most difficult to apply, since it is hard to stipulate those interests without consulting democratic sentiment. Nevertheless, if one accepts a standard realist definition of core interests – territorial integrity and political autonomy – the American foreign policy process has clearly succeeded. Those who endorse declinist views might well argue that future autonomy has been mortgaged by today's economic excesses, but a retrospective judgment confirms that the foreign policy process has never brought the republic as close to danger as, for example, the far different institutional balance of the 1930s. If anything, the process has been skewed toward overstating the external threat, at the cost of interventions such as the Vietnam War.

The more difficult trade-off is between democracy and efficiency, and the trade-off has arguably become steeper in the post-Vietnam foreign policy process. The changes in American foreign policy since 1968 have clearly brought the participation of a larger set of actors in the making of foreign policy. Perhaps the representative character of the numerous interest groups (many based 'inside the Beltway') is questionable, and the engagement of the mass public is often low, but the process is more open, the attentive public is probably larger, and the role of the legislature is far greater. Three issue-areas have epitomized the costs and benefits of the new politics of foreign policy in the 1980s. Central American policy under the Reagan Administration, particularly policy toward Nicaragua, was clearly a failure. Partisan and interest group-driven conflict brought about stalemate between Congress and the President, a stalemate that encouraged the bureaucratic buccaneers of Oliver North and company to undertake secret and illegal actions. The policy did reflect the ambiguities of public opinion described above: both President and Congress could claim to be representing one facet of that opinion. Only after the Bush Administration endorsed a diplomatic track and the Sandinistas took their ill-fated stab at electoral politics did the stalemate end.

South African sanctions appeared headed in the same direction as Central America, but in this instance, the legislature, pushed forward by more intense public disgust with apartheid (though not public support of sanctions) was willing to override a reluctant executive that had already conceded a much milder form of sanctions. The end of democracy was certainly served; a lengthy national debate on the efficacy of sanctions had taken place; the process produced a clear policy outcome (although some would later criticize the implementation of sanctions by the executive). Finally, foreign aid, stepchild of both the foreign policy and the budgetary process, was also an exemplar of the fate of a program lacking a powerful constituency or strong public support, and easily exploited by congressional entrepreneurs to make low-cost points regarding human rights, abortion and other issues. Despite the protests of the Secretary of State and efforts to protect aid programs to the most important clients of the United States, funding for foreign aid declined after 1985 as budgetary pressures mounted. A realist would despair over national interests being sidelined in this way, and the present foreign aid process is a very inefficient way to move money, but it certainly reflects public and much elite opinion on the value of these expenditures.

These three examples of the new politics of foreign policy each concerned the developing world: the costs to the new institutional arrangements were lower in issue-areas of higher risk (in international politics and domestic politics) and more consensus on ends. (Relations with the Soviet Union and with NATO are two examples.) The world emerging in the 1990s, however, is a world with a diminished Soviet threat, one in which issues such as Central America and South Africa will be far more prominent. The Iraqi-inspired crisis in the Gulf is a harbinger of that new world.

Two strategies could lower the costs of a democratized foreign policy without attempting to reconstruct the lost world of Cold War consensus. Future presidents could construct a new consensus without the Soviet threat. George Bush seems to aim at a new 'managerial internationalism': continued American involvement without an overarching 'grand theme'. Perhaps such non-ideological internationalism could succeed on the simple basis of the internationalization of the American economy and society – the United States would remain 'involved' in the way in which European countries are 'involved' internationally, because they must be. The substantial noninternationalist portion of the public could well be captured by other appeals, however, either a populist reaction to continued international involvement or a unilateralist economic nationalism with Japan as the 'threat'. Each of these have found little echo yet among the political elite, but economic downturn or external failure (or perceived decline) could precipitate renewed elite conflict.

With no guarantee of a new political consensus on foreign policy, a second alternative is to reconstruct or reform the foreign policy process so that it functions better in the absence of consensus. Many are the reforms that have been proposed to improve the often cumbersome mechanism by which the United States creates its external policies; few are those that have been chosen. Most reforms follow on a detailed accounting of the political 'failures' in foreign policy-making, yet the reforms themselves are often hopelessly apolitical. Most, it seems, will be implemented through a sheer act of political will. Little attention is given to the incentives that key actors will have to implement such reforms; seldom is their discontent with existing institutional arrangements documented.

A final aspect of the making of American foreign policy is that it has come to resemble other spheres of policy-making: the actors and institutions across foreign policy issue-areas have grown more similar, and foreign policy-making has come to resemble domestic policy processes. Even a formerly arcane and exotic sphere such as intelligence has now taken on the characteristics of executive–legislative relations in other spheres of policy, so much so that the Congressional watchdogs risk being coopted by the intelligence agencies (Treverton, 1990). International monetary policy, also a longstanding realm of experts and bureaucrats, now receives the attention of Congress and interest groups. Any reforms of the foreign policy process then, must embody reforms of American politics and political institutions. To succeed, reforms must satisfy the goals of key political actors. Yet the foreign policy system that has emerged since Vietnam seems to satisfy most of the players most of the time: there have been no more Vietnams, the Soviet threat is fading, and as for economic decline, that, it seems, can be left to future generations. American foreign policy has become American politics by other means, and its future will reflect the future evolution of American politics. Absent dramatic change in the domestic political environment, the politics of foreign policy are likely to change only during junctures of radical alteration in the international environment. And there is little evidence to date that the gradual erosion of America's international economic position or the rapid but benign end of the Cold War will qualify for such a role.

PART FOUR

Current Issues

12

The Budget Deficit

STANLEY E. COLLENDER

Concern about the federal budget deficit has continued to dominate the politics of the United States at the beginning of the Bush Administration and has placed severe constraints on the conduct of public policy. Not only has the size of the budget deficit become a major political problem in its own right, but it has tended to subsume other issues within its embrace. The annual battles over taxation and spending regularly exclude consideration of other substantive questions and have generated considerable partisan bitterness between President and Congress.

The Legacy of the Reagan Years

It is fairly clear that the years 1981 through 1988 – the Reagan years – will be looked upon as a turning point as far as U.S. budget politics are concerned.

Not only did the deficit increase dramatically and remain high compared to almost every prior period in American history, but budget politics were turned completely upside down with previously staunch balanced-budget-advocating Republicans supporting a president who never proposed a balanced budget and previously labelled big-spending Democrats arguing that the deficit had to be eliminated.

As if this was not enough, the budget process was also

changed (some might say revolutionized) not once but twice during the eight years of the Reagan presidency (and then again two years later). These rapid procedural changes left the annual debate over revenues and spending very much up in the air as Congress and the White House struggled to meet the stringent limitations the processes placed both on legislative procedures and proposed solutions to virtually every issue.

It is important to stress that budgetary change did not end with the completion of the Reagan Administration. On the contrary, the actual impact of all of these changes on U.S. budget politics was only felt in full after Ronald Reagan left office. In fact, it is obvious that George Bush only realised the real legacy of the Reagan years once he succeeded Reagan and found that his own plans were severely constrained at almost every turn by what had happened on the budget during the previous eight years.

Since Ronald Reagan campaigned for the presidency in 1980 on a platform of reducing federal spending and came into office in 1981 promising to eliminate the deficit by 1984, it is safe to say that the legacy he left on the budget is far different from that he had planned. In retrospect, however, it is possible if not likely, that American budget policy and politics will be affected for a longer period of time because of what he actually did do rather than what he promised to accomplish.

The Numbers Tell the Story

A quick review of the changes in the budget between 1981 and 1988 – the eight budgets proposed and implemented by Reagan while he was in office – explains much of what happened.

As Table 12.2 shows, in nominal terms the deficit increased to an all-time high of $221.2 billion in fiscal 1986 before levelling off at about $150 billion from fiscal 1987–88. But this was only one of five record highs that were recorded during the Reagan years. Over the eight years the Reagan deficits averaged $167.3 billion, an extraordinary situation when you realize that, prior to Reagan, the U.S. deficit had never even reached $100 billion in any one year.

The Reagan years were also record-setting in constant dollars. The eight Reagan deficits were the highest ever recorded in U.S. in peacetime; the deficit was only higher from 1943–5, at the height of the Second World War.

This was also generally the case with the nominal deficit as a percentage of GNP. Although there were two exceptions in 1975 and 1976, in no years other than those during the Second World War was the U.S. deficit a higher percentage of GNP than it was during the Reagan years.

The best picture as to how the Reagan years changed the U.S. budget comes not from looking at the aggregate figures but from looking at the individual parts. By comparing 1980,

TABLE 12.1   *Steady growth in U.S. revenues and outlays, 1981–8 (millions of dollars)*

Year	Revenues	Outlays
1981	599 272	678 209
1982	617 766	745 706
1983	699 562	808 327
1984	666 457	851 781
1985	734 057	946 316
1986	769 091	990 258
1987	854 143	1 003 830
1988	908 954	1 064 044

Source: U.S. Office of Management and Budget.

TABLE 12.2   *Steady growth in the U.S. deficit, 1981–8 (billions of dollars)*

Year	Nominal Deficit	Constant Deficit*	Nominal Deficit as a % of GNP
1981	−78.9**	−84.6	2.6
1982	−127.9**	−127.9	4.1
1983	−207.8**	−199.2	6.8
1984	−185.3	−171.5	5.0
1985	−212.3**	−190.6	5.4
1986	−221.2**	−193.8	5.3
1987	−149.7	−127.9	3.4
1988	−155.1	−128.1	3.2

* 1982 dollars.
**Record.

Source: U.S. Office of Management and Budget.

the last full year solely under control of the Carter Administration, with 1988, the last full year solely attributable to the Reagan Administration, Table 12.3 shows that three areas – human resources (education, training, social services, health, income security, social security, and veterans benefits); physical resources (energy, natural resources and environment, transportation, community and regional development, and commerce and housing credit); and other (international affairs, space and technology, agriculture, administration of justice, and general government) all fell as a percentage of the budget. Military spending, on the other hand, rose from 22.7 per cent to 27.3 per cent.

But the biggest increase of all was interest on the national debt, which grew by almost 61 per cent, from 8.9 per cent of the budget to 14.3 per cent. During the same period, gross U.S. debt almost tripled, from $908.5 billion to a previously inconceivable $2.6 *trillion*.

TABLE 12.3 *Dramatic changes in U.S. budget components, 1980–8 (millions of dollars)*

	1980 outlays	% of budget	1988 outlays	% of budget
Military	133 995	22.7	290 361	27.3
Human resources	313 374	53.0	533 407	50.1
Physical resources	65 985	11.2	68 275	6.4
Interest on the debt	52 512	8.9	151 748	14.3
Other	44 996	7.6	57 219	5.4

Source: U.S. Office of Management and Budget.

Procedural and Political Changes Followed the Numbers

The growing frustration of having a President who was seemingly devoted to eliminating the deficit but who actually accomplished the opposite, along with that President's almost routine castigation of it for not balancing the budget forced Congress to change the U.S. budget process in 1985. It passed the Balanced Budget and Emergency Deficit Control Act of 1985, commonly known as Gramm–Rudman–Hollings (GRH) because of its three principal sponsors, Senators Phil

Gramm (R.–Tex.), Warren Rudman (R.–N.H.), and Ernest Hollings (D.–S.C.).

Unlike the two previous laws that created the framework of budgeting procedure (the Budget and Accounting Act of 1921 and the Congressional Budget and Impoundment Control Act of 1974), GRH specifically started by defining the deficit as being bad and was designed to eliminate it almost to the exclusion of all other goals. Except in the case of war or an economic turndown, GRH removed all choice as to how large the deficit should be each year and how much it should be reduced. Both questions were specified through the creation of 'maximum deficit amounts', deficit limits that declined each year until the budget was supposed to be balanced.

In addition, rather than simply assuming that Congress and the President would live up to these limits, GRH supposedly guaranteed them through its most radical departure from the previous budget procedures – sequestration. According to the sequestration procedure, if Congress and the White House did not agree on and enact a plan that reduced the deficit to the specified maximum for the year, federal spending was cut automatically by whatever amount was needed to reach the deficit maximum. Half of the cuts would come from military programs and half from domestic programs.

TABLE 12.4   *Gramm–Rudman–Hollings deficit maximums*

	1986	1987	1988	1989	1990	1991	1992	1993
Original	172	144	108	72	36	0		
Revised	–	–	144	136	100	64	28	0

Graham–Rudman–Hollings may have been the most cynical law ever enacted in American history. First, it did not trust law-makers to come up with the appropriate fiscal policy for the nation, so it specified it for them. Secondly, it did not trust them to implement that detailed policy and thus, in effect, placed a sword over the politicians' heads and dared them not to comply with the previously-enacted requirements.

The lack of trust on which GRH was based was a direct result of the antipathy that built up between the Democrats and Republicans and between the White House and Congress on the budget during the Reagan years. This atmosphere of suspicion was evident in virtually every aspect of federal budgeting, although the following five examples provide a good idea about what was happening.

- Starting in 1981 and continuing through the seven other years of the Reagan Administration, the President's economic and deficit projections proved to be wildly optimistic to the point where few outside or inside the Government believed them (Stockman, 1986; Greider, 1981).

- Reagan frequently agreed to raise revenues and then blamed Democrats for increasing taxes.

- In 1985 Senate Republicans agreed to a politically very difficult cut in Social Security benefits only to have the White House side with Democrats at the last minute and back down. It was later assumed that the Republican Senators' support for the social security cut helped the Democrats regain control of the Senate in the 1986 elections.

- Reagan frequently submitted a budget to Congress that was so extreme as to have no chance of being considered and then blamed Congress for not living up to its budget responsibilities.

- Especially in the early years of the Reagan Administration when Caspar Weinberger was Secretary of Defense, Reagan frequently refused to propose any reductions in military spending even though it was clear that politically acceptable tax increases and domestic spending cuts would not be enough to reduce the deficit as required.

In part, Gramm–Rudman–Hollings was intended to overcome the bad blood that developed between all of the participants in the budget debate by deciding some of the most contentious issues in advance. There would no longer be a question as to how large the deficit should be every year because the maximums set that level. Similarly, the amount of deficit reduction would also not be an issue because it would have to be whatever amount was needed to reduce the deficit to the maximum.

Gramm-Rudman–Hollings did not work out quite as expected, however. Rather than overcoming the mistrust between the various budget actors, it helped create more as Congress and the White House found increasingly creative ways for not meeting the deficit maximums. The use of unrealistically optimistic economic forecasts, for example, was hardly eliminated. On the contrary, Congress seemed increasingly content to use the President's rosy economic projections even when it understood that they were, in fact, rosy.

Creative accounting also became increasingly prevalent during the GRH period. For example, rather than cutting spending or increasing taxes to pay for the bailout of the U.S. savings and loan industry in 1989, Congress, at the Bush Administration's insistence, decided to do the transaction 'off-budget', that is, not to count it in the budget totals.

Other creative accounting tricks included accelerating tax payments to bring the revenue into the current fiscal year, moving spending into an adjacent fiscal year, starting a program this year with low costs that expanded rapidly in the future, and assuming deficit reductions early in the year that everyone knew would never be enacted.

One of the most egregious examples of a budget gimmick, not to mention the best indication that Reagan had set a clear precedent that was likely to be followed in the future, occurred during the first few months of the Bush Administration. To meet the GRH requirements, Secretary of Defense Dick Cheney proposed that the first military pay date of fiscal 1990 be moved from Monday, 2 October, to Friday, 29 September, supposedly so that U.S. troops and their dependents would be paid before the weekend began. What Cheney did not say, however, was that the move would also shift the $2.9 billion payment from the first business day of one fiscal year to the last business day of the previous year and, in so doing, reduce the deficit in fiscal 1990 and help meet the GRH requirements while increasing the deficit in fiscal 1989.

By increasing the fiscal 1989 deficit this maneuver contributed to the failure to reach the GRH maximum for that year. However, the GRH sequestration spending cuts could only be triggered once a year – in October, two weeks after the fiscal year began. If, as happened in this case, the deficit exceeded the maximum but the determination was not made until after the October deadline, sequestration did not occur.

The Cheney maneuver, therefore, meant that, even though the 1989 deficit was higher than the amount set by GRH, there was no sequestration that year. And, because it allowed Congress and the Administration to lower the 1990 deficit, the Cheney plan also helped avoid sequestration for that year. It is little wonder that there was little opposition to what Cheney proposed once its implications became known.

These 'blue smoke and mirrors' practices may have lowered some of the budget tensions as hard choices over spending cuts and tax increases were avoided; but it did so by increasing the distrust that existed between voters and Washington. Public opinion polls in the United States show quite clearly that both parties get relatively low marks for dealing with the deficit. They also show a tremendous lack of trust about proposed solutions; few Americans are willing to accept a tax increase because they believe that elected officials will simply spend the additional funds on favored constituencies rather than use it to reduce the deficit.

The public mistrust about the budget has, in turn, led to the most ironic change of all. Hard as it may be to believe, the political, procedural and substantive events in the budget debate that occurred while Ronald Reagan was President make the problem even more difficult to solve than it was before, as proposed solutions are stymied at every turn.

Challenges for the 1990s

All of this leads to the conclusion that there will be three budget challenges in the 1990s: spending, taxes and process.

Spending

As hard as it is to imagine in a budget that will approach or exceed $2 trillion by the middle of the 1990s, thanks to the Reagan years there will be little spending left that will be easy to cut. The reason is that about one-third of the budget will be devoted to fixed costs that cannot be cut at all and another almost half of the budget will pay for politically sensitive benefit 'entitlement' programs.

The fixed costs include two different items. Interest on the U.S. debt will probably exceed 16 per cent of the budget by the mid-1990s as the total U.S. debt exceeds $4 trillion. Contracts signed in prior years, mostly for military procurement, will equal an additional 15 per cent of the budget. Since both interest and entitlements represent legally-binding claims on the government, neither will be able to produce savings no matter how bad the deficit might be.

At least half of the entitlements will be Social Security, a program that will increase in political sensitivity as the post Second World War baby boom generation starts to collect its retirement benefits. Another one-quarter will be Medicare, which provides health care for the elderly, and it too will become increasingly sensitive as the United States population ages. This means that all other entitlements will have to bear the brunt of most deficit reduction efforts. But since the remaining entitlements – such as the federal civil service and military retirement programs, veterans benefits, and welfare – are also quite sensitive, it will be difficult to cut these as well.

The remaining part of the budget will be the most vulnerable. But since it includes military spending (except for prior-year weapons purchases), domestic spending for most federal agencies and such basic public protection services as the FBI, Drug Enforcement Agency, Coast Guard, air traffic controllers and federal jails, it is difficult to imagine how large cuts will be found in these areas either.

It is important to keep in mind that the above analysis does not take into account any new programs. Another California earthquake, or any similar disaster for that matter, will certainly encourage additional federal spending, as will the need to upgrade American infrastructure and take steps to improve the United States competitive position in the world. And a foreign policy or military problem, such as the 1990 Iraqi invasion of Kuwait that led to Operation Desert Storm, could certainly result in unanticipated increases for defense or foreign aid, or both.

How are these new and pent-up demands for spending likely to be met in light of the budget situation that Ronald Reagan left to George Bush? Except in all but the most extreme circumstances, increases in current programs and any new programs will likely have to be funded at the expense of other existing programs. In other words, the debate over U.S. budget priorities will develop into a zero-sum game in the 1990s in which more for one area or program of the budget will mean less for another.

This was immediately evident in the first year of the Bush Administration, when the deficit made it impossible to fund increases in a number of new high-priority areas. For example, although the political upheavals in eastern Europe created demands for increased U.S. foreign aid for the new and more pro-Western governments, the White House and Congress were unable to find those funds without proposing cuts in other foreign aid. Such revisions included diverting some of the aid that had been slated for Israel, a proposal that would have been unthinkable only a year earlier because of that country's extremely high popularity in the U.S.

A second example of zero-sum budgeting was the talk about a 'peace dividend', that is, transferring funds from the military to domestic budget because of the apparently reduced threat to American interests around the world. Many lobbies (and their champions in Congress and the Administration) immediately proposed ways to spend the funds that were no longer expected to be needed by the Pentagon. Even though the extent of the dividend was not known by policy-makers, the possibility of the new pool of available funds sent many interest groups scrambling for months in what some in Washington likened to piranhas in a feeding frenzy.

A third example was the new Budget Enforcement Act (BEA) budget process (see below) that replaced GRH in 1990 and which formalized zero-sum budgeting through 1995. For 1991–3, BEA actually established three separate zero-sum situations – for defense, international, and domestic spending – and required that, except in certain 'emergencies', all additional funding come from existing programs.

Taxes

The tax situation in the 1990s will be similar to that with spending. The fall in popularity of income taxes, combined with the Reagan–Bush rhetoric against any increase, means that Congress will find it hard to support changes in the next decade.

This means that, to the extent that increased revenues are part of the deficit reduction equation at all, Congress and the White House will have to look to something other than the income tax. As was amply demonstrated by the tax portion of the 1990 deficit reduction legislation (the Omnibus Budget Reconciliation Act of 1990), excise taxes and user fees are the most likely vehicles for raising taxes because they will result in high revenues quickly.

A consumption tax of some kind, including a value-added tax, has the potential for raising the most revenue. However, because a consumption tax is so alien to Americans and would be so controversial, it will probably take at least two years for the legislative process on such a tax to be completed and another two years to implement the tax once the legislation is enacted. This means that a consumption tax offers little immediate help in reducing the deficit. As a result, it is not likely to be a part of any deficit reduction effort that occurs in the immediate future.

Process

The Gramm–Rudman–Hollings process was revised in 1990 and its successor, the Budget Enforcement Act, bears little resemblance to it. The major difference between GRH and the Budget Enforcement Act is that, while the 1985 legislation was entirely concerned with reducing the budget deficit, BEA's main purpose is to limit Congress and the President's ability to enact increases in spending and decreases in revenues. The deficit may fall under the Budget Enforcement

Act; but that will be more a result of an improving economy and other fortuitous events than by budget process directives. (Thus, for example, the initial deficit projections made under the Budget Enforcement Act assumed that federal spending for the savings and loan bailout, which in 1991 are expected to be in excess of $100 billion, would be reversed by 1994. At that point the federal government is expected to earn as much as $50 billion a year from selling the assets of the previous-acquired S&Ls.)

The Real Legacy of the Reagan Years

Although Ronald Reagan promised to leave office with a balanced federal budget, the large deficits that he actually left, the bad blood that developed between Democrats and Republicans and Congress and the White House on the budget, and the latest procedural restrictions that were adopted, mean that the 1990s will be characterized by a number of things that Reagan not only did not promise but probably did not anticipate.

Stalemates

After a decade of spending cuts, the choices that Congress and the White House are facing on the budget are not only hard, they are also largely politically unacceptable. Until the enactment of the BEA in 1990, this had been expected to lead to a steady series of stalemates between the House and Senate and between Congress and the President as each tried to outmaneuver the other to avoid the blame for what had to be done. And this is, in fact, what happened in 1990 as congressional and Administration leaders met for almost six months to work out a deficit reduction agreement that would not be politically harmful. As long as BEA is in place, however, the stalemates should disappear because reducing the deficit will not be the primary goal. But if BEA is revised or when it expires at the end of 1995, the deficit and the deficit's consequent stalemates could and probably will quickly return.

Slow Progress on the Deficit

Without some change in outlook, either by the voters or elected officials, there will be only limited progress on the deficit. And this assumes that the economy will continue to grow. If it does not – if, for example, another recession during the mid-1990s follows the one that began in late 1990, the U.S. deficit may increase rather than decrease.

Limited Ability to Respond to New Contingencies

The ultimate problem that the deficit situation is likely to cause is an inability of the United States to plan for and respond to sudden new problems. Unless the problem is considered critical, the deficit has made it all but impossible for the U.S. to undertake any new initiatives if they will cost substantial sums of federal dollars. This means increased competition for the few dollars that will be available and non-federal solutions to problems that in a previous era would have been considered a federal responsibility.

The best example of this is in health care. Because of the limited resources the federal governement is willing to devote to this problem, it generally only gets involved when a crisis of some kind occurs, such as an epidemic or a dramatic increase in infant deaths. This means that the government will be deficit spending only to fund consumption-like expenditures to deal with the human hardship caused by the crisis instead of paying in advance for investments that would make the crisis less likely. From an economic point of view, this is exactly the wrong strategy, and one that is very likely to be more costly in the long-run.

Hidden Taxes

If the federal government cannot spend its own dollars to deal with problems, it will look increasingly to state and local governments to spend theirs. In addition, the federal government will also consider passing costs on to the private sector, mandating that businesses provide more and more comprehensive benefits to their workers in lieu of federal government. If this occurs, the budget debate that has taken place at the federal level during the 1980s could be transferred to other levels of government and to the private sector in the 1990s and so will pervade American politics even more fully in the future than it did in the past.

13

Civil Rights and the Bush Presidency

GILLIAN PEELE

One area of continuing tension in public policy under President Bush has been the field of civil rights. Initially Bush sent out mixed signals about his attitude towards minorities and the extent to which the federal government should attempt to prevent discrimination against them. Thus he balanced a changed tone in the handling of civil rights issues and support for legislation to protect the disabled (which resulted in the Americans with Disabilities Act of 1990) with a veto of the Civil Rights Act of 1990 and equivocation over its successor – the Civil Rights and Women's Equity in Employment Act of 1991. In the heated debate about the merits of these legislative measures passed by an overwhelmingly Democratic Congress, Democrats and Republicans accused each other of playing electoral politics rather than addressing the substantive issues. In fact the Bush Administration, although extremely sensitive to electoral concerns, was also pressured by a range of factors including the attitudes of business on affirmative action, internal divisions and a powerful legacy from the previous Administration.

The Reagan Legacy on Civil Rights

It is hardly surprising that civil rights should raise such passions within the American political system. The status and treatment of minorities within American society has always been a highly sensitive subject for a polity formally dedicated to equality but in practice marked by inequalities of power and status which frequently reflect race and gender. Since the Second World War at least minorities in general (and blacks in particular) have looked to the federal government and to the presidency to create a favorable intellectual climate from their perspective for the handling of such issues as employment practice, educational opportunity and housing. Successive postwar administrations of all parties and the courts had built up an increasingly strong record of using the power of federal government to try to eliminate discrimination from American life.

The Reagan Administration, however, wished to challenge many of the assumptions underlying the federal government's role in the field of civil rights. Although it believed it had public opinion on its side, its aggressive drive to reverse the trend of more than three decades brought it into institutional conflict with the courts and with Congress as well as into head-on confrontation with the liberal civil rights community.

Liberal civil rights groups during the Reagan presidency were very aware that they faced a counter-revolution. For Ralph Neas, the Executive Director of the Leadership Conference on Civil Rights (a pressure group which represents some 180 national organizations) and many other civil rights leaders, the Reagan Administration had compiled the worst civil rights record of any administration in the past fifty years. The Administration's approach was discussed in terms of 'turning the clock back' on civil rights enforcement (Amaker, 1988; Days, 1984).

The causes of the Reagan Administration's attitude towards civil rights need to be briefly highlighted before attempting an analysis of President Bush's approach. There seem to have been three broad reasons for the controversial stance of the Reagan Administration over the period 1981–8.

First, and most generally, the Reagan Administration saw itself as possessing a strong policy mandate. Ronald Reagan had made no efforts to disguise his adherence to conservative positions and indeed he believed that his strong positions on foreign and domestic policy issues were responsible for the magnitude of his victory. Behind Reagan there was a conservative movement which had come together over the late 1970s. This movement – which was far more aggressive and intellectually self-confident than the traditional Republican Party – gave the Reagan Administration a different style from that of previous Republican presidencies (see Chapter 1).

Civil rights issues were themes which differentiated liberals and conservatives in America very clearly. For liberals such remedies as affirmative action and court-ordered busing were necessary to promote the disadvantaged groups in American society. Moreover, for many liberals the simple removal of legalized discrimination was not enough. The achievement of real equality in their view involved both the absence of institutional barriers to progress and the pursuit of a broad strategy of social and economic equality for minority groups. There was thus an unfinished agenda of civil rights and the federal government had a duty to promote policies which would eliminate poverty as well as monitor voting rights and school desegregation.

For conservatives such an approach to public policy was anathema. In their view the constitution gave no warrant for the special treatment of racial groups. By definition such policies as reserving places for minority ethnic groups in the process of university admissions, for example, involved further discrimination against innocent members of the rest of American society. Nor did they approve of the process whereby efforts to preserve minority access to the ballot (the purpose of the Voting Rights Act of 1965) had been transformed into a mandate to ensure that minority groups were proportionately represented and that their voting strength was not diluted in the process of reapportionment (see Chapter 2).

The intellectual arguments against affirmative action had been forcefully presented in the 1970s by such 'neo conservatives' as Nathan Glazer and Irving Kristol (Peele, 1984). The Republican Party had taken up many of the neo-conservatives' arguments about affirmative action and race-conscious remedies. In its platform of 1980, while opposing 'unfair discrimination because of race, sex, advanced age, physical handicap, difference of national origin or religion, or economic circumstances', the Republicans had rejected policies which involved 'bureaucratic regulations and decisions which rely on quotas, ratios and numerical requirements'.

A second reason for the Reagan Administration's stance on civil rights was the extent to which the different elements of the conservative coalition had their own specific agendas which demanded some radical policy initiatives. There was for example a broad opposition within the new Christian right to feminism. Title VII of the civil rights legislation of the 1960s had been broadened to cover not merely minority racial groups but also women; and it was seen by many conservative Christians as being hostile to traditional family values. Partly in response to this newly articulate element in American politics, the Republican Party after 1980 dropped its support of the Equal Rights Amendment.

The conservative Christians had other issues on their agenda in the 1980s. One important concern was the preservation of their private schools which were committed to fostering biblical values in education. These schools had grown in popularity with the implementation of desegregation in the public schools and with what many conservatives saw as a not unrelated breakdown of discipline there. However, the status of these schools was controversial because few of them had any numerically significant ethnic minority enrollment. This ethnic imbalance may or may not have been the result of deliberate discrimination; but it was sufficient to incur the hostility of the Internal Revenue Service which could deny tax-exempt status to institutions which did not conform with the public policy goal of integration.

The tax status of private schools became an issue in the Reagan Administration when Trent Lott (the minority whip in the House) and political appointees within the Justice Department exerted pressure to secure a reversal of federal policy on when an institution (in this case Bob Jones University) might qualify for the benefit of charitable status. The episode was significant because of the way it underlined the radical nature of the new elements in the conservative coalition and the extent to which the Reagan Administration might respond to their agendas even if, as in the Bob Jones case, it involved the unusual steps of reversing long-standing I.R.S policy and reversing a position which the Administration had taken before the Supreme Court.

It was not merely the conservative Christians who wished to redirect the Administration's policies on civil rights. Other elements in the conservative coalition advanced arguments and policy proposals which represented a rejection of much of the welfare liberalism of the previous two decades.

The new right think-tanks such as the Heritage Foundation had their own agenda for the handling of civil rights issues. Thus, in its influential *Mandate for Leadership* series (which offered the Reagan Administration blueprints for implementing the 'conservative revolution') the Heritage Foundation recommended a number of initiatives which the federal government should take to alter the direction of civil rights policy. In 1984 such steps included eliminating federal support for set-aside programmes, opposing the doctrine of comparable worth, and requiring an intent standard in voting rights cases (Butler *et al.*, 1984).

The third cause of hostility to civil rights in the Reagan Administration was its general hostility to two aspects of the American political system which many observers might view as endemic. In line with the thrust of much new right argument in the 1970s and 1980s the Administration advocated a change in the balance between government provision and market provision. Government provision would always be flawed because it would have to respond to electoral influences and sectional interests. The market by comparison was efficient and free from the distortions imposed on policy by entrenched interests. It was, of course, highly relevant in this context that in the field of civil rights policy the major pressure groups were liberal; and in the mind of conservatives such groups as the NAACP, the Leadership Conference on Civil Rights and the ACLU constituted an extremely powerful establishment.

In addition to this sense of the need to resist the liberal establishment, the conservatives were also critical of the role of the courts in the development of civil rights policy. Indeed the perceived usurpation of power by the federal courts and the progress of civil rights policy were intimately linked in the minds of many conservatives (see Chapter 1).

The Reagan Administration came to power with a deliberate strategy for the federal courts and the American legal system. This strategy had a number of elements but involved a careful scrutiny of all judicial appointments to secure ideologically compatible appointees to the federal bench. (H. Schwartz, 1988; Clayton, 1990). Such nominees were not qualified simply by being Republican sympathizers. They had to be ideologically sound which was sometimes established by the litmus test issue of abortion and sometimes involved adherence to the doctrine of original intent as a theory of constitutional interpretation (Levy, 1988).

The Reagan Administration, it should be noted, did not merely wish to alter the direction of policy behind the scenes. It wished to open (and win) a debate about a number of federal government policies in the field of civil rights. In this sphere, the Administration's interpretation of the proper meaning to be accorded to various civil rights and the best method of achieving them would obviously have great legitimacy. As the Heritage Foundation study put it:

> For twenty years the most important battle in the civil rights field has been for control of the language. It is the rhetoric of civil rights that justifiably appeals to Americans' admirable sense of fairness. The battle for the hearts and minds of Americans largely had been won by the time of the passage of the Civil Rights Act of 1964 and the Voting Rights Act of 1965. While later legislation would extend government protection to new areas, such as housing and credit, and new conditions such as sex, age and handicap, the basic vocabulary had already been written into law. Americans and their laws oppose 'discrimination', 'segregation' and 'racism'; they favor 'equality', 'opportunity' and 'remedial action'. The secret to victory, whether in court or

in Congress, has been to control the definition of these terms. (Butler *et al.*, 1984)

There were, however, other institutions in the policy arena who could challenge the interpretation of civil rights provided by the Administration. One was Congress which had written many of the laws which the Reagan Administration wished to see reinterpreted or circumvented. Another rival institution was the judiciary whose interpretations of the Constitution and the laws were the subject of much conservative criticism. In the field of civil rights however there was a third important body, the Civil Rights Commission, which despite its short life had acquired a degree of authority and legitimacy which made it inevitable that the Reagan Administration would attempt to alter its character.

The CRC was seen by the Administration as typical of the ultra-liberal approach to civil rights which it believed the electorate had decisively rejected in 1980. Yet the legitimacy attached to the CRC made its criticisms irritating and the Administration decided that it would be desirable to replace incumbent commissioners with ones whose interpretations of civil rights were more sympathetic to Reaganite views. In the struggle that followed to secure a body more to the Administration's taste, the various elements in the new right and civil rights communities became locked in bitter battle. Although President Reagan succeeded in getting a CRC that was more reflective of the Administration's approach, it was at the price of reconstituting the Commission. And the newly reorganized Commission not merely ceased to produce much in the way of authoritative reports on major policy issues; it also lost legitimacy within the civil rights community to such an extent that Congress was under pressure to cut off its funds or abolish it altogether. In fact Congress did not kill or abolish the Civil Rights Commission but slashed its budget leaving it to the Bush Administration to decide whether to renew its mandate.

The Reagan's Administration's approach to civil rights engendered deep hostility in Congress. Until 1986 the Senate was in Republican hands and most of the running had to be made by the House in attempting to examine Administration policies. However with the Democratic capture of the Senate in November 1986 the Administration lost the initiative in this area and its handling of civil rights issues and its public statements about the judiciary rebounded on it.

A major indicator of the weakened position of the Administration occurred with the Senate's rejection of Robert Bork to the Supreme Court. The Administration's own stance on the character of the judiciary made it inevitable that this nomination would be highly contested once it became clear that Bork would be the swing vote on the Court. The defeat of the nomination in the Senate represented a new determination by the Democrats to oppose Reaganite initiatives in the field of legal power (see Chapter 6).

The Administration was further weakened by the controversy surrounding the Attorney-General, Edwin Meese. Meese had been one of Reagan's closest advisers in the first Administration and in the second he replaced William French Smith. His business associations were always suspect and his involvement with the Wedtech corporation caused the appointment of a special prosecutor to investigate allegations of impropriety in the Justice Department. In August 1988, Meese resigned and was replaced by former Pennsylvania governor Dick Thornburgh.

Yet, although the Bork nomination went down in the Senate and although the discrediting of Meese in a sense removed some of the ideological drive from the Reagan Justice Department, the fact remained that at the end of eight years Reagan and his supporters had achieved one of their chief aims – a conservative Supreme Court. Its impact in the field of civil rights would not be felt until the end of 1989 but then it was felt very heavily as the Supreme Court handed down judgements which narrowed the scope of existing anti-discrimination legislation and supported a much more conservative view of the court's role in redressing inequality.

The Bush Administration and Civil Rights

As with so many other areas of public policy, it was difficult to predict what stance the Bush Administration would take in the area of civil rights and how far it would try to distance itself from the Reagan policies. The 1988 presidential campaign certainly gave supporters of a new approach to civil rights questions little cause for optimism since Lee Atwater's strategy involved negative campaigning which labelled Michael Dukakis an extremist liberal because of his attitudes on parole, the pledge of allegiance and his membership of the ACLU. Atwater himself, of course, came from a background of South Carolina politics and was deeply aware of the potential for using issues such as race, crime and patriotism to erode Democrat support and foster southern Republicanism.

On the other hand President Bush gave the impression of having adopted such a tactic as a necessary evil and took care to distance himself from the strategy once the victory was won. In fact, as some commentators noted, Bush's political career had long displayed a troubling ambiguity on the racial issue combining some 'episodes of moral courage' with incidents that could demonstrate 'either racial insensitivity or a willingness to use the racial card for political gain' (Holmes, 1991). Thus, although Bush voted against the 1964 Civil Rights Act, he later supported the 1968 Fair Housing Act despite opposition within his own conservative Congressional district. Indeed, as Vice-President in the Reagan Administration he worked to strengthen that legislation.

Despite the appeal to racism which many critics saw in Bush's 1988 election campaign, there were also hints that Bush, while he was opposed to rigid quotas, supported affirmative action of a more flexible kind. His support for the extension of the 1964 Civil Rights Act to cover disabled Americans indicated at least that Bush had no principled opposition to further extension of federal efforts to combat discrimination. And because Bush had never been entirely sympathetic to or trusted by the conservative movement, there was the possibility that his Administration would be much more pragmatic than ideological on civil rights questions.

Two other features of President Bush's situation may have given liberals cause for optimism in this policy area. First, the vague policy agenda advanced during the election campaign and the strengthening of the Democratic hold on Congress meant that Bush could claim no personal mandate either for a general set of policies or for specific measures. He would therefore have to work with Congress to create a bipartisan and co-operative environment if his presidency was not to be deadlocked from the inauguration.

Secondly, Congress had itself begun to regain the initiative in this area and to shed some of the nervousness of the contentious civil rights issues which had marked the Reagan presidency. For example in March 1988 it had passed (over a presidential veto) the Civil Rights Restoration Act to reverse the 1984 decision in *Grove City* v. *Bell*, thereby strengthening the scope of the federal government to withhold funds from institutions which discriminated.

At the rhetorical level, Bush made a number of symbolic gestures immediately after the 1988 election. He chose the occasion of the Martin Luther King holiday to stress his commitment to black equality and civil rights. This seemed to mark a deliberate break with the Reagan Administration's approach and certainly distanced him from those members of the conservative wing of the Republican Party (such as Senator Jesse Helms) who had opposed the symbol of the holiday. In fact the gesture fitted neatly with a general political strategy aimed at enhancing support for the Republican Party among blacks. This strategy involved presidential meetings with black political leaders (for example the Congressional Black Caucus) and appearing at major black institutions (Holmes, 1991). If it was high on symbolism rather than substance, it still marked a change from the Reagan Administration. President Reagan did not meet with the Congressional Black Caucus at all during his eight-year presidency.

President Bush's appointments to key civil rights positions were not however uniformly reassuring for those who wanted to see a distinct break with the past. While Attorney-General Thornburgh was kept in place, opinion changed about his political stance. Initially the decision was seen as reflective of Bush's general emphasis on expertise and perhaps a desire to reduce the degree of politicization which the office had experienced under Ed Meese. Yet Thornburgh proved in many ways an ambiguous figure. While he undoubtedly represented a clean and competent appointment by comparison with Meese, Thornburgh had moved right from the time when in the early 1960s he was an active member of liberal pressure groups including the ACLU. It was Thornburgh who advised Bush to float the idea of a constitutional amendment to overturn the Supreme Court's 5–4 decision in *Texas* v. *Johnson* (1989) that federal and state laws against flag desecration were unconstitutional.

Insofar as the Attorney-General had an agenda it appeared to focus on crime and drugs rather than on shifting the balance of the courts or propounding a conservative jurisprudence. To some extent this impression was a reflection of personnel changes as most of the more ideological movers and shakers from the think-tanks and academe left government. Although, there is still room for disagreement between political appointees and career officials, the tension was less marked than in the Reagan Administration.

One damaging episode occurred early in the Bush presidency. The nomination of William Lucas to head the Civil Rights Division of the Department of Justice caused great controversy within the civil rights community. The period in which William Bradford Reynolds had headed this division (combined with the position of special counsellor to the Attorney-General) had been one in which the civil rights community had been faced with an abrasive conservative ideologue in charge of the division most crucial to their concerns.

Lucas was a black with virtually no litigation experience and he appeared to owe the nomination to his work for the Republican National Committee. Testimony before the Senate Judiciary Committee from a former Assistant Attorney–General for Civil Rights, Drew Days III, emphasized the important role of the office in guiding the Administration's policy in this area. Other witnesses pointed both to lack of legal experience and to the poor public record even in administration. Why the nomination to such a sensitive post was allowed to go forward is something of a mystery but it may be that the Administration thought the Democratic majority would not reject a black. If so they were wrong and the Lucas nomination was defeated.

The refusal to confirm Lucas's nomination was attacked by the Republicans as blatant partisanship and racism. In fact one Democrat on the Judiciary Committee (Dennis DeConcini) did vote to confirm Lucas but otherwise it was a straight partisan split. The post was then filled by John Dunne, a well-qualified lawyer, although not one with particular expertise in the area of civil rights.

Congressional opinion on a number of key legal and civil rights issues moved in a more liberal direction generally. In the House, perhaps the key indicator of a shift was the first broadly pro-abortion vote for many years, a majority voted to restore public funding although the legislation was vetoed by President Bush. In 1990 a costly piece of legislation was passed – the Americans with Disabilities Act – giving special protection against discrimination to the handicapped. In both the House and the Senate legislation was introduced to reverse the effect of some of the 1989 Supreme Court decisions on affirmative action and this legislation became the focus for civil rights activists in 1990.

The 1990 and 1991 Civil Rights Acts

The Civil Rights Act of 1990 was designed to modify a number of decisions which the more conservative Supreme Court had handed down in 1989 and which made it more difficult to use the law to sue employers for discriminating against racial minorities and women. Thus in *Wards Cove Packing Company* v. *Atonio* the Court altered what a plaintiff had to prove in order to sustain a claim of bias. Until 1989 employees could invoke the rule in *Griggs* v. *Duke Power Co.* and prove discrimination by showing that an employment practice had the effect of reducing the number of minorities or women in the work force. An actual intention to discriminate did not have to be proved. If a plaintiff demonstrated that the workforce contained fewer minority or women members than might have been expected given the pool of employees available, the court shifted the burden of proof to the employer. To rebut the presumption of discrimination, the employer had to prove that the practice which gave rise to the statistical imbalance was required as a matter of 'business necessity'. In practice, fear of discrimination suits led many employers to use quotas or 'hiring by numbers' to increase their minority and female employees and to ward off criticism.

In *Wards Cove* therefore the Court made cases of what might have been unintentional discrimination much more difficult to establish. The burden of proof was effectively shifted onto the plaintiff who had also to highlight the practices which caused the discrimination more effectively than before. In addition an employer could justify practices which discriminated against minorities by the weaker standard of 'legitimate employment goals' rather than the more stringent *Griggs* standard of 'business necessity'.

The Civil Rights Act of 1990 would have shifted the burden of justifying employment practices back to the employer. And it would have enabled women and religious minorities who had established discrimination against them in employment to be awarded substantial damages by the courts. (The existing law gave only victims of racial bias, not sexual or religious discrimination, the ability to claim punitive damages as opposed to compensation.)

The Humphrey–Hawkins legislation to reverse *Wards Cove* and similar cases was agreed by both the House and the Senate but it was a negotiated bargain reflecting changing attitudes to civil rights generally as well as a good deal of election-year posturing.

President Bush was presented with a dilemma as to whether to veto the legislation. In favor of a veto was the need to maintain the support of the Republican right which immediately prior to the 1990 mid-term elections was angry about his flip-flop on taxes and his incapacity to deliver a budget. Also there was a real need to maintain the support of the business community which adamantly opposed the legislation. Finally there was the argument, pressed by some strategists that the Reagan Democrats – white manual workers disadvantaged by affirmative action – should be considered.

Bush however paused before the veto. No president likes to veto a Civil Rights Act and Bush had worked hard to create a more bipartisan climate and to improve his ratings among blacks. Some liberals within the Administration also urged support and there was the additional factor that a veto would simply prompt the reintroduction of the legislation the next time round, perhaps in less palatable form. In the end President Bush vetoed the legislation in October 1990, alleging that it was a quotas bill. Although Congress attempted to override the veto, it did not have the votes to do so.

Inevitably Bush's veto was attributed by many to electoral calculations. In the mid-term elections, Republicans made much of the quotas issue in an attempt to exploit white fears of employment discrimination which were made more acute by the economic climate. In one close-fought Senate race – in which ultra-conservative Jesse Helms defeated black Democrat Harvey B. Gantt – pro-Helms advertisements showed a pair of white hands crumpling a job rejection letter and implied that the job had gone to a less qualified minority applicant. Although the issue by itself may not have elected anyone, it is probable that the experience of the 1990 mid-terms convinced Republican strategists that the issue could still help the party, especially among blue-collar workers and in the South.

The reintroduction of the Civil Rights Bill in January 1991 therefore seemed likely to encounter stiff opposition from the Republican Party. A number of other factors had made the climate less favorable for the passage of legislation. Most important, Bush's own position had hardened. The question of whether to sign the 1990 legislation was finely balanced; but by the summer of 1991 Bush had apparently mastered the arguments and committed himself firmly against the Congressional version of the bill. (The Administration offered its own version of the legislation in 1991, but it found no favor with House.)

Bush's position with public opinion in mid-1991 was, of course, extremely strong as a result of the Gulf War. Even among blacks he enjoyed a 58 per cent approval rating at a time (June 1991) when his threatened veto of the civil rights legislation was known (Holmes, 1991). By contrast President

Reagan at no time in his presidency surpassed a 50 per cent approval rating among blacks and the average annual approval rating among non-whites during his presidency was 23 per cent.

In addition to Bush's enhanced opposition to the legislation offered by Congress, there was some evidence of strengthened opposition within the administration from John Sununu and Boyden Gray, although colleagues such as Louis Sullivan urged him to sign. The business community's opposition to the legislation had become more apparent despite efforts to bring civil rights leaders and business leaders together in a compromise in early 1991. Small businesses in particular fear that any return to the pre-1989 position could mean additional costly lawsuits which would be very damaging in a recession.

Thus, although the House vote for the legislation (which had been relabeled in an attempt to enhance its appeal to women) was marginally more positive than the 1990 vote, by the summer of 1991 it seemed unlikely that any compromise legislation which President Bush could sign would emerge. At the same time it did not seem that Congress had the necessary votes to override a presidential veto.

The nomination of Clarence Thomas – the black former head of the Equal Employment Opportunities Commission – to fill the vacancy on the Supreme Court left by Thurgood Marshall was another signal that Bush's position on affirmative action and quotas was hardening. Thomas was adamantly opposed to quotas and, the choice was seen as a clever cynical move by Bush. However, Bush was clearly very unhappy with the racist campaign of David Duke in Louisiana's 1991 International race. And as the President's support in the polls started to drop because of his apparent lack of domestic credibility, Bush's attitude to the Civil Rights Bill changed again. In October 1991 he signed a slightly modified bill to the relief of strategists who saw the issue as having the capacity to hurt the President's standing among blacks and whites in 1992. It is highly unlikely, however, that the sudden about-turn will do Bush any good, keep race out of the next election or reduce the inflammatory nature of discrimination issues in U.S. politics.

14

Immigration Reforms: A Mexican–American Perspective

RODOLFO O. DE LA GARZA

U.S. Immigration is currently at a higher level than at any period since the 1920s. This has had important socio-economic effects and has caused considerable political division and controversy. Because many of both the documented and undocumented immigrants have come from Mexico, the Latino community in general, and the Mexican–American community specifically, has found itself in the center of the dispute. Immigration reform has been a test of Mexican–American political influence. Latinos had hoped that their political power would grow dramatically during the 1980s. Instead, they enter the 1990s realizing that their political progress will necessarily be more gradual.

The 1980s: The Decade of the Hispanic

Two factors stimulated the belief that the 1980s would be the 'decade of the Hispanic' – that is a time when Latinos would finally become influential political actors at the national level. The first is the evolution of the Voting Rights Act. The 1965 VRA, which was originally passed to enfranchise Southern blacks, was expanded to include southwestern states when it was renewed in 1975. This created the conditions for Latinos of Mexican origin to begin dismantling the barriers that had historically prevented their full participation in the political process.

Also, between 1970 and 1980, the Latino population increased 61 per cent to a total of 14.6 million. This growth was especially pronounced among Mexican-origin Latinos who increased by more than 90 per cent and account for more than 60 per cent of all Latinos. Approximately 80 per cent of the Mexican origin population lives in Arizona, Colorado, New Mexico, California and Texas. The latter two states are home to 77 per cent of this group, and between 1973 and 1988, the Mexican-origin population in these states increased 91 and 238 per cent respectively (Brischetto, 1989; de la Garza and DeSipio, 1989).

However, as the 1990s drew near, it became obvious that the promise of the decade would be unrealized. Electorally, Latinos in general and Mexican–Americans in particular have had mixed success. They have made great gains in district-level elections. In Texas, for example, there were 1611 Mexican–American elected officials in 1988, up from 565 in 1973. Latino elected officials in California and New York increased 102 and 580 per cent, respectively, during the same period. The total number of Latino congressmen, all but one of whom are Mexican–Americans, doubled to ten between 1978 and 1984.

Nonetheless, neither Mexican–Americans nor other Latinos, enjoyed any victories in elections with major national consequences. New Mexico failed to replace the nation's only Mexican–American senator after Senator Joseph Montoya's defeat in 1976. Similarly, Latinos in general and Mexican–Americans in particular also have had no influence in the outcome of the decade's three presidential elections. The great majority of Mexican–Americans and Puerto Ricans voted for the defeated Democratic candidate in each of these Republican landslides. Cubans, on the other hand, voted Republican, but the Republican victories were so overwhelming that the Cuban vote was not significant in the election results.

In part, this inability to influence electoral outcomes in senatorial and presidential elections reflects the fact that population gains notwithstanding, Latinos generally and especially those of Mexican-origin constitute a much smaller part of the electorate than their numbers suggest. While they make up 8.1 per cent of the nation's population, they are only 4.8 per cent of the eligible electorate. Only two-thirds are of voting age, compared with three-fourths of non-Latinos (Brischetto, 1989). More importantly, as of 1980, 25 per cent of the Mexican-origin population was foreign born and a large proportion remained non-citizens. In California and Texas, approximately 38 and 18 per cent, respectively, of Latinos (the great majority of whom are Mexican) over 19 are non-citizens (de la Garza *et al.*, 1990).

Because of this limited electoral influence, one would expect that the achievements of the Hispanic decade regarding public policy would be equally modest. Consider, for instance, the fact that since 1980 fourteen states including California, Colorado, Arizona and Florida have made English their official language despite intense organized Latino opposition (Combs and Lynch, 1988).

But the most critical test of Latino political power to date has been the controversy over the Immigration Reform and Control Act (IRCA), known as the Simpson–Rodino bill. While Mexican–Americans actively opposed IRCA enactment, it was less salient to other Latinos. As citizens by birth, this bill would have no direct effect on Puerto Ricans. Cubans were relatively unconcerned because IRCA did not threaten the refugee status under which they gained legal resident status. However, IRCA's initially proposed provisions directly threatened the Mexican-origin population in a variety of ways, and Mexican–Americans therefore were among the leaders of IRCA opponents. IRCA enactment therefore indicates that Mexican–Americans had not yet attained the national influence they expected to wield.

Taken as a measure of political influence, the outcome of the immigration debate suggests that Mexican–American influence over policy-making is limited. On the one hand, Mexican–Americans were more influential in shaping IRCA than is generally recognized. They successfully narrowed those provisions that had the most negative portent for Latinos and broadened others that most protected them. Their success reveals a changed position on immigration issues and a new political sophistication that may be the most important product of the 'Decade of the Hispanic'. Nonetheless, IRCA's final form also indicates Mexican–Americans (and Latinos) still have not attained influence sufficient to block legislation which they perceive as eroding their basic civil rights.

Immigration and the Mexican Community

The Treaty of Guadalupe Hidalgo signalled the end to the U.S.–Mexico war (1845–8) and the birth of Mexican–Americans as a distinct U.S. minority. Those Mexicans who for whatever reason remained north of the newly created border automatically became U.S. citizens in 1849.

The new border had no immediate effect on the social and cultural processes of established Mexican communities from the mouth of the Rio Grande in Texas to those in California. Though formally Americans, residents in these towns continued to live as Mexicans. In part this was because in many of these areas several decades passed before Anglos and their institutions were present in sufficient numbers to make themselves felt. In areas where Anglo communities quickly developed, Mexican–Americans were segregated into 'Mexican towns' which remained essentially intact and unchanged (Romo, 1983; Foley, 1988; Montejano, 1987). These settlements retained their cultural character also because movement back and forth between Mexico and the United States continued as if the new border had never been established. These communities were therefore expanded and culturally reinforced by the continuous inflow of Mexicans. From the 1850s then, Mexican immigration was effectively unmonitored and there was no attempt to regulate or prevent Mexican entry to the Southwest until well into the twentieth century. In fact, Mexicans were explicitly excluded from the restrictive immigration legislation of 1924 as a concession to the Southwest's desire for continued Mexican workers (Montejano, 1987, pp. 182–6).

The political consequences of the new border were felt much more quickly. By the 1850s Anglos in the Southwest were dealing with Mexican–Americans much as they had with blacks during Reconstruction. Mexican–Americans were disenfranchised and left with virtually no access to the political process and with no hope that the legal system would help them defend their civil rights, property, and lives. Indeed, their situation became so desperate that, in addition to armed defiance (Rosenbaum, 1981; Acuna, 1988), Mexican–Americans resorted to petitioning Mexican government officials to intervene with U.S. officials in their behalf (Balderama, 1982).

From the latter part of the nineteenth century through to the 1920s, then, the cultural differences between Mexicans (non-citizen residents) and Mexican–Americans were slight. Furthermore, there were few incentives and opportunities for political differences to develop given that Anglos throughout most of the Southwest did not differentiate between Mexican–Americans and Mexicans. With notable exceptions, (Moore, 1970; Montejano, 1987) both were treated as undesirable aliens fit to be workers but not citizens or social equals (Acuna, 1988).

As Anglo institutions took root across the region, they began influencing Mexican-origin communities even as they segregated Mexican-origin people. With the passing decades, small numbers of Mexican–Americans were gradually being resocialized and becoming culturally distinct from Mexican immigrants as they also improved their economic and social status. This fledgling middle class organized groups to protect and improve those tenuous gains and to advance its political status. They did this asserting their 'Americanness' and proclaiming their patriotism. The League of United Latin American Citizens (LULAC), for example, included as one of its goals developing 'within members of our race the best, purest and most perfect type of a true and loyal citizen of the United States of America' (Garcia and de la Garza, 1977, p. 28). LULAC, the nation's largest and most established Mexican–American organization, conducted its business in English and until the 1980s admitted only U.S. citizens.

As Mexican–Americans of all social classes began looking at themselves as Americans rather than Mexicans and evaluating their circumstances by U.S. rather than Mexican standards (Alvarez, 1971), they also redefined their collective self-interest in terms that often were antagonistic to Mexicans. This was fueled by events like the 'repatriations' of the 1930s and 1950s when U.S. authorities rounded up 'Mexicans' and forced them back to Mexico. Despite their protests, many Mexican–Americans fell victim to these round-ups (McKay, 1984; Acuna, 1988). More generally, by the 1950s Mexican–Americans saw Mexican immigrants as depressing wages and displacing them in the labor market. Major Mexican–American organizations therefore mobilized against continued Mexican immigration and in particular to guestworkers brought in under the Bracero program (Allsup, 1982). This opposition was further fueled because, feeling contaminated by the negative stereotypes the public generally held of Mexican immigrants (Menhaca, 1989), many Mexican–Americans hoped to improve their image by distancing themselves from Mexican laborers even if that meant preventing their entry to the United States.

Thus, as Mexican–Americans became active regarding immigration issues, they did so in defense of their rights and status as citizens and in opposition to Mexican immigrants. From the 1930s through the 1960s, this meant that while at a personal level many Mexican–Americans helped Mexican relatives and friends to immigrate legally and illegally, the leading Mexican–American organizations joined forces with organized labor and other restrictionists to reduce Mexican immigration.

The Chicano Movement added a different dimension to this equation. Where earlier activists de-emphasized their Mexicanness to gain socio-political access, Chicano leaders in the late 1960s and 1970s mobilized supporters around Mexican cultural symbols. They charged that American society was closed to anyone of Mexican origin regardless of citizenship and therefore Mexican–Americans should unite with Mexican immigrants to tear down society's racist barriers. Chicanos argued that Mexican immigrants were not a souce of Mexican–American problems but were instead also victimized by Anglo society. Rather than oppose Mexicans, Chicanos called on Mexican–Americans to attack the real source of their problems – Anglo racism.

The Movement changed southwestern politics even though it had spent itself by the early 1980s. It radicalized many Mexican–American moderates who then joined with Chicanos to challenge extant political and social institutions. Among its significant legacies was that it helped reduce the saliency of immigration issues to Mexican–American leaders and replaced them with issues related to equal opportunity and civil rights. Thus, during the 1980s Mexican–American groups have not mobilized against Mexican immigrants (for the first time since perhaps the 1930s). Indeed, in a few cases they have been the principal defenders of immigrant rights (de la Garza, 1989).

Contemporary Mexican–American views on immigration reflect this change. As the struggle over IRCA illustrates, immigration was a major national issue from the late 1970s through 1986, but it was not a major issue to Mexican–Americans. Three surveys found that Mexican–American elites across the nation did not identify immigration among the most important issues affecting their communities (de la Garza, 1982; Brischetto, 1983; Pachon and DeSipio, 1990). The only aspect of immigration issues that was mentioned concerned the need to protect immigration rights (Pachon and DeSipio, 1989). These elites were most concerned about education and social services. General surveys of Mexican–Americans produced similar results (Miller *et al.*, 1984; de la Garza and Brischetto, 1983). More importantly, while Congress was debating IRCA and Texas was holding an election in which immigration was the key issue, a Texas survey asked respondents to rank the importance of the following issues: the environment, unemployment, education, immigration, welfare programs, social security, crime and nuclear war. Immigration had the lowest overall score among Mexican–Americans. They ranked education highest (Polinard *et al.*, 1984).

As has been true historically, however, many Mexican–Americans remain concerned that Mexican immigrants displace them in the job market or depress wages (Miller *et al.*,

1984). In Texas, for example, Mexican–Americans were split regarding one of IRCA's major proposed provisions, levying fines on employers who hired undocumented (illegal) Mexican immigrants. In 1984, they were equally divided on this issue, but by 1986 54 per cent supported employer sanctions. Mexican–American leaders in Washington and the Southwest nonetheless spoke out against this provision because they feared it would lead to widespread employment discrimination against all Latinos. Anglo–Texans supported employer sanctions by majorities of 63 and 70 per cent, respectively, in 1984 and 1986 (Brischetto, 1988).

Although they did not favor more immigration, most Mexican–Americans were supportive of those Mexicans who had already immigrated. In 1984 and 1986, a majority of Texas Mexican–Americans supported legislation to allow Mexicans who had immigrated illegally to legalize their status. The majority of Anglo–Texans opposed legalization in 1984, and 46 per cent were opposed in 1986 (Brischetto, 1988).

This, then, is the background to the role Mexican–Americans played in the IRCA debate. Immigration was not a salient issue to Mexican–Americans. Instead, at the elite and mass level, they were concerned about educational, social welfare and civil rights issues. As is described in the following section, the role that Mexican–American leaders played in the IRCA debate evolved but always had as its focus preventing legislation that might result in discriminatory consequences for Mexican–Americans.

1980–1986: The IRCA Debate

The IRCA debate evolved between 1978–86, a period during which there was a national sense that immigrants were flooding in and that the nation had 'lost control of its borders'. There was particular concern about immigrants from Mexico and other Latin American countries, as the efforts of the Federation for American Immigration Reform (Bean and de la Garza, 1988) and the Official English movement illustrate (de la Garza and Trujillo, 1989). Similarly, an analysis of the vote in 1984 when IRCA narrowly passed the House of Representatives and was killed in conference committee suggests that anti-Mexican attitudes explain much of the pro-IRCA vote (Lowell *et al.*, 1986).

As initially proposed, IRCA contained three major components. First, there were employer sanctions. Secondly, the bill included an amnesty provision allowing undocumented immigrants who had arrived prior to a date to be specified to apply for legal residency. Thirdly, it proposed a renewed guest worker program.

Mexican–American leaders were concerned about each of these. They most opposed employer sanctions because they feared this would lead to employment discrimination against all Latinos. They supported legalization but wanted a more generous grace period than was being proposed by IRCA's authors. Finally, they opposed a guest worker program because historically these programs had resulted in exploitation and abuse of Mexican and Mexican–American workers.

Mexican–American leaders were, however, in a tenuous position. Mexican–American Congressmen and leaders of national organizations were a fledgling presence in Washington in the early 1980s and lacked the resources to block the legislation on their own. Therefore, they used a variety of tactics in their attempts to kill and modify IRCA from 1980 until the bill's passage in 1986 in response to the changing circumstances.

Initially, the National Council de la Raza (NCLR), the MALDEF and LULAC were joined by Latino Congressmen in efforts to kill any new immigration bill. By 1984 when it seemed increasingly likely that some type of immigration reform would pass, the legislators and organizations altered their tactics to include forming alliances with other groups to influence specific provisions in case a bill passed.

The alliances Latino organizations developed varied with each of IRCA's provisions. Led by NCLR, which spearheaded the Latino alliances, Latinos joined forces with the National Chamber of Commerce and other business groups to try to kill the legislation. They worked with the National Council of Churches, labor unions (that included undocumented in their ranks), other ethnic groups and associations of immigration lawyers on the legalization issue. Together with the ACLU they sought to protect against any discriminatory consequences that might arise as a result of employer sanctions. After initially opposing guest worker programs, they negotiated with and then joined forces with growers to develop mutually acceptable provisions.

The legislation divided the ten Latino (nine Mexican–American, one Puerto Rican) Congressmen. They unanimously helped defeat an amendment that would have eliminated provisions barring discrimination based on citizenship status. All but two supported a successful amendment introduced by Congressman de la Garza that required Immigration and Naturalization Service agents to obtain warrants before searching open fields for violations of immigration laws. It is noteworthy that the two nay votes came from representatives of agricultural districts in South Texas. All but the lone Republican supported the defeated amendment that would have allowed a family containing at least one member eligible for housing assistance to receive assistance regardless of the legal status of other household members; by an identical split, they helped defeat an amendment that would have excluded Nicaraguan and Salvadoran immigrants from separate programs of temporary legal status.

The final vote divided the group, with four voting for and six voting against IRCA. Representative Bill Richardson voiced the reluctance with which Latinos voted for IRCA: 'I think this bill is better than nothing. It was the last gasp for legalization to take place in a humane way'.

Mexican–Americans were most concerned about IRCA's potential discriminatory consequences. Initially, it proposed that employers be allowed to check an employee's legal residency status at their own discretion. Fearing this would result in widespread discrimination, Mexican–Americans played the key role in substituting the requirement that all new employees be required to present documents certifying their legal residency. Mexican–American pressures also helped establish the requirement that in November 1989, Congress review the effects of employer sanctions to determine if they resulted in discrimination. If Congress finds IRCA to have caused 'substantial' discrimination, employer sanctions could be terminated. Mexican–American leaders planned to use the mandated congressional hearings sessions to renew discussions on IRCA in general.

Mexican–Americans also were instrumental in modifying key provisions of the legalization program. In addition to voting to add temporary protection for Nicaraguans and Salvadorans, they helped shorten from six to four years the time necessary for an undocumented immigrant to have resided in the United States. They influenced the liberalization of the provisions under which poor immigrants would be eligible for permanent residency. Normally anyone earning less than poverty level wages is classified as a 'public charge' and is therefore ineligible for permanent residency. That requirement would have excluded 30–40 per cent of undocumented Mexican immigrants. IRCA's provisions call for additional information such as employment history, employability and history of participation in social welfare programs to be taken into consideration. Also Mexican–American leaders and their allies won confidentiality requirements which would protect the identity of unsuccessful permanent residency applicants. Without this, it is likely that few undocumented immigrants would have applied for amnesty. In addition, Mexican–Americans lobbied for provisions that made it possible for community agencies to publicize the program and process these applicants and thus help create an environment that would encourage large numbers of applicants.

Mexican–American leaders successfully influenced IRCA's provisions regarding agricultural guest workers. Their adamant opposition to a conventional guest worker program focused attention on the harsh conditions immigrant workers faced and helped put agricultural employers on the defensive. Thus, it was the final provision approved and when it finally passed, IRCA's guest worker program included expanded protections for the workers.

IRCA's passage did not end the immigration debate, however. Congress held hearings on IRCA's effects in November 1989. In addition to examining the legislation's discriminatory consequences, Congress also sought to re-evaluate IRCA more generally in view of reports indicating that illegal immigration continues at a high albeit lesser rate. Mexican–Americans may draw attention to this immigration because it includes a substantial Central American component, whose presence is generating controversy among some Mexican–American communities (de la Garza *et al.*, 1990). In part, the issues at stake are those that historically divided Mexican–Americans and Mexican immigrants, only now Central Americans are the focus of Mexican–American anger. Further fueling this resentment is that some Central Americans are granted refugee status which entitles them to privileges that are denied to Mexican immigrants.

Additionally, Congress has developed legislation that revised the criteria that determine immigration eligibility. Of particular concern are modifications in the provisions regarding eligibility based on family unification, skill and education levels, and economic status. Each of these may reduce significantly the number of Mexican and Latin American immigrants. Revisions in the family unification criteria might eliminate many of the categories citizens currently use to acquire immigration permits for members of their extended families. These provisions have been especially important to Latin Americans because of their familial patterns. Increasing skill and education requirements put Latin Americans at a disadvantage because the overwhelming majority of Latin Americans have limited skill and education levels. A category of visas for investors or affluent applicants will similarly disadvantage Latin Americans. Not only would few be able to apply under this category, but given that there is a fixed number of visas granted each year, creating such a category would reduce the number of visas available to all other applicants.

Conclusion

The role Mexican–American leaders played in the IRCA debate reflects the changed view Mexican–Americans have of immigration. As recently as the 1960s Mexican–Americans mobilized in opposition to Mexican immigrants, but since the 1970s they have focused their attention on issues like civil rights and access to education and social services. Nonetheless, they remain divided in their views of Mexican immigration. While a majority support liberal provisions allowing undocumented immigrants to legalize their status, a majority also thinks that undocumented immigrants displace them in the workforce and therefore they tend to support fines for employers who hire undocumented immigrants.

What Mexican–American elites wanted most from IRCA, therefore, was assurance that it would not result in increased hardships for Mexican–Americans. Their first objective, thus, was to kill the bill. When it became evident that IRCA would pass, Mexican–American leaders successfully struggled to modify its provisions to protect their constituency. Given their limited political clout and fledgling national presence, those successes may be considered a major victory.

For the first time, they displayed the skills necessary to influence Washington politics. Armed with MALDEF's and NCLR's solid research and advice, they marshalled arguments that could not be summarily dismissed. In the early phases of the debate, LULAC led MALDEF and NCLR in strident opposition to IRCA. As it became clear a bill would pass in some form, LULAC's vehemence became counterproductive, and NCLR and the Latino congressmen looked for ways to influence the legislation. Thus, at various times, this resulted in unprecedented coalitions between Mexican–Americans and historic antagonists such as the National Chamber of Commerce and agricultural associations that proved effective.

These accomplishments aside, however, even in its final form, IRCA's enactment is evidence of the marginal status Latinos have in U.S. society and of how limited the achievements of the 'Decade of the Hispanic' have been. IRCA was passed with the recognition that it might generate increased discrimination against Latinos. It may be amended only if it results in 'a widespread pattern of' increased anti-Hispanic discrimination. The General Accounting Office, the agency charged with assessing IRCA's discriminatory effects, admits that there are no guidelines for determining what 'significant' increases are. Ultimately, the definition will be determined politically, that is, by non-Latino legislators deciding how much anti-Latino discrimination they are willing to have Latinos experience.

It is difficult to imagine Congress enacting any legislation which it acknowledges is likely to discriminate against blacks, Jews or other ethnic or minority groups. That Congress passed such legislation affecting Hispanics during the 'Decade of the Hispanics' is perhaps the best indicator of the status Latinos have attained as they enter a new decade.

As Congress reviews IRCA and considers further immigration reforms, Mexican–American leaders will be better prepared to voice Mexican–American concerns regarding their civil rights and economic conditions. The experience from the IRCA debate of learning to establish alliances with historically antagonistic groups as well as with traditional supporters should serve them well as they respond to Congress's new initiatives. The results of the IRCA debate, however, indicate that even the knowledge and experience Mexican–Americans have gained may not be sufficient to prevent the enactment of legislation which they perceive to be adverse to their interests if Anglo legislators and the nation at large favor it.

PART FIVE

Conclusion

15

An Era of Divided Government

MORRIS P. FIORINA

For the past twenty-five years concluding essays in volumes like this one have addressed the prospect of electoral realignment. No more. Realignment – at least as classically conceived – appears to be a dead concept. Since 1964 we have waited for the realignment; and each time the academic consensus has announced, 'No, that wasn't it'. But, classical realignment or not, American politics have been transformed in the past quarter century. In particular, we seem to have settled into a persistent pattern of divided government. Republican standard-bearer George Bush won an easy victory in 1988, carrying forty states with 54 per cent of the popular vote. At the same time, Democratic candidates took 260 of the 435 seats in the House of Representatives, and won 18 of the 33 Senate races, leaving that body too under Democratic control. This split outcome surprised no one; three of the previous eight presidential elections (1956, 1968, 1972) produced the same split, and two more (1980, 1984) placed the Presidency and Senate at odds with the House of Representatives. Of the past nine presidential elections, only three (1960, 1964, 1976) have given one party control of the Presidency and both Houses of Congress. Should George Bush serve two terms and Democratic control of the House continue, American undergraduates in 1996 will not remember any period of unified government – even the Carter interlude will be lost in the mists of early childhood memory.

Given the unmistakable signals provided by reality, political scientists finally are coming to view divided government less as an aberration and more as a given in contemporary American politics. Why do we have divided government, and what are its consequences? This essay addresses those questions, although the discussion can only be suggestive given the current state of research. I will begin by placing the contemporary period in historical context, then proceed to a survey of the explanations offered for the contemporary condition, and conclude with questions about its likely consequences.

Divided Government in Historical Perspective

From the Founding through the 1820s presidents emerged from the congressional caucus, more or less precluding a divided government. With the renomination of Andrew Jackson by popular convention in 1832, American elections have created or continued a condition of divided government for 60 of 158 years, about 40 per cent of the country's history (see Table 15.1). The contemporary era (1952–90) stands out, with a clear majority (13/20) of presidential and mid-term elections producing divided governments, but there are other periods that are unique in their own ways. Consider the period encompassing the first half of the twentieth century. In those 52 years, 22 of 26 national elections resulted in *unified* control, something not matched either before or after. There is some irony here in that historical accounts contrast the highly organized nineteenth century parties and their fiercely partisan members with the less organized and militant parties of this century (McGerr, 1986). According to the literature the regional realignment of the 1890s, the Progressive onslaught, and the rapid social and economic transformation of the country all combined to weaken the parties' capacity to structure the electoral process – to control nominations, to deliver the vote, and to organize officeholders. All of this suggests a monotonic decline in party influence in American politics. On the other hand, a macro-level indicator of the parties' ability to structure American politics – unified control – shows the opposite movement. Split-ticket voting may have risen at the turn of the century, but divided control did not (Rusk, 1970). Rather, the Republicans dominated the first quarter of the century (with a Wilsonian interregnum), while the second quarter saw the Democrats dominate. In neither case was there much in the way of divided control. The few elections that divided control were all mid-terms. The Administration lost Congress at the conclusion of each of the World Wars. The Republicans lost the House in 1910 and in 1930. All in all, the contemporary period is more of a departure from the earlier twentieth century pattern than it is from American history in general.

TABLE 15.1   *Control of national institutions, 1832–1992 (number of elections)*

	Unified	Divided
1832–1990	49	30
1832–1900	20	14
1900–1952	22	4
1952–1992	7	12

Source: Tabulated from *Members of Congress Since 1789*, Washington, D.C.; Congressional Quarterly Inc. (1985): pp. 182–3.

A closer look at the historical record sheds additional light on the present era. Divided government tends to occur in those times identified by political historians as periods of strain (Table 15.2). All of the divided government that occurred in the nineteenth century occurred in the periods 1840–60 and 1874–96. In the first period abolitionism and nativism cross-cut the parties. The period ends with the elections of 1860 which brought unified Republican control and civil war. In turn, fourteen years of unified Republican control came to an end when the Southern Democrats returned to Congress in 1874. The next two decades rank with the contemporary period in terms of divided control. The rapid pace of economic development thrust what had heretofore been local issues into state and national arenas, and the parties' mass bases were rent by ethno-cultural divisions (Kleppner, 1979). What has been called the 'period of no decision' came to an end only with the depression and sectional realignment of the 1890s and the rise of industrial Republican supremacy.

TABLE 15.2 *Major periods of divided government*

	Unified	Divided
1840–1860	4*	6
1874–1896	3	8
1952–1992	7	13
Three period total	14	27
All other	35	4

* Number of elections.

Source: See Table 15.1.

Seen against this background, the contemporary era appears less exceptional. Race, the Vietnam war, and then the complex known as the social issue buffeted the New Deal party system much as slavery, industrialization and wars buffeted its predecessors, with similar results for control of national institutions. There is one respect, however, in which the contemporary period truly is unique. In the present era divided control has been as likely to accompany presidential elections as mid-terms: six of one and seven of the other led is split control (Table 15.3). In previous eras, however, divided control virtually always was the result of a mid-term loss of unified control achieved in the preceding presidential election. Between 1832 and 1952 only 3 of 18 elections that resulted in divided government were in presidential years, and each is somehow special. The 1848 election was a three-way race in which former Democratic President Van Buren ran on the Free Soil ticket, throwing the presidency to the Whigs. In 1876 the Democrats carried the House and won the *popular* vote for President (Tilden was eventually counted out in the Electoral Commission), but failed to carry enough of the contested Senate seats to gain control. And in 1884 the partially insulated Senate again held out against the victorious Democrats. Before Eisenhower's re-election in 1956 winners of two-way presidential races *always* carried the House, and only in 1884 did one fail to carry the Senate.

TABLE 15.3   *Divided government by type of election*

	Presidential	Mid-Term
1832–1992	9	22
1832–1900	3	11
1900–1952	0	4
1952–1992	6	7
1840–1860	1	5
1874–1896	2	6
1952–1992	6	7
Other	0	4

Source: see Table 15.1.

Thus, explanations of divided government in the nineteenth century must focus on asymmetric defection and turnout in mid-term elections, whereas explanations of divided government in the contemporary period must also focus on split-ticket voting. Only in 1954 did a mid-term begin a period of divided government. All other mid-terms in the current era only continued a pattern of divided government established at the previous presidential election.

There is one further comparison that sheds perspective on the contemporary era of divided government. Discussions of divided government invariably focus on the three national elective institutions, but the American states also have experienced a rise in divided control. Burnham (1989) points out that three-quarters of all Americans now live in divided government states. The 1988 elections left 29 split states, the historical high point in a general upward trend (Figure 15.1). As I will argue below, given that most proposed explanations of divided government are based on the national experience, parallel trends in the states suggest that such arguments are incomplete.

Explanations of Divided Government

One of the most commonly offered explanations of divided national government is the first one that should be dismissed: gerrymandering. Some Republican politicos believe that they

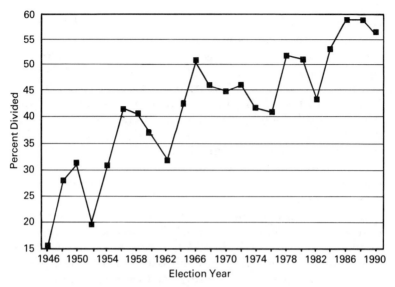

FIGURE 15.1   *Divided states: 1946–90*
Source: *Statistical Abstracts of the US.*

are being cheated out of their fair share of House seats by
districting plans that favor Democrats. This explanation
deserves as much consideration as some Democratic apolo-
gists' explanation for their continued string of presidential
defeats: their candidates do not have as much personality as
the Republican candidates. Several academic studies have
carefully considered the effects of districting and have concluded that the net effects are slight; what Democrats steal in
some states, Republicans usually manage to steal back in
others (Mann, 1987). Rather, the problem the Republicans
have in House elections is simply that they do not get as many
votes as the Democrats. Not since 1952 has the Republican
total exceeded the Democratic total. Still, Republicans complain that even when they come close, as in 1984, they do not
carry a proportional number of seats. That is true, but their
complaint is with the normal operation of the single-member
first-past-the-post electoral system, not with devilishly clever
Democratic gerrymanderers.

   The large gap between the Republican presidential and
congressional votes obviously means that large numbers of

voters are splitting their tickets. In the aggregate the trend is striking. At the beginning of the century it was exceedingly rare for a congressional district to give split majorities to presidential and congressional contenders, but in recent years 40 per cent of all districts have reported such split outcomes (Table 15.4). For the contemporary period we can probe beneath such aggregate results to determine the rates of individual ticket-splitting. Between the 1950s and 1970s ticket-splitting almost doubled from 15 per cent or less of the electorate to 25 per cent or more. The largest jump occurred between 1964 and 1972, the so-called 'time of troubles', with no apparent increase since then (Figure 15.2).

In a period of party decomposition, it is not surprising that ticket-splitting should increase (Burnham, 1965). The weakening of party bonds makes voters more likely to respond to attractive candidates and issues of the other party. But contemporary ticket-splitting has followed a pattern that must be accounted for by a complete explanation of the

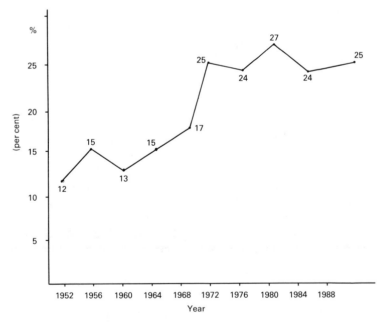

FIGURE 15.2   *House–President ticket-splitting*
Source: See Figure 15.1.

TABLE 15.4   *Congressional districts carried by House and presidential candidates of different parties*

Year	Per cent
1900	3
1908	7
1916	11
1924	12
1932	14
1940	15
1948	21
1952	19
1956	30
1960	26
1964	33
1968	32
1972	44
1976	29
1980	34
1984	44
1988	34

Source: Ornstein, *et al.* (1987), Table 2.14: 1988 figures from *Congressional Quarterly Weekly Report*, July 8, 1989, p. 1711.

behavior: the observed ticket-splitting favors Republican executives and Democratic legislators by a noticeable margin over Democratic executives and Republican legislators (Table 15.5). This pattern obviously is most pronounced in the Republican re-election landslides of 1956, 1972, and 1984, and until 1972 the weakness of two-party competition in the South artificially enhanced the national pattern. But the pattern is a relatively consistent feature of national elections in the contemporary era. Thus, any convincing explanation for divided national government must explain first why split ticket voting increased sharply between the mid-1960s and mid-1970s, and secondly why the split favors Republican presidents and Democratic representatives. Several explanations have been offered.

TABLE 15.5　*Patterns of President–House ticket splitting (per cent)*

Year	Whole Country		Non–South	
	D. President R. House	R. President D. House	D. President R. House	R. President D. House
1952	2	10	3	5
1956	2	14	3	11
1960	4	10	6	7
1964	9	6	10	5
1968*	7	11	7	9
1972	5	25	5	20
1976	9	15	10	13
1980*	9	18	10	16
1984	6	18	5	17
1988	7	18	7	16

* Excludes Wallace/Anderson voters.
Source: American National Election Studies.

Incumbency

Shortly after the 1984 elections columnist William Schneider wrote in *The New Republic*:

> It was incumbency that saved the Democratic Party from ruin. If the government had passed a decree prohibiting incumbents from running for re-election, the Republican Party would probably have gained control of both Houses of Congress and a substantial number of statehouses.

Certainly, the House incumbency advantage is the first explanation that political scientists would offer for the current condition of divided national control. There is a huge literature on incumbency, far too much to review here. Suffice it to note that incumbents have a variety of advantages that enable them to deter strong challenges in the first instance, and to beat them back (usually) when deterrence fails. With the growth of the welfare state, the traditional ombudsman role of the member has expanded, allowing them to construct a 'personal vote' that transcends partisan and ideological considerations (Fiorina, 1989). Incumbents raise great sums of campaign money from PACs and other interested parties, while challengers go begging (Jacobson, 1987a). And Members have taxpayer-provided staff, office and other resources that have a market value of as much as a million dollars per year. Some incumbents do lose, of course, but the losses have become more idiosyncratic – less tied to swings in the national vote (Jacobson, 1987b). And, a final critical piece of the argument, a notable increase in the advantage of incumbency occurred in the late 1960s (Erikson, 1972). The increased incumbency advantage in House elections fits very nicely with the timing of the increase in split-ticket voting.

How does incumbency explain the *pattern* of ticket-splitting? This is less clear. Simple luck may be part of the answer. The Democrats were the House majority in the mid-1960s when the electorate's party affiliations began to weaken, when the role of government expanded, and when new technologies (in polling, direct mail, computerization) began to affect congressional elections. So, even if both parties were equally likely to adapt to the new opportunities, there were more Democrats to make the adaptation than Republicans. This argument carries the counter-factual implication that if the Republicans had managed to capture the House in 1966–8, we would now be seeing either unified Republican governments or a pattern of Democratic Presidents and Republican Congresses.

This counter-factual argument strikes most observers as dubious, suggesting that something more is needed to complete the explanation. It has been suggested that the pro-grovernment philosophy of Democrats makes it easier for them than for Republicans to adopt the new style of politics. Believing in a minimal government role and opposing the existence of many government programs, Republicans may be personally unwilling to perform the kind of constituency service that is a major component of the incumbency advantage. And they may be less likely to seek to expand government for the benefit of their districts. In short, Democratic ideology fits the congressional times better than Republican (Ehrenhalt, 1982, p. 3175). Against this argument stands research showing that Republican incumbents have no less of an electoral advantage than Democrats.

So, while some of the links in the argument are not yet adequately researched, the incumbency-based argument offers a plausible explanation for the current condition of divided control. Divided government is largely an accident. On the basis of performance and issues the contemporary electorate favors Republican presidential candidates. But House elections are affected less by national conditions and issues, and more by the personal qualities and activities of the candidates. That, coupled with some historical inertia produces Democratic Houses.

Still, even the most diligent students of incumbency doubt that it can carry the full explanatory load for divided government. Gary Jacobson states flatly that:

> the incumbency explanation is incomplete and insufficient. It cannot explain why Democrats once again control the Senate (or how they lost it in the first place). It cannot explain why a larger proportion of Republican representatives (4.7 per cent) than Democratic representatives (3.7 per cent) have been defeated in the last five general elections. And it cannot explain why Republicans have not won more open seats. (Jacobson, 1989a.)

Jacobson reports that since 1968 all but 28 seats in the 435 member House of Representatives have come open. But during these two decades of Republican presidential dominance the Republicans have made a net gain of exactly two seats. The Democrats have the same 60:40 edge today that they had in 1968. A little algebra highlights the implications of this fact for incumbency explanations of divided government.

Let d and r be the respective probabilities that the Democrats and Republicans retain an open seat they currently hold, where both d and r are greater than 0.5 (an empirical fact). For a 60:40 split to be preserved after all the seats are put at risk, the following must hold:

$$\frac{60}{40} = \frac{60d + 40(1-r)}{40r + 60(1-d)}$$

Solving, $r = (1.5d - 0.5)$, which implies that $d > r$. *In order to preserve their initial advantage the Democrats must have a higher probability of retaining an open seat than the Republicans.* In fact, Jacobson's tabulations show that between 1968 and 1988 the Democratic probability of holding an open seat was about 0.8, while the Republican probability was only 0.72 (Jacobson, 1990). If the Republicans had achieved parity except for incumbency, they would have narrowed the gap in the House. *That they have not indicates that some other pro-Democratic force(s) is at work.*

There is a further reason to doubt the sufficiency of the incumbency explanation for divided government, but it will be more convenient to introduce it by way of commenting on a second category of explanation.

America is Fundamentally a Democratic Country

Casual discussions of divided government implicitly treat the House of Representatives as the deviant body on which explanation should focus. The Republicans win the Presidency with ease and they have captured the Senate in two recent elections, but the House is beyond their reach. An alternative perspective suggests that we treat the Presidency as the deviant body. After all, the *only* arena in which the Democrats consistently do poorly is the presidential one. In election after election Democrats not only capture the House, but also win two-thirds of the governorships, two-thirds of the state legislatures, the overwhelming number of mayor's races in large cities, and so forth. Thus, the question should not be why Democrats do so well in the House; the question should be why they do so poorly in the presidential races. And here an obvious answer is available.

In the mid-1960s a new issue complex intruded on national politics. Race, drugs, non-traditional sexual practices, prayer in schools, abortion, and other matters shouldered aside more traditional New Deal issues as the motive force underlying the choices of a significant portion of the electorate. From a purely electoral standpoint, the Democrats have always been on the wrong side of such issues (Scammon and Wattenberg, 1970). Thus, optimal Democratic strategy calls for downplaying such issues in favor of less internally divisive ones. But the open presidential nomination process allows controversial constituency groups such as blacks, feminists and gays to achieve high visibility and keep their issues in the spotlight. Add a pinch of bigotry, stir in some diabolical Republican media wizards, and bring to a boil. Presto, we get Republican Presidents as white Southerners and blue-collar workers defect rather than support the agenda of the newer Democratic constituencies.

Meanwhile, in the quieter backwaters of the states and congressional districts Democratic candidates run on more traditional issues and go their separate ways on the social issues. San Francisco Democrats adopt one stance, Cleveland Democrats adopt a different one. By matching Republicans on the new 'gut' issues, Democrats can pull ahead on the basis of their traditional image as the party of ordinary working Americans.

This explanation has great intuitive appeal, and to some extent it certainly must be operating. But like the incumbency explanation, there is reason to doubt its sufficiency. Questions arise when one looks closely at one of its premises: that the country is heavily Democratic below the presidential level. Yes, the Democrats win almost two-thirds of the state level races. This creates a natural impression that they control a comparable proportion of the states (Chubb and Peterson, 1985). But as previously noted, 75 per cent of the American population lives in divided government states. How is the latter figure consonant with the image of Democratic dominance? The answer is that it is not. Rather than simple Democratic dominance at the state level one finds a complex, even baffling pattern of outcomes.

Table 15.6A summarizes the pattern of state outcomes for the past three election cycles. It should be noted that 38 states elect their governors in the off years. Thus the preliminary examination tallies with state government patterns as they existed in 1978, 1982, and 1986. In total the Democrats won the governorship in somewhat more than 60 per cent of the cases. In the legislatures they are even stronger: they hold both houses in two-thirds of the states, and at least one house in more than three-quarters. Amazingly, however, there is *no* relationship between their success in the two arenas. As shown in Table 15.6B, if gubernatorial and legislative success were *totally* independent, the Democrats would have unified control in two-fifths of the states and the Republicans in one-tenth. That is exactly what we see: the pattern of observed governmental patterns is virtually identical to that expected under complete independence. In recent years, knowing which party controls the state legislature tells us precisely nothing about which one controls the governorship.

TABLE 15.6A *Gubernatorial and legislative victories, 1978, 1982 and 1986*

Governors

Democratic	90	0.62
Republican	56	0.38

Legislatures

Democratic	93	0.64
Republican	33	0.22
Split	21	0.14

TABLE 15.6B *Patterns of state government control*

	Number	Proportion	Expected Proportion
Unified Democratic	58	0.40	0.40
Unified Republican	14	0.10	0.08
Divided Democratic Governor	32	0.22	0.22
Divided Republican Governor	42	0.29	0.30

Most Gubernatorial elections occur in mid-term years.
Source: Calculated from Statistical Abstract of the United States.

This is not the place to probe deeply beneath this puzzling finding, but preliminary explorations have turned up further interesting questions. With only half the states divided, but three-quarters of the population living in divided states, divided government must be more common in the more populous states. Once again the pattern is actually a bit more differentiated. *Republican-headed* divided states – consistently the majority – tend to include more populous states, Texas, California, Illinois and Missouri, for example. In contrast, the smaller number of *Democratic-headed* divided states tend to be among the less populous, Kansas, Idaho and Utah, for example. The case of Utah is especially intriguing. On the presidential level this state is so Republican that Democratic candidates barely bother to put in an appearance. The state sends two conservative Republicans, Jake Garn and Orrin Hatch, to the Senate. Republicans typically hold a comfortable majority in the state legislature. And between 1964 and 1980 the Democrats won the governor's race five consecutive times.

In sum, outcomes in the American states are far more complicated than a simple 'Democratic dominance' argument presumes. Moreover, returning to an earlier argument, it is far from clear that one could generalize an incumbency explanation to cover the state outcomes. What the state outcomes tell us is that divided government in the United States is not simply a President-House phenomenon; it is something more systemic, and probably requires a more general explanation. As might be expected divided control at one governmental level is correlated with divided control at another: in 1988 23 per cent of all congressional districts in unified government states turned in split President–House results, as compared to 45 per cent in divided states.

Purposeful Explanations

Popular treatments of divided control tend to emphasize the more-or-less conscious intent of the electorate. In recent years various polls have shown that majorities of voters favor divided control over unified control under either party. For example, an ABC News/*Wall Street Journal* poll taken just after the 1988 election found that voters favored divided control by better than a 5:3 margin. Given the coincidence between such sentiments and electoral outcomes it is understandable that some commentators have advanced the argument that voters deliberately vote to divide control.

Thus Henry Fairlie observed in the *New Republic* on 5 October 1987:

> When the American people split their votes, returning Republican presidents and Democratic congressmen, they know what they are doing. They may be willing to give a

new president the chance to show what he can do, but they cling to their protectors in the House as insurance.

In a similar vein, the editor of *Roll Call* (a Capitol Hill weekly) suggested on 30 October 1989 that:

> Voters may be consciously *choosing* divided government. Despite the dire warnings of stalemate, Americans seem to like the idea of having the White House in the hands of one party and the Congress in the hands of the other – as a sort of extra check and balance, even more than the Constitution provides.

And more anecdotally, election night commentary on the national networks in 1988 openly speculated about the intent of the electorate in giving George Bush a Democratic congress.

Journalists are not the only ones to offer purposeful explanations for contemporary conditions. Such explanations have been cautiously advanced and explored by professors as well. Thus far, purposeful explanations come in three varieties according to whether they emphasize policy balancing, complementary strengths and weaknesses, or 'a pox on both your houses'.

In an earlier article I argued that a simple model of policy balancing by voters generates conclusions that resemble aggregate developments in national elections over the past several decades (Fiorina, 1988). In a system with an independent executive, voters have the option of voting for unified control of legislative and executive institutions, or of voting for divided control. In the latter case assume that voters expect policy to be a weighted average of the positions of the parties that control each institution:

$$\text{Policy} = q(\text{executive party}) + (1 - q)(\text{legislative party})$$

Then with two parties, Democratic and Republican, the voters can choose among four 'platforms'. DD–unified Democratic control, DR–Democratic president/Republican legislature, RD–Republican president/Democratic legislature, and RR–unified Republican control. In a simple left–right space the four positions will be ordered:

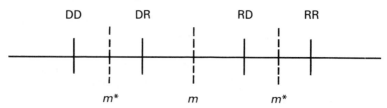

If voters select the platform closest to them, all voters between the midpoints, m^*, will split their tickets, with those to the left of m splitting DR, and those to the right, RD[1]. Notice that when a voter casts a split ticket he or she votes for the presidential candidate of the party nearer him or her and the congressional candidate of the party farther away[2]. This simple model generates a series of hypotheses. Among the most important are three (*ceteris paribus*).

1. Ticket-splitters will be concentrated among those voters whose preferred positions lie between those of the two parties.
2. The more polarized the parties, the greater the incidence of ticket-splitting.
3. The preponderance of the ticket-splitting will be RD rather than DR if more voters are closer to the Republicans on the issues than to the Democrats.

Clearly, the American parties *have* polarized since the 1960s (Miller and Jennings, 1986). Voters whose positions lie between the two parties *are* those most likely to split their tickets. And the average voter today does position him or herself between a Democratic party located to the left and a Republican party located to the right, and on most issues, *closer* to the Republicans (Table 15.7). Thus, a policy-balancing model can explain both the timing of the increase in ticket-splitting and its tendency to favor Republican executives and Democratic legislators. In these and other respects a policy balancing model fits with the broad outlines of electoral behavior.

TABLE 15.7 *Voter policy positions compared with perceptions of party positions**

	Democratic Position	Citizen Position	Republican Position
Liberal–Conservative ideology	3.1	4.3	5.1
Government provision of public services	5.3	3.8	2.9
Aid to minorities	3.0	4.2	4.6
U.S. involvement in Central America	4.5	4.5	3.0
Defense spending	3.2	4.0	5.4
Aid to women	3.1	3.9	4.6
Co-operation with U.S.S.R.	3.2	4.1	4.9
Government responsibility for jobs and living standards	3.1	4.4	4.9

* Each of the eight issues in the table is the subject of a seven-point scale. The figures in the first and third columns are the average positions of the two parties as perceived by the respondents; the middle column is the average self-placement of the respondents.

Source: 1984 NES.

Of course, such models are vulnerable to the immediate objection that they overestimate the sophistication of the electorate. For example, skeptics may object that many people do not even know which party controls the House of Representatives, although the ignorance of the electorate in this respect has been exaggerated. In the three 1980 elections more than 80 per cent of *all* voters knew that the Democrats controlled the House prior to the election. Such criticisms are well-taken, but it must be borne in mind that only 25 per cent of the electorate engages in ticket-splitting. Moreover, that 25 per cent is a slightly unusual section of the electorate – somewhat more educated, interested and attentive, much more politically independent and somewhat more politically efficacious (DeVries and Tarrance, 1972). In addition, in order for the model to work voters need react only to *general* party images; they need not synthesize the myriad proposals of individual candidates. Finally, voters do not need to know who currently controls the legislature; they need only indicate a preference for the pattern of control they would like.

A second intentional explanation has been advanced by Gary Jacobson (1989b). This one builds on the empirical finding that contemporary party images have complementary strengths and weaknesses. Voters view Republicans as the party more likely to promote a healthy economy; but they view the party as less interested in the common citizen and more concerned with economic special interests. The Democrats on the other hand have the edge when it comes to distributing fairly the gains and losses from economic activities. Thus, voters are cross-pressured. They would like the Republicans to bake the economic pie (and protect it from marauding bears and other dangers), but they would like the Democrats to dish it out. What are they to do?

According to Jacobson, a reasonable answer is to vote for Republican presidents and Democratic congressmen. The executive is more important for the determination of overall national policy. Moreover, executive institutions and their personnel have a more national orientation than legislative institutions and their personnel. Thus, placing Republicans in the executive combines party and institutional strengths in the service of allocative efficiency. Conversely, the traditional and major role of Congress is distribution. Placing Democratic majorities in the Congress combines party and institutional strengths in the service of distributive justice.

Jacobson provides no direct evidence in support of his argument. Survey evidence indicates that voters view the parties as having different strengths and weaknesses, but whether those voters who have the hypothesized combinations of views are those who split their tickets remains to be shown. In a number of respects, moreover, Jacobson's argument appears to be incomplete. When did the current pattern of popular perceptions develop? Does it correspond to the timing of the increase in ticket-splitting? For another thing the applicability of Jacobson's argument to ticket-splitting at the state level is open to question. Californians being what they are, perhaps it is conceivable that they choose Republican governors because of perceived Republican superiority in macroeconomics and foreign policy, but this argument appears strained as an explanation of Utah voters' choices of Democratic governors.[3] Finally, like Ehrenhalt's hypothesis, Jacobson's argument about the hypothesized better 'fit' of Democrats to congressional politics suggests that Democrats in Congress should have a larger incumbency advantage than Republicans. But as mentioned earlier, the best estimates suggest that both parties' candidates are equally advantaged by incumbency.

The third purposeful explanation has not yet been formally advanced by any single author, although elements of it emerge in many arguments in the press and popular commentary. For example, David Nyhan, a columnist for the *Boston Globe*, has written:

> Voters generally pick Democrats for Congress and Republicans for president, in hopes they'll keep each other under control, because greed, self-dealing and under the table grabbing are equal opportunity occupations.

This sentiment recalls the traditional curse: 'a pox on both your houses'. According to proponents of this third view of voter behavior, ticket-splitting reflects disenchantment with both parties, a disenchantment that has grown into cynicism about getting acceptable government from either party. The disenchantment does not stem primarily from issue stands, but rather stems from the perceived incompetence, corruption, oppressiveness, and/or arrogance of party elites. When they split their tickets, voters are not simply trying to bring about a moderate compromise between two polarized parties, as in the policy-balancing explanation; rather, voters are seeking to create a deadlock where neither party can do anything, and both dissipate their resources and energy fighting with each other. Rather than bring about moderate government, or to combine each party's best, 'pox' voters have decided that stalemate is their best hope.

While scholars continually track the mood of the American electorate, it is difficult to identify any study that relates variations in that mood to ticket-splitting. This is unfortunate because a quick pass through the 1980 American National Election Study provides some preliminary indications that the 'pox' view bears investigation (Table 15.8). Voters who do

TABLE 15.8   *President/House ticket-splitting in relation to various indicators of alienation and distrust (per cent)*

Don't care which party wins presidential election	36
Do care which party wins	25
No important differences in what parties stand for	34
There are important differences	25
Low on political trust	30
Medium	25
High	25
Never trust government to do what's right*	36
Sometimes trust them	28
Mostly trust them	26
Always trust them*	21
Government too strong for good of country	31
Government not too strong	22
Hardly at all pay attention to public affairs	21
Now and then pay attention	21
Some of the time pay attention	35
Most of the time pay attention	26
Low internal political efficacy	23
Higher	29
Higher still	27
Highest	35
Politics too complicated to understand	26
Not too complicated	32

* Less than 25 cases.

Source: 1980 American National Election Study.

not care which party wins the presidential election, who see no important differences in what the parties stand for, and who believe that the federal government is getting too strong are all about ten per cent more likely to split their tickets than those expressing the opposite sentiments. Voters who are lower on a political trust scale (and some of the component items) are somewhat more likely to split their tickets. Such relationships might only indicate that those on the margins of the political process are more disorganized in their voting, but as the lower panel of the Table shows, ticket-splitters are somewhat more attentive to public affairs and express a higher sense of personal efficacy than straight ticket voters.

And, as remarked earlier, they are somewhat more educated and politically independent. Not all of the various trust, responsiveness and other 'alienation' items show similar relationships, and there are some interesting partisan interactions beneath the simple relationships. But there are enough suggestive relationships here to indicate the need for further research.

Summary

The explanation for the current situation of divided government is now a matter of considerable debate. No well-informed scholar can deny that incumbency explains a large proportion of the current presidential–House division. But it is less clear that a legislative incumbency advantage can explain the state divisions (not to mention the increasing tendency of state electorates to split their two Senate seats between the parties). Nor can incumbency arguments account for the asymmetric pattern of divided government – Republican executives/Democratic legislatures – without positing additional considerations that have yet to be demonstrated. For these reasons some scholars have shown a willingness to consider the hypothesis that some portion of the electorate is engaging in purposeful voting. One need not argue that voters are consciously calculating about their actions. It may only be that certain voters become more receptive to arguments for voting for the other party once they have made a decision for president or congress. Thus balancing arguments should be viewed in 'as if' terms. In the large, the electorate behaves as if voters were engaging in a fairly sophisticated trading off of party positions. But viewed individually, few voters show direct evidence of such concerns. The three arguments surveyed identify the kinds of voters who are most likely to end up dividing their votes.

Consequences of Divided Government

Some commentators believe that the major consequences of divided government are all too obvious. First, split control of national institutions exacerbates problems of co-ordination and coherence that are inherent in the constitutional fabric. Divided government can make an inefficient form of government unworkable. Secondly, split control obscures the accountability of government officials for policies followed and outcomes realized during their tenure. Responsibility is always problematic in a federal system with weak parties and a separation of powers, but split control can obscure responsibility altogether. Although these two concerns resonate with traditional thinking in American politics, it is apparent that our evaluations of divided government have far outrun our understanding of its consequences. The consequences of divided government are more controversial than one might at first sight suppose. And no one has addressed the question of whether these consequences, even if bad, are worse than those that would ensue if unified control were somehow achieved in the contemporary American context. Where one stands on that question hinges critically on why one thinks that divided government has become the norm.

Efficiency and Effectiveness

In a thoughtful recent essay James Sundquist reflects on the contemporary condition of divided government (Sundquist, 1988). With a system of separated institutions, some elected and some appointed, sharing powers that are intricately blended among them, efficiency has never been a strong point of American democracy. What has made the system workable in the past is the unifying force of political party. The development of a persistent condition of divided government removes the critical co-ordinating force of party. Institutional rivalries now are buttressed by partisan rivalry and partisan electoral interest. One would like to believe that the Tom Foleys, George Mitchells, and George Bushs sit down after election, and say, 'Well, that's over; now let's put our differences aside and do what's best for the country'. But we are beyond such elementary school expectations. As Sundquist observes, the congressional majority has no choice but to reject presidential initiatives; to accept them is to acknowledge his competence and sagacity, hence, to support his re-election. Similarly, the President cannot run against Congress in the next election if he admits that congressional initiatives are meritorious. Divided control gives each branch of government an electoral incentive to work for the failure of the branch held by the other.

Thus, it is alleged that problems like the budget and trade deficits fester, foreign policy toward Central America degenerates into bitter partisan stalemate, frustrated presidents go outside normal governmental channels (and the law) in order to achieve their aims, frustrated Congressmen leak secrets and conduct destructive investigations in order to achieve theirs, and government degenerates into a snakepit of no-holds barred partisan struggle (Ginsburg and Shefter, 1990). The normal obstacles of the separation of powers are reinforced manyfold by split control of the separate institutions. Consequently, governing becomes a matter of posturing for the most part, and when actions must be taken, they tend to reflect the lowest common denominator and satisfy no one. The country suffers as costs mount and opportunities fade because the government is incapable of formulating and implementing coherent policies.

This sounds convincing, but not everyone sees it that way. Though a critic of current constitutional arrangements such as Lloyd Cutler attributes the contemporary budget deficits to divided government, academic research is less certain (Cutler, 1989). And though one analyst such as James Sundquist sees little beyond drift and stalemate, another – David Mayhew – finds nothing in the historical record to suggest that periods of divided government are any less productive than periods of unified control (Mayhew, 1989). It might even be argued that periods of divided control are *more* likely to call forth legislation. For example, the expansion of Social Security benefits and coverage was stimulated by the competition between Republican Presidents and Democratic Congresses. Similarly, the Clean Air Act of 1970 emerged stronger than anticipated because of the one-upmanship that went on between President Nixon and presidential aspirant, Senator Edmund Muskie, the responsible Democratic committee chair (Jones, 1975). And though the passage of the 1986 Tax Reform Act is not well understood, part of the explanation seems to be that neither party wished to bear the blame for allowing the legislation to fail. While neither party can accomplish everything it wants to in divided government periods, it seems that the struggle for political credit sometimes makes them as likely to compromise behind some legislation, as to allow the process to stalemate. Moreover one could question whether partisan compromises are inevitably bad. Is it better to have a sharp alternation of policies as when the British Labour Party nationalized the steel industry after the Second World War only to have the Conservative Party promptly denationalize it after coming to power? These are hard questions. Reasonable people will not disagree over them.

Responsibility

A decade ago I wrote an essay entitled 'The Decline of Collective Responsibility in American Politics' (Fiorina, 1980). Writing in an era that exalted popular participation and reacting to the sorry performance of the Carter Administration – the U.S.'s last episode of unified government – I updated the traditional arguments about the importance of party responsibility in American politics. With the weakening of party affiliations in the electorate and the decline of party organization as a force in campaigns, the ability of party to enforce cohesion in government inevitably had followed. Congressmen were re-elected on the basis of their individual records and would run no risks to aid a president of their party whose fate would have little or no bearing on theirs. The result was (among other things) an erosion of electoral accountability. Presidents were held accountable for the state of the economy and other aspects of the larger national well-being, but congressmen could generally escape responsibility for the big picture by running on their personal relationships to their districts and their records of particularistic achievements. After all, no one could plausibly charge that one representative of 435 or one senator of 100 personally was responsible for stagflation or gas lines. An impersonal entity called 'Congress' shared that responsibility with the president. But unlike the president, the collective 'Congress' never appears on the ballot. Thus, the president had come to bear greater political responsibility than his authority justified, while the Congress had come to bear less. The point was not that party responsibility was the ideal, but that the alternative was irresponsibility, not some other form of responsibility. Thus, any reforms or developments that encouraged voters to support the party, not the person, were worth considering and encouraging.

That was over a decade ago, and if responsibility is problematic in American politics even when government is unified, the problem is compounded when government is divided. Presidents blame Congress for obstructing carefully-crafted solutions, while members of Congress attack the president for lack of leadership. Citizens genuinely can not tell who is to blame, and the meaning of election outcomes becomes increasingly confused.

The reluctance of Americans to impose collective responsibility on their leaders often gives American politics a comical tone. During the 1988 election campaign there was a great to-do about George Bush's role in the Iran–Contra affair. How much did he know? How responsible was he? Some elements of the media became obsessed with these questions. Bush was able to turn that obsession to his advantage in the celebrated live encounter with Dan Rather. European observers must have viewed the entire episode as pure silliness. Was Bush responsible? Of course he was. He was a member of the Administration in power and he did not resign in protest; therefore, he was responsible – 100 per cent. The voters cannot mark their ballots: Reagan 75 per cent guilty, Bush 50 per cent guilty, Schultz 35 per cent, Weinberger 20 per cent; they can only mark up or down. The only way to give office-holders the proper incentives is to hold *all* of them *fully* responsible for the decisions with which they are associated. Nothing else will suffice. In contrasting his Vice-Presidential choice to that of Bush, Dukakis argued that if a scheme like Iran–Contra were hatched when Lloyd Bentsen was in the room, the upright Bentsen – unlike Bush – would quickly squelch such madness. Maybe so, but as Madison long ago cautioned, we should not rely on the uprightness of our leaders. The best insurance against a future occurrence like the Iran–Contra affair would have been the destruction of Bush's political career, and Republican losses of ten Senate and forty House seats. Then, we could be relatively confident that when some future scheme was hatched, someone in the room would ask 'Do you remember what happened in 1988?'

Though collective responsibility is a blunt instrument, it is the only one we have. In obscuring responsibility for government actions and the results thereof, divided control exacerbates the already serious problems of responsibility that are inherent in American politics. On this matter I am in substantial agreement with Sundquist. But as always, there is another side to the argument. When we are talking about much of economic and social policy and mundane matters of foreign policy, the accountability argument is compelling. But there are policies that have different, sometimes irreversible effects. A unified Republican government under Reagan would have offered the electorate a clear choice in 1984 and 1988. In the abstract that would be desirable, but one suspects that dead Nicaraguans would take small consolation in the knowledge that Americans had a clear choice in 1984 and 1988. And there always is the theoretical possibility that an aggressive, unified government could follow a policy path that would kill many of its constituents before it ever was held to account at the next election. Divided government may limit the potential for a society to gain through government actions, but it may similarly limit the potential for a society to lose because of government actions.

Intellectual Challenge

The leitmotif of Sundquist's essay of 1988 is the intellectual challenge divided government poses for political science. Sundquist maintains that American political science traditionally has accepted a version of the responsible party doctrine combined with a belief in the critical need for presidential leadership. Many of the major thinkers of American political science – Key, Herring, Schattschneider, and a host of others – lived their entire professional lives in the first half of the twentieth century – the unusual era of unified government (see Table 15.1). Even the next generation lived their formative years during the latter days of that period (Campbell *et al.*, 1960). The result is that almost to this day our general accounts of the operation of American national government presuppose unified party control (Weingast and Moran, 1983; Moe, 1987; Wilson, 1989).

While conceding the dangers in evaluating government operation in different eras, Sundquist contends that the American version of party government did function passably well, at least relative to the current period of divided government. But whether right or wrong, he expresses disappointment that most of his colleagues have not joined the issue, charging that political scientists evade

> what is surely one of the most crucial intellectual questions facing students of American government – one that the previous generation of political scientists explicitly asked and answered ... fence straddling on this issue is not intellectually defensible. Either the dominant pre-1954 view of the desirability of party government and presidential leadership as the model and the ideal was right or it was wrong. That two systems so diametrically opposite as party government and coalition could serve the country equally well is a virtual mathematical impossibility ... One or the other necessarily has to be the superior model for America, and political scientists have a responsibility to determine which it is and inform the country of their judgment. (Sundquist, 1988)

Most of us are willing enough to accept intellectual responsibility (though I doubt that the country waits with bated breath for the pronouncements of political science professors). The problem is that some of us do not see matters quite so clearly as Sundquist. In my view an evaluation of the current state of divided government *must* be equivocal, and it must remain so until we fully understand the reasons that it has come about – why voters are splitting their tickets – as discussed earlier. For Sundquist, divided government is simply an accident: 'the United States has its own unique version of coalition government – not a coalition voluntarily entered into by the parties but one forced upon them by the accidents of the electoral process' (Sundquist, 1988). Evidently regarding party decline, and incumbency as sufficient explanations of the present situation, Sundquist explicitly rejects purposeful explanations because they assume that

> divided government is the people's intent, more or less conscious, rather than the essentially chance outcome of the electoral system that was not designed by those who use it. Clearly the latter is the case: divided government is a historical and procedural accident. (Sundquist, 1988.)

If divided government is only an accidental by-product of a chaotic electoral system, Sundquist's indictment gains force. On the other hand, if purposeful explanations have any validity, Sundquist's case is greatly weakened. Recall Schattschneider's dictum that 'Democracy was made for the people, not the people for democracy' (Schattschneider, 1975). If it can be shown that the ticket-splitting of a significant proportion of the citizenry reflects a lack of confidence in the elites of both parties, who are we to recommend that they make a clear choice? If, in their view, Republican Party elites are people who want to shoot up small countries, who would redistribute from poor to rich, and who view toxic wastes and acid rain as figments of the liberal imagination; while Democratic Party elites are people who feel that true democracy exists only in certain third world dictatorships, who love taxes, and who believe that there are no criminals, only oppressed victims of society; why on earth should citizens be forced to make a clear choice? Or, if voters believe that the Republican Party will concentrate on the prosperity of the whole and ignore the misery of some parts, while the Democratic Party will concentrate on equality at the expense of prosperity, why should they be forced to make a clear choice? Or, if voters believe that unified control under either party will lead to unconstrained looting, why should they be forced to turn over all the keys of government to either party?

If further research on split-ticket voting in American elections concludes that divided government is no more than 'a historical and procedural accident', then a responsible political science must respond to Sundquist's challenge. What are the costs of divided government? And if they are significant, how can the system be made to work better, and how might we return to the more unified conditions of previous times? On the other hand, if further research on split-ticket voting concludes that purpose as well as caprice underlies such behavior, then a different sort of challenge arises. Over the past generation what conditions have led the parties to behave in such a manner that a critical minority of Americans believes that divided government, with its inefficiency and irresponsibility, is preferable to a unified government that would act more efficiently and responsibly but in the service of ends they do not accept?

If the intent of the electorate should prove to be a significant factor underlying the current condition of divided government, then current conditions should be seen as a legitimate part of our constitutional system, however much they may differ from earlier historical experience. The Constitution sought to buttress 'parchment barriers' by pitting ambition against ambition; and the principal means of doing that was to elect public officials at different times, by different people, and for somewhat different reasons. If Americans choose to divide institutional control among the contending parties, they are only availing themselves of an option explicitly provided for in their founding charter. An invigorated separation of powers may be a nuisance or even a danger in an era of activist government, but it certainly is not something alien to American traditions.

Thus, the immediate task is to renew our commitment to the study of the behavior of the American electorate, not only in presidential and House elections, but in Senate elections and in American state elections. Ticket-splitting and other aspects of the relationships between voting for different offices should become a central focus of research, rather than a sideline. As always, political science owes society investigation before evaluation and recommendation.

Notes

1. The location of these cutting points varies with the value of q which determines the positions DR and RD. The larger is q, the closer DR will be to DD, and vice versa.

2. This is a consequence of the assumption made in the analysis that q > 0.5: the executive is more powerful than the legislature in determining the location of the policy.
3. Within the policy-balancing model there are two explanations for the behavior of Utahans. Democratic executives and Republican legislatures are chosen if either (1) the median voter is between the parties but closer to the Democrats (seems doubtful), or (2) in contrast to the national government, the legislature is regarded as the more powerful of the two institutions ($q < 0.5$).

Guide to Further Reading

Chapter 1   Values, Institutions and Policy Agendas

There is an enormous literature on the American political tradition and only a few works can be mentioned here. Hartz (1955) is a useful starting-point for understanding the role of liberalism in America. The conservative perspective is covered in Peele (1984) and Nash (1976). Pole (1978) gives an excellent account of the part the idea of equality has played in political debate. White (1976) looks at the American judicial tradition. The role of religion is covered in Ahlstrom (1975) and Wuthnow (1988). Feminist ideas are conveniently summarized in Castro (1990). The literature on blacks in America is enormous, but the agenda of black politics can be gleaned from reading the *Yearbook of Black America*, published by the Urban League. More general coverage of changing values in America can be found in Matusow (1984) and Phillips (1990).

Chapter 2   The American Electoral System

The literature on representation is vast and ever-changing. Two classic works provide a good starting-point for understanding the American electoral system. Dahl (1956) analyses the premises of the U.S. system of representation; Rae (1974) discusses the uniqueness of American electoral rules.

There are a number of important studies of American voting behavior. These include Campbell *et al.* (1960); Nie *et al.* (1979); and Niemi and Weisberg (1984). The best overview of presidential elections is found in Polsby and Wildavsky (1984) and of congressional elections in Jacobson (1987). The most important study of turnout is Wolfinger and Rosenstone (1980). Tufte (1978) provides a readable study of the economy and elections. An understanding of the role of parties in the electoral process can be found in Wattenberg (1990) and Ranney (1975). Minority politics are examined in two excellent recent studies – Browning *et al.* (1984); and Jackson and Preston (eds) (1991). Finally the seminal role of money in politics is still Jacobson (1980).

Chapter 3   American Political Parties

Accessible introductions to the American party system are McSweeney and Zvesper (1991) and Sorauf and Beck (1988). Sundquist (1983) provides an excellent account of the development of American parties. The classic exposition of the thesis of party decline is Broder (1972). Crotty (1984) and Wattenberg (1990) also present evidence of the decline of the parties. For a discussion of party renewal see Kayden and Mahe (1985) and Sabato (1988). Herrnson (1988) provides an excellent account of the ways in which the parties have adapted to a new electoral environment. The best account of the reform of the presidential selection process is Shafer (1983), though Ceaser (1982) also offers a useful analysis of this subject. For a broader examination of the consequences of party reform see Polsby (1983).

Chapter 4   Presidential Leadership

Memoirs, biographies, and accounts of individual Presidents provide a useful source of material about the presidency. Some of the better accounts of the Reagan Administration are Jones (1988), Hill, Moore and Williams (1990) and Hogan (1990). Mervin (1990) offers a slightly controversial view of the success of the Reagan Administration. Campbell and Rockman (1991) offer a preliminary appraisal of the Bush presidency. More general texts on the presidency include Koenig (1990), Rose (1988) and Berman (1987). Neustadt (1976) remains the most influential work in the study of the presidency. Moe (1985) has challenged conventional thinking about the need for presidents to manage the executive branch. Kernell (1986) pursues the same theme. Two thoughtful and important books on the nature of the presidency are Schlesinger (1974) and Lowi (1985). The best account of the growth of the Executive Office of the Presidency is Hart (1987).

Chapter 5   Congress and Legislative Activism

The literature on Congress is enormous. For a more comprehensive bibliography than it is possible to provide here see Bailey (1990). For a general introduction to Congress see the books by Davidson and Oleszek (1989), Ripley (1989) and Bailey (1989). The collection of essays by Dodd and Oppenheimer (1989) is also invaluable. An extended discussion of the importance of constituency service can be found in the books by Fenno (1978), Johannes (1984), Parker (1986) and Cain, Ferejohn and Fiorina (1987). On roll-call behavior see Clausen (1973), Fiorina (1974) and Kingdon (1989). Recent literature on leadership in Congress has been a little sparse, but useful information is contained in the books by Sinclair (1983), Bach and Smith (1988) and Smith (1989). The best discussion of recent reforms in Congress is Rieselbach (1986). An interesting evaluation of congressional performance is provided by Mezey (1989).

Chapter 6   Constitutional Legitimacy and The Supreme Court

A recent discussion of the role of the Supreme Court in American politics is O'Brien (1986). Hodder-Williams (1980) also provides a good introduction to the Court. Fisher (1988) provides an interesting counter to arguments that the Supreme Court is the final arbiter of the Constitution. For those interested in the recent history of the Supreme Court, McCloskey (1972) covers the Stone, Vincent and Warren Courts, while Blasi (1983) discusses the Burger Court. Rehnquist (1987) provides a lively account of the Court from an insider's perspective. The Reagan Administration's attempts to influence the Court are discussed in Schwartz (1988) and Witt (1986). Accounts of the Bork nomination include Pertschuk and Schaetzel (1990) and Bronner (1989).

Chapter 7   Public Bureaucracy in the American Political System

The classic account of the American bureaucracy is Seidman and Gilmour (1986). Stillman (1987) also provides a good introduction to the bureaucracy. For a discussion of recent attempts to reform the bureaucracy see Gormley (1989) and Goodman and Wrightson (1987).

Chapter 8   The Changing Federal Balance

Recent studies of the changed nature of federal–state relations under the Reagan Administration include Conlan (1988) and Nathan and Doolittle (1987). Also useful, though now dated, are Elazar (1984) and Reagan and Sanzone (1981). For a discussion of urban policy see Gurr and King (1987) and Peterson and Lewis (1986).

Chapter 9   Economic Policy

For a useful overview of the state of the American economy see Obey and Sarbanes (1986). The economic policy of the Reagan era is discussed in Cagan (1986). A more lively account of this period is provided by Stockman (1986). Hibbs (1987) examines the connection between electoral politics and macroeconomic policy, while Stein (1985) provides an overview of presidential economic policy-making from Franklin Roosevelt to Ronald Reagan, and Schick (1983) examines congressional policy-making.

Chapter 10 Social Welfare Policy

Patterson (1981) and Browning (1986) are both good accounts of the development of welfare policy in the United States. Weir, Orloff and Skocpol (1988) also contains much useful information on the background to the current debate about welfare policy. A positive evaluation of the consequences of past policies is provided by John Schwartz (1988). Glazer (1988) offers a stimulating discussion of the limits of social policy. Cottingham and Ellwood (1989) examine the challenges facing welfare policy in the 1990s.

Chapter 11 American Foreign Policy

The literature on American foreign policy is extensive, but can be divided into two broad types. The first provides a historical description of the foreign policy of the United States. Among such works are Ambrose (1985), LeFeber (1989). The second provides an analysis of the way that foreign policy is made. A good recent addition to the literature is Dumbrell (1990). Other important texts include Spanier and Uslaner (1989) and Nathan and Oliver (1987). For the stuggle between Presidents and Congress over foreign policy see Mann (1990), Warburg (1989) and Crabb and Holt (1980).

Chapter 12 The Budget Deficit

General books on the budgetary process include Wildavsky (1984) and Schick (1980). Collender (1991) provides a guide to the current federal budget and is updated regularly.

Chapter 13 Civil Rights in the United States

There is a large literature on the history of the movement; but Taylor

Branch (1988) offers an excellent overview. The handling of civil rights under Reagan is covered in Amaker (1988) and Yarbrough (1985). Individual areas of civil rights have generated their own literature but reference should be made to Kluger (1975) on integration. Voting is provocatively handled in Thernstrom (1987). For an excellent summary of the issues associated with affirmative action see Rosenfeld (1991).

Chapter 14 Immigration Reforms: A Mexican–American Perspective

The literature on immigration reform is limited. Perhaps the best general study is Bean, Vernez and Keely (1989). On the general question of Latino immigration see Brown and Shue (1983). Smith (1980) discusses immigration policy in the broader context of U.S. foreign policy towards Mexico. The growing empowerment of Latinos is discussed in Foley (1988) and Brischetto (1988).

Chapter 15 An Era of Divided Government

The causes and consequences of divided government are examined in Jacobson (1990), Thurber (1991), Mayhew (1991) and Cox and Kernell (1991). Discussions of the need for constitutional reform include Sundquist (1988) and Cutler (1989).

Bibliography

Aberbach, Joel D. (1979) 'Changes in Congressional Oversight', *American Behavioral Scientist*, 22, pp. 493–515.

Aberbach, Joel D. (1983) 'Congress and the Agencies: Four Themes of Congressional Oversight of Policy and Administration', in Dennis Hale (ed.) *The United States Congress*, New Brunswick, NJ, Transaction Books.

Abraham, Henry J. (1972) *Freedom and the Court: Civil Liberties in the United States*, New York, Oxford University Press.

Abraham, Henry J. (1985) *Justices and the Presidents: A Political History of Appointments to the Supreme Court*, New York, Oxford University Press.

Acuna, Rodolfo (1988) *Occupied America*, New York, Harper and Row.

Adamany, David and Joel Grossman (1983) 'Support for the Supreme Court as a National Policymaker', *Law and Policy Quarterly*, vol. 5, pp. 405–37.

Advisory Commission on Intergovernmental Relations (1988) *Significant Features of Fiscal Federalism*, vols 1 and 2, Washington DC, ACIR.

Ahlstrom, S. E. (1975) *A Religious History of the American People*, New York, Image Books.

Aldrich, John H., John L. Sullivan and Eugene Borgida (1989) 'Foreign Affairs and Issue Voting: Do Presidential Candidates "Waltz Before a Blind Audience"', *American Political Science Review*, vol. 83, pp. 123–40.

Allison, Graham (1971) *Essence of Decision*, Boston, Little, Brown.

Allsup, Carl (1982) *The American G.I. Forum*, Austin, Texas, Center for Mexican American Studies.

Alvarez, Rodolfo (1971) 'The Unique Psycho-Historical Experience of the Mexican American People', *Social Science Quarterly*, 52: 2, pp. 15–29.

Amaker, Norman C. (1988) *Civil Rights and the Reagan Administration*, Washington DC, The Urban Institute.

Ambrose, Stephen (1985) *Rise to Globalism*, Harmondsworth, Penguin.

Arnson, Cynthia J. (1989) *Crossroads: Congress, the Reagan Administration, and Central America*, New York, Pantheon.

Aron, Nan (1989) 'Support for the Supreme Court as a National

Policymaker', *Law & Politics Quarterly*, vol. 5, pp. 405–37.

Art, Robert J. and Stephen E. Ockenden (1981) 'The Domestic Politics of Cruise Missile Development, 1970–1980', in Richard K. Betts (ed.) *Cruise Missiles: Technology, Strategy, Politics*, Washington DC, Brookings Institution.

Bach, G. (1971) *Making Monetary and Fiscal Policy*, Washington DC, Brookings Institution.

Bach, Stanley and Steven S. Smith (1988) *Managing Uncertainty in the House of Representatives*, Washington DC, Brookings Institution.

Bachrach, Peter and Morton S. Baratz (1970) *Power and Poverty*, New York, Oxford University Press.

Bailey, Christopher J. (1998a) 'Beyond the New Congress: Aspects of Congressional Development in the 1980s', *Parliamentary Affairs*, vol. 41, pp. 236–46.

Bailey, Christopher J. (1988b) *The Republican Party in the US Senate 1974–1984*, Manchester, Manchester University Press.

Bailey, Christopher J. (1989) *The US Congress*, Oxford, Basil Blackwell.

Bailey, Christopher J. (1990) 'The US Congress: An Introductory Bibliography', *American Studies International*, vol. 28, pp. 32–47.

Balderrama, Francisco E. (1982) *In Defense of La Raza*, Tucson, University of Arizona Press.

Barone, Michael (1990) *Our Country, The Shaping of America from Roosevelt to Reagan*, London, Collier Macmillan.

Bawden, D. Lee (ed.) (1984) *The Social Contract Revisited*, Washington DC, The Urban Institute.

Bean, Frank D. and Rodolfo O. de la Garza (1988) 'Illegal Aliens and the 1990 Census Counts', *Society/Transactions*, 25: 3, pp. 48–53.

Bean, Frank D., Georges Vernez and Charles B. Keely (1989) *Opening and Closing the Doors: Evaluating Immigration Reform and Control*, Washington DC, The Urban Institute.

Beer, Samuel (1978) 'The Public Philosophy', in Anthony King (ed.) *The New American Political System*, Washington DC, American Enterprise Institute.

Bendiner, Robert (1964) *Obstacle Course on Capitol Hill*, New York, McGraw-Hill.

Berman, L. (1979) *The Office of Management and Budget and the Presidency, 1921–1979*, Princeton, Princeton University Press.

Berman, L. (1987) *The New American Presidency*, Boston, Little, Brown.

Bibby, John F. (1980) 'Party Renewal in the National Republican Party', in Gerald M. Pomper (ed.) *Party Renewal in America: Theory and Practice*, New York, Praeger.

Bixby, Ann Kallman (1989) 'Public Social Welfare Expenditures, Fiscal

Year 1986', *Social Security Bulletin*, vol. 52, pp. 29–39.

Blasi, Vincent (ed.) (1983) *The Burger Court*, New Haven, Yale University Press.

Blechman, Barry M. (1990) 'The New Congressional Role in Arms Control', in Thomas E. Mann (ed.) *A Question of Balance: the President, the Congress, and Foreign Policy*, Washington DC, Brookings Institution.

Blondel, Jean (1973) *Comparative Legislatures*, Englewood Cliffs, Prentice-Hall.

Bonomi, Patricia, James McGregor Burns, and Austin Ranney (eds) (1981) *The American Constitutional System Under Strong and Weak Parties*, New York, Praeger.

Boyd, Gerald M. (1989) 'The Bush Style of Management: After Reagan, It's Back to Details', *New York Times*, 19 March.

Branch, Taylor (1988) *Parting the Waters*, London, Macmillan.

Brennan, William J. (1986) 'The Constitution of the United States: Contemporary Ratification', *South Texas Law Review*, vol. 27, 433–52.

Brisbin, Richard A. (1990) 'The Conservatism of Antonin Scalia', *Political Science Quarterly*, vol. 105, pp. 1–30.

Brischetto, Robert (1983) *Mexican American Issues for the 1984 Presidential Election*, San Antonio: Southwest Voter Registration Education Project.

Brischetto, Robert (1988) *Political Empowerment of Texas Mexicans, 1974–1988*, San Antonio, Southwest Voter Research Institute.

Brischetto, Robert (1989) 'Latino Representation and the 1990 Census', in William P. O'Hare (ed.) *Redistricting in the 1990s: A Guide for Minority Groups*, Washington DC, Population Reference Bureau.

Broder, David (1972) *The Party's Over*, New York, Harper and Row.

Broder, David (1988) 'Bush: Competence Plus Disturbing Signals', *International Herald Tribune*, 2 November.

Broesamle, John J. (1990) *Reform and Reaction in Twentieth Century American Politics*, London, Greenwood.

Bronner, Ethan (1989) *Battle for Justice: How the Bork Nomination Shook America*, New York, Norton.

Brown, Peter G. and Henry Shue (1989) *The Border That Joins*, New Jersey, Rowan and Littlefield.

Browning, Robert X. (1986) *Politics and Social Welfare Policy in the United States*, Knoxville, University of Tennessee Press.

Bryce, James (1888) *The American Commonwealth*, London, Macmillan.

Burke, Edmund (1854) 'Speech to the Electors of Bristol', in *Burke's Works*, vol. 1, London, Henry G. Bohn.

Burnham, Walter Dean (1965) 'The Changing Shape of the American

Political Universe', *American Political Science Review*, vol. 59, pp. 7–28.

Burnham, Walter Dean (1975) 'Insulation and Responsiveness in Congressional Elections', *Political Science Quarterly*, vol. 90, p. 411.

Burnham, Walter Dean (1989) 'The Reagan Heritage', in Gerald Pomper (ed.) *The Election of 1988*, Chatham, Chatham House.

Butler, Stuart *et al.* (1984) *Mandate for Leadership II*, Washington DC, The Heritage Foundation.

Cagan, P. (1986) *Essays in Contemporary Economic Problems: The Impact of the Reagan Program*, Washington DC, American Enterprise Institute.

Cain, Bruce (1984) *The Reapportionment Puzzle*, Berkeley, University of California Press.

Cain, Bruce, John Ferejohn and Morris Fiorina (1984) 'The Constituency Service Basis of the Personal Vote for U.S. Representatives and British Members of Parliament', *American Political Science Review*, vol. 78, pp. 110–125.

Cain, Bruce, D. Roderich Kiewiet and Carole Uhlaner (1986) *Minorities in California*, A Report to the Seaver Foundation.

Cain, Bruce, John Ferejohn and Morris Fiorina (1987) *The Personal Vote*, Cambridge, Harvard University Press.

Cain, Bruce, I. A. Lewis and Douglas Rivers (1989) 'Strategy and Choice in the 1988 Presidential Primaries', *Electoral Studies*, vol. 8, pp. 23–48.

California Secretary of State (1986) *California Ballot Pamphlet, Primary Election, June 3, 1986*, Sacramento.

Campbell, Angus, Philip E. Converse, Warren E. Miller and Donald E. Stokes (1960) *The American Voter*, New York, Wiley.

Campbell, Colin (1986) *Managing the Presidency: Carter, Reagan and the Search for Executive Harmony*, Pittsburgh, Pittsburgh University Press.

Campbell, Colin (1991) 'The White House and the Cabinet under the "Let's Deal" Presidency', in Colin Campbell and Bert A. Rockman, (eds) *The Bush Presidency: First Appraisals*, New Jersey, Chatham House.

Caplan, Lincoln (1987) *The Tenth Justice: the Solicitor-General and the Rule of Law*, New York, Knopf.

Caspar, John D. (1976) 'The Supreme Court and National Policy Making', *American Political Science Review*, vol. 70, pp. 50–63.

Castro, Ginette (1990) *American Feminism: A Contemporary History*, New York University Press.

Caves, R. W. (1989) 'An Historical Analysis of Federal Housing Policy from the Presidential Perspective', *Urban Studies*, vol. 26, pp. 59–76.

Ceaser, James W. (1982) *Reforming the Reforms: A Critical Analysis of the Presidential Selection Process*, Cambridge, Mass., Ballinger Publishing.

Ceaser, James W. (1988) 'The Reagan Presidency and American Public

Opinion', in Charles O. Jones (ed.) *The Reagan Legacy*, Chatham, Chatham House.

Chayes, Abram (1982–3) 'The Supreme Court 1981 Term Forward: Public Law Litigation and the Burger Court', *Harvard Law Review*, vol. 96, pp. 4–60.

Chubb, John E. and Paul E. Peterson (eds.) (1985) *The New Direction in American Politics*, Washington DC, Brookings Institution.

Clark, Joseph S. (1964) *Congress: The Sapless Branch*, New York, Harper and Row.

Clausen, Aage R. (1973) *How Congressmen Decide*, New York, St. Martin's Press.

Clayton, Cornell W. (1990) 'The Politics of Justice: The Attorney-General and the Making of American Legal Policy', unpublished D.Phil. thesis, Oxford University.

Clifford, J. (1965) *The Independence of the Federal Reserve System*, Philadelphia, University of Philadelphia Press.

Colie, Melissa P. (1988) 'The Legislature and Distributive Policy Making in Formal Perspective', *Legislative Studies Quarterly*, vol. 13, pp. 427–58.

Collender, S. E. (1991) *Guide to the Federal Budget*, Washington DC, Urban Institute Press.

Columbia Law Review, 'All the President's Men? A Study of Ronald Reagan's Appointments to the US Court of Appeal', *Columbia Law Review*, vol. 87, pp. 766–93.

Comarow, Murray (1981–2) 'A War on the Civil Service', *Bureaucrat*, vol. 10, pp. 8–9.

Combs, M. C. and L. M. Lynch (1988) 'English Plus', *English Today*, vol. 6, pp. 36–42.

Commission on Housing (1982) *The Report of the President's Commission on Housing*, Washington DC, GPO.

Committee on Party Renewal (1980) *Strengthening the Political Parties*, reprinted in Robert Harmel and Kenneth Janda (eds.) (1982) *Parties and their Environments*, New York, Longman.

Committee on Political Parties of the American Political Science Association (1950) *Toward A More Responsible Two-Party System*, New York, Rinehart.

Conlan, T. (1988) *New Federalism*, Washington DC, Brookings Institution.

Converse, Phillip E. (1966a) 'The Nature of Belief Systems in Mass Publics', in David Apter (ed.) *Ideology and Discontent*, New York, Wiley.

Converse, Phillip E. (1966b) 'Information Flow and Stability in Partisan Attitudes', in Angus Campbell *et al.* (eds.) *Elections and the Political Order*, New York, Wiley.

Cooper, Joseph and David W. Brady (1981) 'Toward a Diachronic Analysis of Congress', *American Political Science Review*, vol. 75, pp. 998–1006.

Cooper, Philip J. (1988) *Hard Judicial Choices: Federal District Judges and State and Local Officials*, New York, Oxford University Press.

Corwin, Edward S. (1957) *The Presidency: Office and Power, 1787–1957*, New York, New York University Press.

Corwin, Edward S. (1981) 'The "Higher Law" Background of American Constitutional Law', in Richard Loss (ed.) *Corwin on the Constitution*, vol. 1, Ithaca, Cornell University Press, pp. 79–139.

Council of Economic Advisors (1988) *Report to the President*, Washington DC. GPO.

Cottingham, Phoebe H. and David T. Ellwood (1989) *Welfare Policy for the 1990s*, Cambridge, Harvard University Press.

Cox, Gary and Samuel Kernell (eds) (1991) *The Politics of Divided Government*, Boulder, Col., Westview Press.

Crabb, C. V. and P. M. Holt (1980) *Invitation to Struggle: Congress, the President and Foreign Policy*, Washington DC, Congressional Quarterly Press.

Cronin, Thomas E. (1980) *The State of the Presidency*, Boston, Little, Brown.

Crotty, W. J. (1984) *American Parties in Decline*, Boston, Little, Brown.

Cutler, Lloyd N. (1980) 'To Form A Government', *Foreign Affairs*, Fall, pp. 126–43.

Cutler, Lloyd N. (1985) 'Party Government Under the American Constitution', *University of Pennsylvania Law Review*, vol. 25, p. 134.

Cutler, Lloyd (1989) 'Now is the Time for All Good Men', *William and Mary Law Review*, vol. 30, p. 391.

Dahl, Robert A. (1957) 'Decision-making in a Democracy: the Role of the Supreme Court as a National Policy Maker', *Journal of Public Law*, vol. 6, pp. 279–95.

Davidson, Roger H., David M. Kovenock and Michael K. O'Leary (1969) *Congress in Crisis*, Belmont, Calif., Wadsworth Publishing.

Davidson, Roger H. and Walter, J. Oleszek (1989) *Congress and its Members*, 3rd edition, Washington DC, Congressional Quarterly Press.

Days, Drew (1984) 'Turning Back the Clock: The Reagan Administration and Civil Rights', *Harvard Civil Rights and Civil Liberties, Law Review*, vol. 19.

de la Garza, Rodolfo (1989) 'Mexico, Mexicans, and Mexican Americans in U.S.–Mexico Relations', *Texas Papers on Mexico*, pp. 89–102.

de la Garza, Rodolfo (1982) *Public Policy Priorities of Chicano Political Elites*, Washington D.C., Overseas Development Council.

de la Garza, Rodolfo and Louis DeSipio (1989) 'The Changing Hispanic Political Landscape', in William P. O'Hare (ed.) *Redistricting in the 1990s: A Guide for Minority Groups*, Washington DC, Population Reference Bureau.

de la Garza, Rodolfo and Armando Trujillo (1989) 'Latinos and the Official English Debate in the United States: Language is not the Issue', in *Language and the State: The Law and Politics of Identity*, Edmonton, Alberta, University of Alberta.

de la Garza, Rodolfo, Nestor Rodriquez and Harry Pachon (1990) 'The Domestic and Foreign Policy Consequences of Mexican and Central American Immigration: Mexican American Perspectives', in George Vernez (ed.) *Immigration and International Relations*, Santa Monica, The Rand Corporation.

Derthick, Martha (1979) *Policymaking for Social Security*, Washington DC, Brookings Institution.

Destler, I. M. (1986) *American Trade Politics*, Washington DC, Institute for International Economics.

Destler, I. M., Leslie H. Gelb and Anthony Lake (1984) *Our Own Worst Enemy: The Unmaking of American Foreign Policy*, New York, Simon and Schuster.

Destler, I. M. and John Odell (1987) *The Politics of Anti-Protection*, Washington DC, Institute for International Economics.

Destler, I. M. and Randall C. Henning (1989) *Dollar Politics: Exchange Rate Policymaking in the United States*, Washington DC, Institute for International Economics.

DeVries, Walter and V. Lance Tarrance (1972) *The Ticket-Splitter: A New Force in American Politics*, Grand Rapids, Eerdmans.

Dodd, Lawrence C. and Bruce I. Oppenheimer (eds) (1989) *Congress Reconsidered*, Washington DC, Congressional Quarterly Press.

Drew, Elizabeth (1983) *Politics and Money*, New York, Macmillan.

Dukakis, Michael (1987) 'States Take A Fresh Look At Housing', *Journal of State Government*, vol. 60.

Dumbrell, John (1990) *The Making of U.S. Foreign Policy*, Manchester, Manchester University Press.

Edwards, George C. (1989) *At the Margins: Presidential Leadership in Congress*, New Haven, Yale University Press.

Ehrenhalt, Alan (1982) 'Why a Pay Rise Would Be Good for the GOP', *Congressional Quarterly Weekly Report*, 31 December, 3175.

Eisinger, P. (1988) *The Entrepreneurial State*, Madison, University of Wisconsin Press.

Eisner, R. (1986) 'The Federal Budget Crisis', in David Obey and Paul Sarbanes (eds) *The Changing American Economy*, Oxford, Basil Blackwell.

Elazar, Daniel J. (1984) *American Federalism*, New York, Harper and Row.

Ellwood, D. T. (1988) *Poor Support: Poverty in the American Family*, New York, Basic Books.

Epstein, Lee (1985) *Conservatives in Court*, Knoxville, University of Tennessee Press.

Epstein, Leon D. (1986) *Political Parties in the American Mold*, Madison, University of Wisconsin Press.

Erikson, Robert S. (1972) 'Malapportionment, Gerrymandering, and Party Fortunes in Congessional Elections', *American Political Science Review*, vol. 66, pp. 1234–45.

Eulau, Heinz and Paul Karp (1977) 'The Puzzle of Representation: Specifying the Components of Responsiveness', *Legislative Studies Quarterly*, vol. 2, pp. 233–54.

Farah, Barbara and Ethel Klein (1989) 'Public Opinion Trends', in Gerald M. Pomper (ed.) *The Elections of 1988: Reports and Interpretations*, Chatham, Chatham House.

Feagin, J. R. and J. Gilderblomm (1989) 'Public–Private Partnerships: The Houston Experience', in G. Squiles (ed.) *Unequal Partnerships*, New Brunswick, Rutgers University Press.

Federal Funds Information for States (1988) *Federal Aid for the Homeless*, Brief 89–2, Feburary 17.

Feldstein, M (ed.) (1980) *The American Economy in Transition*, Chicago, Chicago University Press.

Fenno, Richard F. (1959) *The President's Cabinet: Analysis in the Period from Wilson to Eisenhower*, Cambridge, Harvard University Press.

Fenno, Richard F. (1975) 'If, As Ralph Nader Says, Congress Is "The Broken Branch" How Come We Love Our Congressmen So Much?', in Norman Ornstein (ed.) *Congress in Change*, New York, Praeger.

Fenno, Richard F. (1978) *Home Style*, Boston, Little, Brown.

Ferejohn, John F. (1977) 'On the Decline of Competition in Congressional Elections', *American Political Science Review*, vol. 71, pp. 166–76.

Fiorina, Morris P. (1974) *Representatives, Roll Calls, and Constituencies*, Lexington, Lexington Books.

Fiorina, Morris P. (1989) *Congress: Keystone of the Washington Establishment*, 2nd ed., New Haven, Yale University Press.

Fiorina, Morris P. (1980) 'The Decline of Collective Responsibility in American Politics', *Daedalus*, vol. 109, pp. 25–45.

Fiorina, Morris P. (1981) *Retrospective Voting in American National Elections*, New Haven, Yale University Press.

Fiorina, Morris P. (1988) 'The Reagan Years: Turning to the Right or Groping Toward the Middle?', in Barry Cooper, Allan Kornberg and William Mishler (eds) *The Resurgence of Conservatism in Anglo-American Democracies*, Durham, Duke University Press.

Fisher, Louis (1975) *Presidential Spending Power*, Princeton, Princeton University Press.

Fisher, Louis (1988) *Constitutional Dialogues: Interpretation As Political Process*, Princeton, Princeton University Press.

Foley, Douglas E. (1988) *From Peones to Politicos*, Austin, University of Texas Press.

Fossett, J. W. (1983) *Federal Aid to Big Cities*, Washington DC, Brookings Institution.

Frantzich, Stephen E. (1982) *Computers in Congress*, Beverley Hills, Sage.

Fraser, Steve and Gary Gerstle (1989) *The Rise and Fall of the New Deal Order 1930–1980*, Princeton, Princeton University Press.

Freedman, James O. (1978) *Crisis and Legitimacy*, New Haven, Yale University Press.

Freeman, J. Leiper (1965) *The Political Process*, New York, Random House.

Freidman, Benjamin (1988) *Day of Reckoning*, New York, Random House.

Funston, Richard (1975) 'The Supreme Court and Critical Elections', *American Journal of Political Science*, vol. 69, pp. 795–811.

Galbraith, J. K. (1967) *The New Industrial State*, New York, Houghton Mifflin.

Garcia, F. Chris and Rodolpho de la Garza (1977) *The Chicano Political Experience*, North Scituate, Mass., Duxbury Press.

Gilpin, Robert (1987) *The Political Economy of International Relations*, Princeton, Princeton University Press.

Ginsburg, Benjamin and Martin Shefter (1990) *Politics by Other Means*, New York, Basic Books.

Glazer, Nathan (1988) *The Limits of Social Policy*, Cambridge, Harvard University Press.

Goldstein, Judith and Stefanie Ann Lenway (1989) 'Interests or Institutions: An Inquiry into Congressional-ITC Relations', *International Studies Quarterly*, vol. 33.

Goodman, M. R. and M. T. Wrightson (1987) *Managing Regulatory Reform*, New York, Praeger.

Goodsell, Charles T. (1984) 'The Grace Commission: Seeking Efficiency for the Whole People?', *Public Administration Review*, vol. 44, pp. 196–204.

Gormley, William T. (1989) *Taming the Bureaucracy: Muscles, Prayers and Other Strategies*, Princeton, Princeton University Press.

Gormley, William T. (1991) 'The Bureaucracy and Its Masters: The New Madisonian System in the US', *Governance*, vol. 4, pp. 1–18.

Gottlieb, Stephen E. (1982) 'Rebuilding the Right of Association: The Right to Hold a Convention as a Test Case', *Hofstra Law Review*, vol. 11, p. 191.

Gottschalk, Peter and Sheldon Danziger (1984) 'Macroeconomic Conditions, Income Transfers, and the Trend in Poverty', in D. Lee Bawden (ed.) *The Social Contract Revisited*, Washington DC, Urban Institute.

Greeley, Andrew M. (1972) 'Political Attitudes Among American White Ethnics', *Public Opinion Quarterly*, Summer, pp. 213–22.

Greenstein, Fred (1982) *The Hidden-Hand Presidency: Eisenhower as Leader*, New York, Basic Books.

Greenstein, Fred (ed.) (1983) *The Reagan Presidency: An Early Assessment*, Baltimore, Johns Hopkins University Press.

Greider, William (1981) *The Education of David Stockman and Other Americans*, New York, Dutton.

Grofman, Bernard (ed.) (1990) *Political Gerrymandering and the Courts*, New York, Agathon.

Gurr, T. R. and D. S. King (1987) *The State and the City*, Chicago, University of Chicago Press.

Haggard, Stephen (1988) 'The Institutional Foundations of Hegemony: Explaining the Reciprocal Trade Agreements Act of 1934', *International Organization*, vol. 42, pp. 94–5.

Hansen, A. (1964) *The Postwar American Economy: Performance and Problems*, New York, W. W. Norton.

Harmel, Robert and Kenneth Janda (1982) *Parties and their Environments*, New York, Longman.

Harris, R. A. and S. Milkis (1989) *The Politics of Regulatory Change*, New York, Oxford University Press.

Harrison, B., C. Tilly and B. Bluestone (1986) 'Rising Inequality', in David Obey and Paul Sarbanes (eds) *The Changing American Economy*, Oxford, Basil Blackwell.

Hart, John (1987) *The Presidential Branch*, Oxford, Pergamon.

Hartman, Robert W. (1984) *Pay and Pensions for Federal Employees*, Washington DC, Brookings Institution.

Hartz, Louis (1955) *The Liberal Tradition in America*, New York, Harcourt Brace Jovanovich.

Hays, Samuel (1987) *Beauty, Health and Permanence: Environmental Politics in the United States, 1955–1985*, Cambridge, Cambridge University Press.

Heller, W. (1986) 'The Public Policy Experience', in David Obey and Paul Sarbanes (eds) *The Changing American Economy*, Oxford, Basil Blackwell.

Herrnson, Paul S. (1988) *Party Campaigning in the 1980s*, Cambridge, Harvard University Press.

Hess, Stephen (1976) *Organizing the Presidency*, 1st ed., Washington DC, Brookings Institution.

Hess, Stephen (1988) *Organizing the Presidency*, 2nd ed, Washington DC, Brookings Institution.

Hibbs, D. A. (1987) *The American Political Economy*, Cambridge, Harvard University Press.

Hill, D., R. Moore, and P. Williams (eds) (1990) *The Reagan Presidency*, Basingstoke, Macmillan.

Hodder-Williams, Richard (1980) *The Politics of the U.S. Supreme Court*, London, Allen and Unwin.

Hodder-Williams, Richard (1988) 'The Strange Story of Judge Robert Bork and a Vacancy on the United States Supreme Court', *Political Studies*, vol. 36, pp. 613–37.

Hodder-Williams, Richard (1990) 'Litigation and Political Action: Making the Supreme Court Activist', in Robert Williams (ed.) *Explaining American Politics*, London, Routledge.

Hoffman, David (1989) 'On Panama, Bush Characteristically Cautious: Scowcroft Shunning Role of Crisis Manager, Maintained Informality', *Washington Post*, 15 October.

Hogan, Joseph (ed.) (1990) *The Reagan Years*, Manchester, Manchester University Press.

Holmes, Stephen A. (1991) 'When the Subject is Civil Rights, There are Two George Bushes', *New York Times*, 9 June.

Horner, Constance (1989) 'Securing Competence and Character in the Public Service', *Governance*, vol. 2, pp. 115–23.

Horowitz, Donald (1977) *The Jurocracy*, Lexington, D.C., Heath.

Huntington, Samuel P. (1973) 'Congressional Responses to the Twentieth Century', in David B. Truman (ed.) *The Congress and America's Future*, Englewood Cliffs, Prentice-Hall.

Huntington, Samuel P. (1988–9) 'The US – Decline or Renewal?', *Foreign Affairs*, vol. 67, pp. 76–96.

Huston, R. (ed.) (1968) *Roles of the Attorney-General of the United States*, Washington DC, American Enterprise Institute.

Ingraham, Patricia W. (1987) 'Building Bridges or Burning Them? The President the Appointees, and the Bureaucracy', *Public Administration Review*, vol. 47, pp. 424–5.

Ingraham, Patricia W. and Carolyn Ban (eds) (1984) *Legislating Bureaucratic Change: The Civil Service Reform Act of 1978*, Albany, State University of New York Press.

Irons, Peter (1988) *The Courage of their Convictions: Sixteen Americans Who Fought Their Way to the Supreme Court*, New York, The Free Press.

Jackson, Brooks (1988) *Honest Graft: Big Money and the American Political Process*, New York, Knopf.

Jacobson, Gary (1978) 'The Effects of Campaign Spending in Congressional Elections', *American Political Science Review*, vol. 72, pp. 469–91.

Jacobson, Gary (1980) *Money in Congressional Elections*, New Haven, Yale University Press.

Jacobson, Gary (1987a) *The Politics of Congressional Elections*, Boston, Little, Brown.

Jacobson, Gary (1987b) 'The Marginals Never Vanished', *American Journal of Political Science*, vol. 31, pp. 126–41.

Jacobson, Gary (1989a) 'Congress: A Singular Continuity', in Michael Nelson (ed.) *The Elections of 1988*, Washington DC, Congressional Quarterly Press.

Jacobson, Gary (1989b) 'Meager Patrimony: Republican Representation in Congress after Reagan', in Larry Berman (ed.) *The Reagan Imprint*, Baltimore, Johns Hopkins University Press.

Jacobson, Gary (1990) *The Electoral Origins of Divided Government: Competition in U.S. House Elections, 1946–1988*, Boulder, Westview Press.

Jaffa, Harry V. (1986–7) 'What were the "Original Intentions" of the Framers of the Constitution of the United States?', *University of Puget Sound Law Review*, vol. 10, pp. 343–448.

Jentleson, Bruce (1990) 'Diplomacy', in Thomas E. Mann (ed.) *A Question of Balance*, Washington DC, Brookings Institution.

Johannes, John R. (1984) *To Serve The People*, Lincoln, Neb., University of Nebraska Press.

Johnson, Frank (1977) 'Judicial Action is a Duty – Not an Intrusion', *Judges Journal*, 16-4-11.

Jones, Charles O. (1975) *Clean Air: The Policies and Politics of Pollution Control*, Pittsburgh, University of Pittsburgh Press.

Jones, Charles O. (1982) *The United States Congress*, Homewood, Ill., Dorsey Press.

Jones, Charles O. (ed.) (1988) *The Reagan Legacy*, Chatham, Chatham House.

Jordan, A. Grant (1981) 'Iron Triangles, Wooly Corporatism, and Elastic Nets: Images of the Policy Process', *Journal of Public Policy*, vol. 1, pp. 95–123.

Katz, Michael (1986) *In the Shadow of the Poorhouse: Social History of Welfare in the United States*, New York, Basic Books.

Katz, Michael (1989) *The Undeserving Poor: From the War on Poverty to the War on Welfare*, New York, Pantheon.

Katzmann, Robert A. (1990) 'War Powers: Toward a New Accommodation', in Thomas E. Mann (ed.) *A Question of Balance: the President, the Congress, and Foreign Policy*, Washington DC, Brookings Institution.

Kayden, X. and E. Mahe (1985) *The Party Goes On*, New York, Basic Books.

Kennedy, Paul (1987) *The Rise and Fall of the Great Powers*, New York, Random House.

Keohane, Robert O. (1984) *After Hegemony*, Princeton, Princeton University Press.

Kernell, Samuel (1986) *Going Public: New Strategies of Presidential Leadership*, Washington DC, Congressional Quarterly Press.

Key, V. O. Jr. (1966) *The Responsible Electorate*, Cambridge, Harvard University Press.

Kiewiet, Roderick and Douglas Rivers (1985) 'The Economic Basis of Reagan's Appeal', in John E. Chubb and Paul E. Peterson (eds) *The New Direction in American Politics*, Washington DC, Brookings Institution.

Kindleberger, Charles (1973) *The World in Depression, 1929–1933*, Berkeley, University of California Press.

King, D. S. (1987) *The New Right: Politics, Markets, and Citizenship*, London, Macmillan.

King, D. S. (1990) 'Economic Activity and the Challenge to Local Government', in D. S. King and J. Pierre (eds) *Challenges to Local Government*, London, Sage.

King, D. S. (1991) 'Citizenship as Obligation in the US: Title II of the Family Support Act of 1988', in Michael Moran and Ursula Vogel (eds) *The Frontiers of Citizenship*, London, Macmillan.

Kingdon, John W. (1984) *Agendas, Alternatives, and Public Policies*, Boston, Little, Brown.

Kingdon, John W. (1989) *Congressmen's Voting Decisions*, 2nd ed., New York, Harper and Row.

Kleppner, Paul (1970) *The Cross of Culture*, New York, Free Press.

Kleppner, Paul (1979) *The Third Electoral System, 1853–1892: Parties, Voters and Political Cultures*, Chapel Hill, University of North Carolina Press.

Kleppner, Paul *et al.* (1981) *The Evolution of Electoral Systems*, Westport, Greenwood Press.

Kluger, Richard (1975) *Simple Justice*, New York, Random House.

Koenig, Louis W. (1990) *The Chief Executive*, 5th ed., New York, Harcourt, Brace, Jovanovich

Krasner, Stephen D. (1978) 'United States Commercial and Monetary Policy: Unravelling the Paradox of External Strength and Internal Weakness', in Peter J. Katzenstein (ed.) *Between Power and Plenty: Foreign Economic Policies of Advanced Industrial States*, Madison, University of Wisconsin Press.

Krislov, Samuel (1962–3) 'The *amicus curiae* brief: from friendship to advocacy', *Yale Law Journal*, vol. 72, pp. 694–721.

Ladd, Everett Carll (1981) 'Party "Reform" Since 1968: A Case Study in Intellectual Failure', in Patricia Bonomi, James McGregor Burns and Austin Ranney (eds) *The American Constitutional System Under Strong and Weak Parties*, New York, Praeger.

LaFeber, Walter (1989) *The American Age*, New York, W. W. Norton.

Lakoff, Sanford and Herbet York (1989) *A Shield in Space?*, Berkeley, University of California Press.

Lasser, William (1985) 'The Supreme Court in Periods of Critical Alignment', *Journal of Politics*, vol. 47, pp. 1174–87.

Lawson, Kay (1987) 'How State Laws Undermine Parties', in A. James Reichley (ed.) *Elections American Style*, Washington DC, Brookings Institution.

Lazarsfeld, Paul, Bernard Berelson and Hazel Gaudet (1968) *The People's Choice*, 3rd ed., New York, Columbia University Press.

Lee, Eugene (1985) 'California', in D. E. Butler and Austin Ranney (eds) *Referendums*, Washington DC, American Enterprise Institute.

Levine, Charles H. (1988) 'Human Resource Erosion and the Uncertain Future of the U. S. Civil Service: From Policy Gridlock to Structural Fragmentation', *Governance*, vol. 1, pp. 136–8.

Levy, Leonard W. (1988) *Original Intent and the Framers' Constitution*, New York, Macmillan.

Lindsay, James M. (1991) *Congress and Nuclear Weapons*, Baltimore, Johns Hopkins University Press.

Lippman, Walter (1955) *Essays in Public Philosophy*, New York, Mentor.

Lowell, B. Lindsay, Frank D. Bean and Rodolfo de la Garza (1986) 'The Dilemmas of Undocumented Immigration: An Analysis of the 1984 Simpson-Mazzoli Vote', *Social Science Quarterly*, vol. 67, pp. 118–27.

Lowenstein, Daniel Hays (1988) 'Constitutional Rights of Major Political Parties: A Skeptical Inquiry', unpublished paper.

Lowenstein, Daniel Hays (1990) 'On Campaign Finance Reform: The Root of All Evil is Deeply Rooted', *Hofstra Law Review*, vol. 18, p. 301.

Lowi, Theodore J. (1964) 'American Business, Case Studies, and Political Theory', *World Politics*, vol. 16, pp. 677–715.

Lowi, Theodore J. (1972) 'Four Systems of Policy, Politics, and Choice', *Public Administration Review*, vol. 32, pp. 298–310.

Lowi, Theodore, J. (1985) *The Personal President*, Ithaca, Cornell University Press.

McCloskey, Robert G. (1972) *The Modern Supreme Court*, Cambridge, Harvard University Press.

McConnell, Grant (1966) *Private Power and American Democracy*, New York, Knopf.

McCubbins, Matthew D. and Thomas Schwartz (1984) 'Congressional Oversight Overlooked: Police Patrols Versus Fire Alarms', *American Journal of Political Science*, vol. 28, pp. 165–79.

McCue, Ken (1984) 'The Structure of Individual Decisions in American Elections: The Influence of Relevant Alternatives', unpublished Ph.D. thesis, California Institute of Technology.

McGerr, Michael E. (1986) *The Decline of Popular Politics*, New York, Oxford University Press.

McGuigan, Patrick B. and Dawn M. Weyrich (1990) *Ninth Justice: the Fight for Bork*, Washington DC, Free Congress Research and Education Foundation.

McKay, David (1985) *American Politics and Society*, Oxford, Basil Blackwell.

McKay, R. Reynolds (1984) 'The Impact of the Great Depression on Immigrant Mexican Labor: Repatriation of the Bridgeport, Texas Coalminers', *Social Science Quarterly*, vol. 65, pp. 354–63.

Mackenzie, G. Calvin (1981) *The In-and-Outers*, Baltimore, Johns Hopkins University Press.

Mackinnon, Catherine 'Francis Biddle's Sister: Pornography, Civil Rights and Speech', in *Feminism Unmodified: Discourses on Life and Law*, Cambridge, Harvard University Press.

MacKinnon, Catherine (1989) *Towards A Feminist Theory of the State*, Cambridge, Harvard University Press.

McSweeney, Dean and John Zvesper (1991) *American Political Parties*, London, Routledge.

Maddison, A. (1982) *Phases of Capitalist Development*, Oxford, Oxford University Press.

Magleby, David, Walt Klein and Sue Thomas (1982) 'The Initiatives in the 1980s: Popular Support, Issue Agendas, and Legislative Reform of the Process', unpublished paper.

Malbin, Michael (1979) *Unelected Representatives*, New York, Basic Books.

Mann, Thomas (1987) 'Is the House of Representatives Unresponsive to Political Change?', in A. James Reichley (ed.) *Elections American Style*, Washington DC, Brookings Institution.

Mann, Thomas E. (1990) *A Question of Balance: The President, The Congress, and Foreign Policy*, Washington DC, Brookings Institution.

Mann, Thomas and Norman J. Ornstein (eds) (1981) *The New Congress*, Washington DC, American Enterprise Institute.

Marshall, R. (1986) 'Working Smarter', in David Obey and Paul Sarbanes (eds) *The Changing American Economy*, Oxford, Basil Blackwell.

Marshall, Thomas R. (1989) *Public Opinion and the Supreme Court*, Boston, Unwin, Hyman.

Mashaw, Jerry L. (1983) *Bureaucratic Justice*, New Haven, Yale University Press.

Mastanduno, Michael, David A. Lake and John G. Ikenberry (1989) 'Toward a Realist Theory of State Action', *International Studies Quarterly*, vol. 33, 457–74.

Matusow, Allen J. (1984) *The Unravelling of America: A History of Liberalism in the 1960s*, New York, Harper and Row.

Mayhew, David R. (1974) *Congress: The Electoral Connection*, New Haven, Yale University Press.

Mayhew, David R. (1989) 'Does it Make a Difference Whether Party Control of the American National Government is Unified or Divided', unpublished manuscript.

Mayhew, David R. (1991) *Divided Party Control: Does it Make a Difference?*, New Haven, Yale University Press.

Mead, L. (1985) *Beyond Entitlement: The Social Obligations of Citizenship*, New York, Free Press.

Meese, Edwin III (1985) 'The Attorney-General's View of the Supreme Court: Towards a Jurisprudence of Original Intention', *Public Administration Review*, vol. 45, pp. 701–4.

Meese, Edwin III (1986–7) 'The Law of the Constitution', *Tulane Law Review*, vol. 61, pp. 979–90.

Menhaca, Martha (1989) 'Chicago-Mexican Cultural Assimilation and Anglo-Saxon Cultural Dominance', *Hispanic Journal of Behavioral Sciences*, vol. 11, pp. 203–31.

Merton, Robert K. (1968) *Social Theory and Social Structure*, Glencoe, Ill., Free Press.

Mervin, David (1990) *Ronald Reagan and the American Presidency*, London, Longman.

Mezey, Michael L. (1989) *Congress, the President, and Public Policy*, Boulder, Westview Press.

Miller, Lawrence W., Jerry L. Polinard and Robert D. Wrinkle (1984) 'Attitudes Toward Undocumented Workers: The Mexican American Perspective', *Social Science Quarterly*, vol. 65, pp. 482–94.

Miller, Warren E. and Donald E. Stokes (1963) 'Constituency Influence in Congress', *American Political Science Review*, vol. 57, pp. 45–56.

Miller, Warren E. and M. Kent Jennings (1986) *Parties in Transition*, New York, Russell Sage.

Milner, Helen (1988) *Resisting Protectionism: Global Industries and the Politics of International Trade*, Princeton, Princeton University Press.

Moe, Terry M. (1985) 'The Politicized Presidency', in John E. Chubb and Paul E. Peterson (eds) *The New Direction in American Politics*, Washington DC, Brookings Institution.

Moe, Terry M. (1987) 'An Assessment of the Positive Theory of "Congressional Dominance"', *Legislative Studies Quarterly*, vol. 12, pp. 475–520.

Moe, Terry M. and Gary Miller (1983) 'Bureaucrats, Legislators, and the Size of Government', *American Political Science Review*, vol. 77, pp. 297–323.

Montejano, David (1987) *Anglos and Mexicans in the Making of Texas*,

1836–1986, Austin, University of Texas Press.

Moore, Joan (1970) 'Colonialism: The Case of the Mexican American', *Social Problems*, vol. 17, pp. 463–71.

Moynihan, Daniel P. (1973) *The Politics of a Guaranteed Income*, New York, Vintage.

Murphy, Walter F. (1962) *Congress and the Court: A Case Study in the American Political Process*, Chicago, University of Chicago Press.

Murray, Charles (1984) *Losing Ground*, New York, Basic Books.

Nagel, Stuart (1965) 'Court-curbing Periods in American History', *Vanderbilt Law Review*, vol. 18, pp. 925–44.

Nash, George (1976) *The Conservative Intellectual Movement in America*, New York, Basic Books.

Nathan, J. A. and J. K. Oliver (1987) *Foreign Policymaking and the American Political System*, 2nd ed., Boston, Little, Brown.

Nathan, Richard P. and Fred C. Doolittle (1987) *Reagan and the States*, Princeton, Princeton University Press.

National Governors' Association (1987a) *Making America Work*, Washington DC, NGA.

National Governors' Association (1987b) *Policy on Welfare Reform*, Washington DC, NGA.

Navasky, Victor S. (1971) *Kennedy Justice*, New York, Athaneum.

Neustadt, Richard E. (1976) *Presidential Power*, New York, Wiley.

Nie, Norman H., Sidney Verba, and John R. Petrocite, (1976) *The Changing American Voter* Cambridge, Havard University Press.

Niemi, Richard G. and Herbert F. Weisberg, (1976) *Controversies in American Voting*, San Fransisco, W. H. Freeman.

Newland, Chester A. (1983) 'A Midterm Appraisal – The Reagan presidency: Limited Government and Political Administration', *Public Administration Review*, vol. 43, pp. 1–21.

Nightingale, D. S. and L. C. Burbridge (1987) *The Status of Work-Welfare Programs in 1986*, Washington DC, Urban Institute.

Nolan, Janne E. (1989) *Guardians of the Arsenal: the Politics of Nuclear Strategy*, New York, Basic Books.

Norton, H. (1977) *The Employment Act and the Council of Economic Advisers*, Columbia, University of South Carolina Press.

Nye, Joseph S. (1984) *The Making of America's Soviet Policy*, New Haven, Yale University Press.

Nye, Joseph S. (1990) *Bound to Lead*, New York, Basic Books.

Obey, David and Paul Sarbanes (eds) (1986) *The Changing American Economy*, Oxford, Basil Blackwell.

O'Brien, David (1986) *Storm Center: The Supreme Court in American Politics*, New York, Norton.

O'Brien, David (1988) *Judicial Roulette*, New York, Priority Press.

O'Connor, Karen (1983) 'The Role of the Solicitor-General in Supreme

Court Litigation, *Judicature*, vol. 66, pp. 256–64.

O'Connor, Karen and Lee Epstein (1984) 'A Legal Voice for the Chicano Community: The Activities of the Mexican–American Legal Defense and Education Fund', *Social Science Quarterly*, June, pp. 245–56.

OECD (1988a) *National Accounts: 1960–1986*, Paris.

OECD (1988b) *Economic Outlook, June 1988*, Paris.

Olsen, Mancur (1965) *The Logic of Collective Action*, Cambridge, Harvard University Press.

Olsen, Mancur (1982) *The Rise and Decline of Nations*, New Haven, Yale University Press.

Ornstein, Norman J. (1981) 'The House and the Senate in the New Congress', in Thomas Mann and Norman J. Ornstein (eds) *The New Congress*, Washington DC, American Enterprise Institute.

Orren, Gary R. and Nelson W. Polsby (eds) (1987) *Media and Momentum*, Chatham, Chatham House.

Pachon, Harry and Louis DeSipio (1990) 'Latino Legislators and Latino Caucuses', New Directions for Latino Public Policy Research Working Paper 11, Center for Mexican American Studies, University of Texas.

Palmer, John L. and Isabel V. Sawhill (eds) (1982) *The Reagan Experiment*, Washington DC, Urban Institute.

Palmer, John L. and Isabel V. Sawhill (eds) (1984) *The Reagan Record*, Washington DC, Urban Institute.

Parker, Glenn R. (1986) *Homeward Bound*, Pittsburgh, University of Pittsburgh Press.

Parker, Glenn R. and Roger H. Davidson (1979) 'Why Do Americans Love Their Congressmen So Much More Than Their Congress?', *Legislative Studies Quarterly*, vol. 4, pp. 53–61.

Parry, Robert and Peter Kornbluth (1988) 'Iran-Contras Untold Story', *Foreign Policy*, vol. 72, pp. 3–30.

Patterson, James T. (1981) *America's Struggle Against Poverty, 1900–1980*, Cambridge, Harvard University Press.

Peele, Gillian (1984) *Revival and Reaction*, Oxford, Clarendon Press.

Pertschuk, Michael and Wendy Schaetzel (1990) *The People Rising: The Campaign Against the Bork Nomination*, Washington DC, Thunder's Mouth Press.

Peters, B. Guy (1986) 'Burning the Village: The Civil Service under Reagan and Thatcher', *Parliamentary Affairs*, vol. 39, pp. 79–97.

Peters, B. Guy (1988) *Comparing Public Bureaucracies: Problems of Theory and Method*, Tuscaloosa, Ala., University of Alabama Press.

Peters, B. Guy (1989) 'Regulation of Administrative Data Collection in the United States', *The Journal of Behavioral and Social Sciences*, vol. 29, pp. 1–14.

Peterson, G. E. (1984) 'Federalism and the States', in J. Palmer and I. Sawhill (eds) *The Reagan Record*, Cambridge, Ballinger.

Peterson, G. E. (1986) 'Urban Policy and the Cyclical Behaviour of Cities', in G. E. Peterson and C. W. Lewis (eds) *Reagan and the Cities*, Washington DC, The Urban Institute.

Peterson, Paul E. (1981) *City Limits*, Chicago, University of Chicago Press.

Phillips, Kevin (1970) *The Emerging Republican Majority*, New Rochelle, Arlington House.

Phillips, Kevin (1983) *Post-Conservative America*, New York, Random House.

Phillips, Kevin (1990) *The Politics of Rich and Poor*, New York, Random House.

Piccigallo, P. R. (1988) 'Taking the Lead: The States' Expanding Role in Domestic Policymaking', *Journal of American Studies*, vol. 22, pp. 417–42.

Pichirallo, Joe (1988) 'Governor is Expected to be Bush's Chief of Staff', *International Herald Tribune*, 17 November.

Pitkin, Hanna Fenichel (1967) *The Concept of Representation*, Berkeley, University of California Press.

Pole, Jack (1978) *The Pursuit of Equality in American History*, Berkeley, University of California Press.

Polenberg, R. (1966) *Reorganizing Roosevelt's Government*, Cambridge, Harvard University Press.

Polinard, Jerry L., Robert D. Wrinkle and Rodolfo de la Garza (1984) 'Attitudes of Mexican Americans Toward Irregular Mexican Immigration', *International Migration Review*, vol. 18, pp. 782–99.

Polsby, Nelson W. (1983) *Consequences of Party Reform*, Oxford, Oxford University Press.

Polsby, Nelson and Aaron Wildavsky (1984) *Presidential Elections*, 6th ed., New York, Scribeners.

Pomper, Gerald M. (1977) 'The Decline of Party in American Elections', *Political Science Quarterly*, vol. 92, p. 21.

Pomper, Gerald M. (ed.) (1980) *Party Renewal in America: Theory and Practice*, New York, Praeger.

Porter, Roger (1980) *Presidential Decision Making: The Economic Policy Board*, Cambridge, Cambridge University Press.

President's Special Review Board (1987) *The Tower Commission Report*, New York, Bantam.

Pressman, Jeffrey L. and Aaron Wildavsky (1973) *Implementation*, Berkeley, University of California Press.

Pritchett, C. Herman (1954) *Civil Liberties and the Vinson Court*, Chicago, University of Chicago Press.

Pritchett, C. Herman (1961) *Congress Versus the Supreme Court, 1957–1960*, Minneapolis, University of Minneapolis Press.

Rae, Nicol C. (1989) *The Decline and Fall of the Liberal Republicans: From 1952 to the Present*, Oxford, Oxford University Press.

Ranney, Austin (1975) *Curing the Mischiefs of Faction*, Berkeley, University of California Press.

Ranney, Austin (1981) 'The Working Conditions of Members of Parliament and Congress: Changing the Tools Changes the Job', in Norman J. Ornstein (ed.) *The Role of the Legislature in Western Democracies*, Washington DC, American Enterprise Institute.

Ranney, Austin (1985) 'The United States of America', in D. E. Butler and Austin Ranney (eds) *Referendums*, Washington DC, American Enterprise Institute.

Reagan, M. D. and J. G. Sanzone (1981) *The New Federalism*, 2nd ed., Oxford, Oxford University Press.

Rehnquist, William H. (1987) *The Supreme Court: How it Was, How it Is*, New York, Morrow.

Reichley, A. James (1985) 'The Rise of National Parties', in John E. Chubb and Paul E. Peterson (eds) *The New Direction in American Politics*, Washington DC, Brookings Institution.

Reichley, A. James (ed.) (1987) *Elections American Style*, Washington DC, Brookings Institute.

Reynolds, William Bradford (1982) 'Justice Department Policies on Equal Employment and Affirmative Action', *Proceedings of New York University 35th Annual Conference on Labor*, pp. 443–53.

Reynolds, William Bradford (1983) 'The Justice Department's Enforcement of Title VII', *Labor Law Journal*, vol. 34, pp. 259–65.

Rieselbach, Leroy N. (1986) *Congressional Reform*, Washington DC, Congressional Quarterly Press.

Rimlinger, Gaston V. (1971) *Welfare Policy and Industrialization in Europe, America, and Russia*, New York, Wiley.

Ripley, Randall B. (1989) *Congress: Process and Policy*, 4th ed., New York, Norton.

Robinson, Donald A. (1980) 'The Place of Party in Democratic Ideas', in Gerald Pomper (ed.) *Party Renewal in America*, New York, Praeger.

Romo, Ricardo (1983) *East Los Angeles: History of a Barrio*, Austin, University of Texas Press.

Rose, Richard (1988) *The Post-Modern President*, Chatham, Chatham House.

Rosenbaum, Robert J. (1981) *Mexicano Resistance in the Southwest*, Austin, University of Texas Press.

Rosenfeld, Michel (1991) *Affirmative Action and Justice*, New Haven, Yale University Press.

Rusk, Jerrold (1970) 'The Effect of the Australian Ballot Reform on Split Ticket Voting: 1876–1908', *American Political Science Review*, vol. 64, pp. 1220–38.

Rusk, Jerrold and Helmut Norpoth (1982) 'Partisan Dealignment in the American Electorate: Itemizing the Deductions Since 1964', *American Political Science Review*, vol. 76, pp. 522–37.

Sabato, Larry J. (1978) *Goodbye to Good-Time Charlie*, Lexington, Mass., Lexington Books.

Sabato, Larry J. (1981) *The Rise of Political Consultants*, New York, Basic Books.

Sabato, Larry J. (1988) *The Party's Just Begun*, Glenview Ill., Scott Foresman.

Sabato, Larry J. (ed.) (1989) *Campaigns and Elections*, Glenview Ill., Scott, Foresman.

Salamon, Lester M. (1982) 'The Presidency and Domestic Policy Formulation', in Hugh Heclo and Lester M. Salamon (eds) *The Illusion of Presidential Government*, Boulder, Westview.

Salisbury, Robert H. and Kenneth A. Shepsle (1981) 'US Congressman As Enterprise', *Legislative Studies Quarterly*, vol. 6, pp. 559–76.

Savas, E. S. (1987) *Privatization: The Key to Better Government*, Chatham, Chatham House.

Scammon, Richard and Benjamin Wattenberg (1970) *The Real Majority*, New York, Coward, McCann and Geoghegan.

Schattschneider, E. E. (1975) *The Semi-Sovereign People*, New York, Dryden Press.

Schick, Allen (1980) *Congress and Money*, Washington DC, Urban Institute.

Schick Allen (ed.) (1983) *Making Economic Policy in Congress*, Washington DC, American Enterprise Institute.

Schieffer, Bob and Gary Paul Gates (1989) *The Acting President*, New York, E. P. Dutton.

Schlesinger, Arthur M. (1974) *The Imperial Presidency*, New York, Popular Library.

Schlesinger, Arthur M. (1981) 'Can The Party System Be Saved?', in Patricia Bonomi, James MacGregor Burns and Austin Ranney (eds) *The American Constitutional System Under Strong and Weak Parties*, New York, Praeger.

Schlesinger, Joseph A. (1985) 'The New American Political Party', *American Political Science Review*, vol. 79, p. 1152.

Schmidhauser, John R. and Larry R. Berg (1972) *The Supreme Court and Congress: Conflict and Interaction, 1945–1968*, Glencoe, Free Press.

Schneider, William (1987) '"Rambo" and Reality: Having it Both Ways', in Kenneth A. Oye, Robert J. Lieber and Donald Rothchield (eds)

Eagle Resurgent? The Reagan Era in American Foreign Policy, Boston, Little, Brown.

Schwartz, Bernard (1986) *Swann's Way: The School Busing Case and the Supreme Court*, New York, Oxford University Press.

Schwartz, Herman (1988) *Packing the Courts: the Conservative Campaign to Rewrite the Constitution*, New York, Scribners.

Schwartz, John (1988) *America's Hidden Success*, New York, Norton.

Segal, Jeffrey A. (1988) '*Amicus* briefs by the Solicitor-General during the Warren and Burger Courts', *Western Political Quarterly*, vol. 41, pp. 135–44.

Seib, Gerard F. (1989) 'Bush in Assembling Staff of His Administration Takes the Experienced but not the Power Hungry', *Wall Street Journal*, 17 January.

Seidman, Harold and Robert Gilmour (1986) *Politics, Position, and Power*, New York, Oxford University Press.

Selig, Joel L. (1985) 'The Reagan Justice Department and Civil Rights: What Went Wrong', *University of Illinois Law Review*, pp. 785–835.

Shafer, Byron (1983) *Quiet Revolution*, New York, Sage.

Shafer, Byron (1988) *Bifurcated Politics*, Cambridge, Harvard University Press.

Shastri, Amita (1986) 'Social Services and California's Minorities', Appendix to Bruce E. Cain *et al.*, *Minorities in California*, A Report to the Seaver Foundation.

Shepsle, Kenneth A. (1989) 'The Changing Text Book Congress', in John E. Chubb and Paul E. Peterson (eds) *Can The Government Govern?*, Washington DC, Brookings Institution.

Shonfield, A. (1965) *Modern Capitalism: The Changing Balance of Public and Private Power*, Oxford, Oxford University Press.

Sinclair, Barbara (1981) 'Majority Party Leadership Strategies For Coping With The New US House', *Legislative Studies Quarterly*, vol. 5, pp. 391–414.

Sinclair, Barbara (1983) *Majority Leadership in the U.S. House*, Baltimore, Johns Hopkins University Press.

Smith, Peter H. (1980) *Mexico: The Quest for a U.S. Policy*, New York, Foreign Policy Association.

Smith, Steven S. (1989) *Call to Order*, Washington DC, Brookings Institution.

Sommers, A. T. with L. R. Blau (1988) *The US Economy Demystified*, Lexington, Lexington Books.

Sorauf, Frank J. (1988) *Money in American Elections*, Glenview, Ill., Scott Foresman.

Sorauf, Frank J. and Paul Allen Beck (1988) *Party Politics in America*, 6th ed., Glenview, Ill., Scott Foresman.

Spanier, John and Eric M. Uslaner (1989) *American Foreign Policy*

Making and the Democratic Dilemma, 5th ed., New York, CBS College Publishing.

Stahl, O. Glenn and James J. McGurrin (1986) 'Professionalizing the Career Service', *The Bureaucrat*, vol. 15, pp. 16–21.

Stedman, M. A. and J. D. Holden (1987) 'States, Localities Respond to Federal Housing Cutbacks', *Journal of State Government*, p. 60.

Stein, H. (1969) *The Fiscal Revolution in America*, Chicago, University of Chicago Press.

Stein, H. (1985) *Presidential Economics: The Making of Economic Policy from Roosevelt to Reagan and Beyond*, New York, Simon and Schuster.

Steiner, Gilbert Y. (1971) *The State of Welfare*, Washington DC, Brookings Institution.

Stevens, John Paul (1985–6) *UC Davis Law Review*, vol. 19, pp. 15–21.

Stillman, R. J. (1987) *The American Bureaucracy*, Chicago, Nelson-Hall.

Stockman, David (1986) *The Triumph of Politics*, London, Coronet.

Stone, C. and H. Sanders (eds) (1987) *The Politics of Urban Development*, Lawrence, Kan., University Press of Kansas.

Subcommittee on Economic Goals and Intergovernmental Policy of the Joint Economic Committee (1982) Hearing on Enterprise Zones, 97th Congress, 1st session, January 11.

Subcommittee on Investment, Jobs and Prices of the Joint Economic Committee (1984) Hearing on 'The President's 1984 National Urban Policy Report', 98th Congress, 2nd session, June 20.

Sundquist, James L. (1981) *The Decline and Resurgence of Congress*, Washington DC, Brookings Institution.

Sundquist, James L. (1983) *Dynamics of the Party System*, Washington DC, Brookings Institution.

Sundquist, James L. (1986) *Constitutional Reform*, Washington DC, Brookings Institution.

Sundquist, James L. (1988) 'Needed: A Political Theory for the New Era of Coalition Government in the United States', *Political Science Quarterly*, vol. 103, pp. 613–35.

Sununu, John (1988) 'The Spirit of Federalism: Restoring the Balance', *Intergovernmental Perspective*, 14.

Swanstrom, T. (1989) 'No Room at the Inn: Housing Policy and the Homeless', *Journal of Urban and Contemporary Law*, 35.

Symposium (1985) 'Gerrymandering and the Courts', *UCLA Law Review*, vol. 33, p. 1.

Talbott, Strobe (1988) *The Master of the Game: Paul Nitze and the Nuclear Peace*, New York, Alfred Knopf.

Taylor, Paul and David Broder (1988) 'Perfecting a Negative Campaign', *International Herald Tribune*, 29–30 October.

Thelen, David P. (1981) 'Two Traditions of Progressive Reform, Political Parties and American Democracy', in Patricia Bonomi, James

McGregor Burns and Austin Ranney (eds) *The American Constitutional System Under Strong and Weak Parties*, New York, Praeger.

Thompson, K. W. *The President and the Public Philosophy*, Baton Rouge, Louisiana State University Press.

Thernstrom, Abigail (1987) *Whose Vote Counts?*, Cambridge, Harvard University Press.

Thurber, James (ed.) (1991) *Divided Democracy*, Washington DC, Congressional Quarterly Press.

Tocqueville, Alexis de (1945) *Democracy in America* (ed.) Phillips Bradley, New York, Vintage Books.

Toffler, Alvin (1980) 'Congress in the Year 2000', *GAO Review*, Fall, pp. 38–48.

Treadway, J. M. (1985) *Public Policymaking in the American States*, New York, Praeger.

Treverton, Gregory F. (1990) 'Intelligence: Welcome to the American Government', in Thomas E. Mann (ed.) *A Question of Balance: the President, the Congress, and Foreign Policy*, Washington DC, Brookings Institution.

Tribe, Laurence H. (1985) *God Save this Honorable Court*, New York, Random House.

Tribe, Laurence H. (1990) *Abortion: The Clash of Absolutes*, New York, Norton.

Tufte, Edward R. (1975) 'Determinants of the outcomes of midterm Congressional Elections', *American Political Science Review*, vol. 69, pp. 812–26.

U.S. Department of Housing and Urban Development (1982) *The President's National Urban Policy Report 1982*, Washington DC, GPO.

U.S. Department of Housing and Urban Development (1984) *The President's National Urban Policy Report 1984*, Washington DC, GPO.

Vernon, Raymond and Debora L. Spar (1989) *Beyond Globalism: Remaking American Foreign Economic Policy*, New York, The Free Press.

Vose, Clement E. (1972) *Constitutional Change: Amendment Politics and Supreme Court Litigation Since 1900*, Lexington, Heath.

Walker, David B. (1989) 'American Federalism: Its Historic Conditioners, Current Condition, and Future Prospects', unpublished paper.

Walker, Samuel (1990) *In Defence of American Liberties: A History of the ACLU*, New York, Oxford University Press.

Waller, Douglas C. (1987) *Congress and the Nuclear Freeze*, Amherst, University of Massachusetts Press.

Walters, Ronald W. (1988) *Black Presidential Politics in America: A Strategic Approach*, New York, State University of New York Press.

Warburg, Felix (1989) *Conflict and Consensus: the Struggle Between Congress and the President over Foreign Policymaking*, Grand Rapids, Ballinger Publishing.

Wattenberg, M. P. (1990) *American Parties in Decline*, Cambridge,

Harvard University Press.

Weberg, L. B. (1988) 'Changes in Legislative Staffs', *Journal of State Government*, 61.

Weingast, Barry R. and Mark J. Moran (1983) 'Bureaucratic Discretion or Congressional Control? Regulatory Policymaking by the Federal Trade Commission', *Journal of Political Economy*, vol. 91, pp. 765–800.

Weinraub, Bernard (1989) 'Sununu, the Chief of Staff is Learning the Ropes the Hard Way', *New York Times*, 6 February.

Weir, Margaret, Ann Shola Orloff and Theda Skocpol (eds) (1988) *The Politics of Social Policy in the United States*, Princeton, Princeton University Press.

Weisskopf, T., S. Bowles and D. Gordon (1983) 'Hearts and Minds: A Social Model of U.S. Productivity Growth', *Brookings Papers on Economic Activity*, No. 2.

White, E. (1988) *The American Judicial Tradition*, Oxford, Oxford University Press.

Wildavsky, Aaron (1984) *The Politics of the Budgetary Process*, 4th ed., Boston, Little, Brown.

Wilson, James Q. (1966) *The Amateur Democrat*, Chicago, University of Chicago Press.

Wilson, James Q. (1989) *Bureaucracy: What Government Agencies Do and Why They Do It*, New York, Basic Books.

Wilson, William Julius (1987) *The Truly Disadvantaged*, Chicago, University of Chicago Press.

Wilson, Woodrow (1914) *Congressional Government*, London, Constable.

Wirth, F. (1985) 'The Dependent City? External Influences Upon Local Government', *Journal of Politics*, vol. 47, pp. 83–112.

Witt, Elder (1986) *A Different Justice: Reagan and the Supreme Court*, Washington DC, Congressional Quarterly Press.

Witte, Edwin E. (1963) *The Development of the Social Security Act*, Madison, University of Wisconsin Press.

Wolfinger, Raymond E. (1972) 'Why Political Machines Have Not Withered Away and Other Revisionist Thoughts', *Journal of Politics*, vol. 34, p. 365.

Wolman, H. (1990) 'The Reagan Urban Policy and its Impacts', in D. S. King and J. Pierre (eds) *Challenges to Local Government*, London, Sage.

Woolley, J. (1984) *Monetary Politics: The Federal Reserve and the Politics of Monetary Policy*, New York, Cambridge University Press.

Wright, John R. (1985) 'PACs, Contributions and Roll Calls: An Organisational Perspective', *American Political Science Review*, vol. 79, pp. 400–14.

Wuthnow R. (1988) *The Restructuring of American Religion*, Princeton, Princeton University Press.

Yarborough, Tinsley E. (ed.), (1985) *The Reagan Administration and Civil Rights*, New York, Praeger.

Index

abortion 15, 23, 27, 30, 31, 36,
  141, 162, 163, 268, 299
Administrative Procedures Act
  (1946) 175, 176
AFL–CIO 215
Aid for Families with Dependent
  Children (AFDC) 32, 191,
  195, 206, 231, 238, 239, 242
Allegheny County v. *American Civil
  Liberties Union* (1989) 163
Allen, Richard 95
Alliance for Justice 149
American Civil Liberties Union
  147, 298, 304, 318
American Family Association 15
American–Israeli Public Affairs
  Committee (AIPAC) 269
American Prospect 27
Americans with Disabilities Act
  (1990) 294, 305
Amicus Curiae 148, 153
Anti-Ballistic Missile Treaty
  (ABM) 264
Arab Gulf 264–5
Asian-Americans
  definition 52
  demographic changes 1–2, 37
Aspin, Les 262, 263
Atwater, Lee 24, 110, 302

Baker, James 95, 96, 97, 99,
  100–1, 104, 105, 111–12,
  113–14, 260
Bakker, Jim 23
Balanced Budget and Emergency
  Deficit Control Act (1985) 7,
  226, 283–8, 290

Barrow v. *Baltimore* (1833) 145
Bennett, William 24
Bentsen, Lloyd 349
bilingualism 51, 52
black Americans 4, 10, 303, 307–
  8
  churches 24
  Democratic Party 17, 18, 33–4,
    35, 39, 47–9, 50–1
  demographic changes 1
  elected officials 34
  poverty 32, 49
  see also civil rights, Voting
    Rights Act
Bob Jones University 298
Bork, Robert 31, 139–40, 142–3,
  150, 153–4, 156, 159, 164,
  301
Boskin, Michael 106
Bradley, Tom 49
Brady, Nicholas 105, 106, 109
Brennan, William 144, 162
Bretton Woods 251
Brock, William 69
Brown, Ron 27
Brown v. *Board of Education,
  Topeka, Kansas* (1954) 155,
  156, 160
Bryce, James 135
Brzezinski, Zbigniew 255
Buchanan, Patrick 101
Buckley v. *Valeo* (1976) 44, 56
budget 7, 10–11, 25, 124–5, 221,
  222–5, 280
  Bush 286–7, 289
  National Debt 288
  Reagan 280–7, 288, 291

budget – *cont.*
  spending 288–90
  taxes 290, 292–3
Budget and Accounting Act
  (1921) 284
Budget Enforcement Act (1990)
  7, 289–90, 291
Budget Review Board 99
Bumpers, Dale 118–19
Bundy, McGeorge 255
Bureau of Budget *see* Office of
  Management and Budget
bureaucracy 3, 8, 92, 97
  agencies 171–4
  Bush 165–70, 186, 187, 259–
    60
  Congress 172, 173–4, 175
  Executive Schedule 169
  future 187–8
  General Schedule 168–70
  morale 185–6
  pay 178–9
  personnel system 168–71,
    177–8
  politicization 91, 92, 181–2
  President 165, 166–7
  Reagan 166–70, 177–85
  reform 182–5
  role 167
  rule-making 175–7
Burger, Warren 142, 144, 158
Burke, Edmund 78
Bush, George 198, 244, 346,
  349–50
  agenda 102, 245
  bureaucracy 165–70, 185, 187,
    259–60
  child care 30
  civil rights 294, 295, 300, 301–
    5, 306–7, 308
  competence 104
  Congressional relations 109–
    12, 113, 115, 124–5
  economic policy 10, 103, 226–
    8, 287
  election 102–3, 324, 349
  foreign policy 10, 273–4, 275
  ideology 21–2, 24–5, 35
  Iraq 6, 26, 112–13, 273–4, 276
  Panama 6, 106–7, 114
  style 104, 106–7
  Supreme Court 144
  welfare policy 245–7, 248
  White House 104–8, 114
Byrd, Robert 131

Campaign Finance Reform 54,
  55–6, 70
campaign technology 18–19, 44,
  47, 53–4
Cannon, Joseph 130
Carpenter, Ted Galen 26
Carter, Jimmy 69, 79, 90, 92, 93,
  96, 103, 170, 184, 215, 218,
  219–20, 226, 239, 250, 255,
  268, 272, 348
Cato Institute 23, 26
Census (1990) 1, 10
Central Intelligence Agency
  (CIA) 170, 256, 264
Cheney, Richard 103, 286–7
child care 30, 31, 33
Children's Defense Fund 31
civil rights 10, 18, 27, 34, 49,
  112, 115
  Bush 294, 295, 300, 301–5,
    306–7, 308
  Civil Rights Act (1990) 294,
    305–8
  Civil Rights and Women's
    Equity in Employment Act
    (1991) 294
  Reagan 295–301
Civil Rights Act (1964) 146, 192,
  302
Civil Rights Commission 300
Civil Rights Restoration Act
  (1988) 303
Civil Service Reform Act (1978)
  170, 181
Clark, William 95, 96, 99
Clean Air Act (1970) 347
Clean Air Act (1990) 123
Clinton, William 206
Commentary 23
Committee on the Present

Danger 268
Common Cause 56, 57
Congress 3, 4, 7–8, 30, 36, 88,
    90, 103, 109–10, 113, 146,
    155, 200, 214, 243, 248, 303,
    315, 322, 324, 326
  budget 124–5, 213, 280, 284,
    285, 290, 291
  bureaucracy 172, 173–4, 175
  'bureaucratization' 128
  casework 121–2
  civil rights 294, 300, 305–8
  committees 117–18, 126, 127,
    132–3, 261, 262
  computers 119–20
  constituencies 117–25, 137,
    266
  'electoral connection' 46, 262
  floor procedures 126, 132–3,
    261
  foreign policy 255, 260–7,
    269–71
  leadership 84, 115, 126, 127,
    129–34
  mail 119–20
  media coverage 118
  new members 127
  parochialism 46, 47, 122–6,
    136
  party organization 66
  party unity 66, 85, 129–31
  performance 134–7
  policy-making 115–16, 122,
    123–5, 126, 137
  schedule 120
  seniority 131
  staff 45, 120–1, 123, 126, 127–
    8, 261
  Supreme Court 140, 143–4
Congressional Black Caucus 35,
    303
Congressional Budget and
    Impoundment Act (1974)
    284
Congressional Budget Office
    126, 127, 128
Congressional Research Service
    127

conservation 2, 3, 16, 19, 20–6,
    35, 141, 296–7
  courts 8, 142–3
  federalism 198–9
  poverty 33
Council of Economic Advisors
    (CEA) 213
courts 3, 8, 59, 146, 149, 152,
    155, 299
  see also Supreme Court
Cousins v. *Wigoda* (1975) 76
Cox, Archibald 153
Cranston, Alan 121
Culler, Terry W. 166–7, 180

Daley, Richard 49
Darman, Richard 109, 110
Davis v. *Bandemer* (1986) 42
Days, Drew 304
Deaver, Michael 95, 96, 99, 100
Deconcini, Dennis 121, 305
Defense Department 255–9
Democratic Leadership Council
    27, 131
Democratic National Committee
    (DNC) 48, 71, 74, 75, 83
Democratic Party
  black Americans 17, 18, 33–4,
    35, 47–8, 50–1
  Congress 131
  dominance 68
  ideology 17–18, 20–1, 25, 27,
    147
  Latinos 17, 47–8, 50–1, 310
  'nationalization' 69, 71, 75
  neo-conservatives 22
  populism 27–9
  progressivism 73
  voters 39, 42, 48
  see also political parties
Democratic Party v. *Wisconsin ex rel.*
    La Follette (1981) 76
Department of Housing and
    Urban Development (HUD)
    199, 201, 244
Deukmejian, George 49
Devine, Donald 166–7
Dinkins, David 35

direct mail   70–1
divided government   4–5, 11, 38,
     88, 141, 146, 161, 164, 165,
     211–12, 324–5
  consequences   345–53
  explanations   40–2, 328–45
  historical perspective   325–8
  states   336–8, 342–3
Domestic Policy Council   107–8
Dornan, Robert   26
drug policy   123, 125
Dukakis, Michael   28, 48, 77, 79,
     102, 302, 349
Dunne, John   305

Eastern Europe   10, 47, 251, 289
economic policy   9, 20
  balance of payments   225
  Bush   10, 103, 226–8, 287
  conflict   212–14
  Congress   213–14, 220–2
  deficit   224, 280–93
  economic growth   211, 224,
     225
  fiscal policy   213, 216, 217,
     219–20, 225–7
  inflation   216, 219, 222, 225
  micro-policy   214–16
  'misery index'   220
  monetary policy   213–14, 216,
     217, 219–20
  'New Economic Policy'   218–19
  partisanship   217
  Presidents   212–13, 221
  Reagan   10, 32, 93, 197, 215,
     222–5, 227, 280–7
  'supply-side economics' 222–4
  taxation   217, 222, 223, 227
Economic Policy Board   97
Economic Policy Council   107–8
economic populism   27–8
education   123
Eisenhower, Dwight   89, 116,
     242, 327
electoral system
  dealignment   38
  decentralization   38
  realignment   324
  rules   37–8
  see also campaign finance,
     electorate, gerrymandering,
     incumbency, political parties,
     ticket-splitting
electorate
  diversity   37, 39, 47–55
  education   118
El Salvador   256
Enders, Thomas O.   257
environmental protection   112,
     115, 125, 146
Environmental Protection
     Agency   146
Equal Rights Amendment (ERA)
     16, 31
Eu v. *San Francisco County
     Democratic Central Committee*
     (1989)   81
Evans, Daniel   261
Executive Office of the President
     (EOP)128, 212–13

Family Assistance Plan   251
Family Support Act (1988)   33,
     205–6, 207
Farrakand, Louis   35
federalism   9, 157–8
  'entrepreneurial States'   203–4
  federal grants   196–7, 199, 207
  models   191–5, 207–9
  national urban policy   200
  new federalism   191, 195–6,
     202–5
  Reagan   190, 191, 195–203
  States rights   190
Federal Deposit Insurance
     Corporation (FDIC)   210
Federal Election Campaign Act
     (1971)
  1974 Amendments   70
  1979 Amendments   81
Federal Register   175
Federal Reserve   9, 212, 213–14
  Federal Open Market
     Committee   214
  Federal Reserve Board   214,
     218, 220, 223, 225, 227

Federation for American
    Immigration Reform 316
feminism *see* women's movement
Finney v. *Hutto* (1977) 151
flag burning 16, 164
Foley, Thomas 346
Food and Drug Administration
    (FDA) 171
Ford, Gerald 69, 108, 184, 218,
    219, 226, 233, 241
foreign policy 10
    anti-decline thesis 250–1
    arms control 250, 255, 263,
        265, 266
    Central America 250, 256, 257
    Cold War 250, 252, 253, 260,
        273, 276
    Congress 260–6, 269–71
    conservatives 25–6
    decline thesis 250–1
    democracy 275–7
    domestic roots 251–4
    interest groups 267–71
    national interest 274–5
    public opinion 271–4
    Soviet Union 250
    see also Bush, Eastern Europe,
        El Salvador, Iraq, Panamana,
        Nicaragua, Reagan, Soviet
        Union, State Department
Fortas, Abe 142
Free Congress Research and
    Education Foundation 149
Fried, Charles 154
Friedersdorf, Max 101

Gantt, Harvey B. 307
Garretty, John 150
General Accounting Office
    (GAO) 127
Gephardt, Richard 28
gerrymandering 41–2, 329
Gingrich, Newt 25
Ginsburg, Douglas 143
Glazer, Nathan 297
Glenn, John 121, 263
Goldberg, Arthur 158–9
Goldwater, Barry 70

Gore, Albert 48, 263
Grace Commission 182, 183–4
Graham, Daniel 257
Gramm, Phil 281–2
Gramm–Rudman–Hollings *see*
    Balanced Budget and
    Emergency Deficit Control
    Act (1985)
Gray, C. Boyden 110–12
Gray, William 35
Great Society 15, 25, 33, 217
Greenspan, Alan 227
Grenada 93
Griswold v. *Connecticut* (1965) 159
Grove City v. *Bell* (1984) 303
Gulf War 6–7, 25, 26
    see also Iraq

Hainesworth, Clement 143
Haldeman, H. R. 95
health care 125
Helms, Jesse 35, 303, 307
Heritage Foundation 298, 299–
    300
Hispanics *see* Latinos
Hollings, Ernest 284
Horner, Constance 185
Horton, Willy 102
House of Representatives 116,
    126, 127, 131
    Democratic Caucus 129
    reform 134
    Rules Committee 129, 132,
        133
    Speaker 129, 131, 132
housing policy 115, 123, 125,
    201–2, 243–4
Humphrey, Hubert 73
Hussein, Saddam 113

ideology 2–3, 15
    see also conservatism, liberalism
immigration 10, 37, 115
    level 309
    Mexicans 309, 312–16, 320,
        321–2
    Nicaraguans 318, 319
    Salvadorians 318, 319

Immigration Reform and Control
    Act (1986)   311–12, 315,
    316–20, 321, 322
incumbency   43–7, 332–5
initiatives   58–9
INS v. *Chadha* (1983)   152
interest groups   2, 3–4, 16–17,
    35–6, 37, 118, 142–4, 147–
    52, 173, 174, 175, 260, 267–
    71, 295, 304
Internal Revenue Service   297
International Monetary Fund
    212
International Trade
    Commission   270–1
Iran–Contra scandal   6, 90, 92,
    101–2, 258–9, 265, 349–50
Iraq   6, 26, 112–13, 273–4, 276
'Iron Triangles'   173–4
Israel   269–70

Jackson, Andrew   325
Jackson, Jesse   24, 28, 34–5, 48–9
Jackson, Robert   150
Japan   227, 251
Jencks, Christopher   27
Jews   18, 35, 39, 47
Johnson, Frank   150
Johnson, Lyndon   15, 142, 217,
    225, 233, 241
Joint Economic Committee   217
Justice Act (1870)152
Justice Department   141, 152,
    154–5, 297–8, 301, 304

Kean, Thomas   205
Keating, Charles   121
Kemp, Jack   24, 244
Kennedy, Anthony   143, 164
Kennedy, Edward   27, 31
Kennedy, John F.   233
Kennedy, Paul   250
Kennedy, Robert F.   153, 164
Kirk, Paul   48
Kirkpatrick, Jeanne   100
Kissinger, Henry   255
Koch, Ed   49
Koch, June   199

Kristol, Irving   23, 297

Latinos
    bilingualism   51, 311
    definition   51–2, 310–11
    democratic party   17, 47–8,
        310
    demographic changes   1–2, 37,
        50, 310–11
    elected officials   310, 317, 318
    enfranchisement   309–10
    poverty   32, 50
    Republican Party   310
    Voting Rights Act (1965)   60–
        1, 309–10
Lawyers' Committee for Civil
    Rights   149
Leadership Conference on Civil
    Rights   31, 295, 298, 302
League of United Latin American
    Citizens   313, 317, 321
League of Women Voters   57
Lebanon   93, 264
Lee, Rex   154
Legislative Strategy Group   99,
    106
liberalism   2, 19, 27–9, 141, 220,
    296–7
    poverty   33
    Supreme Court   142, 144
Library of Congress   128
Lincoln Savings and Loan   121
Lott, Trent   297
Lucas, William   304–5

Mannatt, Charles   71
Marbury v. *Madison* (1803)   147
Marshall, Thurgood   144
Martinez, Bob   30
Mayaquez   264
McCain, John   121
McCree, Wade   153–4
McFarlane, Robert   99, 101
McGovern, George   70, 79
McGovern–Fraser Commission
    74–6
Mead, Lawrence   33
Meese, Edwin   95, 96, 97, 99,

100, 141, 154, 155, 157, 301,
  304
Mexican–American Legal
  Defense Fund 50
Mitchell, George 131–2, 346
Mondale, Walter 48, 77, 79
Montaya, Joseph 310
Moral Majority 15
Morrison v. *Olson* (1988) 152
Moynihan, Daniel P. 207, 231,
  246
Murray, Charles 33
Muskie, Edmund 347

National Association for the
  Advancement of Colored
  People 50, 147, 148, 298
National Association of
  Manufacturers 267
National Chamber of Commerce
  317, 321
National Conservative Political
  Action Committee 119
National Conventions 73–6
National Council of Churches
  317
National Council de la Raza 317,
  321
National Governors' Association
  204, 206–7
National Organization of
  Women 31
National Republican
  Congressional Committee
  70
National Republican Senatorial
  Committee 70
National Security Agency 170
National Security Council 97,
  101, 106–7, 256
naturalization 52–3
Neas, Ralph 295
New Deal 3, 18, 20, 34, 47, 156,
  190, 232
Nicaragua 11, 115, 256, 263–4,
  275
Nitze, Paul 258

Nixon, Richard 55, 89, 91, 94,
  97, 116, 142, 218–19, 233,
  238, 239–40, 241, 260, 347
Noriega, Manuel 106, 107
North Atlantic Treaty
  Organization 23, 25, 276
North, Oliver 258, 275
Nunn, Sam 111, 262

Obey Commission 134
O'Connor, Sandra Day 142, 163,
  164
Office of Economic Opportunity
  241
Office of Information and
  Regulatory Affairs 198, 208
Office of Management and
  Budget 91, 94, 109, 124,
  128, 198, 212, 213, 222
Office of Personnel
  Management 166–7, 180,
  185
Office of Policy Development 95
Office of Technology
  Assessment 126, 127
Omnibus Budget Reconciliation
  Act (1981) 196, 203, 205,
  206, 240
O'Neill, Thomas 'Tip' 131, 133
Open Housing Act (1968) 146
Organization of Petroleum
  Exporting Countries 219,
  220, 251

Panama 6, 106–7, 114
Patterson Committee 134
Pearson–Ribicoff Report 134
People for the American Way
  149
Pepper, Claude 236
Pepper Commission 247
Pierce, Samuel 199
Plessy v. *Ferguson* (1896) 154
Political Action Committees 18–
  19, 45, 56–7, 61, 118, 119
political machines 67–9

political parties 2, 3, 5, 15, 17–20, 37, 62
  fund-raising 57–8
  identification 39, 64–5, 85
  litigation 81–2, 83
  polarization 340
  office-holders 65–6
  organization 66–72
  reform 58, 76–80
  renewal 63–4, 69–72, 80–4, 85
  weakness 42, 54, 63–4, 69
  see also Democratic Party, Republican Party
Porter, Roger 106, 108
poverty 15, 17, 20, 28, 31–3, 244–5
Powell, Lewis 142, 150
Presidents
  agenda-setting 6, 15
  bureaucracy 165, 167
  Cabinet 91
  elections 24, 28–9, 327
  foreign policy 254, 255–60
  'imperial' 89
  'managerial' 92
  modern 190, 191
  national constituency 5, 15
  nomination 73, 85, 335
  performance 91–3, 113–14, 126
  power 124
  staff 91
  Supreme Court 140
  see also individual presidents
primary elections 67–8
  Presidential 58, 73–5, 81–2
Princeton University 27
progressivism 63, 67, 72–80, 82, 325
Protestantism 24, 39
Public Health Service 171
Public Interest 27

Quayle, Dan 103
Quayle Committee 134

Reagan, Ronald 15–16, 17, 77, 108, 142, 250, 262, 274

agenda 94, 142
bureaucracy 166–7, 177–88, 195, 256, 258, 259–60
Cabinet 90, 93, 96–9
civil rights 34, 295–301
competence 92–3
defense policy 94
economic policy 10, 32, 93, 197, 215, 222–5, 227, 280–7
federalism 190, 191, 195–203, 208
foreign policy 254–60, 264, 267, 272
housing policy 201–2
ideology 20–1, 23, 24, 35, 93, 141, 199–200, 296
Inaugural Address 195
popularity 90–1, 307–8
presidency 3, 5–6
State of the Union Address (1988) 124
style 89, 90–9, 104
welfare policy 229, 230, 240–5, 246, 248, 249
White House 94–5, 99–102, 113–13
reapportionment 4
referenda 58–9
Regan, Donald 99–102, 105
Regents of the University of California v. *Bakke* (1978) 148, 163
Rehnquist, William 142, 143, 164
Republican National Committee 41, 69–70, 71
Republican Party
  Congress 129–31
  conservatism 22
  elections 38
  fund-raising 69–71
  ideology 17–18, 20, 21, 297, 33
  'nationalization' 69–70, 75
  voters 69–71
'retrospective voting' 46
Reynolds, William Bradford 141, 154, 304

Reynolds v. *Sims* (1964)   153, 155
Richardson, William   318
Richmond v. *J.A. Croson Co.*   163
Riegle, Donald   121
Robb, Charles   27
Roe v. *Wade* (1973)   30, 163, 164
Rollins, Edward   101
Roman Catholics   23, 24, 39, 47
Roosevelt, Franklin   73, 93, 156, 190, 210–11, 212, 242
Rudman, Warren   284

Savings and Loan crisis   8
Scalia, Antonin   142, 164
Schafly, Phyllis   31
Scowcroft, Brent   105, 108
Securities and Exchange Commission   210
Senate   116, 126, 127, 129, 131–2, 300–1
  Democratic Policy Committee   132
  Democratic Steering Committee   132
  Ethics Committee   121
  reforms   134
  Rules Committee   134
  unanimous consent   133
Senior Interagency Groups   97
Shelby, Richard   121
Shultz, George   255
Silber, John   35
slavery   14–15
social security   32, 230–1, 242–3, 246
Social Security Act (1935)   191, 205, 229, 230, 231
Solicitor-General   152–4
Souter, David   8, 31, 144, 164
South Africa   266, 270, 275–6
Southwest Voter Registration Project   50
Soviet Union   25–6, 250, 251, 254, 276
Starr, Paul   27
State Department   255, 256
Stewart, Potter   142

Stockman, David   98, 99, 124, 222, 240
Strategic Defense Initiative   256–9
Sununu, John   24, 104–6, 109–10, 114
Super-Tuesday   48–9
Supreme Court   8, 16, 31, 36, 41–2, 56, 59, 60, 76, 81, 82, 191, 193, 298, 301, 305
  agenda   140, 146
  appointments   140, 142–4, 155, 163, 299
  Bush Administration   144
  Congress   140, 143–4, 160
  docket   149, 160–2
  ideology   142
  jurisprudence   155, 156–9
  legitimacy   138–40, 143, 144, 145, 156, 164
  political nature   150–2, 156
  power   147
  Reagan Administration   139
  reputation   140
  role   145
  see also individual cases
Svahn, John   101
Swann v. *Charlotte-Mecklenburg County Board of Education* (1970)   151

Tashjian v. *Republican Party of Connecticut* (1986)   81
Tax Reform Act (1986)   203, 347
Teeter, Robert   104–5, 109
Teller, Edward   257
Tennessee Valley Authority   170–1
Texas v. *Johnson* (1989)   304
Thatcher, Margaret   21
Thomas, Clarence   8, 308
Thornburg v. *Gingles* (1986)   60
Thornburgh, Richard   301, 303, 304
ticket-splitting   40–3, 64, 326, 330–1, 333, 340, 343
Tocqueville, Alexis de   135, 138
Tower, John   103, 111

Tower Commission 101–2
Treasury Department 212, 213
Treaty of Guadalupe Hidalgo 312
Tribe, Lawrence 14
Truman, Harry 242, 252

United States v. *Darby Lumber Co.* (1942) 146
Urban League 27

Van Buren, Martin 327
Vance, Cyrus 255
Veterans Administration 175
Vietnam War 25, 92, 107, 126, 127, 129, 251, 252, 253, 260, 264, 268, 271, 274, 327
Volcker, Paul 220
Volcker Commission 187
Voting Rights Act (1965) 4, 60–1, 146, 192, 296, 309–10
Vrodouak, Ed 49

Wallace, George 166
War Powers Resolution 264–5, 266
Wards Cove Packing Co. v. *Antonio* (1989) 305
Warren, Earl 142, 144, 158, 160
Washington, Harold 49
Washington Legal Foundation 149
Watergate Scandal 69, 89, 92, 119, 126, 127, 129
Watt, James 184

Webster v. *Reproductive Services of Missouri* (1989) 30, 163
Weinberger, Caspar 255–6, 285
Weld, William 35
welfare policy
  Bush 245–7
  cost 232–3, 240–1
  federalism 229–30
  growth 232–7
  privatization 248
  public assistance 229, 231–2, 236
  Reagan 229, 230, 239, 240–5, 248, 249
  reform 115, 205–7, 230, 238–40
  social insurance 229, 230–1, 232, 235
  social security 230–1, 242–3, 246
West Virginia State Board of Education v. *Barnette* (1943) 145
White, Byron 164
Wickard v. *Filburn* (1943) 146
Wilder, Douglas 35
Wildmon, Donald 15
Wilson, Woodrow 135
women's movement 3, 15, 29–31, 32–3, 297
Wright, Jim 115, 133
writ of certiorari 149–50, 152, 153, 160

Young, Coleman 35